Historical Media Memories of the Rwandan Genocide

To my daughter,
Liell "Kanyana" Pollack

These are the stories of just a few of the thousands of children who lost their lives in the genocide against the Tutsi. Their lives are as dear, and we mourn them no less, after the passing of years.

As you leave this section, you will find stories of children who survived. They are committed to living together, not as Hutu or Tutsi, but as Rwandans.

Introduction text to the Children's room at
The Kigali Genocide Memorial

Historical Media Memories of the Rwandan Genocide

Documentaries, Films, and Television News

Tommy Gustafsson

EDINBURGH
University Press

Edinburgh University Press is one of the leading university presses in the UK. We publish academic books and journals in our selected subject areas across the humanities and social sciences, combining cutting-edge scholarship with high editorial and production values to produce academic works of lasting importance. For more information visit our website: edinburghuniversitypress.com

© Tommy Gustafsson, 2024

Grateful acknowledgement is made to the sources listed in the List of Illustrations for permission to reproduce material previously published elsewhere. Every effort has been made to trace the copyright holders, but if any have been inadvertently overlooked, the publisher will be pleased to make the necessary arrangements at the first opportunity.

Edinburgh University Press Ltd
13 Infirmary Street, Edinburgh, EH1 1LT

Typeset in 10.5/13pt Goudly Old Style
by Cheshire Typesetting Ltd, Cuddington, Cheshire

A CIP record for this book is available from the British Library

ISBN 978 1 3995 1733 1 (hardback)
ISBN 978 1 3995 1734 8 (paperback)
ISBN 978 1 3995 1735 5 (webready PDF)
ISBN 978 1 3995 1736 2 (epub)

The right of Tommy Gustafsson to be identified as the author of this work has been asserted in accordance with the Copyright, Designs and Patents Act 1988, and the Copyright and Related Rights Regulations 2003 (SI No. 2498).

Contents

List of Figures	ix
Acknowledgments	xii

1. Introduction: Historical Media Memories of the Rwandan Genocide — 1

Part One The Apocalypse, April to July 1994

2. Swedish Television News in 1994 — 31

Part Two The Creation of a Transnational Historical Media Memory of the Rwandan Genocide, 1994–2005

3. The Creation of a Transnational Historical Media Memory of the Rwandan Genocide in the International Production of Television Documentaries, 1994–2003 — 65
4. The Creation of a Global Public Consciousness, 2004–2005 — 80
5. Telling the Truth: Documentary Films and Public Consciousness — 108

Part Three To Maintain a Historical Media Memory on a Global Level, 2004–2021

6. The Difficulties of Maintaining a Historical Media Memory in Feature Films — 119
7. Emblematic Images and the Maintenance of a Historical Media Memory in Documentaries — 137
8. Women, AIDS, and Rape — 146
9. Reconciliation and Gacaca Documentaries — 153
10. Historical Revisionism and Historical Negationism — 167

Part Four The Use of Historical Media Memories in Rwanda, 2001–2021

11 The Genocide against the Tutsi in Rwandan Film and Television   191

Notes   235
Bibliography   271
Filmography of the Rwandan Genocide   282
Index   288

Figures

1.1 The "Genocide Fax," sent by Roméo Dallaire to the UN in New York on January 11, 1994 — 25
2.1 Piles of corpses lying by the road in *Rapport*, April 19, 1994 — 46
2.2 Children fighting over a sack of flour, interpreted symbolically as a fight between ethnicities in *Rapport*, May 3, 1994 — 48
2.3 Images of corpses lying by the side of a road, filmed from a moving truck, and used to illustrate the first use of the word "genocide" in *Nyheterna*, May 6, 1994 — 50
2.4 UN General Secretary Boutros Boutros-Ghali admits that the UN has failed to put together a second peace mission to Rwanda during a press conference in *Rapport*, May 26, 1994 — 56
2.5 Paul Kagame states that he "will not negotiate with the government, for it is composed of murderers," in *Rapport*, June 7, 1994 — 58
2.6 Cheering Hutus welcoming the French troops in Opération Turquoise in *Rapport*, June 24, 1994 — 59
3.1 Men with machetes at a roadblock in *Rwanda: How History Can Lead to Genocide* (1995) — 70
3.2 Corpses by the side of the road in *The Triumph of Evil* (1998) — 71
3.3 and 3.4 Images from the evacuation of KPH, showing Western journalists "shooting" Tutsi refugees as well as hundreds of refugees being abandoned, with the European woman being dragged away in the bottom-right corner of the image in *The Triumph of Evil* (1998) — 73
3.5 The Nick Hughes footage in *The Last Just Man* (2003) — 74
4.1 Paul (Don Cheadle) has a gun put to his head and is encouraged by soldiers of the Presidential Guard to shoot his

own family, of Tutsi origin, to prove that he is not a traitor to his ethnicity in *Hotel Rwanda* (2004)   83

4.2 The use of editing, framing, and music to "teach" audiences about the Western failure in Rwanda, thereby creating an emancipatory understanding of history as something unwritten and changeable in *Hotel Rwanda* (2004)   91

4.3 and 4.4 The replica of the "The Nick Hughes Footage" and the allusion to "The River of Corpses," which both create an audiovisual shield for audiences watching *Hotel Rwanda* (2004)   94

4.5 An enhanced version of the emblematic image "Corpses by the Road" in *Shooting Dogs* (2005)   101

5.1 The use of Western talking heads. US State Department spokesperson Christine Shelley's reluctance to define what was going on in Rwanda as genocide at a press briefing on April 28, 1994, in *Ghosts of Rwanda* (2004)   109

5.2 and 5.3 Two variants of "Corpses by the Road" in *Ghosts of Rwanda* (2004) and *Shake Hands with the Devil: The Journey of Roméo Dallaire* (2004), respectively   110

5.4, 5.5 and 5.6 The emblematic images "Bloated Corpses in the River," "The River of Corpses," and "The Man with a Machete" in *Shake Hands with the Devil: The Journey of Roméo Dallaire* (2004) and *Ghosts of Rwanda* (2004), respectively   112

6.1 The fictive Roméo Dallaire (Roy Dupuis) interacts with "Corpses by the Road" in *Shake Hands with the Devil* (2007)   121

6.2 Witnessing the genocide through a small window in the Netflix melodrama *Trees of Peace* (2021)   128

6.3 Emmanuel (Edouard Bamporiki) at a re-education camp for Hutu perpetrators in *Kinyarwanda* (2011)   132

6.4 Recreation of the emblematic image "The River of Corpses" in *'94 Terror* (2018)   134

7.1 A variant of the emblematic image "Skeletons and Clothes" in *Kill Them All! Rwanda: The Story of an Unimportant Genocide* (2004)   137

7.2 The personal and at the same time professional testimony of Dr. James Orbinski, which acts as a human bridge to African pain in *Triage: Dr James Orbinski's Humanitarian Dilemma* (2007)   141

8.1 Eight-year-old Marianna points out the corpses of her parents in *Blodsarvet* (1995). The caption reads: "They cut off mom's head and dad was shot"   149

8.2	Marianna and her son at the Ntarama Genocide Memorial in *Mothers of War* (2009)	151
9.1	Forgiveness as a "divine" act. An already convicted perpetrator is forgiven by a white Christian woman whom he has never met before in *Hunting My Husband's Killers* (2005), one of several Christian reconciliation films on the Rwandan genocide	155
9.2	Rwandans preparing for Gacaca in *Gacaca: Living Together Again in Rwanda?* (2002)	160
9.3	Kwasa and his "American mommy," Suzette Munson, in *Life after Death* (2014)	164
10.1	The *génocidaire* Théoneste Bagosora at his ICTR trial in *From Arusha to Arusha* (2008)	170
10.2	BBC reporter Jane Corbin walks around the crash site, where debris from the plane that carried Rwandan President Juvénal Habyarimana still lies around in the backyard of the former presidential residence in *Rwanda: The Untold Story* (2014)	177
10.3	The use of animations to circumvent the use of real imagery of the genocide against the Tutsi in *Black Earth Rising* (2018)	187
11.1	Commemoration meeting during commemoration week in Kigali in April 2015. Photo: Taliah Pollack	195
11.2	One of the captions at the beginning of *Keepers of Memory* (2004) which deviates from the official historical media memory of the genocide in Rwanda	207
11.3	The television set in the first room of the Kigali Genocide Memorial, where visitors can watch a three-minute film about the history of Rwanda, with a focus on the colonial influence of Belgium. Photo: Tommy Gustafsson	208
11.4	The Hutu street boys in *Through My Eyes: A Film about Rwandan Youth* (2004)	210
11.5	The explicit use of violence in the reconciliation film *The Pardon* (2009)	218
11.6	Rugamba (Edouard Bamporiki) visits his father in prison in *Long Coat* (2009)	221
11.7	The Madman (Jp Uwayezu) in *Grey Matter* (2011)	229
11.8	"The Nick Hughes Footage" used as a nightmare in *Umurabyo* (2015)	232

Acknowledgments

During the spring semester of 2015 I worked and did research at the University of Rwanda in Kigali, and I returned for additional research trips in 2016/2017. I would like to thank my dear colleagues at the School of Journalism and Communication, foremost Joseph Njuguna, Jean-Pierre Uwimana, Margaret Jjuuko, and Edward Kabuye Mwesigye, for their friendship and support. Likewise, I am grateful for the help I received from the staff at The Kigali Genocide Memorial and Nyamata Genocide Memorial Centre. I also had the opportunity to meet with Arthur Asiimwe, the Director General of the Rwanda Broadcasting Agency (RBA), Jean-Damascène Gasanabo, Director General of the National Commission for the Fight against Genocide (CNLG), and Eric Kabera, CEO of Kwetu Film Institute, who in various ways guided me in my research on the historical media memory of the genocide against the Tutsi in Rwanda. The research in this book has been made possible through generous research grants from the Swedish Research Council and Riksbankens Jubileumsfond. Lastly, I would like to thank my wife, Taliah Pollack, for her love and never-ending support.

1
Introduction: Historical Media Memories of the Rwandan Genocide

Steven Spielberg's *Schindler's List* (1993) is often hailed as the supreme example of a Holocaust film, that is, a film about genocide. Despite the fact that this is a feature film based on historical events with all the limitations to accuracy that that entails, since its premiere it has been used around the world as an audiovisual history textbook that has the power to move, inspire but also to teach its audiences about certain aspect of genocide in general, and about the genocide of the European Jews during the Second World War in particular.[1] However, *Schindler's List* has been subjected to severe criticism for being outright false, un-educational, commercial, oversimplified, for obscuring the majority of victims, for being too sentimental, and for having a happy Hollywood ending that radiates with "positively repulsive kitsch."[2] The question of historical accuracy seems to be in direct opposition with the film medium's ability to inspire, and to reach and inform audiences about historical events like genocides. Is it even possible for audiences to acquire some sort of historical knowledge which is not immediately undermined by the film medium's inherent way of telling a story?

While *Schindler's List* probably is the most commercially successful film ever that deals with genocide as its main theme, grossing approximately US$321 million at the box office worldwide, it still remains one of Spielberg's least successful films commercially, far behind blockbusters such as *E.T.: The Extra-Terrestrial* (1982) and *Jurassic Park* (1993).[3] The accusations aimed at Spielberg for making money out of the Holocaust are grossly unfair, especially considering that Spielberg founded the USC Shoah Foundation Institute for Visual History and Education, partly with the earnings from *Schindler's List*.[4] However, in a Bourdieuian sense *Schindler's List* contributed to Spielberg's—and even Hollywood's as an institution—cultural prestige with its seven Academy Awards, eighty-four international film prizes, and an official endorsement by President Bill Clinton.[5] Nonetheless, the commercial element of the international film industry tends to smear, or be used to smear, even the most accurate historical film, and only the more artful and supposedly uncommercial films, such as

Nuit et brouillard (*Night and Fog*, 1956), appear to be allowed to deal with solemn historical subjects such as genocide.[6]

As a poor countryside cousin, *Hotel Rwanda* (2004) has often been compared to *Schindler's List* as the "African" or the "Black *Schindler's List*," and Paul Rusesabagina, the main protagonist in *Hotel Rwanda*, is often referred to as a "Black Oscar Schindler."[7] This is of course a demeaning way to refer to this historical film, the real-life person, and, not least, the gruesome genocide that took place in Rwanda in 1994. However, within the realms of genocide films, this diminishing process appears to be unavoidable since the Holocaust is the genocide *par excellence*. All genocides, and all audiovisual representations of genocide, will consequently always be given a lower profile in comparison, at least when considered in a Western context. But what happens if one tries to consider the many variables for a global or transnational context for the memorization of genocide? Is it possible to create transnational historical media memories of historical events, and if so, how is a process like that fashioned between the local, the national, and the transnational?

Besides the obvious fact that both these films focus on narratives that tell stories about extraordinary individuals who stood up against the seemingly unstoppable machinery of genocide, there are several additional similarities between *Schindler's List* and *Hotel Rwanda* that highlight the challenging relationship between film and history in general, and audiovisual representations of genocide in particular. Just like *Schindler's List*, *Hotel Rwanda* has been hailed as the quintessential film on the Rwandan genocide that "documents for a mass audience what it was like."[8] The film is regularly used as an audiovisual history textbook to teach pupils about the genocide, and it is probably the most widespread audiovisual representation of the Rwandan genocide to date.[9] However, mirroring the critique of *Schindler's List*, *Hotel Rwanda* has been subjected to severe criticism for being oversimplified in its explanation of the genocide, for being historically inaccurate, for being too sentimental, for having the obligatory happy Hollywood ending, and certainly for being too commercial in its approach, despite the fact that it only generated US$34 million at the box office worldwide, a mere tenth of the revenue of *Schindler's List*.[10] But unlike the memorialization of the Holocaust, the memory of the Rwandan genocide is still in the process of being shaped, and that means that criticism of *Hotel Rwanda* does not stop with the typical Hollywood bashing, but instead incorporates quite serious and highly political allegations.

American English scholar Jonathan D. Glover claims, for example, that the film, although inadvertently, participates in the "mythology of the genocide that supports the RPF's official narrative of events."[11] The Zimbabwean media scholar Nyasha Mboti claims that the soundtrack, especially the use of the South African pop song "Umqombothi" at the beginning of the film, actually promotes genocide; the direct opposite of director Terry George's intention.[12] South African film scholar Tanja Sakota-Kokot points out, rather obviously considering that the film is about genocide, that "*Hotel Rwanda* does not focus on positive representations of Africa, but rather, through the continued representation of violence and anarchy, creates a very specific representation of the fundamentalist Other."[13] And South African historian Mohamed Adhikari has, on the contrary, launched devastating criticism of *Hotel Rwanda* as a film that shies away from explicit violence; advocating a happy and upbeat ending which "strikes a false note [. . .] because it actively encourages uninformed viewers to conclude that with the RPF about to capture Kigali, the genocide will soon come to an end."[14]

These analyses of *Hotel Rwanda* demonstrate the tension that surrounds this genocide and its audiovisual representations. The latter readings combine concerns about, yet again, simplified and corrupted audiovisual representations of Africa with what could, in comparable readings of the Holocaust, be labelled as revisionist interpretations of history. The unavoidable simplification of historical narratives in audiovisual representations of the past seems to be, in the case of Rwanda, interpreted as malicious condensations that deliberately alter the past instead of being perceived as unfortunate but narratively necessary abridgements.

The purpose of this book is to study how the audiovisual historical media memory of the Rwandan genocide has developed and been shaped as a global media event, from 1994 up until today. The main source material will consist of the approximately 200 feature films, short films, documentaries, television series, as well as television news items on the Rwandan genocide that have been produced and distributed at a global level over the last thirty years, making the Rwandan genocide the most audiovisually recreated genocide, second only to the Holocaust. The main research questions are: (1) How is the historical memory of the Rwandan genocide constructed, re-represented, and used in these audiovisual productions? (2) How are transnational historical media memories created and then upheld at a global level? (3) What happens to media memories when they travel from the local, through the national, to the global, and then back again?

This is a broad survey of films on the Rwandan genocide, which include productions from thirty-nine different countries,[15] and the aim of this book is to introduce readers to this extensive production, the majority of which are still quite unknown, both to the general public but also in the scholarship about audiovisual representations of the Rwandan genocide, where about twenty films and documentaries repeatedly continue to be discussed and criticized, while the vast majority of films, especially those produced in Rwanda, are unresearched and thus outside of the perceived historical media memory of the Rwandan genocide. In addition to the films and television news reporting, a vast number of source materials will be used, such as international film reviews, articles, debates, books, and interviews, but also teaching guides, official Rwandan documents, and UN reports. Although not an aim in itself, the reader will also be introduced to the scholarship and critical literature on the Rwandan genocide in general, and audiovisual representations of the Rwandan genocide in particular.

Film and History

Film and history have always had a complicated relationship. During the almost 130 years of film history (and over seventy years of television history) professional historians have been very hostile towards the act of communicating or teaching history by audiovisual means. The idea that film and television would even have the ability to produce and convey serious historiography is something that runs counter to what most of us are taught even in elementary school, where film and television are regarded suspiciously as deceptive media, or as mere entertainment.[16] This historic aversion is based primarily on two integrated positions: a socio-historical and a media-historical position.

The socio-historical position is connected to film and television's traditionally low social status as, first and foremost, commercial and entertaining media without the ability to teach anything useful, and if they conveyed any knowledge, it was believed to be dangerous ideas about violence, sex, and the unlawful taste of leisure rather than morally uplifting history lessons. More than a century of heated debate about the film medium's seduction of children and youth, women, and the working class—with still ongoing worldwide regulations such as film censorship—is evidence of this lingering negative attitude.[17] What follows is a cultural hierarchy where the written word always stands above the audiovisual representation. That is, history produced within academia as well as popularly written history will automatically be deemed to be more accurate and truer in comparison with cinematic history.

Although historians and other gatekeepers have complained constantly about and have criticized the shortcomings of cinematic history, this lamenting seldom includes a serious discussion about the fact that audiovisual historiography has been, without a doubt, the most influential form of mediation of historical knowledge and understanding to the general public around the world—with the exception of large parts of the African continent—in the twentieth and twenty-first centuries.[18] The audiovisual communication of history through film and television has the ability to reach tens of thousands more people in comparison to the circulation of, for example, a PhD dissertation in history. Cinematic history thus constitutes a competitor to the history produced at universities and as teaching materials. The competitive situation and the cultural hierarchy contribute to a reality where cinematic history can be dismissed without any further reflections on the role that film and television actually play. Given that very many individuals are affected by and base much of their understanding of society on these audiovisually displayed histories—be they inaccurate or not—this detail alone should turn cinematic history into a more significant issue for the historical sciences than it is currently.

The media-historical position is related to the fact that cinematic history must always dramatize the past and simplify historic events by showing a selection of events, people, and details.[19] Film and television narratives can by default, therefore, be criticized as false ahistorical creations; a critique generally based on factual errors and oversimplifications in specific examples such as the already mentioned films *Schindler's List* and *Hotel Rwanda*. However, this does not mean that film and television producers of cinematic history simply make up their stories as they go along, without a basis in history. Leading authorities on a subject are, as a rule, engaged as historical experts on the relevant period in order for everything to be as historically accurate as possible in the finished product. Despite this, big budget historical films such as *Gladiator* (2000) harbor hundreds and hundreds of historical inaccuracies that professional historians and film critics alike often see as their designated task to correct.[20] The producers of cinematic history, however, are not primarily looking to reproduce an exact historical truth; they want to produce a successful film or a television series that has to take into account both economic and stylistic factors. The style of the film includes the component of history as part of the cinematic presentation and its narrative strategy, which in turn is structured by contemporary conventions about how a certain period ought to be portrayed for audiences to perceive it as realistic. One of the criticisms aimed at *Gladiator* was the fact that the marble statues in the film were white and not painted as they demonstrably had been during Antiquity. However, the general perception of these statues of Antiquity is that they are white, because this is what audiences have learned over a period of more than 100 years from looking at photographs in school textbooks, and after having watched numerous feature films and television documentaries about Antiquity where the "truth" about the white statues has been etched into memory. For this reason, the statues stayed white in *Gladiator*, despite the fact that the history professors, the director, and the production designer knew very well that this was an anachronism.[21]

The criticism of cinematic history as something that is fabricated and therefore untrue lies close to the fact that professional historians too are bound to dramatize and simplify their material as they write history. As historian Hayden White once pointed out, this means that even scholarly history constitutes a sort of fiction based on facts.[22] This can be exemplified by the circumstance that people generally tend to confuse the *concept of history* with the *concept of the past*. While the past is what really happened once, history is always a meager *representation* of the past. Hence, the composition of history, either with words or audiovisually, is just a pale imitation of the past since no historian could take all historical facts into consideration when writing history; facts that thereto must be interpreted to create a story. Professional historians use source criticism as a method, weighing sources against each other and judging their authenticity, their temporality, and their tendency. This approach is aimed at an objective historiography, but in the end even the most painstakingly meticulous historian must make selections and interpretations of her/his source material. As a result, a subjective element will always exist in all history produced. However, owing to the cultural hierarchy of the book and the film—but also because historians safeguard their profession, among other ways by criticizing cinematic history for being fabricated—this circumstance is rarely problematized.[23] The only exception is when historians blatantly violate the basic minimum requirements for the history profession, as is the case with revisionist historians such as David Irving and Robert Faurisson, both outspoken deniers of the Holocaust.[24]

Written, scholarly history and cinematic history can thus be said to exist in the same public arena of *historical culture* where the creation of historical memories and representations must be analyzed as an ongoing process—a struggle—where images and words, and the interpretation of those images and words, bounces between the national and the transnational, and between different media such as books, films, television, and the Internet.[25] American historian Robert A. Rosenstone has stated that while scholarly history is based on facts, the end result—the book or the article—always transgresses those facts when put out into a world full of moral arguments, metaphors, and symbolism. Moreover, Rosenstone stresses that cinematic history too is based on facts, although perhaps on a looser basis, but that the end result—the film, the documentary, or the television series—nevertheless is put out into the same arena of historical culture where it is analyzed and interpreted with the same moral arguments, metaphors, and symbolism. It is in this arena, or this intersection of historical culture, where it becomes valuable to study cinematic history; that is, as a history of the past that undoubtedly affects people's view of the past and of society, precisely as does the history taught in school and in textbooks.[26]

The relationship between film and history, and between television and history, has almost exclusively been an Anglo-American field of research. European research on the subject, for instance, has been more scarce, and symptomatically the preponderance of European research on cinematic history has been on American historical films and US film culture.[27] The main reason for this is

Hollywood's dominance when it comes to the production of expensive historical fictions with global impact, such as *Saving Private Ryan* (1998), *Rome* (2005-2007), and *Boardwalk Empire* (2010-2014). Likewise, the British tradition with great costume dramas such as *Brideshead Revisited* (1981), *Gandhi* (1982), and *Downton Abbey* (2010-2015) falls under such Anglo-American dominance. Prolific scholars such as Rosenstone, American historian Robert Brent Toplin, and British film scholar Andrew Higson have all emphasized that the historical sciences no longer can afford to ignore the actual impact of film and television as mediators of historical knowledge. Instead of simply dismissing cinematic history, they assert that film and television must be examined according to their own inherent medial conditions, i.e., as media with different features, codes, and conventions when it comes to creating historical milieus and historical knowledge and understandings of the past.[28]

However, research within the field of film and history has been undertheorized or focused on details. Furthermore, the field can be divided into two: between those who critically reject history on film and those who positively embrace history portrayed on film, and to the latter group belong scholars like Rosenstone and Toplin. What both groups usually have in common is a focus on specific examples, either on errors and oversimplifications or on how certain historical films work. The singular example may then stand as an example for a larger group of historical films or perhaps for a certain historical period—often according to the hypothesis, or perhaps truism, that historical films always are connected to their production context, which in different ways affects the historical period the films depict.[29] But what exactly is affecting the film from a contextual point of view, and which criteria to choose (budget, technical, actors, geographical, educational, etc.), is often not established nor even related to each other. On the other hand, there is an impetus within the field on a focus on symbolism and semiotics as a way to understand how cinematic history works. Here the works of American film scholar Vivian Sobchak and French film theorist Christian Metz are often cited, particularly *The Persistence of History: Cinema, Television and the Modern Event* and *The Imaginary Signifier*, which both have their strengths but which fall short when it comes to an overall understanding of what cinematic history entails, especially when considering criteria such as the implications of repetition, change over time vis-à-vis the historical period/event portrayed, and an understanding of how cinematic history is relayed on a transnational level.[30] Further, the focus on singular examples of cinematic history, in combination with semiotic and/or psychoanalytic theories, has led to studies that often reject the commercial film for studies of more artful and thus, seemingly, more valuable films.[31] Needless to say, all film projects are commercial in some sense and by rejecting commercial films or films with a classical realist narrative, the researcher ignores the fact that Hollywood films usually reach much larger audiences than a European art film or an experimental film. This is not to say that the latter type of films are not worthy of research, rather the opposite, but I think it is damaging to constantly create a quite pointless dichotomy between commercial and valuable films. Both types of films should be included and analyzed, as both types circulate in the same historical culture.

Another dichotomy is the one between narrative fiction films and documentaries in relation to cinematic history. There are, of course, differences between Hollywood feature films and historical documentaries mainly produced for television. However, the main difference lies in the reception and in the different expectations that these genres raise, rather than in the execution *per se* when considered from the viewpoint of source criticism and historical accuracy. Both genres are representations of the past; in no way more true or more false due to their structure and narrative mode.[32] However, the expectations of reality and truthfulness connected to the historical documentary are as old as the film medium itself. Swedish historian Ulf Zander has pointed out that the requirement of realism was associated to the historical film, even from an early stage, and that a belief in the proverb "The camera never lies" was linked to the notion that historians could find the truth in documents and other artifacts during the first decades of the twentieth century. Nonetheless, with the professionalization of the historical sciences, all films were automatically disqualified as source material—except for what was considered as documentary material in actualities, documentaries, and newsreels. Zander claims that this "documentary prejudice" actively contributed to "instill the differences between the documentary film and commercial feature film."[33]

While the historical feature film has been thoroughly scrutinized and criticized by historians, film critics, and teachers over the years, the historical documentary has not been subjected to the same criticism. There is only one full-length study which specifically addresses the relationship between the documentary genre and history, written by Swedish historian David Ludvigsson. In *The Historian-Filmmaker's Dilemma*, Ludvigsson examines how history is used in a modern society, and how the past is audiovisually mediated in historical documentaries that were made for Swedish public television between 1968 and 2000. The study has a distinct producer's perspective and the analyses are structured according to the cognitive, moral, and aesthetic considerations that the filmmakers had to make.[34]

Furthermore, as a historian, Ludvigsson asks if film and television producers/directors can, or perhaps should, be regarded as historians on an equal footing with scholarly historians. Rosenstone and Toplin, for instance, have championed the idea that film and television producers/directors ought to be considered as proper historians, since they communicate historical knowledge.[35]

While Ludvigsson concurs with the idea that television producers mediate and sometimes produce history, he is reluctant to see cinematic history as legitimate. In the same spirit, he downplays the television medium's importance as a mediator of historical knowledge based on the somewhat outdated conception that television audiences are more passive than active and he claims, in addition to this, that "people do not trust in the television's stories anyway."[36]

This is, once again, a case in point for how the historical sciences safeguard their profession by criticizing cinematic history in a way that neglects to give an adequate answer to the question of how we are supposed to regard and value audiovisually communicated history, and its possible effects, in a modern media society. However, it is a mistake to dismiss film and television producers/directors out of hand as less important on the basis only that they are not academically trained historians. Considering the impact that films and television programs do have, producers of cinematic history should indeed be viewed as serious-minded historians. Their audiovisually communicated histories cannot be seen as mere entertainment or fiction, and of course not as impeccable stories about the past above all scrutiny. Instead, these productions should be examined in the same objective and vigorous way as written history is assessed. Obviously, different media require different methods. Nevertheless, the same basic questions need to be addressed pertaining to the history produced for film and television. This includes a discussion of the scope and impact of cinematic history; how audiovisual history is communicated aesthetically and pedagogically, as well as how cinematic history relates to written history. In short, how cinematic history contributes to our understanding of the past.

In order to realize a new approach within the field of film and history—and to avoid the unfruitful dichotomies between commercial and valuable films and fictional and documentary films—this book will analyze a large body of films and documentaries on the Rwandan genocide. These films and documentaries will be analyzed side by side, rather than as opposites. The step from specific examples to analyzing a large body of films on a historic event is rare within film and history. One inspiring exception is American film scholar Aaron Kerner's *Film and the Holocaust*, where he discusses a large body of films on the Holocaust, based on genre.[37] My approach will be mainly chronological, but also thematic and geographical, with the intention of being able to trace how a historical media memory is created, sustained, and then divided into memories, nationally and transnationally. In addition, I will emphasize the creation of *emblematic images*, that is, images that are repeated and constantly recycled in the creation and in the maintenance of a historical media memory. The concepts of change and repetition are therefore of vital importance, which will add something new to the field of film and history.

Film and Genocide

Research on film and genocide, and especially films about the Rwandan genocide, is seldom located within the field of film and history. In fact, much of the criticism does not emanate from film studies or history but comes instead from scholars based in a multitude of different subjects, such as law, cultural studies, languages, human rights, Christian studies, and peace and conflict studies.[38] Many scholars who write about film and genocide have remarkably shallow knowledge of how the medium of film works, and of how to discuss its position within society without falling back on handy clichés. Often, this results in quite basic criticism of the films that is in accordance with the general social attitude that says that film and television are merely unreliably entertainment media.

One of these misconceptions is the constant reference to *Hotel Rwanda* as a "blockbuster."[39] The concept of a blockbuster film can refer either to a huge financial success or to a high-concept film, that is, a high-budget production aimed at the mass market—often associated with pre-sold properties, merchandising, and heavy marketing campaigns—that is deliberately created to become a commercial triumph. Audiences are thus manipulated to a certain degree to endorse these type of films rather than to choose for themselves at the box office.[40] Examples of blockbuster films are *The Dark Night* (2008), the *Pirates of the Caribbean* franchise (2003–2017), and *Avengers: Endgame* (2019). *Hotel Rwanda* was not a runaway commercial success, and it cannot be characterized as a preconceived blockbuster film since it was a moderately budgeted film (with an estimated budget of US$17.5 million)[41] without the support of an intensive marketing campaign with the intention to make huge amounts of money. Hence, to identify *Hotel Rwanda*, as well as other films with a genocide theme, as Hollywood blockbusters is not only incorrect, it is also a disparaging technique to reduce these films to a core of commercial (and illicit) values that unavoidably taints the subject matter and its message—no matter how historically correct or incorrect these films are.

Obviously, there are other reasons in play than just the commercial one when the decision is made to produce a film, a documentary, or a television series about genocide. Such reasons are often idealistic and/or ideological; they can be educational (that the film in question can teach and inform audiences about genocide); they can be moral (never let it happen again); they can be religious (to promote reconciliation and forgiveness); they can be political (pointing the finger); or they can arise out of a guilty conscience. Of course, further down the line the motivations, as we shall see, can even border on the exploitative and the offensive according to the reception by some audiences, but the main motivation is hardly ever economic because, as Greg Barker, the director of *Ghosts of Rwanda* (2004), quite bluntly puts it: "if you ask them, people don't particularity want to see films about genocide."[42]

Over the last forty-five years genocide has become a relatively common narrative in film and television productions, in particular pertaining to the numerous representations of the Holocaust. The seminal breakthrough came with the success of NBC's television miniseries *Holocaust* (1978), which was televised in the US and most Western European countries and received tremendous ratings in 1978 and 1979. Prior to 1978, representations of genocide were all but absent from the screens, with only a few rare and explicit exceptions, such as the two Polish films *Ostanti etap* (*The Last Stage*, 1948) and *Ulica Graniczna* (*Border Street*, 1948), or the critically acclaimed but also controversial documentary *Night and Fog*—a film that, for example, was heavily censored in Sweden, with no fewer than nine cuts, mostly concerning archival footage of mutilated corpses.[43] In addition to this, some thirty American and European films were made between 1945 and 1978 in which the Holocaust featured in the background of the main narrative, for example in films like *Die Letzte Chance* (*The Last Chance*, 1945), *The Stranger* (1946), *Sterne* (*Stars*, 1959), *Exodus* (1960), and *The Odessa File* (1974). Nonetheless, the Holocaust was generally considered to be a sensitive subject at best, and, at worst, an impossible subject that, for reasons of morality, could not be exploited in the arts in the aftermath of the Second World War. The latter, and clearly dominant, position was expressed by a number of influential intellectuals, such as Theodore Adorno and Eli Wiesel, and applied irrespective of whether the artistic representation concerned films, paintings, or novels, as it was claimed that a conventional dramatization of the Holocaust would inevitably lead to mere trivialization.[44] The exceptions were more intellectual films in the European art cinema tradition such as *La caduta degli dei* (*The Damned*, 1969) or *Il portiere di note* (*The Night Portier*, 1974), i.e., films that failed to reach a wider audience and that therefore had a limited effect on the historical consciousness of the Holocaust.[45]

In addition to the sense of trivialization and a fear that the Holocaust could be turned into a Hollywood theme park, there are several additional reasons, some carrying more weight than others, for this often-fierce antagonism towards an explicit rendering of the Holocaust that kept the subject away from the screen. American film scholar Miriam Bratu Hansen points out, among other things, the problems associated with the limitations of the classical narrative, and the question of cinema subjectivity in an article on *Schindler's List*:

> A fundamental limitation of classical narrative in relation to history, and to the historical event of the Shoah in particular, is that it relies on neoclassicist principles on compositional unity, motivation, linearity, equilibrium,

and closure—principles singularly inadequate in the fate of an event that by its very nature defies our narrative urge to make sense of it, to impose order on the discontinuity and otherness of historical experience.[46]

The strong sentiment that genocides, especially the Holocaust but also the Rwandan genocide, are events that to all intents and purposes are impossible to make sense of within the realm of the arts does have several implications. First, it clashes forcefully with the resilient notion of the Enlightenment's faith in the power of knowledge; that is, the belief that "if only people knew, they would act."[47] Second, since the educational idea often constitutes the guiding principle for the production and even existence of genocide films and television programs, this creates a contradiction in objectives. Historically, the reluctant attitude towards portraying genocide has in fact contributed to thwarting the creation of public memories of genocides, which in turn has led to a situation where genocides can, and are, overlooked, mythologized, and thus reduced as historical events, as in revisionist histories of the Holocaust, the Armenian genocide, and the Rwandan genocide.[48] When the alternative of respectful silence is weighed against the shortcomings of film and television narratives, the question must be asked as to whether silence really is the better option, not least in light of the fact that audiovisual media have been the primary vehicle for communicating historical knowledge and remembrance during the twentieth and twenty-first centuries.[49]

The overall attitude towards the Holocaust can be exemplified by political theorist Hannah Arendt's often quoted phrase "banality of evil," coined at the Adolf Eichmann trial in Israel in 1961.[50] This prosaic elucidation is symptomatic, in that it does not explain anything but instead reduces the Holocaust to an irrational act of evil, clearly part of the paradigm in which the Holocaust and other genocides are perceived as unexplainable. Nick Hughes, television journalist and director of *100 Days* (2001), argues that "you cannot show the true horror of genocide [. . .] because you are dealing with masses and masses, hundreds of thousands of silent, individual deaths, and that's extremely hard to describe or even imagine."[51] British scholar and filmmaker, Piotr A. Cieplak, agrees and develops this truism in relation to films on the Rwandan genocide, claiming that:

> the uniqueness of the concept of genocide stems from the fact that it cannot be understood or explained, beyond its socio-political and historical conditioning. It is beyond human comprehension and manifests itself in the lack of possibility of closure evoked by Adorno and Bernstein. Thus, all that can be achieved through this technique of approximative 'othering' is a categorization of the film within the constraints of western genres, somewhere

between a melodrama and an action thriller, which, in themselves, act as limiting frameworks.[52]

However, as Bratu Hansen asserts, the Holocaust has predominantly been dependent on mass-mediated forms of memory.[53] Following the enormous impact of the television series *Holocaust*, the Holocaust became the genocide narrative *par excellence*, quickly developing into an accepted and even normalized subject despite the fears of its philosophical detractors. Aaron Kerner points out the fact that *Holocaust*, "[f]or all its lackluster qualities [. . .] perhaps had more material effects than all the representations of the Holocaust combined."[54] After 1980, the production of Holocaust or Holocaust-related films virtually exploded out of its previous semi-suppression. Consequently, the number of feature films and feature-length documentaries produced between 1979 and 2023 exceeded 500, and the number is still growing. But if genocide really is "beyond human comprehension" that would mean that all these films and television programs are either made up, with flawed connections to the past (which constitutes a strong view among their critics), or it can also mean that they can actually communicate some kind of historical knowledge to their audiences. One thing is beyond dispute, and that is that the impact of *Holocaust*, and later of *Schindler's List*, has contributed to the public and academic discourse on the Holocaust, generating debate and academic research. This could certainly be understood as if cinematic history has contributed to make this incomprehensible genocide a little more comprehensible. Now, the question is not *if* genocides can be represented but rather *how* genocides are depicted and rationalized within film and television narration.

By comparison, other genocides, such as those committed in Belgian Congo 1884-1908, German South-West Africa 1904-1907, the Ottoman Empire 1915, Indonesia 1965-1966, Cambodia 1975-1979, and East Timor 1975-1999, have in no way spawned an equal number of films, with only singular exceptions such as *The Killing Fields* (1984), *Ararat* (2002), *The Act of Killing* (2012), or *The Year of Living Dangerously* (1982) where the Indonesian anti-communist genocide acts as a backdrop. Even atrocities committed against minorities other than Jews within the realm of the Holocaust—*The Porajmos* (the Romani people genocide), the persecution of homosexuals, the Euthanasia program, the murdering of some 3 to 4 million Soviet prisoners of war in 1941/1942—are hardly ever discussed in public. It goes without saying that these genocides seldom have been transformed into commercial feature films or docudramas nor broadcast repeatedly as documentaries on prime-time television. The outcome of this silence is that these genocides remain absent from public memory and, consequently, are not part of any local, national, or transnational historical consciousness. The danger of this non-memorialization can be illustrated by the continued and open discrimination of the Romani people in European Union member nations such as Italy, Hungary, Romania, Czech Republic, and Slovakia.[55]

In addition to the Holocaust, the one exception to this general lack or utter avoidance of audiovisual depictions of genocides is the large number of films, documentaries, and television programs produced about the Rwandan genocide. Thus far, approximately forty narrative feature films and short films, and approximately 160 feature-length documentaries and documentary shorts, have been made, making the Rwandan genocide the second most audiovisually recreated genocide. Together these films form a powerful audiovisual historical media memory of the Rwandan genocide on a global scale. First, nearly all these films, in one way or another, have been made with the purpose of informing and spreading knowledge about an "unknown" genocide. Second, many of these productions of cinematic history tend to emphasize a moral viewpoint aimed at the failure of the Western powers to intervene. Third, most of these films, fictional or factual, draw from the same type of emblematic images to illustrate, rather than to explain, the genocide.[56] These films are thus often didactic, *and* they frequently adopt a Western viewpoint at the same time as they utilize images that prowl between the bestiality of depicting the incomprehensible and representing Africa as sheer otherness. The term bestiality is not used here to refer to the horrific scenes of the genocide but, instead, echoing Adorno's idea of involvement through representation, that "the very act of attempting to represent a thing as incomprehensible as genocide creates a set of challenges and choices that need to be faced."[57] Collectively it can be said that these films work to communicate the message that the events in Rwanda constituted a horrific episode in human history that never can be allowed to happen again, similar to the intention and message of most genocide films.

Then again, films on the Rwandan genocide are still in the midst of development. With few exceptions, the films and television programs produced thus far fit into two overall genres only, those of the solemn drama and the factual documentary—the expected genres for films dealing with genocide—whereas Holocaust films have outgrown these genres and at this point have the ability to be rendered as action films, thrillers, exploitation films, pornography, horror films, avant-garde films, and as straightforward comedies. Notable examples of the latter genre are *Train de vie* (*Train of Life*, 1999), *Jacob the Liar* (1999), and especially Roberto Benigni's *La Vita è Bella* (*Life is Beautiful*, 1997), which was warmly greeted all around the world, winning three Academy Awards, but was also criticized ferociously as a revisionist Holocaust film that was even said to justify the extermination of the Jews in the twentieth century.[58] In spite of this, I would argue that with the exception of high-profile films such as *Schindler's List*, *Life is Beautiful*, and *Hotel Rwanda*, most films on genocide, especially if they are perceived as educational documentaries, generally are not criticized but instead are embraced as important mediators of the past, often solely on the grounds of their profound subject matter.[59] The idea that audiovisual representations of genocide are inapropriate is thus unproductive and, to some degree, even preposterous.

Here attention will be given to the total output of audiovisual representations of the Rwandan genocide. This is, almost certainly, an impossible task since no one can get access to and watch every film clip ever made of the genocide. Nevertheless, the aim is to trace how a transnational historical media memory of the Rwandan genocide has developed since 1994, but also how this memory is transformed into media memories. To accomplish this in a manageable way, the analysis will be divided into four parts that consider different forms of audiovisual source materials and genres as well as the correspondence between local, national, and transnational levels of the global media landscape.

The first part of the book is a study of Swedish television news reporting on the Rwandan genocide as it took place between April and July 1994. At this local level the question of actual space allowed for the genocide will be deepened by questions of how the genocide first was portrayed, constructed, and explained in a Western context. In accordance with this, the reporting will be evaluated as a part of the international media reporting of the genocide to examine in what way the Swedish impetus correlates to similar portrayals on a global scale. The second part of the book analyzes how a transnational historical media memory was slowly created between 1994 and 2005, and how the repeated use of a number of emblematic images, first shown as television news around the world in 1994, contributed to the creation of a global public consciousness vis-à-vis the Rwandan genocide. Part three analyzes how the official historical media memory of the Rwandan genocide has been maintained on a global level from around 2004 up until today, a period that has seen an explosion of the number of films and documentaries about the Rwandan genocide, following the impact of *Hotel Rwanda*, in a similar way that the TV series *Holocaust* impacted the audiovisual representations of the Holocaust. However, during this period, the moral and educational themes are supplemented by other themes that include a special focus on women, AIDS, and rape; reconciliation films; and revisionist films that challenge the official historical media memory of the Rwandan genocide. The fourth and final part of the book is a return to the national perspective and analyzes how the genocide is portrayed in Rwandan film and television productions, focusing on how Rwanda, as a nation, creates its own audiovisual historical media memory of the genocide and how this memory is incorporated into the ongoing reconciliation process and a new national identity.

All four parts will have separate introductions and a contextualization of the source materials and of the subject matter, and, subsequently, analyses of the audiovisual material in relation to context (e.g., theory, history, geography, reception, genre) and previous research. While the chronological approach will enable a focus on repetition and change over time, research on the Rwandan genocide, and particularly on audiovisual representations of the Rwandan genocide, will be presented and discussed along the way and, when appropriate, in direct relation to the films analyzed.

Global History and Transnational Historical Media Memories

Global history or world history is usually defined as a field of historical study that examines history from a global perspective, often by looking for common patterns that emerge across cultures. Global historians tend to use thematic approaches that revolve around either integration or difference. In the former case integrational processes are studied to examine how, for example, history has drawn people of the world together.[60]

Nevertheless, history is predominantly, almost by default, a national subject taught in schools to promote national objectives. Of course, schools and other educational outlets communicate history which moves beyond narrow national borders, but this international history should not be confused with global history. International history is certainly equivalent to the history of the world, but it is typically also a history of the world told from a certain (national) perspective, where the Eurocentric perspective has upheld a dominant position on account of the lingering consequences of colonialism and post-colonialism. Is it therefore productive or even conceivable to talk about global or transnational memories in the same way as when writing global history? American historian David L. Ransel differentiates between global, international, and transnational history, arguing that:

> global history strives for comprehensiveness, while international history, which continues to use nation as its primary category of analysis, seeks to transcend the old diplomatic history by investigating not just interstate relations but cultural, social, political, labor, and other institutional contacts and influences between countries that affect state governments. Transnational history, in contrast, is concerned primarily with connections: how people, ideas, institutions, technology, and commerce flow across national borders and link up with or influence people and processes in other countries.[61]

Basically, a collective memory is when a group of people share the same memory. A nation can choose to memorialize certain events in the past to create (a sense of) national unity. Traditionally, that is since the nineteenth century, wars and symbolic representatives of the nation such as kings (and sometimes queens) and presidents have been used to mold this memory, usually in the form of a "golden era" of the past but sometimes also in the form of a historic disaster that helped to shape the modern nation-state.[62] In this case, the Rwandan genocide is clearly one such historic disaster that is used to create a sense of national unity in order to shape a modern nation-state.

Transnational history and thus transnational media memories are undeniably similar to collective national memories but with two decisive differences: (1) a transnational media memory must reach, and thereby include, more people, and in order to do that the memory needs (2) a suitable vehicle, at the same time as it has to transcend the notion of the national to capture people's imagination. Transnational media memories could thus be understood as the intermediation of ideas and notions of the past that flow over national borders and connect people on a global level. In this process audiovisual and visual media such as film, television, and photography have played a major role during the twentieth and twenty-first centuries. Even more so than books. A case in point is the well-known news photographs that have contributed to create transnational media memories on a global level: "The Assassination of Lee Harvey Oswald" (1963), "The Execution of Viet Cong Suspect Nguyen Van Lem" (1968), "The Blue Marble" (1972), "Children Fleeing a Napalm Strike" (1972), "The Tank Man at Tiananmen Square" (1989), "Falling Man from World Trade Center" (2001), and "Hooded Detainee as Abu Ghraib Prison" (2004)—most of which incidentally emanate from live documentary film footage.

The concept of *transnational historical media memories* is thus dependent on audiovisual media—and its proven ability to override national, cultural, and language borders—to a higher degree than national memories. This interconnected world-system, defined by an audiovisual transnationalism, began with the rapid worldwide spread of the invention of the film medium around 1900, and has since accelerated with television, VHS, DVD, computers, the Internet, and smartphones. With its circulation of stills and moving images, information, and media created memories, audiovisual transnationalism has over the years developed into an audiovisual lingua franca or "the global force that link[s] people or institutions across nations."[63] It is a key concept for the comprehension of the globalized mass media market.

British film scholars Elizabeth Ezra and Terry Rowden even claim that audiovisual media "rapidly is displacing literature [. . .] as the textual emblematization of cosmopolitan knowing and identity," dubbing the phenomenon "Global Cine-literacy."[64] While I am not sure that this cine-literacy has overtaken the hegemonic position of the written word on a national level, or even reached the kind of geographical scope to be labeled as global, I am quite certain that it has affected the communication and the notion of historical media memories at a global level.

Here it is reasonable to reflect on the concept of transnational historical media memories, especially regarding the concept of the transnational as an equation to globalization. We all know that Hollywood, with its big-budget historical films, dominates the world market and that audiences are presented with American versions of "world history" in, for example, heavily criticized films such as *Black Hawk Down* (2001) and *U571* (2000). Many scholars and film critics therefore automatically associate globalization, particularly pertaining to audiovisual culture, to a commercial Coca-Colonization or an Americanization of the world.[65] However, regarding historical films and transnational historical media memories, this simplified view must be problematized.

First, although it is often obvious that historical Hollywood feature films tend to splice the truth, this is not a fruitful way to approach these films, particularly by dismissing them for being too commercial, as was the case with films such as *Schindler's List* and *Hotel Rwanda*. The preoccupation with historical inaccuracies in Hollywood feature films—a gatekeeping task often performed by film critics and not by historians—tends to become a meticulous search to prove this commercialism rather than turning into a discussion of what this communication of history actually means for our historical knowledge and memories. Certainly, historical inaccuracies can become important on certain levels (i.e., genocide denial) but as Robert Brent Toplin has claimed in a defense of the historical Hollywood film, the preoccupation with small "lies" has led to the failure to recognize the larger "truths"; that the film medium has the ability to teach history on a cognitive level that surpasses any popular science book, textbook, or dissertation, and this on a global level.[66]

Second, while criticism can be aimed at narrative feature films based on actual historic events such as *Hotel Rwanda* for being constructed, commercial, and untrue, the same criticism does not usually apply to the documentary genre and television news since these genres in themselves are commonly believed to be mediators of reality. As previously mentioned, the documentary genre has seldom been under scrutiny within the field of film and history and I believe that the main reason for this, besides the notion that documentaries connote reality, is the fact that the genre is not considered to be "American" *per se*, with all its implications.

The documentary genre has rarely been associated with Hollywood when it comes to, for example, classical narrative, subjects, or the claim that the outcome consists of dreamlike fabrications of "real life." Documentaries, and especially documentaries on genocide such as *Shoah* (1985) or *Shake Hands with the Devil: The Journey of Roméo Dallaire* (2004), are conversely taken seriously, and are often hailed as important regardless of their national origin or subject matter—or that they in fact make selections and construct their histories out of the past, as does any feature film.[67] That is, if they do not completely go against established historiography. The transnational element of the genocide documentary therefore seems to work on the level of transparency; that is, the national origin of the sender does not seem to matter since the subject matter of genocide concerns us all on a transnational and idealistic level, summarized and consolidated by the United Nation's Convention on Genocide from 1948, as of today ratified by 152 states.[68]

However, audiovisual transnationalism is not omniscient as it does not apply to all audiences everywhere. A comparison can be made with the eco-documentary, and here the BBC's heavily awarded wildlife television documentary series *Planet Earth* (2006) and *Life* (2009) are cases in point where the breathtaking images and the factual presentation are seemingly not aimed at a particular national body but to the world at large, as in the motto: "this concerns us all." In this case the transnational level acts as if it is neutral, but it is aimed at predominantly Western audiences, comfortably reclining in their living rooms in front of the television set. As we will see, something similar happens when the seriousness of genocide is transferred from Europe to Africa or any other "dark" places outside of the Western Hemisphere.

Third, the view that equates globalization with Americanization must ignore other clearly transnational film and television industries, which create their own transnational historical media memories, for example Bollywood in India, Hong Kong, and Egypt, and Nollywood in Nigeria with its local upshoots like Hillywood in Rwanda. All these film industries are in fierce competition with Hollywood, and they also dominate many of the markets outside of North America and Europe.

Is there a way to escape Western dominance in global history? Ransel states that most scholars try to escape a Eurocentric point of view but that this is just an aspiration. However innovative a scholar is he/she will inevitably have to use "analytical categories that are necessarily culture-bound such as 'nation' and 'civilization'."[69] History is therefore always culture-bound. But should historians and media scholars therefore abandon any attempts at writing global history from a "global" perspective? This is not the place to answer that philosophical question, but a parallel question is whether it is possible to study transnational historical media memories without a Eurocentric (or even a Hollywood) perspective?

I would say that the solution is not to try to avoid it altogether but to be aware of how a Eurocentric perspective has affected the source material, and what impact this can have on the analysis. In this case, how have different but yet interconnected transnational historical media memories been created about the Rwandan genocide via television news, feature films, and documentaries.

Why are these audiovisual memories created in a certain way? How is history portrayed and discussed? What functions do images that mediate information, knowledge, and interpretations of the "incomprehensible" have in different contexts? For example, there is no doubt that many of the films and documentaries produced by Western countries place a strong focus on the failure of the UN and thus a guilty Western consciousness. Does this substantial Eurocentric perspective on the genocide have any implications? Perhaps at the expense of a history of what actually happened? As German historian Jörn Rüsen maintains, "there is an inevitable logic involved here: once memory moves beyond commemorating the past and contemplates its role in the present and its significant for the future, it has to find ways to integrate negative, even traumatic events of the past to form a new historical identity."[70] In this case we are talking about multiple transnational historical media memories that both contemplate their role in the present at the same time as they commemorate the past; sometimes on a collision course with each other, and often from different geographical and political perspectives, but all with an aim towards the future, either to proclaim "never again" or in a pursuit of a new national identity.

Rwandan History and a Historical Overview of the Rwandan Genocide

This is not an exhaustive recapitulation of what happened in Rwanda in 1994. This brief recapitulation should instead be seen, and used, as a necessary overview of historical information needed before the analysis of television news, documentaries, and narrative feature films commence. As with all other genocides, the one in Rwanda is contested in different ways. This means that there exists more than one history about these events in the past, interpreted through more than one perspective. Nonetheless, this overview is based on what established historians and other scholars generally have agreed took place in Rwanda in 1994.

However, first it is necessary to clarify what to call the genocide and the use of the term the "Rwandan genocide." The Rwandan genocide is a term that is used internationally and that has been established as the normative term in a similar way that the "Holocaust" has come to signify the genocide of European Jews. In Rwanda, the use of this term is contested because Rwandans feel the focus does not end up on the perpetrators. A parallel is that the Holocaust is not called the German genocide, nor the genocide in Germany, which would be the equivalent to the genocide in Rwanda.[71] Instead, Rwanda has officially adopted the term "the 1994 genocide against the Tutsi" to better describe the genocide. This term in a sense is officially sanctioned at an international level, after lobbying from Rwanda, by the UN via resolution 2150 that was voted for in 2014. The resolution recognized the genocide and the importance of fighting genocide denial, and in it, there is a wording of the genocide that has been accepted in Rwanda as the normative one, namely "the 1994 genocide against the Tutsi in Rwanda, during which Hutu and others who opposed the genocide were also killed."[72] In this book, the terms "the Rwandan genocide" and "the genocide against the Tutsi" will be used alternately but not interchangeably. While the term "the Rwandan genocide" signifies an overall image and understanding of the genocide, mainly from a Western perspective, the term "the genocide against the Tutsi" is used to establish exactly what happened. In Chapter 11, on how Rwanda has created its own films on the genocide, the shorthand "genocide" will be used, because it appears as self-evident in that context.

However, the genocide in Rwanda has a pre-history that is crucial for the understanding of the events that took place in 1994 and how the genocide later was memorialized and made into history.

Rwanda is a small and densely populated country with a history that dates back to at least the fourteenth century as the Kingdom of Rwanda.[73] Rwanda was one of the last African countries to be colonized in the European dash for Africa in the late nineteenth century. Europeans did not set foot in the country until 1894, and it was not until 1898 that Germany overtook the country and then ruled it as a colony. The Germans were ousted in 1916, as they lost all colonies after the First World War, and Belgium thereafter administrated Rwanda and Burundi as part of the Belgian Congo until its independence in 1962.[74]

Political scientist Catharine Newbury has written perhaps the most empirically thorough study on the division of Hutu and Tutsi, *Cohesion and Oppression*, released in 1988—before the genocide—in which she considers 100 years of Rwandan history prior to its independence in 1962. Newbury criticizes the alleged primordial perspective that has governed previous research on Rwanda in particular, and Africa in general, which has viewed political life as mere "tribal" or "ethnic" activities.[75] She clearly establishes that the categories of Hutu and Tutsi existed prior to the European colonization, but that Hutu and Tutsi categories were based on class rather than ethnicity—comparable to the social division between nobles and peasants in Europe before the nineteenth century—and that it was not unusual for a Hutu farmer to advance to a Tutsi noble, or vice versa.[76] These categories of status were slowly turning into ethnic identities even before the colonization; mostly as a result of the Tutsi monarchy's tightening grip over the state building process—promoting "Tutsi" in the process—in an effort to exercise power over the whole country. This in turn led to a more rigid division of ownership of land and cattle, the traditional class indicators in Rwanda, and thus to a harsher implementation of clientship relations between Tutsi and Hutu.[77]

The European colonization meant that first the Germans but above all the Belgians picked up on the "primordial" categories and ruled Rwanda according to a concept of "divide and conquer"—favoring Tutsi, the noble minority, over Hutu, the rural majority. With the introduction of the scientific concept of the day—race—during the interwar years these ethnic categories soon became even more rigidly defined, making it virtually impossible to pass from one category to the other, and all while social division continued to deepen.[78] From the 1930s onwards this categorization was implemented with the use of identity cards, which would carry immense importance during the genocide in 1994.[79]

Newbury argues that the dual colonial system for the Hutu created both the category of "Hutu" as well as political awareness, based on "ethnicity," within the group.[80] In the last years of Belgian rule the inflexible educational and religious division—upheld by the Roman Catholic Church with the intention of creating a Christian aristocracy composed of Tutsi—loosened and many Hutus were able to circumvent Tutsi oppression by instead working for the Europeans, who in turn washed their hands in face of the imminent surrender of the colony.[81] In fact, by the time of the popular revolution in 1959, which overturned the Tutsi monarchy and lead to Hutu rule, the ethnic consciousness had grown so strong among the Hutu that their political leadership refused to abandon the use of ethnic categorization in the identity cards.[82]

While Newbury placed emphasis on the ethnic and political division, Ugandan academic Mahmood Mamdani discusses Hutu and Tutsi as created racial categories as a way to explain the genocide. He states that it is necessary to distinguish between ethnic and racial violence, as "ethic violence can result in massacres, but not in genocide."[83] Consequently, this turned into a question of settlers against natives in Hutu political propaganda by the revolution in 1959, where the Tutsi were constructed as foreign invaders; that is, as a different race—something which continued and then was intensified in the years leading up to the genocide in 1994.[84] The creation of the Hutu Power movement, with its supremacist ideology, and the publication of the anti-Tutsi propaganda list, the "Hutu Ten Commandments," in 1990, are prime examples of how the notion of race was cemented.[85]

From 1962 the roles in Rwanda were thus reversed as Tutsis were now kept out of political power and persecuted. Several outbursts of genocidal violence also took place over the years, resulting in tens of thousands of deaths, so that, by 1990, approximately 900,000 Rwandan refugees lived in the neighboring countries of Uganda, Burundi, Zaire, and Tanzania.[86]

In 1987, children—both Hutu and Tutsi—of those who had fled over the years formed the Rwandan Patriotic Front (RPF) in Uganda with demands for the re-patriotization of the refugee diaspora to Rwanda.[87] In 1990 the RPF invaded northern Rwanda, initiating a successful low-intensity war that ranged on and off for the next two years until peace negotiations started in 1992, eventually leading to the Arusha Peace Agreement in 1993. The peace agreement was meant to instigate political and military reforms, and the implementation of a new constitution. A broad interim government was supposed to be appointed until democratic elections could be held. Furthermore, an international and neutral peacekeeping force was to be stationed in Rwanda, supervising the demobilization of the two fighting forces and making sure that the refugees could return.[88]

On October 5, four weeks after the Arusha Peace Agreement was supposed to be set in motion, the UN's Security Council adopted resolution 872, which established United Nations Assistance Mission for Rwanda (UNAMIR). It would then take an additional six months before the full peacekeeping force of 2,539 troops arrived in Rwanda, on March 22, 1994.[89] During this interval of time the violence escalated, supported by governmental propaganda aired by Radio Télévision Libre des Mille Collines (RTLM), and the peace process gradually fell into pieces.[90]

At approximately 8.20 pm on April 6, 1994, the plane carrying the presidents of Rwanda and Burundi, Juvénal Habyarimana and Cyprien Ntariyamira, respectively, was shot down outside Gregoire Kayibanda International Airport, killing all its passengers. Within an hour of the plane crash, roadblocks were set up in Rwanda's capital city, Kigali, signaling the start of the quickest and most gruesome genocide in modern history, as some 800,000 to 1 million people were murdered within the following 100 days.

Already in this summary paragraph three significant events and figures are contested. First, the plane crash is usually singled out as the signal to begin the genocide, and the dispute has been about which faction launched the rocket attack that killed the two presidents, Hutu extremists in FAR (Rwandan Armed Forces) or the rebels in the RPF? Several investigations have been made and the great majority of them point to the Hutu extremists being responsible. In 2012, a French investigation reevaluated the physical evidence and the testimonies from several of the previous investigations, confirming that the missile came from Kanombe Base, controlled by FAR forces, including the Presidential Guard, thus freeing the RPF of accountability.[91]

Second, the plane crash has been interpreted as a catalyst for the genocide; a view that fitted well with the initial reporting from Rwanda that, as we shall see in the next chapter, described the events that unfolded in 1994 as "civil war" governed by "chaos" and "anarchy" and triggered by "tribal quarrels." This, of course, blurred, and for some still blurs, the fact that the genocide was methodically planned with the purchase of weapons, the training of the militia Interahamwe, the establishing of detailed death lists of Tutsis and moderate Hutus all over the country prior to the genocide, and the plan to kill off Belgian UN soldiers with the intention of forcing the UN to withdraw its troops so that genocide could be perpetrated without interference from external forces.[92] This is partly documented in the so-called "Genocide Fax" that the Force Commander for UNAMIR, General Roméo Dallaire, sent to the UN after having met with an informant from the top level of the Interahamwe in January 1994.[93] French historian Gérard Prunier dates the idea of a "final solution" back to 1992, when President Habyarimana started to negotiate with the RPF.[94] All of these facts, plus the fact that roadblocks were set up and the killing began no more than an hour after the president's plane went down, heavily point the finger at Hutu political and military extremists for shooting down the plane, and as the instigators and perpetrators of the genocide against the Tutsi.

Third, there is still, due to the chaos of the situation, no consensus on the number of people killed during the genocide in Rwanda in 1994. The Rwandan government states that "more than one million" Tutsis and moderate Hutus were killed in the genocide, claiming that "over 80 percent of the Tutsi population" was killed.[95] The UN estimates the death toll at 800,000; while Human Rights Watch states that the genocide "claimed more than half a million lives."[96] Then of course there are the revisionists who claim that the genocide did not happen, that it only was a conspiracy, that it was a double genocide or that the genocide in fact was aimed against the Hutu.[97] In the face of the actual evidence available and the numerous testimonies from survivors, which included more than 95,000 orphans, these allegations are unreasonable.[98]

The killing began during the night of April 6–7 and was aimed at prominent moderate politicians, among them Prime Minister Agathe Uwilingiyimana, who was next after the president in the political succession. Almost all the moderate Hutu leadership was wiped out during this first night of targeted killings.[99] UNAMIR had sent fifteen UN soldiers to protect the Prime Minister. Five of them were of Ghanaian origin and were let go when soldiers from FAR came to assassinate Uwilingiyimana, but the ten Belgian UN soldiers were taken to Camp Kigali where they were tortured, mutilated, and hacked to death with machetes. According to the plan, a few days later the Belgian government decided to withdraw its troops, which were the largest and most well-equipped in UNAMIR.[100] Without the Belgian soldiers the UN's Security Council first decided to withdraw UNAMIR altogether on April 21 but then left a skeleton crew of 270 soldiers supported by around 200 local authorities.[101] On May 17, six weeks into the killings, the UN passed resolution 918, which would reinforce UNAMIR. However, the new soldiers did not start arriving until about a month later, and the role of UNAMIR II was confined to preserving security and stability.[102]

The evacuation of expatriates was immediate and almost complete. Belgian and French paratroopers arrived early in the morning of April 9, bringing

OUTGOING CODE CABLE

DATE: 11 JANUARY 1994

TO: BARIL\DPKO\UNATIONS NEW YORK
FROM: DALLAIRE\UNAMIR\KIGALI

FAX. NO: MOST IMMEDIATE-CODE CABLE-212-963-9852 INMARSAT:
FAX NO: 011-250-84273

SUBJECT: REQUEST FOR PROTECTION FOR INFORMANT

ATTN: MGEN BARIL.
ROOM NO. 2052

TOTAL NUMBER OF TRANSMITTED PAGES INCLUDING THIS ONE: 2

1. FORCE COMMANDER PUT IN CONTACT WITH INFORMANT BY VERY VERY IMPORTANT GOVERNMENT POLITICIAN. INFORMANT IS A TOP LEVEL TRAINER IN THE CADRE OF INTERHAMWE-ARMED MILITIA OF MRND.

2. HE INFORMED US HE WAS IN CHARGE OF LAST SATURDAYS DEMONSTRATIONS WHICH AIMS WERE TO TARGET DEPUTIES OF OPPOSITION PARTIES COMING TO CEREMONIES AND BELGIAN SOLDIERS. THEY HOPED TO PROVOKE THE RPF BN TO ENGAGE (BEING FIRED UPON) THE DEMONSTRATORS AND PROVOKE A CIVIL WAR. DEPUTIES WERE TO BE ASSASSINATED UPON ENTRY OR EXIT FROM PARLIAMENT. BELGIAN TROOPS WERE TO BE PROVOKED AND IF BELGIANS SOLDIERS RESORTED TO FORCE A NUMBER OF THEM WERE TO BE KILLED AND THUS GUARANTEE BELGIAN WITHDRAWAL FROM RWANDA.

3. INFORMANT CONFIRMED 48 RGF PARA CDO AND A FEW MEMBERS OF THE GENDARMERIE PARTICIPATED IN DEMONSTRATIONS IN PLAIN CLOTHES. ALSO AT LEAST ONE MINISTER OF THE MRND AND THE SOUS-PREFECT OF KIGALI WERE IN THE DEMONSTRATION. RGF AND INTERHAMWE PROVIDED RADIO COMMUNICATIONS.

4. INFORMANT IS A FORMER SECURITY MEMBER OF THE PRESIDENT. HE ALSO STATED HE IS PAID RF150,000 PER MONTH BY THE MRND PARTY TO TRAIN INTERHAMWE. DIRECT LINK IS TO CHIEF OF STAFF RGF AND PRESIDENT OF THE MRND FOR FINANCIAL AND MATERIAL SUPPORT.

5. INTERHAMWE HAS TRAINED 1700 MEN IN RGF MILITARY CAMPS OUTSIDE THE CAPITAL. THE 1700 ARE SCATTERED IN GROUPS OF 40 THROUGHOUT KIGALI. SINCE UNAMIR DEPLOYED HE HAS TRAINED 300 PERSONNEL IN THREE WEEK TRAINING SESSIONS AT RGF CAMPS. TRAINING

Figure 1.1 The "Genocide Fax," sent by Roméo Dallaire to the UN in New York on January 11, 1994

journalists with them who worked in Rwanda for a couple of days and then left again on April 12 with the paratroopers, when the evacuation was finished. In addition, US Marines entered Rwanda from Burundi, effectively evacuating all American citizens by April 10.[103] This meant that world media were not present in Rwanda between mid-April and June 23 when French troops arrived for Opération Turquoise. Linda Melvern states that the number of reporters "never rose above a maximum of fifteen," and in Kigali only five journalists remained.[104]

The genocide against the Tutsi began during the night of April 6–7. Hutu military leaders and commanders used the murder of the president, blaming it on the RPF, as the reason for the Hutu population to defend itself against the "foreign invaders." Years of political hate propaganda now paid off as many average citizens of Hutu origin listened to their leaders, and the inflammatory rhetoric on the radio, and followed the call to kill.[105] Initially, the genocide was most organized in the Gisenyi province, were Hutu leaders presided over large numbers of Interahamwe militia and Hutu civilians.[106] During April 7 the killings then spread to Kigali, Ruhengeri, Kibuye, Kibungo, Gikongoro, and Cyangugu provinces.[107] The provinces of Gitarama and Butare both had moderate governors, one of them Tutsi, hence why the killing there was postponed until April 9 and April 19, respectively, when the governors were arrested and murdered.[108] The genocide did not affect areas under RPF control, which included the northern part of Byumba province and the eastern part of Ruhengeri.[109]

Gérard Prunier estimates that during April and the first two weeks of May, the Presidential Guard, the gendarmerie and the Interahamwe militia, aided by local Hutu populations, committed the vast majority of the killings; he suggests that up to 800,000 Rwandans may have been murdered during that period.[110] In cities, identification was made possible by numerous roadblocks crewed by the military and Interahamwe militia, where each person had to present their national identity card, which specified their ethnicity. Persons of Tutsi origin—men, women, and children—were immediately taken aside and butchered, leaving numerous corpses by the side of the roads. In rural areas, the identification process was more personal since all families knew each other, making it easy for the killers, who often were neighbors, to identify and kill the Tutsi population.[111]

Most of the victims typically were brutally killed with machetes or with blunt objects, although some army units used rifles and grenades. The rape and sexual mutilation of Tutsi women, even deliberately infecting them with HIV, was another very common weapon, and it is estimated that between 250,000 to 500,000 girls and women were raped.[112] Local officials and radio stations, most notably RTLM, encouraged ordinary citizens to kill their neighbors, even giving specific instructions on where to find them during live broadcasts.[113] A series of massacres was committed around the country, for example at the École Technique Officielle in Kigali on April 11, where over 2,000 people were murdered after the Belgian UNAMIR soldiers withdrew; and in Nyange on April 16, where more than 1,500 Tutsis, who had sought refuge in a Roman Catholic church, were killed by local Interahamwe militia assisted by the parish priest, using bulldozers to knock down the church building; and in Nyarubuye, where 20,000 Tutsi and moderate Hutus, who had sought refuge in the Roman Catholic church, were killed on April 14 and 15.[114] Rwanda is one of the most Christian countries in Africa and it is estimated that 11 percent of those who perished in the genocide were murdered in churches.[115]

The RPF began an attack over the Demilitarized Zone on April 8, and slowly but progressively ended the killings wherever they made territorial gains. The genocide was thus effectively ended in April in the provinces of Ruhengeri, Byumba, Kibungo, and Kigali.[116] The advancement of the RPF created a tidal wave of Hutu refugees, as some 250,000 fled into Tanzania from the eastern provinces in the last days of April.[117] Quite early on there were reports that the RPF committed atrocities in revenge killings, incidents that were wrongfully interpreted by the press as if the RPF too was a part of the genocidal killings in Rwanda.[118]

Towards the end of May and throughout June the killings became gradually more inconspicuous and sporadic in the remaining provinces, as most of the Tutsi population had already been murdered by this point. On June 23, 2,500 French soldiers entered the provinces of Cyangugu, Kibuye, and Gikongoro in the south-west for the United Nations-mandated mission Opération Turquoise. This was intended as a humanitarian mission, but the soldiers were not able to save any significant number of lives. In fact, the genocidal authorities of the fleeing interim government welcomed the French and continued to slaughter Tutsis who came out of hiding to seek protection from the French.[119] On July 4, the RPF took Kigali and on July 18 it completed its conquest of the country, with the exception of the zone held by Opération Turquoise until August 21, as they took control over the Gisenyi province.[120]

The RPF victory initiated "The Great Lakes refugee crisis" as over 2 million Rwandan refugees, mostly of Hutu origin and including Interahamwe and government officials who had carried out the genocide, fled to neighboring countries. By the end of August, the UNHCR estimated that there were 1.5 million refugees in thirty-five camps just around Goma in Zaire, an additional 270,000 refugees in Burundi, and a further 570,000 in Tanzania.[121]

The genocide thus ended with a refugee crisis of "Biblical proportions" that would gravely destabilize the whole region and eventually propel it into what is called Africa's World War (the First and Second Congo War, 1996–1997 and

1998–2003 respectively), a conflict that involved nine African countries, as well as twenty armed groups: several coup d'états and continued refugee problems. It is estimated that an additional 4–5 million human beings died because of the wars, starvation, diseases, and massacres committed between 1994 and 2003.[122] Yet Africa's World War is virtually unknown in the West. After a massive aid campaign in Goma, the world community withdrew once again and returned to its policy of non-intervention. Attention was instead directed towards the accomplishments of Rwanda, which had risen Phoenix-like out of the ashes to become one of Africa's most stable and successful nations.

Part One

The Apocalypse, April to July 1994

2
Swedish Television News in 1994

The news media played a fundamental role during the Rwandan genocide, both locally in Rwanda where hate propaganda fueled the killings, and internationally where the media are perceived to have fatally misinterpreted and even ignored the events. Criticism of the international media has been harsh and uncompromising, especially pertaining to the non-effect that the coverage is said to have had since that is linked to the international community's inaction.[1] This view implies that a more accurate way of conveying news and information could have prevented the genocide as, supposedly, it would have created outbursts of moral indignation among the public and those in power and, ultimately, a more forceful intervention. This ideal conception represents the essence of much of the research carried out on the media's role in the Rwandan genocide.

In *One Hundred Days of Silence: America and the Rwanda Genocide*, political scientist Jared A. Cohen chronicles US foreign policy in relation to the genocide and how non-intervention was justified within the American bureaucracy. Media is heavily blamed for not putting any significant pressure on the government, and when the genocide finally made the news the focus was on "the bodies and the horror, rather than on the details of the conflict," according to Cohen. Instead, the high-speed pursuit and arrest of footballer and actor O. J. Simpson easily overshadowed the genocide for weeks in American news reporting during June 1994.[2]

Spanish NGO and journalist Virginia de la Guardia blames the few news corporations, claiming that the fierce competition, coupled with new digital technologies, endangers serous reporting because it leads to a search for the most dramatic story, which essentially flares up and then quickly fades away without any follow-up. The rivalry also means that the media focus can only be on one world crisis at a time. This conspicuous concentration of news organizations "means that cost, objectivity and private and public sources are much more inter-linked than ever before," and that the globalization of the media in fact has led to a concentration on cheaper local news items, such as crime in the US, where reporting on crime has gone up 600 percent, at the expense of foreign news.[3]

Most elaborate is the collection of texts in *The Media and the Rwanda Genocide*, where academics and journalists discuss the relation between the media and the genocide in no less than thirty-five short essays ranging from how radio and print media were exploited in the genocide, through how Western and African media covered the genocide, to reflections on how media could prevent genocide.[4] The international media coverage is here firmly connected to media's accountability, and according to the anthology the critique of the international news coverage of the Rwandan genocide can be divided into three main arguments: (1) There were only a few journalists in place in Rwanda and their news pieces were rarely picked up according to the "Chad Rule,"[5] (2) The initial reporting of the genocide was grossly inaccurate,[6] (3) There were very few television images from the genocide and as a result nothing with which to make attention-grabbing television.[7]

These observations are seldom situated in the relevant context of historical culture, thus not posing vital questions about what relevance and function the media reporting has in a longer, historical perspective. Internationally, there have been several studies of the genocide *per se*, often with a short historical recapitulation of Rwanda's colonial past, but outside of brief statements about the lack of interest from Western media these studies seldom investigate media's role in relation to the past or the future.[8]

However, the aim of this chapter is not to criticize the media for failing to report on the genocide. In fact, as we shall see, the television media coverage was, at the very start at least and when balanced against other coincident world events like the election in South Africa and the crisis in Bosnia, often both extremely swift and well informed, albeit from a predisposed colonial angle in the sense that the coverage to a great extent depended on already pre-constituted conceptions of Africa as an immature continent pertaining to political, economic, and humanitarian issues. The aim instead is to analyze how a historical media memory of the Rwandan genocide came to be shaped, from the start, in the guise of a guilty Western conscience. The mantra, "everybody knew, but no one did anything," has, accordingly, become an important part of the global media memory and is therefore also a recurrent theme in feature films and feature-length documentaries such as *Hotel Rwanda* (2004) and *Ghosts of Rwanda* (2004).

To get a fresh view on how this historical media memory came to be shaped on both a national and transnational level, the focus is going to be on Swedish television news coverage of the genocide as it occurred between April 6 and July 14, 1994. Here the question of the actual time and space allotted for the genocide will be combined with questions of how the genocide was first portrayed, constructed, and explained for a Western audience. The analysis will be evaluated as part of the international media reporting of the genocide in order to examine in what way the local-national, that is the Swedish, impetus correlates to the constructions and explanations of the genocide on a global level.

The local-national level thus operates as a contrast to the worldwide media conglomerates, and the interlinked globalization that they represent. At the same time, the actual use of audiovisual material for the mediation of information and knowledge supports the idea of a formation of historical media memories on a global level, exemplified by the fact that international news agencies sell the same images of international events to news stations all over the world.

There are three reasons that make the Swedish impetus valuable. First, Sweden does not have the same explicit colonial past as for example Belgium or France, and accordingly was not part of the European scramble for Africa at the end of the nineteenth century.[9] Second, during the Cold War, Sweden situated itself as "the third alternative" between the USA and the Soviet Union and thus created a traditional self-image as the world's conscience; giving support to countries and organizations in the "Third World" such as Vietnam and the African National Congress (ANC) in South Africa. Third, since 1946 Sweden has been one of the United Nation's most dedicated advocators, even adjusting its foreign policy according to UN rules and regulations.[10]

The Context of Swedish Television

Swedish public television (SVT) started its broadcasts with one single channel in 1956. Like most Western European countries with state-owned or partially state-owned television channels, SVT was modeled after the public service broadcasting agenda of the BBC; that is, financed by licenses rather than by commercial advertisement spots. From the very beginning SVT was guided by governmental principles and directives. Television in Sweden was thus regulated with regard to the number of channels, airing time, and program content. The objective was, and still is, to transmit an evenly distributed programming of news, knowledge, and entertainment in an impartial way with the aim being to improve society by informing its viewers.[11] In some ways SVT resembles, for instance, American PBS as both strive for impartial and strict adherence to objectivity and balance in all programs. But where the US federal government is prohibited from interfering or controlling what is broadcasted on PBS, the Swedish directives have had great influence on the programming of SVT, although direct government interference is prohibited. PBS was also founded as a counterweight to the three privately owned US networks at the time, while SVT held an actual monopoly in Sweden.

In 1969 SVT started a second channel. It would then take another twenty-two years until a third channel, the commercial advertisement financed TV4, was permitted to transmit on the terrestrial analogue net, the technique with the ability to reach all viewers in Sweden at the time. Even though a commercial entertainment satellite channel, TV3, had started to transmit in Swedish from London in 1987, followed by a few cable-net based film and entertainment channels, SVT's near monopoly was firmly in place by 1994—actually making Sweden the last country in Western Europe to permit commercial television.[12]

Regarding television news, SVT's *Rapport* (Report) is, and has been since it started in 1969, the most established and most viewed news program in Sweden, irrespective of audience category, with a prime-time scheduling every evening at 7.30 pm. The commercial channel TV4 initially placed its main news program, *Nyheterna* (The News), in the same time slot, 7.30 pm, but after dwindling ratings the program was soon moved up to 10 pm, where it was in 1994. These are the two Swedish television news programs that will be at the center of this chapter. I will analyze *Rapport*'s news coverage of the genocide in Rwanda for all of the 100 days that it lasted, but I will also include the first sixty-five days of *Nyheterna*'s reporting for comparison. Hence, *Rapport* represents the esteemed credo of public service broadcasting, while *Nyheterna* represents the only commercial alternative available in 1994 with a similar reach. Both news programs operated under the same governmental rules and regulations, which were to provide the viewers with "impartial objectivity" when it came to news reporting.[13]

Nevertheless, TV4's *Nyheterna* was for many years regarded as a mere lightweight contender in comparison to SVT's *Rapport*, a perception that *Nyheterna* played on as it introduced a lighter atmosphere in the studio, always ending the program—and becoming somewhat infamous for it—with a funny, down-to-earth piece of news. For example, on April 7 the funny news item was that all American Winter Olympians had been invited to dinner at the White House, with the exception of Tonya Harding, the scandalous figure skater who had hired a goon to break the leg of her main competitor Nancy Kerrigan. *Nyheterna*'s leading story the same evening had been that chaos had broken out in a small Central African nation-state named Rwanda.

Understating Atrocities and Suffering in News Media

There are, obviously, specific circumstances in motion about how genocide is circulated as a media event in a transnational context. The first thing to point out is that genocide is a highly unusual event and, consequently, a "live" news item with hardly any previous points of reference. Some might object to this, referring to all films and television programs on genocide, i.e., the Holocaust, which are available. But can knowledge about the Holocaust be functional to identity genocide *in medias res* for journalists on the ground? French journalist Anne Chaon, present in Rwanda during the genocide, says that: "Journalists are neither historians nor sociologists. They do not work in the quiet of their study. Their reports become part of history, but history is knitted day by day, before their eyes. They don't benefit from the distance required to quickly understand the whole scene."[14]

This is in a romantic sense true, but the fact is that journalists do not work in a void. Behind them there is (if you are not a freelance, that is) an editorial staff and an editorial office that serves as support and as gatekeepers. And although there are many allegations from journalists that their news pieces were censored or not even picked up by print media and television, the different editorial offices also had a duty to frame the story, that is to put it in a relevant context for their audiences. To my knowledge no one chose to frame the genocide in Rwanda in the known context of the Holocaust until very late. For example, in the US ABC's Roger Winter made the first comparison to the Holocaust on July 18, the same day that the Rwandan Patriotic Front (RPF) took control over the Gisenyi province and ended the genocide.[15]

Consequently, this means that journalists in general, whether in television studios or out in the field, are without any expert knowledge of genocide and therefore easily fall back on the handy employment of Third World stereotypes, as was the case in Rwanda, where most journalists reported on the massacres as ongoing "chaos," "anarchy," and "civil war."[16] Chaon states that "Rwanda was a cruel disillusionment, a major failure," despite the fact that "[r]eporters were there. Pictures were available. Stories were filed," thus arriving at the somewhat apologetical conclusion that "if the people you speak to do not want to listen, you can't force them."[17] The conundrum here is why people do not listen. Is it dependent on the use of Third World stereotypes, especially pertaining to Africa, that twisted the story or is it because of the phenomenon of compassion fatigue?

In *States of Denial: Knowing about Atrocities and Suffering*, British sociologist Stanley Cohen has argued that the mass media, especially television, almost have a monopoly in creating cultural images of suffering and atrocities. Cohen identifies several formal elements in this imagery. For example, that the use of negative imagery in news of suffering from "Third World" countries—starving children, war victims, refugee camps—as the "normal" state results in a cultural and eventually personal denial in the West that simply alienates rather than engages people in front of their television sets.[18] At the same time, the cultural belief in visual images, and that they can have a visceral impact, continues to be strong:

Sophisticated technology can spread images of live atrocities around the world in minutes. But self-evident truths will not be self-evidently accepted.

However informative, reliable, and convincing they are, accounts of atrocities and suffering do little to undermine overt forms of denial. Humanitarian organizations are living relics of Enlightenment faith in the power of knowledge: *if only people knew, they would act.*[19]

It should be noted here that denial is a cognitive mechanism that necessitates what Cohen calls the *denial paradox*: in other words, that the denial in itself—we didn't know—in fact reveals that the person/organization/country actually did know what they denied, otherwise it would not be necessary to deny anything.[20] In view of this, Cohen dismisses several traditional rationalizations of denial, such as the psychoanalytical defense mechanism of the unconscious and the thesis about compassion fatigue, due to information overload and desensitization.[21] In its place he distinguishes several more precise basics of denial relevant for the purposes of this book: (1) *The use of euphemisms* as a way to reallocate an event to another class of events, (2) *Moral distance*, as repetition of images of suffering increases their remoteness, (3) *The Chad rule*, "no one wants to hear about Chad," as whole zones of the world are overlooked as they are not seen as newsworthy, leading to (4) *Ethnic amnesia*, as Western media, for instance, ignored or simply "forgot" that genocidal massacres in Burundi and Rwanda commenced before 1994.[22]

Lastly, Cohen argues for the perspective that denial, in the sense of shutting out awareness of others' suffering, in fact should be seen as the normal state of affairs and not as an abnormal condition as it, according to Cohen, "is quite abnormal to know or care very much about the problems of distant places."[23] "The empirical problem is not to uncover yet more evidence of denial, but to discover the conditions under which information is acknowledged and acted upon."[24]

The First Week

As stated above, the international news coverage of the Rwandan genocide has been criticized along three main lines: (1) There were only a few journalists in place in Rwanda and their news pieces were rarely picked up according to the "Chad Rule," (2) The initial reporting of the genocide was grossly inaccurate, (3) There were very few television images from the genocide and as a result there was nothing with which to make attention-grabbing television.

These objections are broadly in line with how Swedish television news programs handled the events in Rwanda at the outset of the genocide, were it not for the first week's speedy and well-informed coverage. Starting on April 7, and through to April 13, both *Rapport* and *Nyheterna* reported on the events in Rwanda at a reasonably fair length every evening, with segments of two to three

SWEDISH TELEVISION NEWS IN 1994

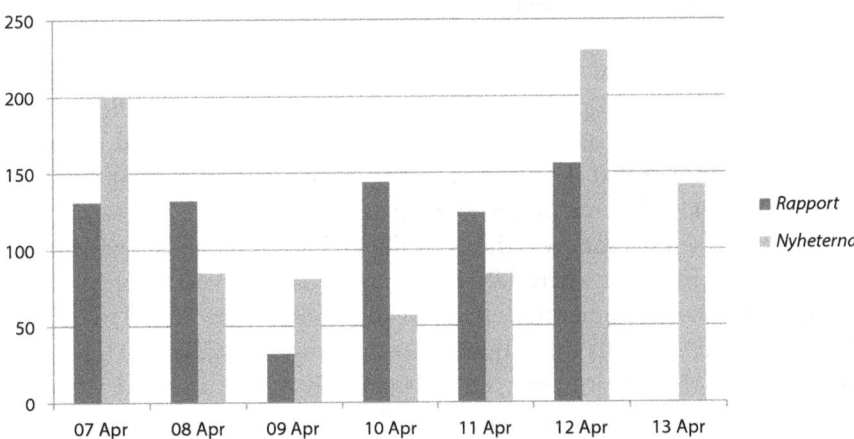

Chart 2.1 The time in seconds devoted to the outbreak of the genocide in TV2's *Rapport* and TV4's *Nyheterna* between April 7 and April 13, 1994. Altogether, *Rapport* allotted 11.59 minutes of its news time to the genocide, while *Nyheterna* allotted 14.42 minutes, that is, 5.7 percent and 9.5 percent, respectively. *Rapport* has a run time of thirty minutes. *Nyheterna* runs for twenty-five minutes, except on Saturdays when the program has a shorter run time of approximately five minutes

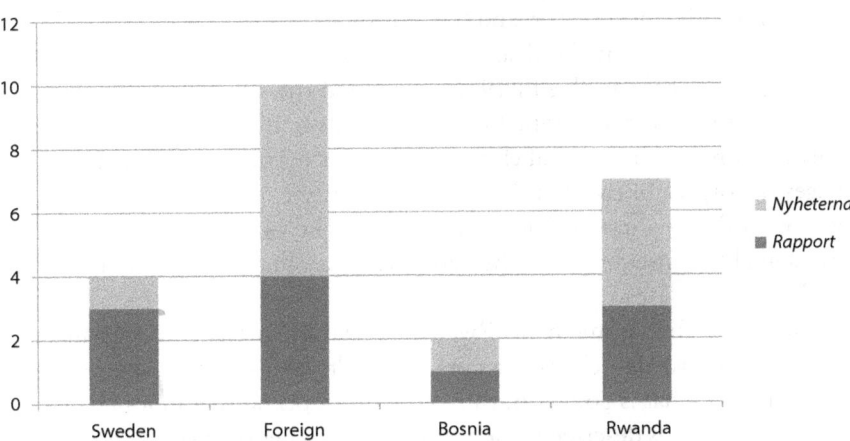

Chart 2.2 Top news stories according to geographical location in *Rapport* and *Nyheterna* between April 7 and April 13, 1994

minutes. Furthermore, *Rapport* had Rwanda as its leading story on April 8, 10, and 12, while Rwanda represented the top news item at *Nyheterna* on April 7, 8, 11, and 12.

On the first day, the reporting in both programs is a bit sketchy when it comes to the latest information. The viewers are informed that fighting has broken out; that the presidents of Rwanda and Burundi have died in a plane crash (*Nyheterna*) or that the plane has been shot down (*Rapport*); and that the prime minister and three unarmed Belgian UN-observers have been killed. While *Nyheterna* puts some emphasis on the UN involvement, showing a brief clip from a conference where UN spokesman Fred Eckhard informs on the Belgians fate, and then mentions that several UN observers are still uncounted for, *Rapport* leaps directly into a historical explanation: "This is how it has been in Rwanda for thirty years: power struggles and ethnic cleansing with extremely brutal elements."[25] Over a sequence of archive footage—images of a gathering of threadbare-looking Rwandans; molested corpses on a street and corpses floating by in a river; and a lone soldier looking out over a river—the reporter states that this disorder has produced 3 million refugees and that hundreds of thousands of people have been killed over the years. The television audience is then informed that peace negotiations were held until yesterday between the "two great native-populations, the majority Hutu with about 85 percent of the population and Tutsi, with 15 percent," and in addition that, "The antagonism between the two peoples are of ancient date; the minority Tutsi has by tradition had the most power, and the old colonial power, Belgium [illustrated with archive footage in black-and-white of Rwandan soldiers and the final lowering of the Belgian flag in 1962] aggravated the situation by favoring the Tutsis according to the colonial concept, divide and conquer." The reporter continues on to draw a parallel with the recent massacres in Burundi—more images of corpses in rivers and images from refugee camps—and ends the segment with the prediction that the murders of the two presidents could have unimaginable consequences: "the future can become even bloodier than the past."

Nyheterna's first segment on Rwanda is sparser in terms of explanations. Here three key words—"chaos," "anarchy," and "tribes"—are consistently used as shorthand for what is going on, thus evoking a primordial rationalization of events. The crisis is described as a historic civil war between two tribes that has ranged on and off since the country's independence. The illustrations used are similar to those in *Rapport*: archival footage of corpses, soldiers, the countryside, and also a panoramic view of what seems to be an endless line of refugees. Moreover, *Nyheterna* uses what is probably the most recurring archival footage to illustrate "Africa," namely images of ordinary Africans, that is, not refugees, walking along a red dusty road carrying necessities.

To compensate for the lack of historical background and explanation *Nyheterna* includes two items which differentiates it from *Rapport* on this first day. First, it includes a telephone interview with a Swedish missionary worker stationed in Rwanda, who says that there has been gunfire through the same morning and that, "something has, so to speak, lingered in the air for a long time here in Rwanda, though nobody imagined that it would lead to this." Second, and more importantly, is the use of an interview with a commentator or "studio expert" of foreign affairs. Here the presentation shifts from an expository mode to an interactive mode as the female studio anchor rotates her chair to face the male expert. The studio lighting is dimmed and shot/reverse shot is used to create a more intimate atmosphere, although the TV4 logo is always visible behind both participants as they discusses the situation, mostly reiterating what has already been said and shown in the reportage. Then the following fatalistic and foresighted exchange takes place:

Studio anchor: Ministers, members of parliament and UN personnel are murdered. What will the UN do now?
Expert: Yes, it seems as if UN soldiers still patrol some parts of the capital city, but nobody knows if they have any control over the situation, and since UN personnel is both killed and threatened, the UN should reasonably consider an intervention. However, it is not impossible that the UN finds the situation to be so hopeless that they decide to evacuate their personnel.
SA: There is essentially a slaughter going on, and if people continue to kill each other in this way, how long can this go on before the world has to intervene?
E: Yes, this has been going on for a long time as we said, tens of thousands of people have died and no one in the world have really cared about it. What is happening now could perhaps change this view in some way, but the risk is obviously great that *we* simply let this continue; letting them beat each other to death and turn our backs once more.

Even though nobody really seemed to know what was going on at this early stage, the creation of a historical media memory of the genocide in Rwanda starts here, just twenty-four hours into the carnage. And it starts out as a guilty Western conscience over an already abandoned Africa.

The archival footage that illustrates the two news segments, and the research carried out, reveal a somewhat ambitious approach towards the events in remote Rwanda. So far, Swedish television news programs do not suffer from ethnic amnesia, but rather from predisposed colonial discourses that plainly recreate Africa as otherness; not really even as part of the us and them dichotomy.

The euphemisms used, particularly by *Nyheterna*, reinforce the view of the situation in Rwanda as a lost cause. Further, the illustrative images do not promote engagement in the Enlightenment way, that is, that faith in the power of knowledge promotes action, but instead do the opposite simply because they are embedded in this predisposed colonial context—with its near automatic negative representations of Africans—of which Sweden undeniably always has been a part.[26]

The rest of the first week's reporting follows a similar stylistic pattern, with news segments that open with a map of Africa where the tiny dots of Rwanda and Burundi are, always together, enlarged while the newscaster announces the latest developments. After that the reportage itself begins, often intertwined with telephone interviews with "eyewitnesses" and essentially illustrated with the exact same archive footage as the first day. However, as early as April 8 (*Nyheterna*) and April 9 (*Rapport*), the story of Rwanda both multiplies into stories and is distorted. This change is largely caused by the imprecise information available, not least the lack of up-to-date television images. Is it this lack of images that changes the story, or does the story change due to the available images?

The events in Rwanda continue to be presented as a story of civil war and relentless violence, even though the estimated death tolls reported rose rapidly from hundreds, to thousands, and then to tens of thousands within three days—a figure that did not change over the following month. When these numbers, and the euphemisms used in connection with them—"orgies of murder," "blood orgies," "bloodbath"—are not associated with genocide *per se*, the account of what is happening becomes quite suspect. First, it reinforces the primordial perspective as both news programs maintain that the events in Rwanda are caused by ancient "tribal quarrels." Second, this out-of-control "anarchy" connotes the colonial narrative of savages against civilization—with the unspoken threat that this could turn from a black-on-black situation to a black-on-white affair—which is highlighted by the fact that African victims are merely quantified, whereas "civilized" victims such as nuns, priests, aid workers, and UN soldiers are individualized.

This selective individualization alters the story of Rwanda, and it quickly turns into a very Eurocentric one, where the center of attention now is on the efforts to save white expatriates—turning the genocide into a mere backdrop for the rest of the first week. This is emphasized by the only news footage that is added between April 8 and April 10, namely a mix of images of Belgian paratroopers, trucks, airplanes that take off, and, one day later, images of white expatriates at Gregoire Kayibanda International Airport, waiting to be airlifted out of Rwanda.

The interviews, mostly conducted by telephone, which both *Rapport* and *Nyheterna* televised daily, add to the Eurocentric viewpoint as the interviewees are either Swedes or Americans. These interviews are used as "live" eyewitness accounts, that is, as a substitute for a severe lack of actual facts, thereby involuntarily enhancing the colonial perspective on the information given. The interviews are short and edited, but collectively they nevertheless communicate a similar story; one of anarchy and ruthless killings that, as they seem to be indiscriminate, are experienced as a threat to the expatriates. An American interviewed at the airport said: "There was a Rwandan tank that pulled up beside a guy on the road, I don't know if he was a thief or the wrong tribe, but he was begging on his hands and knees beside the road and they shot him in the head three times."[27] A Swedish missionary explained: "[T]his last night has been worse, with firing close by our house; it feels worrying, and then one starts to think about what could happen if *they* broke through the walls and threatened us."[28]

The only exceptions were two very short statements made by RPF representatives that *Nyheterna* chose to televise, probably to differentiate itself from SVT. In the first, RPF's spokesperson Claude Dusaida advises French troops, there to evacuate expatriates, not to intervene in the conflict[29]—a warning which in context performs the function of yet another threat against Europeans. The second statement was made by the then General Secretary of the RPF, Major Theogene Rudasingwa, who explains that the RPF does not accept the new, hastily put together interim government, which it sees as a violation of the Arusha Peace Agreement[30]—something that the Swedish studio reporter later misinterprets by drawing the conclusion that it is the peace agreement that is the cause of the conflict.

It should not come as any surprise that the presence (and eventual evacuation) of twelve Swedish missionaries in Rwanda added a national spice to the reporting that kept interest alive in the wake of the "Chad rule." *Nyheterna* even tried to make something of the fact that the Swedish consul had gone missing for a few hours, but, overall, the Swedes are used as neutral and somewhat surprisingly unaware bystanders to a Rwanda gone berserk. Swedish missionary Leif Angnestrand, who had lived in the country for fifteen years, blamed the "bloodbath" on the fact that the Western world had forced democracy on Rwanda: "So now *they* have divided themselves into smaller political parties and this in turn has induced that tribal thinking enters the picture; regionalism enters the picture, dependently of where one lives in the country and what family one belongs to, these things slips into the party structures even if it's not allowed."[31] Even if the information disclosed here is both subjective and very limited it is precisely this closeness that makes these interviews work as smaller pieces within a larger, colonial story.

A number of television journalists flew in on the same planes that brought in French and Belgian paratroopers during those days, and most of them left on the same planes for safety reasons on April 12.[32] These journalists traveled across Kigali, and sometimes out in the countryside, on the trucks that collected expatriates and for a couple of days a window opened up for a new—and what was to become emblematic—kind of television footage of the genocide as the cameramen filmed numerous corpses lying on the side of the road from the platforms of their moving trucks. On April 11 and 12 *Rapport* also aired—following a warning to its viewers—a few seconds of the now well-known footage by British cameraman Nick Hughes of people being killed with machetes in the street, filmed in extreme long shot.[33]

The arrival of new and "live" footage could potentially have had the ability to change the story, and perhaps even shift the focus to the ongoing genocide. However, by then the Eurocentric perspective had already created a vast moral distance that not even Nick Hughes's revealing film could change. In the edited context in which this new footage is shown, the images do not denote genocide, but instead just alienating savagery. Over a montage with running and shouting French soldiers in Kigali, the Nick Hughes footage, and a French soldier who aims his weapon at an unseen threat from a jeep travelling at high speed, the Swedish reporter explains:

> It is dangerous in Kigali, dead dangerous. Aid workers in Rwanda's capital city claim that ten thousand have been beaten to death in five days, that is, two thousand every day. Most of them have, as shown here, been hacked to death. The nervousness of the French paratroopers is understandable. They are now escorting the expatriates out of the bloodbath.[34]

And on April 12, these words were used to put the Hughes footage in context: "The ongoing civil war in Rwanda has, here and there, turned into genuine slaughter. Some speak of thousands of dead."[35]

That same day the evacuation of expatriates ended. Or as the Force Commander of the UN troops, Roméo Dallaire, stated: "I mark April 12 as the day the world moved from disinterest in Rwanda to the abandonment of Rwandans to their fate. The swift evacuation of the foreign nationals was the signal for the *génocidaires* to move towards the apocalypse."[36] Symptomatically, on that evening *Rapport* devoted most of its news segment on Rwanda to talk with the twelve evacuated Swedish missionaries, who by then had arrived safely in Nairobi, Kenya. On the question of how it felt to leave colleagues behind, one of the missionaries replied:

> When the situation becomes this impossible, even if one wants to help them, perhaps psychological or in some other way, you really don't help them. As a foreigner you can cause trouble for them, and in all wars, for-

eigners do not represent something good, just uncertainness. And since we are talking about dark skinned people [said with an uncertain smile], and we are white; they aren't able to hide us, and we cannot hide them, without this being noticed.[37]

The resignation expressed by the missionaries, no doubt genuine when it came to the concern they felt for their Rwandan colleagues left behind, nevertheless supports the determinate notion that nothing could be done. The consistent Eurocentric perspective in the television news reporting is reinforced in this way, both by emphasizing the perceived threat towards the white expatriates and by the creation of a moral distance between "them and us" based on predisposed colonial discourses on Africa as otherness.

Media Silence and the Refugee Crisis

After the first week's intensive reporting, the story of Rwanda all but disappeared from Swedish television. Over the following five weeks, from April 14 to May 18, that is, while the most intensive killing took place during the genocide, *Rapport* returned to the developments in Rwanda on thirteen occasions, of which five consisted of brief news announcements, averaging nineteen seconds, while *Nyheterna* returned to it on fourteen occasions. Consequently, during these five weeks there were long stretches of silence, especially during the remaining weeks of April, as is shown by Chart 2.3. *Rapport* had twenty-two days of silence while *Nyheterna* had twenty-one over the same period. The first week's focus on Rwanda, with 5.7 percent (*Rapport*) and 9.5 percent (*Nyheterna*), respectively, of news time, fell to 2.0 percent and 3.3 percent, respectively, for April. This can be compared to the US's television networks, ABC, CBS, and NBC, that together allotted thirty-two minutes, or 1.5 percent of their news time, to the genocide in April.[38]

As has been noted, this media silence can be explained partly by the competition with other world events, such as the concurrent crisis in Bosnia and the election in South Africa.[39] In the subsequent five weeks Bosnia also featured as the top news story on *Rapport* and *Nyheterna* on six and nine occasions, respectively, whereas reporting on the election in South Africa reached a peak by the end of April, representing the lead story on five and eight occasions, respectively. Rwanda, in comparison, was the top news story on one occasion on *Rapport* and on three occasions on *Nyheterna* during those five weeks.

Nonetheless, Sweden, being a small country, has traditionally had a more balanced ratio of domestic and international news, with a distribution of 60/40 or even 50/50 percent—demonstrated by the fact that *Rapport* and *Nyheterna* featured international news as the lead story on nineteen and twenty-five days,

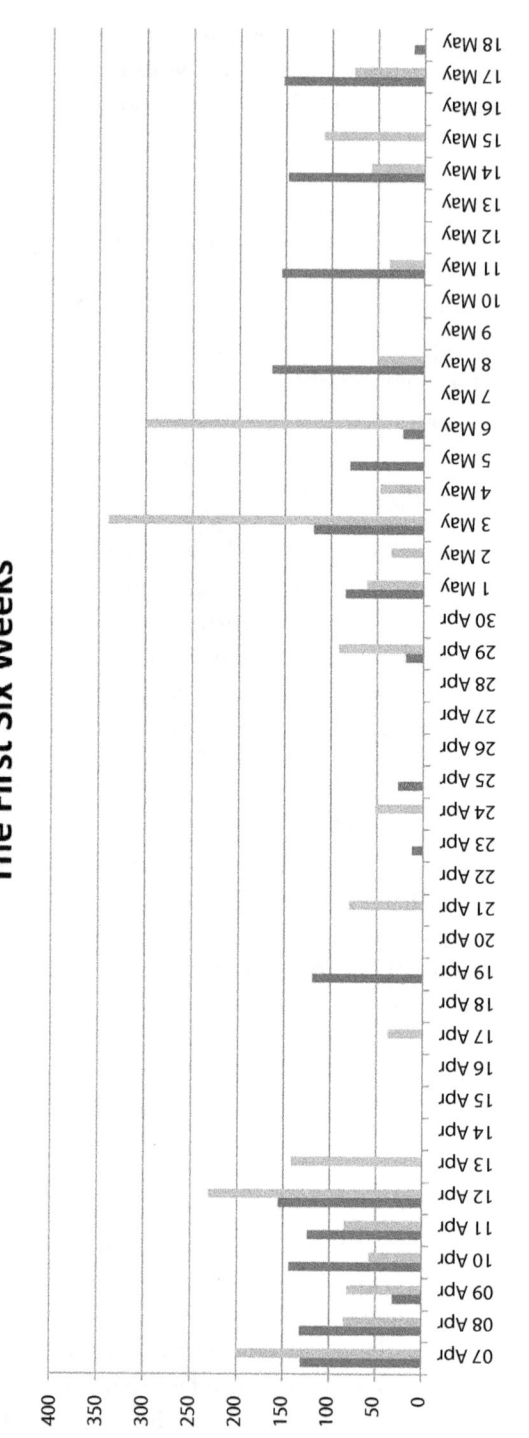

Chart 2.3 The time in seconds devoted to Rwanda in TV2's *Rapport* and TV4's *Nyheterna* between April 7 and May 18, 1994

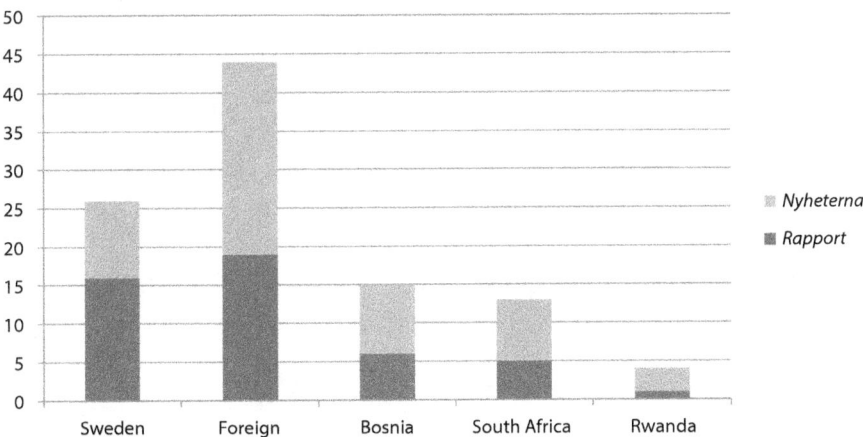

Chart 2.4 Top news stories in *Rapport* and *Nyheterna* according to geographical location between April 14 and May 18, 1994

respectively, out of the thirty-five days in the period under review. In comparison, the USA had a distribution of 73/27 percent between domestic and international news in the same period.[40] Thus, a more valid reason for the sharp decline in interest must be located elsewhere.

When *Rapport* temporarily returns to Rwanda on April 19, the news segment is more incoherent than before, almost certainly because the previous unifying link, the Eurocentric interest, is now gone. What is left is the ongoing slaughter, still disguised as a bloody and irrational African civil war that the UN is powerless to prevent. The segment is mainly illustrated with footage of soldiers from the Rwandan Armed Forces (FAR) firing mortars and standing guard, and cheering RPF soldiers waving their Kalashnikovs in the air. Also shown is previously untelevised footage of piles of dead bodies lying by the roadside taken from a moving vehicle, probably taken by the evacuated journalists and therefore a few days old.

In an effort to explain what is happening viewers are told that most of the dead "probably belongs to the minority people, Tutsi, and since they are believed to support the Tutsi rebels, who are invading the country from the north, they have been slaughtered by murder gangs from the majority people Hutu."[41] This identification of the victims, although vague, and the perpetrators, is in fact a definition of genocide. However, in the existing context that did not serve as a clear-cut definition, and especially not when *Rapport*, holding on to the rule of impartiality, allowed the accused Hutu side to respond, airing a short interview with the prime minister of the interim government,

Figure 2.1 Piles of corpses lying by the road in *Rapport*, April 19, 1994

Jean Kambanda: "I believe that the government represents the people and that the people are now in control over the country." The Swedish voiceover then continues with: "But the problem is that the government is not supported by the whole country. The Tutsi rebels, who represent the traditional noble class, the feudal lords, and the elite within the army, are now trying to take back their past positions."[42] In other words, to explain the mass killings Swedish public television actually uses textbook Hutu hate propaganda.

The segment ends on a note that the West is powerless in the face of this immense irrationalism, illustrated with footage of humiliated and enraged Belgian UN soldiers slicing and tearing up a blue beret with an army knife at the airport. The final images are of fleeing Rwandan refugees, while the voiceover bleakly concludes: "in principle the murdering is now underway all around the country and there will probably not be peace until the two peoples are separated for good."[43]

Nyheterna relates the same story with similar explanations during these semi-silent weeks of April, claiming, among other things, that "the killing is an act of revenge on the former Tutsi masters in Rwanda,"[44] thus displaying ethnic amnesia by neglecting to mention the fact that the Hutus had held the political power in Rwanda for more than thirty years prior to the genocide. The one difference between the two is that *Nyheterna* was keener to report the death figures. During the first week the reported death toll rose rapidly from 100s, to 1,000s, to 10,000s in both news programs, but it then took until April 21 for *Nyheterna* to report that, according to the International Red Cross's (ICRC) estimations, "100,000 people are believed to have been killed in the infighting,"[45] a figure that *Rapport* hesitated to use for another ten days.[46]

This perceived powerlessness of the West thus becomes a form of denial that blurs the line between the past and the present.[47] Even though the atrocities take place in the present, the explanation for them is exclusively placed in the past, making it both irrational and unattainable for a "Western" solution, i.e., democracy, capitalism, or UN peacekeeping. The notion of powerlessness affects the news reporting as it, seemingly, becomes difficult to try to explain this savage irrationalism where standard Western solutions do not apply.[48] Consequently, the repetition of images of forever multiplying piles of dead bodies does not only increase the moral distance between the West and the rest, it also represents poor mediated news in the sense that it avoids or is unable to put these images in a comprehensible narrative structure. And without a necessary narrative logic, *Rapport* and *Nyheterna* thus leave behind the events in Rwanda for two full weeks, apart from the above-mentioned news announcements that briefly highlight a growing refugee problem, broken ceasefires, and failed peace negotiations.

When Swedish television returns to Rwanda at the end of April/beginning of May, the story is changing. There is still a focus on the "impetuous" killings in the "civil war," but the news segments on both *Rapport* and *Nyheterna* have now shifted their focus to the enormous refugee crisis which is rapidly building up on the border to Tanzania. Slightly exaggerated statements like, "The world's largest refugee camp,"[49] "The greatest stream of refugees in modern time,"[50] and "Soon the entire population of Rwanda, 7 million, are on the run,"[51] are used to describe what is going on. Coupled with new and abundant footage of ICRC refugee camp sites and telephone interviews with Swedish aid workers who explain that they "probably can handle the food situation for another ten days,"[52] this in fact represents the moment that sets the events in Rwanda on a more familiar track, thus making it comprehensible to Swedish viewers.

The killings and the "tribal quarrels" of the ongoing genocide are thus explained by the recognizable paradigm of a relentless African refugee problem that the West can, if not solve, then at least temporarily ease with its resources. In accordance with this logic, images of children fighting over a sack of flour in a refugee camp are explained by the fact that they are "mortal enemies at home and therefore have a hard time sharing food with each other."[53] Footage of bloated corpses floating in the Akagera River on the border between Rwanda and Tanzania is interpreted within the refugee paradigm, as the corpses are the result of the inexplicable killings which now are polluting the drinking water for the refugees.[54]

The use of primordial and virtually instinctive colonial explanations and euphemisms continues throughout these decisive weeks. There is talk about a

Figure 2.2 Children fighting over a sack of flour, interpreted symbolically as a fight between ethnicities in *Rapport*, May 3, 1994

"blood feud,"[55] Swedish NGOs explain that the refugees can build their own "huts" with plastic brought in,[56] and during a state visit to Sweden, Burundi's Foreign Minister Jean Marie Ngendahayo first blames the outbreak of violence on the fact that democracy have been forced on Burundi and Rwanda, and then uses a child analogy about African nations that could be interpreted as a sign of colonial internalization but more likely is used to cater to a Western audience in an "logical" way: "Once you start a process you have to finish it. A mum cannot give birth to a child and say: 'OK, I am finished here. I have waited nine months; now this child has to support itself.' You have to help it to work and to eat, and to feed him, to breast him, and so on during many, many, eh, long period."[57]

The development in Swedish television news follows a similar pattern for how Western media handled the Rwandan genocide. As the South African election ended on April 28, the wave of refugees into Tanzania is turned into news.[58] However, Jared A. Cohen claims, by comparison, that US media does not rediscover Rwanda and the refugee crisis until May 16. That is, after President Clinton had publicly declared that the USA would not intervene in countries in which they had no interest and the UN Security Council was still discussing the possibility of setting up a military intervention force.[59] And the main shift in the Rwandan story did not occur until after the civil war ended on July 18—when the world's attention turned to the refugee catastrophe in Goma, Zaire, where more than 2,000,000 Rwandans, mostly Hutus, had escaped.[60] Hence, from a media point of view these weeks should be understood as a transition period in which the refugee crisis is used to explain the genocide and vice versa.

The massive refugee crisis added to the colonial viewpoint, for among the huge numbers of people paraded in front of the television cameras, the only ones who were individualized were the white NGOs. There are only two exceptions: short clips of physically and psychologically injured refugees, mostly children, who are sometimes named but mostly not, who are given a second to look into the camera and say things like: "I saw when they shot our parents."[61]

The other exception is a few laconic interview clips with named soldiers and official representatives of the RPF who, in a sense, fulfill the colonial angle, for example by rejecting the new UN peacekeeping initiative.[62] Notwithstanding this, in hindsight they also initiate the creation of an alternative historical media memory to that of the guilty conscience of the West, which in May gets its main nourishment from whitewashing explanations such as the USA's debacle in Mogadishu, Somalia, and the fact that the Belgians withdrew early.[63] For instance, on May 8, RPF soldier Tony Kulamba, sitting in front of a group of saved Tutsi children, informs the journalist that: "Our soldiers have been picking them up in the bush, others we have picked among the dead bodies."[64] On May 14, after the Swedish studio voiceover had clarified that "the government and its militia are believed to be behind most of the killings," there followed a short interview with a defensive militia man in Kigali, the General Secretary of the RPF, Theogene Rudasingwa, who is cited at a press conference declaring: "At the end of the day, the task of establishing law and order in Rwanda, the task to stopping the massacres, and making sure that such massacres never, never recur in our country, belongs to us as Rwandese people."[65]

These short statements are largely obscured by the rest of the coverage during this period, and they could easily be interpreted within the prevailing colonial viewpoint, but the RPF nevertheless both claims to represent the Rwandan people, and to be trying to actually do something about the situation. The creation of this alternative historical media memory would eventually have a significant impact on policies, laws, and politics in Rwanda, as we shall see in Part Three.

The Use of the Word Genocide

Although the refugee crisis is used to explain and perhaps even obscure the genocide, the beginning of May nevertheless marks what is often interpreted as the critical occasion when the word "genocide" was used for the first time. Definitions are always important and in this case the evasion of the word "genocide" was partly dependent on colonial ignorance. However, it is also closely connected to an avoidance to make any commitments to intervene according to UN's Genocide Convention; perhaps most infamously exemplified by US State Department spokesperson Christine Shelley's reluctance to define what was going on in Rwanda as genocide at a press briefing on April 28.[66]

On May 5, *Rapport*'s well-known studio anchor issues a warning to sensitive viewers before that evening's segment on Rwanda begins. Over footage of people standing on a bridge, looking at mutilated and bloated corpses floating by in a river, and images of a huge accumulation of bloated corpses at a creek, the reporter announces: "From the bridge overlooking Akagera river between Tanzania and Rwanda one has a good view of the consequences of the genocide that is taking place in Rwanda. Sometimes the onlookers can count one corpse every minute, and survivors say that most of the victims come from the minority group, Tutsi."[67] This is the first time that SVT's *Rapport* used the word genocide to characterize the events in Rwanda.

The day after, on May 6, *Nyheterna* had an unusually long news segment on Rwanda (see Chart 2.3). As part of a long and intricate explanation as to why the USA no longer would act as the "world's police," the studio voiceover states that the "Americans blamed their loss of honor on the UN. Now the US sees the UN's inability in Bosnia and does not intervene in Rwanda despite the fact that the biggest genocide, and the greatest stream of refugees since the Second World War, is underway," a statement which is illustrated by short clips of archival footage from Somalia, and footage taken from a moving truck during

Figure 2.3 Images of corpses lying by the side of a road, filmed from a moving truck, and used to illustrate the first use of the word "genocide" in *Nyheterna*, May 6, 1994

the evacuation of expatriates from Rwanda one month earlier.[68] This is the first time that TV4's *Nyheterna* uses the word genocide, and here they also put it into the context of the Second World War, thus making an implicit comparison to the Holocaust.

However, the word "genocide" was used as early as April 11 by French journalist Jean-Philippe Ceppi—as revealed by journalist Linda Melvern among several others—and on April 23 the influential *The New York Times* used the word "genocide" in an editorial to describe what was taking place in Rwanda.[69] Hence, there is obviously not a straight or logical link between the act of defining something as genocide, and actually acting upon that definition. I am therefore doubtful that the simple and scattered use of the word "genocide" in global media can be counted as a definition so strong that the UN's Genocide Convention became valid. Not because that there was not a genocide underway against the Tutsi in Rwanda, but because the definition of this genocide was lost in a morass of colonial prejudices.

This can be demonstrated by the fact that Swedish television news, after its original definition of the violence in Rwanda as genocide on May 5 and 6, did not continue to define it as genocide. In fact, over the remaining seventy days of the official 100 days that the genocide lasted, *Rapport* only used the word "genocide" on four further occasions (see Chart 2.5) and instead continued to alternate between definitions such as "civil war"[70] and "ancient ethnic tensions."[71] "Genocide" was used on three occasions in May. On the 14th, Bernard Kouchner, the former French Minister of Health, declared it to be "genocide"; anticipating Opération Turquoise.[72] On May 22, the word "genocide" was used by a studio reporter to describe the violence against the Tutsi: "The world's passivity in the face of the genocide has accelerated the rebel offensive."[73] However, on May 26, genocide is used together with the word "epidemic" as a way to describe how "the neighboring countries have been affected by Rwanda's genocide epidemic," due to the mass of bodies that by then were turning up in Lake Victoria.[74]

The word "genocide" with all its implications is clearly not used as the natural term for what was going on. Instead, three other types of descriptions are exploited to illuminate the violence in Rwanda. The first is the use of death figures, which by the end of April had been estimated to be between 100,000 and 200,000, until the ICRC more than doubled these numbers to 500,000 on May 14. However, the figure of 500,000 was then altered to the previous, lower figure of 200,000 throughout the genocide (see Chart 2.5), creating uncertainly.

The second type of description is the abundant use of different kinds of graphic circumlocutions to describe the events, such as "the insane killing in Rwanda,"[75] "the slaughter,"[76] "the bloodbath,"[77] "the hideous brutality,"[78] and "the Rwandan death squadrons' cruelty is unimaginable and the survivors'

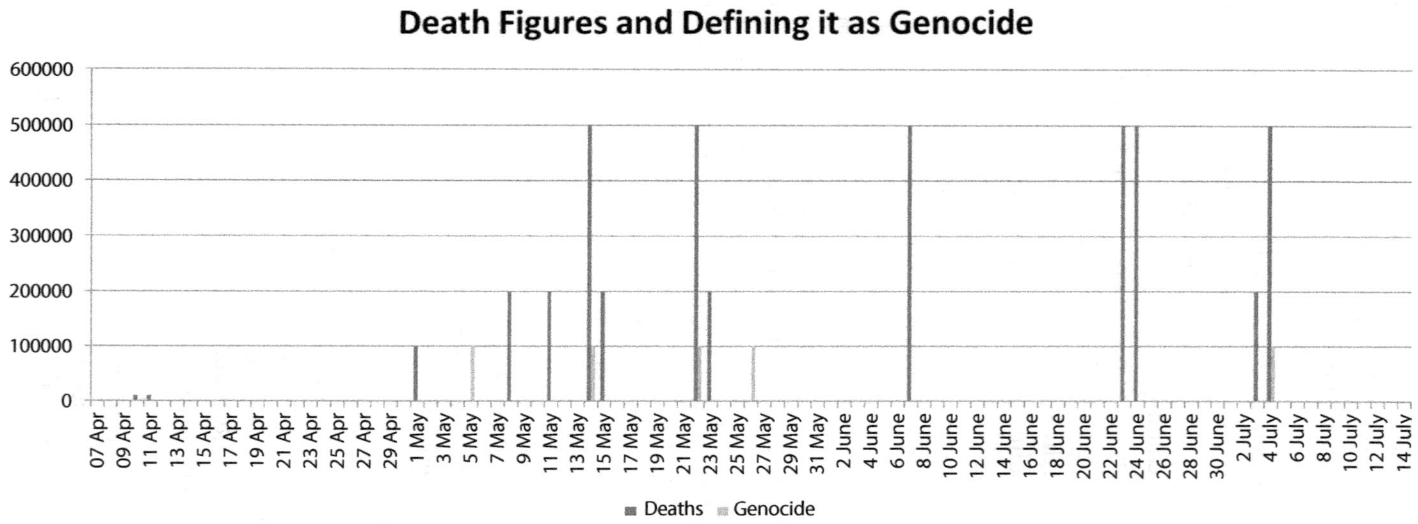

Death Figures and Defining it as Genocide

■ Deaths ■ Genocide

Chart 2.5 Stated death figures and the use of the word "genocide" to define the violence in Rwanda in TV2's *Rapport* between April 7 and July 14, 1994

injuries are often horrific."[79] These vivid descriptions are always coupled with the third type of descriptive means, namely the use of endless images of corpses lying at the roadside, corpses piled up, bloated corpses floating in a river, and mutilated refugees.

The extraordinary death figures and the graphic descriptions coupled with the images of anonymous corpses, all presented from a colonial viewpoint, most certainly contributed to create a moral distance, as the constant repetition of images of suffering tends to increase their remoteness. It should be noted that the use of the word "genocide" did not have a general impact, either locally on Swedish television viewers or globally on the world community, according to the Enlightenment's faith in the power of knowledge or the UN's Convention on Genocide.

One important reason for this, which is seldom considered, is the fact that genocide in this case did not denote genocide in a way that people (at least from a Western point of view) could understand by relating it to something understandable, such as the Holocaust, the definitive genocide. And here I am not talking about the abstract concept of the Holocaust, but instead of the more concrete cinematic version of the Holocaust present in film and television culture. As we have seen, there were no explicit linkages made to the Holocaust as a historic didactic parallel. This could be because, on the one hand, the Holocaust was considered too unique and therefore not comparable with Rwanda, threatening to degrade the significance of the Holocaust as an historical event. On the other hand, the lack of comparison could have been influenced by material explanations, such as the fact that the Holocaust was not considered compatible with the genocide in Rwanda image wise, explanation wise or how the genocide was physically perpetrated.

Furthermore, the genocide against the Tutsi was never considered as a historical fact during most of this period; that is, the ongoing historic events remained elusive throughout. It is therefore legitimate to consider whether genocide only can be thought of, and used, as a phenomenon to describe past events rather than as an alarm clock to raise awareness in the present. To illustrate this difference between past and present there is a big gap in *Rapport*'s use of the word "genocide" from its fourth usage on May 26 to the fifth and final occasion of its use on July 4, the same day that the RPF took Kigali, when it was used as a historical fact to describe something that had already happened, as the studio reporter relates that, "It was to stop the genocide in Rwanda that France, with a slim majority, received the UN's approval to send in troops."[80]

Further Developments and the Creation of Historical Media Memories

During the remaining fifty-seven days of the genocide, from May 19 to July 14, as the killings became more sporadic, the reporting thinned out even more and *Rapport* only returned to the developments in Rwanda on seventeen occasions, of which five consisted of brief news announcements, averaging eighteen seconds. As with the preceding five weeks this meant that there were long stretches of silence. In fact, on four occasions a whole week or more passed by with no new news (see Chart 2.6). The first week's focus on Rwanda, with 5.7 percent of news time, which dropped to 2.0 percent over the next five weeks, was now down to 1.5 percent. Only on one occasion was Rwanda the top news story on *Rapport*.

In between the long stretches of silence during these eight weeks it is possible to distinguish several developments that would, in different ways, influence the creation of historical media memories based on global media reporting. The preceding period had what would seem like a proper ending as the UN Security Council, on May 17, decided to send 5,500 soldiers to Rwanda in order to stop the violence and create peace.[81] However, this was not the happy "Hollywood" ending that everybody had hoped for. As was reported in the news during the following weeks, few nations were willing to contribute troops or equipment until after the violence had ended. Out of the forty-two countries approached by the UN, including Sweden, only four African states promised to send troops. On May 26, UN General Secretary Boutros Boutros-Ghali admitted during a press conference that the UN had failed: "I have tried; I was in contact with different heads of state and beg them to send troops. I was in contact with different organizations and tried my best to be able to help them to find a solution to the problem. Unfortunately, and with great humiliation, I failed. It is a scandal; I am the first one to say that and I am ready to repeat it."[82]

In fact, this development constitutes a game changer for how the genocide would be perceived as a historical event on a global level in the coming years. Although the media reporting was, as we have seen, characterized by a strong guilty Western conscience from the beginning, the Eurocentric perspective nevertheless contributed to create a vast division between "us" and "them." This division was closely tied to the violent and threatening irrationalism attached to the "them," as in "Africans," in the news reporting. However, what is happening here with the failure of the UN to assist is a transformation of the Western notion of "they" do not want "our" help, to "we" do not want to help "them."

Perhaps not surprisingly, over the following weeks *Rapport*'s news reporting on Rwanda is characterized by a return to the safer and more familiar refugee

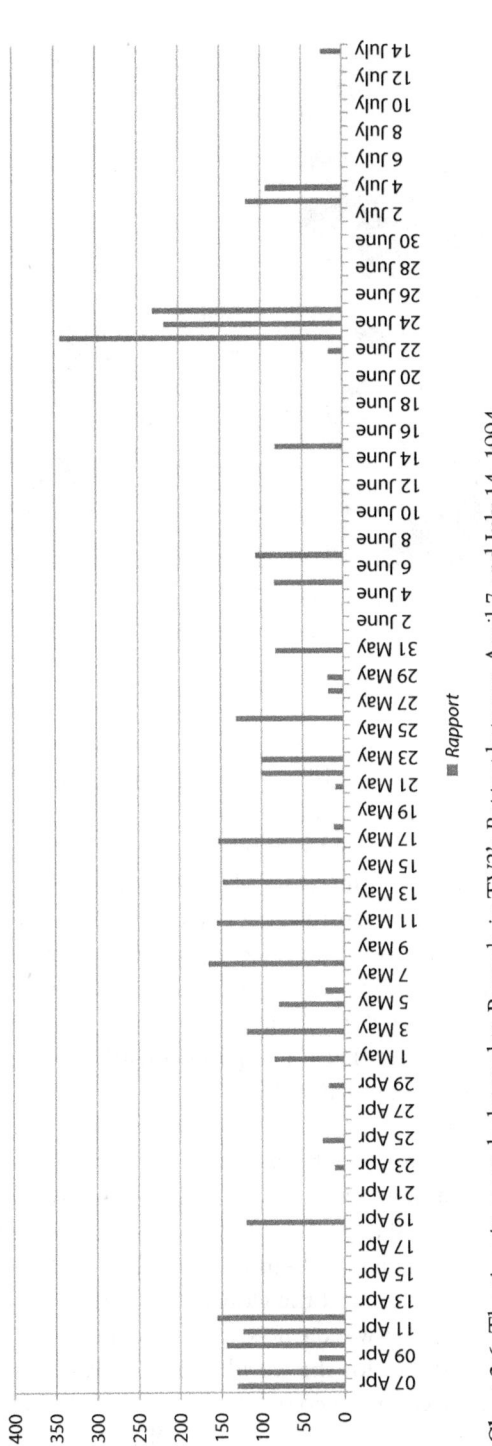

Chart 2.6 The time in seconds devoted to Rwanda in TV2's *Rapport* between April 7 and July 14, 1994

Figure 2.4 UN General Secretary Boutros Boutros-Ghali admits that the UN has failed to put together a second peace mission to Rwanda during a press conference in *Rapport*, May 26, 1994

paradigm. However, the refugee crisis is no longer used to explain the genocide and vice versa as it was before, probably because by now the situation is undeniably more transparent and therefore a distinction can be made between the refugee problem, the civil war, and the genocidal violence. For example, there is no longer any doubt as to who is being targeted, namely the Tutsi.[83] On June 15, the segment on Rwanda ends with the fatalistic observation: "To Rwanda's Tutsi minority, it is a race against the clock, because if the world community does not intervene and stop the war or if the rebels do not take over the country, there will not be a Tutsi minority left to talk about."[84] A week later the reporter verifies that: "The government's death patrols have tried to exterminate the Tutsi population."[85]

The civil war raged on, and by the end of May it was obvious that the RPF, reputed to control two-thirds of the country, was going to win the war, while the UN remained powerless and the interim government and the FAR fled. From the end of May the RPF also had the opportunity to, partially, take control over what was reported—and ultimately therefore to affect the future creation of both the local and the global historical media memory of the genocide. The news from Rwanda now emanated mainly from three locations: (1) the UN as a stand-in for the world community, (2) refugee camps outside of Rwanda, (3) refugee camps controlled by the RPF located inside of Rwanda. The UN level symbolizes the failure of the West, while the reports from the huge refugee camps followed the stereotypical colonial viewpoint focusing on NGOs. However, at this late stage most journalists in Rwanda, with the few exceptions of those "embedded" with the UN, such as Mark Doyle, were associated or "embedded" with the advancing RPF forces. There is an understandable reason for this, as journalist Annie Thomas explains: "Honestly, for my intellectual comfort, I would have been much more comfortable on that side than being with militiamen, their machetes still dripping with blood, professing how much they loved France."[86]

Journalists must aim to retain their journalistic standards and to be impartial, but the fact is that the interim government is all but absent on Swedish television news from the end of May. This is unmistakably a result of the transparency of what was going on in Rwanda which left no doubt as to who were the perpetrators of the genocide. Out of decency, and for moral reasons, the government side had therefore disqualified itself. This does not mean that the impartiality criterion was completely forgotten. As British journalist Mark Doyle commented: "There were [. . .] serious attempts to 'balance' what was essentially an unbalanced story,"[87] meaning that the news needed moral equivalence and, therefore, on a few occasions, claimed that the RPF had committed massacres of Hutus of their own out of "revenge."[88] This also provided a reasonable explanation as to why the Hutu population fled in such numbers ahead of the advancing RPF army.

Nonetheless, the story was tilted to the RPF's advantage, and they could therefore continue to formulate an alternative historical media memory that both ran parallel to and was intertwined with the story of the guilty Western conscience. For example, *Rapport* uses the David and Goliath analogy throughout these 100 days, naming the RPF as the "guerilla" compared to the "Government army."[89] On June 7, another short interview is conducted with a RPF soldier, who is certain of victory: "We are stronger than them, and tactically we are speedier, that is why we have captured all these positions." In the same report "the guerrilla leader," Paul Kagame, is reported to have said, "I will not negotiate with the government, for it is composed of murderers."[90] One week later this perspective is reinforced as *Rapport* starts its segment on Rwanda with the news that sixty adolescent Tutsi boys have been abducted from a church and "massacred by the dreaded Hutu militia." The government is thereafter described as having no control over its own forces, followed by the predisposed statement from the studio reporter that: "There is no reason for the Tutsi dominated guerilla to negotiate peace when the bloodbath continues."[91]

After yet another week of silence two things coincide with each other. The French humanitarian intervention Opération Turquoise is launched, and arriving with the soldiers on June 23 are a number of journalists, including

Figure 2.5 Paul Kagame states that he "will not negotiate with the government, for it is composed of murderers," in *Rapport*, June 7, 1994

Marika Griehsel and Simon Sandford, the only Swedish television journalists in Rwanda at any time during the genocide.[92] This resulted in the three longest reports on Rwanda throughout the entire period (see Chart 2.6 above), with average segment times of 4.24 minutes, the longest being 5.43 minutes on June 23.

As when the UN Security Council took the decision to send new troops to Rwanda one month earlier, the French intervention could have changed the story. However, the French mission was not hailed as the humanitarian breakthrough that was much needed. Instead, from the very beginning the mission was viewed with doubt, as *Rapport* informed its viewers that the UN Security Council only approved the French plan with great hesitation. The studio reporter then questions "what France can do now, about ten weeks too late," and concludes that France has always supported the Hutu government, that is, the *génocidaires*.[93]

With Swedish journalists on the ground the segment then turns into stories of human interest with a focus on the refugee crisis within the country, illustrated by an abundance of footage of anonymous injured and sometimes starving victims. Tellingly, Marika Griehsel chooses to interview an NGO from the ICRC and then a Belgian priest in the care of an orphanage. Only nineteen seconds are devoted to two one-sentence interviews with two survivors, a man and a woman: "I am the only adult left in my family. I still have my children, but I can't cook. I have no food." It is in connection to this interview that Griehsel

Figure 2.6 Cheering Hutus welcoming the French troops in Opération Turquoise, in *Rapport*, June 24, 1994

declares as fact that "The government's death patrols have tried to exterminate the Tutsi population,"[94] thus defining it as a genocide against the Tutsi.

The next day the story about Opération Turquoise was continued but was also muddled by the fact that the studio reporter confuses Hutu and Tutsi, claiming that government troops have been protecting Tutsi in a camp as French soldiers arrived. We are also shown cheering people who welcome the French troops. Griehsel continues the reportage, mentioning the "ancient ethnic tensions," and interviews a refugee of Indian descent who, paradoxically, asserts that Rwanda did not make any difference between Hutu and Tutsi. She then visits a refugee camp located in RPF-controlled Ruhango, illustrated with images of apathetic Tutsi refugees, and states that: "The rebels say that this is the price people have to pay for a future peace,"[95] which could be interpreted to mean that out of the genocide a new Rwanda will rise. On the third consecutive day with extra-long coverage, Griehsel and Sandford have already moved on to neighboring Burundi, where the antagonism between Hutu and Tutsi is also found.[96] Opération Turquoise was not even mentioned that evening, and it would not return to the news for another ten days.

On July 3, the segment on Rwanda starts with the news that the RPF for the first time have opened fire on the French troops, which in the reportage are seen protecting Hutu refugees outside of Butare. But here again the RPF assumes precedence as the voiceover states that "The guerrilla believes that the French support the government that is accused of the murder of 100,000s of

Rwandans."[97] The next day the RPF took control over Kigali, and in order to stop their advancement France established a security zone in the south-west of Rwanda. Illustrated with images of French paratroopers the reporter notes that "The French troops are not neutral anymore. Their new task is to stop the advancing Tutsi guerrilla." The reporter then recapitulates the failure of Opération Turquoise and the success of the RPF in what turns out to be the final comment on the ongoing genocide:

> It was to stop the genocide in Rwanda that France, with a slim majority, received UN approval to go in with troops. Many warned against that a former colonial power would go in and create peace, especially as the French already have supported, trained, and armed the Hutu dominated government army. First, the French really did endeavor to be neutral; their mission was to evacuate the civilian population, to end the senseless killings that had claimed nearly half a million people's lives. Now, the French soldiers are waiting for reinforcement twenty kilometers from the Tutsi guerrilla. A European colonial power against a rebellious African minority.[98]

After yet another ten days of silence *Rapport* returned to Rwanda on July 14 for a short update about the escalating refugee crisis in Goma, Zaire, where more than 1 million Hutu refugees had crossed the border.[99] This announcement marked the turning point as the global media directed all its eyes and ears to the "the largest ever concentration of refugees in recorded history." More than 500 journalists gathered in Goma for the coming weeks which resulted in huge media coverage, especially when compared to the meager coverage of the genocide.[100] Oxfam's logs for credit card donations to help Rwanda is revealing in this instance: May: 1,000 donations; June: 134 donations; July: 6,000 donations; August: 2,500 donations; and September: 100 donations.[101]

The creation of a historical media memory is not a singular and straightforward event. Over a period of 100 days Swedish television news programs followed what turned out to be an irrational logic as the reporting oscillated between extensive coverage of the developments in Rwanda followed by long periods of total silence. The colonial frame of interpretation, with the use of euphemisms and ethnic amnesia, combined with the strong and pervading Eurocentric perspective on the events, contributed to create a waste land of moral distance as well as a historical media memory characterized by a guilty Western conscience. However, the seemingly inexplicable violence is eventually explained via the use of the familiar refugee paradigm, but the constant repetition of images of suffering refugees and what I have termed emblematic images of the genocide—the abundant use of images of corpses lying on the side of the road filmed from moving trucks; piled up corpses; and bloated corpses floating in rivers—reinforced their remoteness even further for television audiences. This in turn contributed to a strong sense of rational Western denial.

Although the story had two notable opportunities to turn into a "happy" ending—that is, on May 17 when the UN Security Council decided on UNAMIR II, and on June 23, when France launched Opération Turquoise—this did not happen and instead these failures are incorporated into the Eurocentric historical media memory characterized by a guilty conscience. However, as we shall see in Part Two on the creation on a transnational historical media memory of the Rwandan genocide, these failures are interpreted in different ways depending on whose memory is it and how the filmmakers decide to shape the cinematic memory of the genocide.

When the transparency of the situation eventually made it possible to make distinctions between the refugee problem, the civil war, and the ongoing genocide, the refugee crisis was no longer needed to explain the genocide. The genocide and the refugee crisis were therefore permanently separated as historical media memories by mid-July as the genocide was officially ended by the RPF and the massive media coverage from Goma begins.

In addition, there was a progressively strong build-up towards the creation of an alternative historical media memory during the last eight weeks of the genocide as the RPF, increasingly, was able to control the angle of the news reported through "embedded" journalists who, perhaps not surprisingly given the circumstances, tended to report favorably about the rebels and against the blood drenched and government sanctioned *génocidaires*. Thus, even at this early stage the RPF take charge, and claim the position to represent the whole people of Rwanda. This is not empty rhetoric but is in fact a fully conscious tactic for the future creation of a Rwanda where ethnic identities are suppressed in favor of national unity. However, this nationalistic approach to the creation of a historical media memory tends to generate tensions, and sometime even revisionist historical recollections of the genocide against the Tutsi, as will transpire in Chapter 10, on revisionism, and in Chapter 11, on Rwanda's own creation of a historical media memory of the genocide.

Part Two

The Creation of a Transnational Historical Media Memory of the Rwandan Genocide, 1994–2005

3

The Creation of a Transnational Historical Media Memory of the Rwandan Genocide in the International Production of Television Documentaries, 1994-2003

The creation of a transnational historical media memory of the Rwandan Genocide is based on the television news reporting during the genocide in 1994, but as was shown in the previous chapter there was no distinct narrative storyline between the start and the end of the genocide. Due to the inherent "liveness" of television news, a multitude of stories emerged, disappeared, and intertwined. Sometimes these stories contradicted each other, and nearly always these stories were constructed and explained from a Eurocentric perspective. How is it then possible to fit all these stories within one single media memory that a feature film or a documentary film can recreate? Is it even meaningful to talk about the Rwandan genocide as a single media memory or should we use the plural term, media memories, to better grasp the creation of a transnational historical media memory?

American historian of ideas Jeffrey Andrew Barash shows that collective memory—memories that are shared by groups rather than individuals, even on a global level—have undergone great changes due to the impact of modern mass media; especially pertaining to memories produced by film and television. While cinematic history has the capacity to simulate direct experience this process also limits or even muddles the connection to a historical past. Barash emphasizes that mass media select, articulate, and broadcast certain events and thus bestow them with public significance. However, the representation of communicated events are not just facsimiles of the past nor the present but are always charged with an autonomous symbolic sense (e.g., Eurocentric, colonial) through which public awareness is channeled and sedimented into a collective memory. While this autonomous symbolic sense can simulate direct experience, it also tends to suppress most of what is not deemed as customary or normal.[1]

To talk about one transnational historical media memory of the Rwandan genocide is therefore both straightforward and misleading because the creation of this media memory is doubtlessly shaped by an autonomous symbolic sense based on a Eurocentric worldview consisting of a guilty Western conscience, ethnic amnesia, and ignorance—and the last criterion especially opens for a historiography that does not at all lead to a single historical media memory. When predominantly Western filmmakers started to try to make sense of what happened in Rwanda in 1994, they also started to create narratives (with a beginning, a middle, and an end) out of the scattered television images (soon to be emblematic images) and stories/testimonies they could gather. Out of necessity, they thus arranged and selected the available images and testimonies, and this process, seen from a top-down perspective, did not immediately create a single media memory but instead created media memories. Nevertheless, from the very beginning a dominant transnational media memory of the Rwandan genocide was created, but this memory never existed in isolation.

At the same time, although Western television news displayed a faltering (and sometimes ignorant) interest in the Rwandan genocide, the subsequent significant international production of cinematic history via feature films and documentary films counterbalances this failed interest, thus turning this genocide, in retrospect, into an event of great public significance. However, an important difference to highlight here is that even though Barash uses international media events such as the Romanian Revolution, the Balkan Wars, and the O. J. Simpson trial, he limits himself to American media as conveyors of collective memories, equating this with global media.[2] The significant production of international feature films and documentaries on the Rwandan genocide is, in comparison, truly transnational because films and documentaries on the Rwandan genocide have been produced and co-produced in no less than thirty-nine countries.[3] Furthermore, this production process spans over a period of nearly thirty years, to date, which reasonably leaves room for repetition, change, and diversity pertaining to the historical media memory of the genocide against the Tutsi in Rwanda.

In this second part of the book a chronological approach divided across three chapters will be used to facilitate the large body of films on the Rwandan genocide, and the sometimes contradicting and/or intertwined storylines. The audiovisual material is analyzed in a two-part process to show how a historical media memory developed and how this eventually solidified into a collective memory based on, essentially, mass recreated moving images. This process involves the emblematic images televised as live news items in 1994, the many documentaries produced, as well as a few feature films that together have contributed to construct a collective historical memory for general audiences around the world. Although documentaries, mainly made for television, and historical feature films, mainly made for distribution in cinemas, are, on the surface, very different when it comes to narrative, the use of images, and authenticity aesthetics, these productions will be discussed side by side as examples of cinematic history that equally contributed to constitute collective memories with global impact.

Chapter 3 explores the first productions of the Rwandan genocide, mainly television documentaries, and thus the origin of the transnational historical media memory with the establishment of emblematic images, and how the memory at this early stage consisted of a cobweb of remembrances and accusations. This is a largely ignored but still respectable body of documentaries made before the arrival of the quintessential film *Hotel Rwanda* (2004). The following two chapters will take a closer look at the six major films made in 2004 and 2005 that both created a global public consciousness and kickstarted a large international production of films and documentaries to commemorate the genocide against the Tutsi. Chapter 4 analyzes the feature films *Hotel Rwanda*, *Shooting Dogs* (a.k.a. *Beyond the Gates*, 2005), and *Sometimes in April* (2005), while Chapter 5 analyzes the landmark documentaries *Ghosts of Rwanda* (2004), *Shake Hands with the Devil: The Journey of Roméo Dallaire* (2004), and *Rwanda: Do Scars Ever Fade?* (2004).

A Cobweb of Remembrances and Accusations, and the Establishment of Emblematic Images, 1994–2003

Films on the Rwandan genocide made before 2004 are rarely mentioned in literature on the media memory of the genocide.[4] I have, nonetheless, identified thirty-five documentaries and one feature film, *100 Days* (2001), which, although made by British director Nick Hughes, will be discussed at length in Chapter 11 as a Rwandan production due to the large involvement of Rwandan personnel and the subsequent impact it had on the Rwandan film industry. An exception to this academic void is Fergal Keane's *Journey into Darkness* (1994), an episode of *Panorama*, BBC's longest-running current affairs show, which graphically told the story of the massacre at Nyarubuye, where approximately 35,000 people died. The episode was broadcast on June 27, that is, during the genocide, and is therefore often hailed as the first documentary on the genocide against the Tutsi in Rwanda.[5] However, a French television team was in neighboring Burundi at the start of the genocide when President Juvénal Habyarimana's plane was shot down on April 6. By chance, they shot a documentary, *Burundi–un suicide African* ("Burundi–an African Suicide," 1994), on the ethnic tensions between Hutus and Tutsis in Burundi and Rwanda that aired on May 5 on Swedish Public Television.

Burundi–un suicide African was made by two just-of-out-film-school youngsters, Guillaume Tanzini and Joseph Bitmaba, who adopt an outsider's, if not unenlightened, perspective on the developments in Burundi and Rwanda. The film spends an unusual amount of time showcasing traditional Burundian dancing and drumming performances. Even so, the film focuses on the competition between two Burundian political parties—the Union for National Progress (UPRONA) and the Front for Democracy in Burundi (FRODEBU). The filmmakers thus translate the political tensions to racial tensions, landing in the perennial historical explanation whereby Belgian colonialism is to blame for cementing the differences between Hutus and Tutsis by exploiting conceived racial differences. This is coupled with interviews with Burundian officials, among them, François Ngeze—briefly head of state between October 21 and 27, 1993, in place of the assassinated president Melchior Ndadaye—who explains that the regional conflict in former Ruanda-Urundi is the outcome of European democracy being forced on Africa. Most audiovisual material consists of interviews and milieu overviews, but some stills and archival footage are used to show the result of the 1965, 1972, 1988, and 1993 massacres. Among these are moving images of beached and bloated bodies, which also figured as one of the emblematic images from the Rwandan genocide in television news around the world the same year. Nonetheless, these filmmakers are the first to touch upon the theory of the double genocide, that is, that the Rwandan Patriotic Front (RPF) committed a parallel genocide against the Hutu population in 1994, probably unaware of its revisionist implications. At this early stage television news around the world reported on the slaughter as a barbaric civil war, rather than as a planned genocide against the Tutsi population. In the end, the documentary comes off as a bit whimsical, trying on for size all sorts of explanations, but unable, due to lack of knowledge, to reach a viable conclusion.

The subsequent documentaries are all made after the genocide ended and they can be divided into two main groups—with one exception: Anne Aghion's *Gacaca: Revivre ensamble au Rwanda?* (*Gacaca: Living Together Again in Rwanda?*, 2002), which is part of a quadruplet of films released between 2002 and 2009 that will be discussed in Chapter 9, on reconciliation and Gacaca documentaries—that reveal an ongoing process, a struggle, over a historical media memory that had not yet been cemented. Furthermore, these films can be analyzed as different ways to communicate and, above all, to explain the history of the genocide by looking at the causes and reasons raised within them.

The first group of films fall back on the conventional historical explanation that could be found in television news and in *Journey into Darkness* and *Burundi-un suicide African*, where the political and eventually the genocidal violence is seen mainly as a result of the mechanisms set in motion during the colonial era. Examples of such documentaries are *Rwanda, l'histoire qui mène au génocide* (*Rwanda: How History Can Lead to Genocide*, 1995), *Une république devenue folle: Rwanda 1894–1994* (*A Republic Gone Mad: Rwanda 1894–1994*, 1995), parts of *Chronicle of a Genocide Foretold* (1996), *The Dead Are Alive: Eyewitness in Rwanda*

(1995), and *L'Afrique en morceaux: la tragdie des Grands Lacs* ("Africa in Pieces: The Tragedy of the Great Lakes," 2000). These films, for example, conveniently omit the more than thirty years hiatus of Hutu rule after the popular revolution in 1959, and this, in a sense, exonerates the instigators and perpetrators of the genocide against the Tutsi in 1994. The only partial exception to this is *The Dead Are Alive: Eyewitness in Rwanda*, where the Rwandan Catholic Church is blamed in tandem with the colonial powers.[6]

The French television documentary, *Rwanda: How History can Lead to Genocide*, directed by Robert Genoud, is a case in point. This documentary explores how the colonization of Rwanda by Germany and especially Belgium created the historical conditions for the genocide in 1994. The premise is that history in Rwanda has been falsified by Westerners and Rwandans alike, and that history was thus used by Hutu extremists to gain power and to promote the genocide against the Tutsi. Interwoven within that are interviews with three average Hutus who relate their personal experience of growing up in Rwanda with the ethnic divisions between Hutus and Tutsis. All three opposed the dictatorship of President Habyarimana but at the same time they, as well as all the talking heads that participate in the documentary, among them Belgian political scientist Filip Reyntjens, underline the fact that it was the Belgian colonizers, in collaboration with the Catholic Church, that fueled the ethnic divisions. To illustrate how these seeds were sowed, Genoud uses archival footage from old German and Belgian documentaries with the original soundtracks. These archival films are thus used as "evidence" without considering the fact that they are purely propaganda films. The implication of this indiscriminate use is that the Tutsi population is incriminated due to its leadership's favoritism by the colonizers. The Hutu revolution in 1959/1962 thus becomes a "natural" outcome of the ethnic divisions, and the genocide becomes the natural consequence of RPF's invasion in 1990. The genocide against the Tutsi is only touched on during the last five minutes of the documentary, when footage of men with machetes at a roadblock as well as numerous takes of corpses lying by the road is used to illustrate the result of Belgian colonization.

Closely connected to these films are documentaries that locate the explanation for the genocide in more contemporary political circumstances. A few films directly accuse France and Belgium for their involvement and even support for the *génocidaires*, such as *Rwanda: The Bloody Tricolour* (1995) and *France in Rwanda: A Guilty Neutrality* (2001). Another group of films lays the blame for the failure directly on the United Nations (UN) and the peacekeeping mission UNAMIR—films such as *Sitting in a Volcano* (1995), *UN Blues* (1995), *The Triumph of Evil* (1998, a.k.a. *When Good Men Do Nothing* in the UK), *The Genocide Factor: Genocide: The Horror Continues* (2000), and *The Last Just Man* (2001).

Figure 3.1 Men with machetes at a roadblock in *Rwanda: How History Can Lead to Genocide* (1995)

One filmmaker stands out during this first formative period as an originator of this colonial angle, British journalist Steve Bradshaw who made three key television documentaries: *A Culture of Murder* (1994), *Rwanda: The Bloody Tricolour*, and the Frontline documentary, *The Triumph of Evil*. *The Culture of Murder*, which aired on the BBC's *Panorama* on August 22, 1994, is typically filmed on location in Goma in the aftermath of the genocide, focusing on the plight of the refugees, thus turning the attention away from the actual victims of the genocide to the perpetrators and accomplices who are, in this refugee paradigm, perceived as victims. *Rwanda: The Bloody Tricolour*, on the other hand, has its focus on France's deep and troubling involvement in Rwanda's internal affairs before and during the genocide. As British international relations scholar Georgina Holmes has pointed out, this documentary and fellow BBC documentaries such as *Journey into Darkness*, *A Culture of Murder* and *Facing Up to Genocide: Valentina's Story* (1997) all follow what she dubs "the BBC's institutional narrative," which tends to explain the planning of the genocide with emphasis on external involvement, and in which the role of Hutu extremists and the RPF are seldom, if ever, referred to.[7]

Perhaps the most striking example of this Eurocentric outlook is *The Triumph of Evil*, where Bradshaw investigates what he calls the "West's do-nothing strategy,"[8] which is not dependent on ignorance but on an active strategy to avoid the violent developments in Rwanda at any cost—thus allowing the genocide to take place. This is mainly accomplished with the help of Western talking heads, both by using archival footage, such as that of US State Department spokesperson Christine Shelley's infamous refusal to label the violence against the Tutsi as genocide during a press conference on April 28, 1994—which is here used for the first time as audiovisual "historical evidence" in a documentary, but also by contemporary interviews with some of who would eventually become recurring key witnesses for the creation of a historical media memory of the Rwandan genocide. The most prominent among these witnesses are Lieutenant-General Roméo Dallaire, the Canadian Force Commander of UNAMIR, and Colonel Luc Marchal, the highest-ranking officer of the Belgian UN troop to Rwanda. The film then in turn explores the Clinton administration's disinterest (due to the Somalia debacle in 1993), the Belgium government's call to withdraw the UN peacekeeping mission (due to the ten murdered Belgian soldiers), the "UN Club" (that is, the UN bureaucracy), claiming that the vote for a stronger UN force on May 17 was nothing but a sham, and finally the US Defense Department's opposition to blocking Rwandan radio channel RTLM (Radio Télévision Libre des milles Collines), which aired hate propaganda before the genocide and then detailed instructions on how to locate victims during the genocide.

Furthermore, *The Triumph of Evil* is one of the first documentaries to take thorough advantage of the emblematic images aired as television news in 1994—that is, images of corpses lying by the side of the road filmed from moving trucks, piles of corpses, bloated corpses floating in a river, and the Nick Hughes footage—which, used as they are as illustrations rather than explanations, tend to reinforce the audiences' remoteness. However, as we shall see

Figure 3.2 Corpses by the side of the road in *The Triumph of Evil* (1998)

later, the randomness of these television images will, within documentary film narrative, be constrained to predictability due to precise selection and editing.

Nonetheless, *The Triumph of Evil* introduces another first of what would eventually become emblematic footage of the West's abandonment of Rwanda, i.e., footage of the evacuation of expatriates from KPH (Kigali Psychiatric Hospital), also known as Ndera Psychiatric Center, in April, 1994.[9] These powerful images show hundreds of Tutsi refugees, as well as patients, who had taken refuge at the hospital, protected by Belgian UN peacekeeping forces, pleading with the soldiers to evacuate them, even begging the soldiers to shoot them rather than hand them over to the Interahamwe militia waiting outside. The footage includes a row of European reporters with cameras opposite these refugees, "shooting" them while the Tutsis raise their arms in the air at the same time as they go down on their knees, begging. During this, a sobbing European woman dressed in a pink top is dragged by two French soldiers to a waiting truck. According to survivors, people tried to block the convoy by lying down on the road as the French drove off, but the soldiers fired in the air. Immediately after the convoy left the Interahamwe entered the premises and killed 2,000 Tutsis, including the patients of the hospital.[10]

Overall, these films mainly process a guilty Western conscience. An integral part of the historiography in these films is thus an inherent Eurocentric outlook on the events. In fact, the Eurocentric perspective is so strong that Africans seemingly cannot even take responsibility for their own actions and are accordingly reduced to being part of a colonial account of events. This in turn could have contributed to a strong sense of rational Western denial, as was discussed in Chapter 2 on television news reporting, but this is not the case, as the hammering in of one type of media memory actually reinforced the collective memory of the genocide against the Tutsi in Rwanda. The use of a few recurrent emblematic images is therefore vital for the creation of this transnational historical media memory.

The KPH images later appear in *The Last Just Man* and *A Good Man in Hell* (2003), both titles referring to Roméo Dallaire, the commander of UNAMIR. While the former is a Canadian documentary with many similarities to *The Triumph of Evil*, especially in its use of images and its almost sole focus on the UN, but from a Canadian interest viewpoint, the latter is a short film made for the United States Holocaust Memorial Museum as part of the exhibit of video resources of the museum as audiovisual evidence.[11] In addition to the KPH images, these two films also uses images of corpses lying on the road. Furthermore, *The Last Just Man* uses the Nick Hughes footage, also seen in *The Triumph of Evil*, while *A Good Man in Hell* uses images of a man at a roadblock who is waving his machete at the passing lorry from where the camera operator filmed the sequence.

Figures 3.3 and 3.4 Images from the evacuation of KPH, showing Western journalists "shooting" Tutsi refugees as well as hundreds of refugees being abandoned, with the European woman being dragged away in the bottom-right corner of the image in *The Triumph of Evil* (1998)

Finally, a Swedish educational documentary, *Ramp om historia–Rwanda* ("Ramp on History–Rwanda", 2003) takes this Eurocentric perspective to the extreme as a young reporter, Max Landergård, nineteen years old at the time, is sent to Rwanda to make a documentary about the genocide. He confesses that he only knew that "some people were killed" and that "machetes were involved" before he arrived, locating himself firmly in the position of Western denial, exemplified by the fact that he frequently uses the words "unreal"

Figure 3.5 The Nick Hughes footage in *The Last Just Man* (2003)

and "unexplainable" as he visits genocide memorials such as Ntarama and Nyamata. The documentary includes vivid testimonies from Tutsi survivors as well as an interview with a female Hutu perpetrator, but there is no attempt to explain or to contextualize the genocide, other than a short reference to the Belgian colonization and a quite crude comparison with the Holocaust, made by Linda Melvern. Instead, this educational documentary, aimed at Swedish schoolchildren, exploits an abundance of unexplained emblematic images such as the Nick Hughes footage, numerous variants of corpses by the road, images of bloated corpses in a river, the KPH images, and extensive images of skeletons and clothes at the genocide memorials.

Over time, when analyzing these early documentaries on the Rwandan genocide, seven types of emblematic images emerge which stand out in comparison to other moving images and which to a significant degree have contributed to the creation of a transnational historical media memory. Henceforth they are referred to as such:

1. "The Nick Hughes Footage" of people being killed and clubbed at a roadblock, shot with an extreme long shot from the roof of the French school in Kigali during the first week of the genocide.
2. "Corpses by the Road," that is, images of corpses lying by the side of the road filmed from the platforms of moving trucks. There are several variants but one, filmed during the first week when journalists traveled the country with paratroopers to collect expatriates, is used repeatedly and shows the scattered corpses of men and women, with dried

blood underneath them, lying by a street gutter as the camera passes them by.
3. "Piles of Corpses," usually filmed from a moving vehicle showing piled corpses several feet high. Here, too, there are several different variants, most of them filmed during the first week.
4. "The River of Corpses," which shows a panorama shot of a "river" of corpses that covers an entire road.
5. "The KPH Images," showing the evacuation of expatriates from Kigali Psychiatric Hospital in April, 1994.
6. "The Man with a Machete"; there are several versions but there are two main alternatives, one showing a man waving his machete at a roadblock, the other showing a man with a machete and knife, both filmed during the first week.
7. "Bloated Corpses in the River," which shows corpses floating in the Akagera river between Rwanda and Tanzania. There are a few variants, and they are filmed a couple of weeks into the genocide.

It should be noted that certain kind of images are hardly used at all in these early documentaries, and these are images of decaying corpses in churches and schools, images of bones and skulls, and additional images of remains (clothes, mummified bodies at memorials). This footage was mostly filmed at the end of the genocide or, when it comes to human remains, several years after the genocide. That is, they were mostly available at this time but their eventual importance for the creation of a transnational media historical memory of the genocide against the Tutsi was not yet activated. Eventually, however, these images would be turned into the eighth emblematic image of the Rwandan genocide.

8. "Skeletons and Clothes," consisting of images of decomposed bodies which turn into skeletons, often with their clothes still on. This footage was filmed at the end of the genocide when journalists were allowed back into the country. There is also a variant of this footage, as these skeletons and clothes were collected, preserved, and displayed as "proof" of the genocide, for example in the genocide memorials in Murambi and Nyamata.

Alternative and Revisionist Documentaries

Many of the seven emblematic images are used in documentaries which in different ways deviate from the dominant and guilt-driven historical media memory of the Rwandan genocide. The most prolific, and nowadays repressed and forgotten, of these films were produced in the first years after the genocide. A case in point is the so-called "Rwanda series," a collection of documentaries made by Canadian filmmakers Yvan Patry and Danièle Lacourse in 1995 and 1996, which include *Hand of God, Hand of the Devil* (1995), *Sitting on a Volcano*, and a three-part television documentary series, *Chronicle of a Genocide Foretold* (1996).

Patry and Lacourse made several trips to Rwanda where they, above all, documented the aftermath of the genocide. The first film, *Hand of God, Hand of the Devil*, has a distinct Canadian outlook since it tells the story of Canada's historical role in colonial Rwanda with missionary work and the start of Université nationale du Rwanda in Butare, which was established in 1963 in cooperation with the Congregation of the Dominicans from the Province of Quebec. This is in stark contrast to the Belgian handling of Rwanda illustrated with, e.g., archival footage of skull measurements. The genocide is nonetheless rushed over. In order to illustrate the genocide speedily, the filmmakers use excerpts of "The Nick Hughes Footage," "Corpses by the Road," and "The Man with a Machete" footage, thus establishing the inexplicable gruesomeness and otherness in comparison to the "civilized" Canadians.

This storytelling becomes even more complex by the fact that the actual focus of the documentary is the murder of two Canadian priests and missionaries who had protested against corruption and human rights violations after the genocide; that is, when the new RPF-led government was in the midst of consolidating its control over the war torn country. This interest not only shifts the focus away from the genocide, but the investigation of the missionaries' death leads into an exploration of RPF's post-genocide activates, where the RPF is blamed for ordering the murders of the Canadians. In addition, the filmmakers' interviews suspect *génocidaire* detainees in Butare prison during the fall of 1994.

After the genocide, approximately 100,000 Hutus were imprisoned, suspected of genocide, often under appalling conditions since the capacity of Rwanda's prison system was exceeded five- to tenfold. Furthermore, the genocide had shattered Rwanda's court system as judges and lawyers had been killed or had fled the country, law books had been burned, and courthouses had been destroyed.[12] This meant that prisoners, guilty or not, were kept for years without proper trials and sentencing. The interviews which were conducted illustrate these appalling conditions and, at the same time, they work to undermine the RPF's legitimacy. All prisoners, unsurprisingly, denied any involvement in the genocide, which creates ambiguity among audiences, but the voiceover also comments on this, saying that "among the ones we talked to in prison there was a mayor, a priest, teachers, and children," thus implying that these normal-looking people could not be the same monsters who had been actively involved in the gruesome genocide. The logical outcome is that the RPF has imprisoned innocent people without trial, making the RPF, if not the monsters, then the antagonists, in the documentary.

The second documentary, *Sitting on a Volcano*, was filmed at the same time as the previous film and is a continuation of its theme as the filmmakers follow the exodus of Hutu refugees to Goma. Here they portray the misery of the tent camps, and the mass deaths due to the cholera epidemic, portraying Hutu refugees as innocent victims squeezed between gangs of Hutu extremist war criminals and the RPF. The film starts with an interview with some Hutus who claim to have fled because they looked like Tutsis, which is not questioned by the filmmakers and comes off as a prevarication. Then the filmmaker allows Augustin Bizimana, the defense minister of the interim government, to proclaim that the RPF "exterminated its people," that is, the revisionist theory of a double genocide.[13] Bizimana was charged with thirteen counts of genocide, including extermination, murder, rape, and torture, and was wanted internationally for twenty-five years, until it was established that he had died in the year 2000.[14] What is more, the filmmakers then return to the Butare prison, essentially repeating the portrayal of the misery of the "innocent" detainees as shown in *Hand of God, Hand of the Devil*. And as if this was not enough, the documentary explores the Kibeho massacre during which the Rwandan Patriotic Army (RPA), the military wing of the RPF, most likely killed between 4,000 and 5,000 returning Hutus in a refugee camp on April 22, 1995.[15] However, the Rwandan government's official estimate is that only 338 Hutus were killed, and this incident is still a highly sensitive subject to this day.

The three-part documentary series, *Chronicle of a Genocide*, made the following year, is based on two trips to Rwanda, but it also rehashes much of the audiovisual material used in the two previous documentaries. The first and second parts, "Blood Was Flowing Like a River" and "We Were Cowards," mostly follow the dominant structure for the historical media memory of the Rwandan genocide, as they recap the colonial view and the Western guilt around the genocide, intercut however with newly filmed interviews that contribute to a more personal take on events. Still, the third part, "We Feel Betrayed," once again examines the aftermath of the genocide as the Hutu majority is subjected to crimes against humanity, according to the filmmakers. Here the filmmakers return to several of the people and places visited previously, such as Butare prison.

Patry and Lacourse's "Rwanda series" could be labeled as a forgotten or suppressed historical media memory. For example, in a book on identity and trauma in Rwanda, American historian Randall Fegley wrongly dismisses the three-part television series and the filmmakers in one sentence—seemingly unaware of the previous two documentaries—for "self-censoring their work under pressure from government official[s]."¹⁶ However, at the time, these documentaries certainly were in a minority but their approach to the genocide was not unique. In Swedish television documentary *Blodsarvet* ("The Blood Legacy," 1995) the genocide against the Tutsi is not even mentioned and the sole focus is on the aftermath with interviews with child refugees, Hutu prisoners, and, for instance, Mathieu Ngirumpatse, former President for Mouvement Révolutionnaire National pour le Développement (MRND), who unopposed is allowed to say about the genocide: "We should use the correct term. People did not kill each other, they fought." Ngirumpatse was sentenced to life in prison for the crime of genocide, crimes against humanity, and war crimes by the International Criminal Tribunal for Rwanda (ICTR) in 2014.¹⁷

This alternative approach to the genocide largely depends on filmmakers' journalistic approach and, possibly, their ignorance of the history of the region and the actual happenings of the genocide at this early time. The fact that international interest in Rwanda was first awakened by the biblical refugee catastrophe following the genocide thus parallels the fact that many journalists and documentary filmmakers who turned their interest towards Goma and the refugees there were ignorant and often characterized Hutus as victims rather than as perpetrators or accomplices. When the enormous scale of the genocide became apparent to the outside world, this in turn created another interest in the killers *per se*, interviewing them in order to find out just how they possibly could have killed their relatives, friends, and neighbors in this gruesome and upfront personal way. This is, for instance, the approach taken by the Japanese documentary short *Naze rinjin wo koroshitaka* ("Why Did They Kill Their Neighbors," 1998), where the audience is allowed to follow a young male perpetrator who was forced to kill his older sister. This is alsothe theme in the American *Rwanda: Out of Darkness* (1998), and the Belgian *The Dead Are Alive: Eyewitness in Rwanda* (1995). Another more explicit example is *World of Death* (1994), which simply could be characterized as a shockumentary, an exploitation film in documentary format that emphasizes spectacle and sensationalism, rather than objectivity,¹⁸ here on the suffering in war, dealing with refugees from Rwanda, but also the war in Bosnia-Herzegovina, and the executions of former top government officials in Liberia. The Hutu refugee perspective is likewise present in Hupert Sauper's—director of the Oscar nominated *Darwin's Nightmare* (2004)—documentary *Kisangani Diary* (1998), on the massacre of Hutu refugees in Democratic Republic of Congo in April, 1997.

The Hutu perspective and the interest in the killers, often as "innocent" or equal victims, paves the way for an alternative historical media memory of the genocide against the Tutsi. As mentioned, this alternative approach probably had logistical reasons since the refugees were easier to access than for the journalists to venture into a war-devastated Rwanda, where the rotting corpses lay silent. However, the focus on the false notion of a double genocide, while mixing it with the RPF's somewhat harsh handling of the Hutu majority, has a strong tendency to obscure the actual genocide, creating something that is bordering on historical revisionism.

Nonetheless, although produced by Westerners these films rarely process the guilty conscience of the West as in the dominant historical media memory of the Rwandan genocide, as the blame is to be found elsewhere. In addition, audiovisually these alternative documentaries pride themselves for using newly taken footage and domestic interviews rather than relying on archival footage and European and American talking heads, which tends to give back some agency to Africa and Africans. Still, the power of the emblematic images still lingers over many of the analyzed films, as especially "The Nick Hughes Footage," "Corpses by the Road," and "The Man with a Machete" footage reestablish a lasting impression of gruesomeness and otherness for television audiences around the world. This, once again, reinforces the notion of a collective and audiovisually based transnational historical media memory of the genocide against the Tutsi in Rwanda.

4
The Creation of a Global Public Consciousness, 2004-2005

While the films made before 2004 have received comparatively little attention among audiences and in academia, they nevertheless laid the groundwork for an audiovisual historical media memory of the Rwandan genocide. However, in connection to the ten-year commemoration of the genocide in 2004-2005, three feature films and at least seventeen documentaries were produced and released. Of these twenty productions, six principal films reached wide audiences and contributed to put the genocide against the Tutsi in public consciousness on a global scale.

The feature films, *Hotel Rwanda*, *Shooting Dogs*, and *Sometimes in April*, and the three feature-length documentaries, *Ghosts of Rwanda*, *Shake Hands with the Devil: The Journey of Roméo Dallaire*, and *Rwanda: Do Scars Ever Fade?*, have been particularly noticed and examined to the extent that it would appear as if no other films on the subject existed. *Hotel Rwanda* grossed approximately US$34 million at box offices worldwide, and received three Academy Award Nominations and a further sixteen film awards, including several human rights recognitions.[1] Add to that rentals and sales on DVD, frequent television broadcasts, and the regular use of the film as an audiovisual textbook to teach pupils about the genocide on a global scale, and *Hotel Rwanda* doubtless is the quintessential film on the Rwandan genocide.[2] Edouard Kayihura and Kerry Zukas, authors of the harshly critical book *Inside Hotel Rwanda: The Surprising True Story . . . And Why It Matters Today*, even claim that *Hotel Rwanda* is the most seen, or even perhaps the only, film on Rwanda and/or Africa that American schoolchildren are shown during their entire education.[3] This is however not entirely true; several films on Africa have been more commercially successful, for example *Blood Diamond* (2006) which grossed US$171 million worldwide, and there is even a more commercially successful film which takes place in Rwanda, *Gorillas in the Mist: The Story of Dian Fossey* (1988), starring Sigourney Weaver, which grossed US$61 million worldwide.[4] Nonetheless, Kayihura and Zukas's and others' reaction to *Hotel Rwanda* demonstrates the assumed (and presuming negative) impact of the film, most probably because it is seen as the only film on the genocide against the Tutsi. *Shooting Dogs* was not as successful at the box office but has had a widespread release on television, DVD, and as an audiovisual teaching tool in schools.[5] Similarly, the HBO-produced *Sometimes in April* has aired on PBS, and has been released on DVD and as school teaching material.[6] Of the three documentaries, *Ghosts of Rwanda* was produced by PBS as part of its highly esteemed Frontline series, as was *Triumph of Evil* six years earlier. *Rwanda: Do Scars Ever Fade?* was produced by The History Channel and *Shake Hands with the Devil* by the Canadian Broadcasting Corporation. All three films have aired numerous times on television around the world, have been released on DVD, are used in teaching situations, and have been bestowed with a number of documentary film nominations and awards, for example at CPH:DOX and the Sundance Film Festival.[7]

Hotel Rwanda

As discussed in the introductory chapter, *Hotel Rwanda*, although not the first film on the genocide against the Tutsi, has to a great extent formed and consolidated the historical media memory of the genocide for general audiences around the world. The original reviews were highly positive, and the only major objection concerned the fact that director Terry George and screenwriter Kier Pearson had made the choice not to restage a more audiovisually graphic version of the genocide. In *The Villiage Vocie* reviewer Michael Atkins wrote:

> Mostly, the carnage—up to a million killed in three months, in a country smaller than Massachusetts—is told to us secondhand, or glimpsed in distant scuffles. Like the majority of movies about the last century of holocausts, *Hotel Rwanda* is as earnest and tasteful as its creators. To capture the white-hot terror of social calamity, someone a little more lawless and fierce might be called for.[8]

However, most reviews proclaimed *Hotel Rwanda* to be a film of tremendous importance.[9] A Swedish reviewer wrote: "This is a goddamn must-see in order to take notice of one of the most horrible contemporary genocides! Rarely has a film felt so important."[10] The main initial didactical issue thus seemed to be whether *Hotel Rwanda* had the capability to enlighten the world about an "unknown" genocide or whether the option to make a "child friendly"[11] version somehow would cloud the historical recollection, and thus the importance, of events. Consequently, the initial discussion did not touch on any historical inaccuracies in the film, which strongly indicates the "unknownness" of the subject matter.

But how do you introduce an unknown history to uninformed audiences? Here three aesthetic and narrative strategies relevant for the pedagogical transfer of cinematic history will be highlighted: (1) The ordinary-man-turned-into-hero trope, (2) The dramaturgical conveying of historical information and knowledge, and (3) The use of (mainly) off-screen violence.

Historian Robert Brent Toplin has argued that "[v]irtually all Hollywood perspectives on history offer biographical approaches to their subject, presenting issues and events in terms of experiences of one or two principal figures."[12] This personalization, or individualization, allows cinematic history to, in a pedagogical way, handle broad questions that is related to the individual character's experience that in turn functions as a stand-in for audiences.

Hotel Rwanda tells the story of the genocide through the eyes and experiences of Paul Rusesabagina, a real-life hotel manager at the luxury Hôtel des Mille Collines in Kigali who is credited for saving 1,286 refugees, mostly Tutsis, from being murdered.[13] The ordinary-man-turned-into-hero is a trope frequently employed in cinematic history when filmmakers have to treat a huge and sometime unruly subject that has to be condensed in order to create a working story of 90 to 120 minutes of screen time. *Schindler's List* (1993) is of course a case in point, but the same trope is used in diverse historical films such as *God afton, Herr Wallenberg* (*Good Evening, Mr. Wallenberg*, 1990), *JFK* (1991), *The Patriot* (2000), *Erin Brockovich* (2000), *Jin ling shi san chai* (*Flowers of War*, 2014), and *Alone in Berlin* (2016).

In *Hotel Rwanda* Rusesabagina is presented as an urbane character who knows all the right people, but he is also a people's person who can connect with all layers of society, that is, with both Hutus and Tutsis of all walks of life, as well as with Western expatriates and the UN peacekeeping personnel. He thus becomes the perfect stand-in for audiences, or as Roger Ebert writes in his review: "This is not the kind of man the camera silhouettes against mountaintops, but the kind of man who knows how things work in the real world, who uses his skills of bribery, flattery, apology and deception to save these lives who have come into his care."[14]

The character development portrays a man who puts his family first at all costs to becoming a man who, risking his own life, works tirelessly to save the lives of strangers. A pivotal and intensely dramatic scene is when Rusesabagina, of Hutu origin, has a gun put to his head and is encouraged by soldiers of the Presidential Guard to shoot his own family, of Tutsi origin, to prove that he is not a traitor to his ethnicity. With them are several people who have been in hiding at Rusesabagina's house since the outbreak of violence, and who have been forced on him, becoming his responsibility. At first, he haggles just for his wife and children but then he sways and bribes the hostile officer to set the rest

Figure 4.1 Paul (Don Cheadle) has a gun put to his head and is encouraged by soldiers of the Presidential Guard to shoot his own family, of Tutsi origin, to prove that he is not a traitor to his ethnicity in *Hotel Rwanda* (2004)

of the group free. From here on, he uses the personal skills described by Ebert with altruistic motives.

It is no wonder that so many reviews compared the Rusesabagina character with that of Oscar Schindler, both being suave characters who use their social skills (and money) to save people from being exterminated.[15] However, the big difference is that Rusesabagina is not a crocked character from the start, needing to be straightened out (or to grow like man) as the Schindler character is. This innocence could be exemplified by the fact that Rusesabagina, in the diegetic world, is taken by surprise by the start of the genocide. The identifiability of Rusesabagina as an ordinary man is therefore greater for audiences already from the start, and I would argue that this is enhanced by the fact that he is played by African-American actor Don Cheadle.

Critics such as American Francophone scholar Alexandre Dauge-Roth have argued that the focus on individual heroes such as Rusesabagina and Schindler makes the "genocide bearable." That is, the focus on survivors, according to Daugh-Roth, overshadows the gruesomeness of the genocide against the Tutsi and the European Jews, respectively, since these idealized "heroic" versions tends to hide "the murderous and heinous behaviors of the majority" and even eclipse the historical circumstances that made the genocide possible.[16] In other words, according to this interpretation audiences are somehow tricked into believing that there is no off-screen space or, rather, off-screen history; that what you see and hear are the only things that happened. This is an old argument that can be traced back to the criticism of Hollywood as a manufacturer of false dream scenarios, found in Theodore Adorno's and Max Horkheimer's seminal study *Dialectic of Enlightenment* (1947), where the authors argue that the "culture industry" is a factory which produces homogenized cultural goods, films in particular, which are used to manipulate modern mass societies into compliance and passivity.[17] But is the focus on an ordinary-man-turned-into-hero trope actually something dangerous, and even grounds for genocide denial, as Daugh-Roth asserts in his study of responses and memorialization in relation to the Rwandan genocide?[18]

It is possible to analyze this audiovisual use of history on two levels. The first one concerns cinematic history as a truthful conveyor of the past. Since the one-to-one representation of the past in films and other cultural outputs is unattainable (and undesirable), then the question of how cinematic history contributes to our understanding of the past is actualized. Dauge-Roth chooses to blatantly attack *Hotel Rwanda* for its factual errors and simplifications claiming, quite rightly, that the film "offers a selective, incomplete, and even misleading version of history."[19] However, this critique is excessively general and could in fact be aimed at all historical films and television programs ever made.

The second level concerns what role cinematic history has in the public arena of historical culture. Is it to teach history, is it to raise awareness, or is it simply to entertain its audiences? Depending on what perspective its users/audiences are employing, these roles are fluent and multiple. For a secondary school history teacher, a historical film can be used to teach history on a didactical as well as an emotional level (what was it like?), and even provide a moment of entertainment (in comparison to the "dull" history textbooks) that actually have the potential to create awareness and/or an interest among pupils to look for more information about the subject in question.[20] For an ordinary cinemagoer, or for someone who flips through the television channels and ends up watching a historical film, the first incitement could perhaps be entertainment, but that does not prevent the film also raising awareness, rather the opposite, especially so when it comes to "unknown" history that is presented with emotional (and perhaps sentimental) impact.

For Dauge-Roth the distinction between the two levels are far from transparent since he, and many other critics with him, compliment *Hotel Rwanda* for playing a "significant role in raising awareness in the West of the genocide of the Tutsis."[21] Critics thus tend to credit the film medium for having the ability to create awareness (on a global scale), but at the same time cinematic history is dismissed because it communicates either the "wrong" history or a simplified version of the past. The use of narrative strategies that equate "entertainment" for the conveying of awareness thus seem to be out of the question for detractors of cinematic history. But narrative and stylistic devices are an integral part of the film medium's inherent logic. Is it then really a viable position to dismiss an entire medium in itself? And what does it mean to create awareness?

To better understand the creation and the function of collective memories and (global) awareness you could inject the concept of *historical consciousness* into the equation. According to Swedish historian Klas-Göran Karlsson, historical consciousness is:

> a mental procedure in which the contemporary human being orientates him-/herself and his/her life situation temporally, in the light of experiences and knowledge of the past, and of expectations for the future. [T]he process is always two-sided. Whether we talk analytically about historical consciousness as a kind of metanarrative, or didactically of historical consciousness as a human competence, it mediates on the one hand a more "deterministic" insight into the fact that the human being is created and conditioned by history, on the other a more "emancipatory" understanding that the human being creates and conditions history, thereby transcending various historical boundaries. Historical consciousness does not only process historical concepts, facts, ideas, and notions, but also values, principles, attitudes, and actions.[22]

Although collective historical consciousness is a more complex phenomenon than the individual one, involving larger historical and social preconditions, the process of awareness is never fashioned in a historical vacuum. Historical consciousness "must and can only be empirically analyzed from the concrete manifestations of historical culture. The general idea is that the historical narrations that are more or less explicitly expressed in history-cultural sources give evidence of how individual and collectives [. . .] use representation of history for guidance."[23] That is, audiences already have (different) experiences and knowledge located in the historical culture that precondition the contemporary interpretation of the audiovisual rendering of the past, which is then used to form a perspective on the future. It is therefore incorrect to claim that audiences are tricked into believing that there is no off-screen history, outside of what is presented in a historical film such as *Hotel Rwanda*.

The original and very positive reception of *Hotel Rwanda* revealed that this film indeed contributed to the creation of historical awareness about the genocide against the Tutsi in Rwanda. Although the film in question, on the first level, is not a one-to-one representation of the historical events, *Hotel Rwanda*, on the second level, nevertheless figures on the public arena of historical culture where it teaches audiences about the genocide. One important question therefore is whether the accusations of the many and diverse historical inaccuracies that have been aimed at the film and its producers somehow overshadow its capability to create historical awareness. According to the hypothesis that historical films always have more to say about their own production context rather than about the historical period they depict, Swedish film scholar Mats Jönsson claims that cinematic history reflects different views of history from a contemporary bound matrix based on economic, aesthetic, and political factors.[24] Although not a financial success *per se*, the producers of *Hotel Rwanda* nevertheless were receptive to the concurrent matrix as they ventured into this high-risk project—and the use of the ordinary-man-turned-into-hero trope is a sign of that sensitivity.

Hence, the question is not about right or wrong history so much as what sort of history is presented, and how it is presented aesthetically and dramaturgically. However, when it comes to *Hotel Rwanda* and the choice of the ordinary-man-turned-into-hero trope there is a life-size complication as to the choice of Rusesabagina as that particular hero. Seldom in the history of historical films has there been so much controversy surrounding the main character in a film about genocide. At least three full-length monographs have been written about the acting hotel manager Paul Rusesabagina and his putative or self-proclaimed actions to save 1,268 refugees at Hôtel des Mille Collines in Kigali. The first book, *An Ordinary Man: An Autobiography*, is written by Rusesabagina and contains a somewhat enhanced version, compared to the film at least, of the events in 1994.[25] Then there are two books that, firstly, question and reject Rusesabagina's efforts during the genocide and, secondly, smear *Hotel Rwanda* and its producers. In *Hotel Rwanda: Or the Tutsi Genocide as Seen by Hollywood*, Alfred Ndahiro and Privat Rutazibwa raise a sharp critique against "Hollywood":

> We refuse to allow the entertainment industry, the machine for making money out of the misfortunes of humanity that is the Hollywood film business, to impose on the minds of an unfortunately ill-informed public stereotypes that may guarantee the commercial success of a work of fiction, but distort and even deliberately pervert the truth about the genocide of the Rwandan Batutsi.[26]

Ndahiro and Rutazibwa's book is based on interviews with survivors who stayed at the Hôtel des Mille Collines during the genocide, while Kayihura and Zukas's *Inside Hotel Rwanda: The Surprising True Story . . . And Why It Matters Today* is based on Kayihura's own experiences at the said hotel in April and May 1994. Kayihura acknowledges *Hotel Rwanda*'s importance for raising awareness and the film's educational efforts but throughout the pages the critique of "Hollywood" in general, and Terry George and Kier Pearson in particular, becomes more rigid until Kayihura straight-out accuses "Hollywood" of "potentially causing a genocide and the overthrow of a country by propping up an imposter."[27]

Rusesabagina is, on the one hand, accused of enriching himself at the expense of the refugees at the hotel and for grossly exaggerating his own efforts in saving lives during the genocide. On the other hand, he is accused of supporting the *génocidaires* because of his good contacts with high-profile perpetrators such as Colonel Théoneste Bagosora and Interahamwe leader Georges Rutaganda (a relationship that in the film is portrayed as a way to negotiate with the *génocidaires*).[28] What complicates matters further, making *Hotel Rwanda* even more controversial for its detractors, are Rusesabagina's conspicuous activities after the release of *Hotel Rwanda*, which turned him into a worldwide celebrity, and earned him a number of rewards, including the Presidential Medal of Freedom, granted by President George W. Bush in 2005.

Journalist and author of several books on the Rwandan genocide Linda Melvern claims that the "success story" of the Hôtel des Mille Collines was used, both during the genocide and today, as a propaganda tool to deny the genocide.[29] Rusesabagina, who wrote about the genocide as a genocide against the Tutsi in his autobiography, has in recent years increasingly started to promote the theory of a double genocide in 1994. He also claims that the RPF is still committing a genocide against the Hutu.[30] There is furthermore an ongoing feud between Rusesabagina and Rwandan President Paul Kagame, who publicly has denounced Rusesabagina for being a fraud and accused him of financing terrorists.[31] Doubtless, these accusations are political (from both directions) and it should be mentioned that Alfred Ndahiro worked as a public relations advisor to Kagame, while Edouard Kayihura worked as a deputy prosecutor in charge of the department of prosecutions of the crime of genocide and crimes against humanity before the Tribunal of the First Instance of Kigali. In response to Rusesabagina's accusation of Rwanda being a repressive dictatorship still based on ethnicity, Kayihura tellingly uses a euphemism to defend what is obviously the presence of political violence in Rwanda:

> [T]hey illustrate that nations are built as omelets are—with the cracking of more than a few eggs along the way—and that history looks back and judges even more heroic men, men such as Washington, Adams, and Jefferson, as fully capable of making errors of judgement, though at the time these patriots believed these decisions were in the nation's best interest.[32]

On August 31, 2020, Rusesabagina was arrested as he was taking a flight to Burundi, which was forced down in Kigali, where he was charged with nine counts of terrorism related to his association with the National Liberation Front (FNL), the armed wing of PDR-Ihumure. After a televised trial he was convicted on terrorism charges and sentenced to twenty-five years in prison on September 20, 2021.[33]

Rusesabagina himself, so apparently part of the dominant historical media memory of the Rwandan genocide via *Hotel Rwanda*, is thus straying from and, in the process, increasingly altering the same memory. But does that change the content and the impact of *Hotel Rwanda* for general audiences? Does it matter that Rusesabagina, conceivably, charged people for food and drinks during the genocide or that he threatened to kick out refugees from the Hôtel des Mille Collines? The questioning of Rusesabagina's humanitarian endeavors by political opponents and some scholars is serious, but that does not prevent teachers from using *Hotel Rwanda* in their education to promote democracy, human rights, and all people's equal value[34]—ultimately what the film is all about.

Of course, the accusations aimed at Rusesabagina are extremely challenging and if, in comparison, Oscar Schindler's or Raoul Wallenberg's humanitarian endeavors would turn out to be false or exaggerated then the films and television program about them would perhaps be deemed unusable. However, the difference is that films and television series like *Schindler's List* and *Wallenberg: A Hero's Story* (1985) essentially are *about* the title characters while *Hotel Rwanda*'s first mission is to tell the story about the genocide against the Tutsi in Rwanda, and in which Rusesabagina just happens to be at the center of events. That the real-life Paul Rusesabagina, subsequently, used his fame to, perhaps, take unlawful credit and to make (money and) a better life for himself, that is an entirely different subject.

Besides using the ordinary-man-turned-into-hero trope as a guide into the story of the Rwandan genocide, the filmmakers also employed dramaturgical means to communicate historical information and knowledge about the genocide to uninformed audiences. Here two principal scenes will be scrutinized. The first concerns an often-criticized scene where audiences, early in the film, learn about the differences between the Hutu and Tutsi ethnic groups. In the one-minute scene, newly arrived cameraman Jack Dalgish has a conversation with a Rwandan journalist, Benedict, in the hotel bar:

> Jack: So, what is the actual difference between a Hutu and a Tutsi?
> Benedict: According to the Belgian colonists, the Tutsis are taller and more elegant. It was the Belgians that created this division.
> J: How?
> B: They picked people, those with thinner noses, lighter skin. They used to measure the width of people's noses. The Belgians used the Tutsi to run the country. Then when they left, they left the power to the Hutus, and of course, the Hutus took revenge on the elite Tutsis for years of repression. I am telling the truth, Paul?
> Paul: Yes, unfortunately [. . .] Benedict is our finest journalist in Kigali, an expert on the subject.
> J: So, what are you, Paul?
> P: I am Hutu.

Jack (turning to two women in the bar): Excuse me, honey. Can I ask you a personal question? Are you a Hutu or a Tutsi?
Women 1: I am Tutsi.
J: And your friend, Tutsi?
Woman 2: No, I am Hutu.
Jack (turning back to Benedict): They could be twins.

Dauge-Roth condemns this scene as especially damaging, even claiming that it promotes "genocide denial," that is, genocide ideology, a legal term used in Rwanda to prevent denial of the genocide against the Tutsi under the threat of severe punishment. However, this legal term tends to exclude all moderate Hutus and others killed during the genocide.[35] Dauge-Roth believes that this genocide denial is expressed by the phrase "of course" in the dialogue above. The "of course," according to Dauge-Roth, legitimizes the genocide as "revenge and self-defense: the oppressed Hutus attacking their former Tutsi masters."[36] First, this is a highly angled interpretation of *Hotel Rwanda*, a film that scarcely can be perceived as apologetic towards the killer Hutu regime. Sociologist Zine Magubane, among others, points out that *Hotel Rwanda* contains a powerful critique of the international community, and that the film promotes African and not, as is often the case, European heroism.[37] Second, this interpretation does not consider the medial context or acknowledge a fundamental structural component of cinematic history. According to Toplin, critics tends to forget that a "dramatic film cannot deliver a comprehensive assessment of its subject. To make history understandable and exciting, filmmakers have to narrow the scope of their portrayals. The subject of the movie is also rather tightly focused on one situation from the past."[38]

Certainly, Jack's casual character is a stand-in for uninformed (Western) audiences that must be provided with necessary historical knowledge in a swift and condensed way. "Hotel Rwanda" or the Hôtel des Mille Collines, is thus the place or the situation that the filmmakers, director Terry George and screenwriter Kier Pearson, have chosen to make a film about a, largely, unknown genocide. Taking that into consideration—and the fact that a two-hour film seldom has more than ten to twenty book-size pages of dialogue[39]—then the one-minute dialogue must be perceived in another light. First, we can establish that the purpose of the film and this dialogue is not to promote genocide denial; the purpose, which is rather hard to misinterpret, is to deliver information about the historical-ethnic tensions in Rwanda before the 1994 genocide. And, second, it is to make a statement that the colonial structures that governed Rwanda, and Africa in general, were morally wrong and even ludicrous, which is duly mirrored by Jack's baffled reaction to the women's announcement of their ethnic identities in the bar.

If filmmakers try to pack too much information into their productions, then they run the risk of losing their audiences, because fact-laden historical dramas can, according to Toplin, "confuse and tire audiences."[40] The outcome then is a film that is not seen—a counterproductive pedagogical strategy for a film with historical-pedagogical intentions[41]—and that filmmakers could experience difficulties raising money for upcoming projects. That is a lose-lose situation.

Critics of historical films tend to concentrate their critique on dialogue and words, all in accordance with how professional historians try to weigh written sources against each other in order to reconstruct or de-construct the past. Paradoxically, this means that images and the use of sound are overlooked for analyses of dialogue and plot, thus failing to see the "subtle yet impressive ways that movies deliver messages."[42]

Another pivotal sequence in which *Hotel Rwanda* employs dramaturgical means to communicate historical information about the genocide while simultaneously sending a message to uninformed audiences comes halfway through the film. Following the scene in which Colonel Oliver has told Paul that "Africans are dirt" and that the West is abandoning Rwanda, the evacuation of expatriates starts with the sound of heavy rain, a BBC radio news broadcast informing audiences that the UN is withdrawing from Rwanda, and Andrea Guerra's absorbing violins on the soundtrack. We see white expatriates being escorted out of the hotel by black bellhops with umbrellas, surrounded by uniformed Belgian and French soldiers. Buses are waiting outside the hotel in the rain, thus creating a space that separates Rwandans from expatriates and soldiers. In this four-minute sequence separations are plentiful, as men, women, and children are forcefully split up according to origin in an emotional fashion that is underscored by the bleak sight of rain and the music on the soundtrack. One of these separations which becomes personal for audiences is when Jack has to leave his new Tutsi girlfriend, trying to give her and Paul money as a poor substitute for life. When Jack leaves for the buses, a bellhop runs after him in the pouring rain with an umbrella, and Jack tries to make him leave, then turning to his fellow colleague, saying: "Jesus Christ, I am so ashamed." As he enters the bus, a voice is heard calling: "Wait! Wait!" Before Jack looks out the front window, the lingering violins on the soundtrack merge with the children's choir from Wyclef Jean's Golden Globe nominated song "Million Voices," creating a powerful audio background. The camera then cuts to a large group of people entering the hotel premises, Catholic priests and nuns running alongside Rwandan refugees in the rain, with one of the nuns carrying a French flag as a symbol of truce. However, they are soon informed of the fact that the evacuation is not for Rwandans. Here, Terry George and cinematographer Robert Fraisse create a visual barrier of soldiers center frame which literally separates nuns and priests from Rwandans. Furthermore, this

Figure 4.2 The use of editing, framing, and music to "teach" audiences about the Western failure in Rwanda, thereby creating an emancipatory understanding of history as something unwritten and changeable in *Hotel Rwanda* (2004)

emotion-raising framing is emphasized by an elevation of the pitch of the children's choir on the soundtrack. The sequence ends with a slow pan of the bus windows through which the expatriates silently weep, stare, look away in shame, and even take photographs. This is followed by a shot/reverse shot of the hotel entrance where, now, only Rwandans take shelter from the rain, looking back at the bus with a soaked Paul in the foreground.

At a concrete level, this sequence teaches audiences that the Western powers, the US, France, Belgium, and the UN, had the chance but chose not to stop the genocide against the Tutsi. With authoritative pedagogical technique *Hotel Rwanda* teaches audiences about an "unknown" genocide, but what is equally important is that audiences, as they are watching the film, realize that what is taking place on the silver screen or television set could have been prevented. This realization has the potential to influence the historical consciousness among its viewers as *Hotel Rwanda* tells a story about past events in order to awaken expectations for the future among contemporary audiences, thereby creating an emancipatory understanding of history as something unwritten and changeable.[43]

Still, this historical consciousness is produced at an emotional level, as demonstrated in the above example, using carefully selected and composed music, framing, and images. This means that it is a historical consciousness characterized by guilt or shame that is advocated. Once again, Jack acts as a stand-in for primary Western audiences, openly expressing the shame he feels as an onlooker and a bystander. However, whereas guilt narratives tend to cultivate division and distance, shame has the potential to trigger critical self-evaluation. As social psychologist Tamara Ferguson et al. claim, guilt and shame can be hard to distinguish from one another because both are emotions of self-assessment.[44] Nonetheless, guilt and shame differ in the approach to the self. Guilt concentrates on her-/himself as the doer of the deed while shame concentrates on the flawed self. Guilt does not therefore relate to what a person is but to the actions committed.[45] This means that the character, Jack, cannot feel guilty about UN's decision to leave, but he can feel shameful about it and of course guilt that he, as an individual, is abandoning the Rwandans. This emotional historical consciousness is thus transferred to audiences who have chosen to see a historical film about genocide. With this transference of shame comes enlightenment, which is why films like *Hotel Rwanda* and *Schindler's List* are used in school teaching. That is, not primarily because of their cognitive values but because of their emotional impact.

The third and final strategy to be discussed concerns *Hotel Rwanda*'s use of (mainly) off-screen violence. How do you introduce an "unknown" history of a gruesome genocide without using explicit displays of violence to convince audiences? According to director Terry George, this was a deliberate choice to reach larger audiences—not to make more money, but to inform more people—and, from that perspective, showing explicit genocidal violence was seen as counterproductive.[46] As mentioned in the introductory chapter, the criticism of this choice by filmmakers goes both ways. On the one hand, historian Mohamed Adhikari aimed harsh criticism against *Hotel Rwanda* for concealing the violence and advocating a "happy ending."[47] On the other hand, film scholar Tanja Sakota-Kokot pointed to the fact that the film, through its representations of "violence and anarchy, creates a very specific representation of the fundamentalist Other [and] this representation focuses on the negative aspects of a culture and creates a fixed identity of Africa."[48] But what is violence and what are representations of violence?

Philosopher Vittorio Bufacchi talks about two different ways of thinking about violence: as a violent *act* (force) and as an *abuse* (violation). The most common understanding of violence is a combination of a violent act and an abuse, that is, violence is by definition something that is perceived as (morally) bad. However, violence exists in several forms, often with a distinction between good and legal violence and bad and illegal violence. What distinguishes these two approaches is partly due to the "legality" of violence and is partly due to the social context of violence. All nation-states, for example, maintain violent monopolies (enforced by the police and the military), which in turn means that all civilian violence (except self-defense) is defined as illegal. The view is based on the law but also on a social agreement saying that it is wrong to violate or kill another human being. Thus, a person who kills or violates another person commits not only an illegal act but also an immoral act. Nonetheless, the smallest common denominator is the active *act* of violence aimed against another human being or object. The actual abuse, the immorality, is more difficult to define. Excessive violence is generally considered to be evil (for example, police brutality), whereas such an action as the USA's use of two atomic bombs at the end of the Second World War could be justified as something necessary and even good.[49]

A way to define and handle the philosophical aspect of violence is to analyze it from different perspectives: from the perpetrator's point of view (violence as intentional destructive force) and from the victim's point of view (violence as violation). An alternative approach, suggested but unexplored by Bufacchi, "is to define violence from the point of view of an impartial spectator or third party."[50] This third perspective overlaps the position of film and television audiences, but is the position of the spectator ever really impartial or neutral? In research on media violence and its impact, films and television (and more rarely literature) are very often accused of creating aggressions among their (young) spectators.[51] What other meanings can audiovisual violence obtain: aesthetic, moral, narrative, didactic?

British cultural studies scholar Roger Bromley argues that the "constant showing of streets littered with corpses as one of the iconic signifiers of the genocide in Western representations is deeply problematic and most gratuitous."[52] Dauge-Roth describes this as a "quasi absence of images" in the sense that images of anonymous corpses are not able to "be more than just an illustration of the deadly trace left by the macabre 'dance of death,'" at the same time as the anonymity obscures a "visible distinction between the Tutsi bodies and those of the Hutus."[53] When looking at a wider range of films on the genocide against the Tutsi in Rwanda, the repetition of images of scattered corpses does most certainly have a numbing effect, fostering a feeling of guilt that simultaneously creates a moral distance to the past.[54] However, when looking at the images of violence and off-screen violence in *Hotel Rwanda*, as a singular but quintessential cinematic representation of the genocide, then it becomes more difficult to accept the notion of a numbing effect. This depends in part on the dramaturgical means used that encourage emotions and individual identification, which, in combination with the feeling of shame, stimulates audiences to take notice and to remember.

Nonetheless, violence and images of atrocities and suffering could, in themselves, have a distancing effect for certain audiences; a consequence that the filmmakers were trying to avoid. Despite its criticism, *Hotel Rwanda* is not totally absent of genocidal violence. In fact, the filmmakers use allusions and reproductions of three emblematic images in a minimalistic way: "Corpses by the Road," "The Nick Hughes Footage" as cameraman Jack Daglish films people in long shot being killed at a roadblock, and "The River of Corpses."

Because the action mostly takes place on the hotel premises, "Corpses by the Road" is used only sparingly, while the replica of the "The Nick Hughes

Footage" is even more remote since it is shot from a distance and then played on a very small monitor in the diegetic world, creating a sort of audiovisual shield for audiences. The allusion to "The River of Corpses" is integrated into the story as Paul and Gregoire, after a recommendation from Interahamwe leader George Rutaganda, take "the river road" back to the hotel after a supply run. A fog covers the road and thus the fact that it is blocked by a river of corpses, which halts the advance of the van they are driving. Paul gets out of the van and falls flat over some bodies. In his immediate field of view is a little girl with closed eyes, hands clasping her ears, lying dead. A shocked Paul flinches back and looks around to discover a large number of bodies in the mist. Although some blood is visible on some of them, no mutilations are shown, just leaving the sheer number of corpses—and Paul's reaction to them as he is about to throw up and puts a handkerchief to his mouth—for audiences to grasp the gruesomeness and the overwhelming scale of the genocide. This could perhaps be a too minimalistic approach but how should the filmmakers

Figures 4.3 and 4.4 The replica of the "The Nick Hughes Footage" and the allusion to "The River of Corpses," which both create an audiovisual shield for audiences watching *Hotel Rwanda* (2004)

have gone about trying to recreate something as immense and incomprehensible as genocide? *Hotel Rwanda*'s critics leaves this question unanswered.

Nevertheless, the filmmakers go outside of this criticized comfort zone several times, most effectively in the scene that comes just before "The River of Corpses" scene. When Paul and Gregoire arrive at George Rutagunda's place there are visible signs of the immense loathing that motivated a commercial side of the genocide,[55] and when Paul enters the gates, audiences are shown a terrible side of the genocide, namely women kept in cages as sex slaves, or as Rutagunda defines them: "Tutsi prostitutes and witches." Paul expresses concern but business comes first. However, when Rutagunda threatens des Mille Collines's guests, Paul questions him just to find out, underscored by ominous music, the horrible and ungraspable truth about what is happening outside of the hotel:

Rutagunda: Soon all the cockroaches will be dead.
Paul: You do not honestly believe that you can kill them all?
R: And why not? Why not? We are halfway there already.

On a more personal level, Paul and his family, including the extended "refugee family" at the hotel, are living under constant threat of violence. Narratively, this persistent threat is a violation of their freedom, but it also works to create suspense and attachment for audiences, mostly towards Paul but also towards the Tutsi victims. Sakota-Kokot has argued that this alignment with Paul only works stylistically because Paul and his family are associated with "'Western' habits/traits," and that this is the result of racist, colonial notions where the "Hollywood blockbuster [. . .] demands that you look through the eyes of a white star, a white hero."[56] That might be so, but the fact is that Paul is black and he is the hero of *Hotel Rwanda*, regardless of the circumstance that he wears Western costumes. The violations against him and his non-white "family" are unmistakably perceived as an (morally bad) abuse by audiences, irrespective of their skin color.

Dauge-Roth's notion of a "quasi absence of images," as corresponding to the lack of real-life images of explicit violence from the Rwandan genocide, appears to be quite ignorant in relation to how cinematic history works and how it is received. One could claim that the film medium has the task of discussing and problematizing violence and its moral implications, and in order to do that the violence can and must be portrayed in illegitimate and legitimate ways that confirm and exceed both visually graphic and moral limitations.

You could make a comparison with the many cinematic representations of the Holocaust based on the same concern that Dauge-Roth raises, that the lack of actual images of violence is problematic for later cinematic representations of a genocide. As with the genocide against the Tutsi in Rwanda, the genocide against the European Jews generated very few audiovisual documents of actual killing, and the same goes for photographic evidence of active atrocities and violence.[57] Another similarity is that a significant part of the historical media memory of the Holocaust, like the Rwandan genocide, therefore is characterized by a sense of *fait accompli*. That is, existing films and photographs consist of already dead, mutilated, starving, and decomposing bodies, in piles, scattered along a yard or a road, or in mass graves. Hence, historical films on these two genocides have to portray, or chose to portray, violence in a way that exceeds the existing and scarce audiovisual information sources. There are, for example, no visual records of gas chambers in operation but the nominal breakthrough for the television miniseries *Holocaust* (1978) put the use of the unimaginable gas chamber in the imagination of audiences, even though you are never actually allowed to look inside one during an execution. As American film studies scholar Aaron Kerner states: "Such images are prone to be treated as fetish objects, and by acquiescing in the available visual archival material—figured as representative of *the* Holocaust—we might heedlessly accept these 'substitute' images for those things that have no visual representation."[58] The gas chamber therefore has become *the* way of killing in people's imagination, in the same way as the machete has come to represent the genocidal violence in the Rwandan genocide.

An interesting outcome of these cinematic imaginations is that the genocide against the Tutsi is perceived as worse and as more appalling than the Holocaust. As Canadian comparative literature scholar, Madelaine Hron, writes: "Most appalling though, is the sickening proximity the killers had to their victims, and their vicious means of killing. Instead of gassing them or shooting them, most killers hacked their victims to death with machetes or other farming implements."[59] It is possible to interpret Hron's comparison as that gassing and shooting were more humane methods of killing, thus indicating that the Rwandan killers were inhumane and uncivilized Africans in comparison with the civilized Germans, who killed by bureaucratic and industrial means.

This is of course a historical as well as a moral and a philosophical question. Is it really better to gas people to death rather than to beat and hack them to death? The fact is that most people in the Holocaust died of starvation, beatings, and as slave labor, not of gassing—but in most cinematic renderings these forms of crude, gory, and active violence are usually toned down. The understanding of violence as something morally bad is therefore not a constant. Instead, there exist several levels of moral distinctions that do not just differentiate between notions of legal and illegal violence but also between more or less evil violence. When it comes to the genocide against the Tutsi as something *more* appalling, then, this belief is based on outdated colonial delusions that position Africans in general as "wild," "barbaric," and "unruly." In view of this interpretation, Terry George's lenient take on violence thus becomes less racist.

Echoing this is the fact that most Holocaust films do not put violence and gore on display, but instead try to depict the genocide through different types of abuses of personal freedom, which could include active violence and death but seldom in graphic close-up. These abuses are (usually) aimed at the protagonists, thus creating an alignment between the historical Jews and contemporary audiences. Although many critics have scorned Holocaust films for trivializing, especially films made outside the documentary genre, this criticism rarely concerns the circumstance that these films contained too little violence. This could be understood as a paradox since violations such as the loss of personal property, relocation, and ghettoization hardly equal the actual experience of witnessing the murder of 6 million European Jews. The choice to use off-screen violence is therefore not a vicious revision of the past but instead is a way to be more inclusive towards audiences that are to be introduced to "known" genocides such as the Holocaust as well as to "unknown" genocides such as the genocide against the Tutsi in Rwanda.

Shooting Dogs and *Sometimes in April*

Hotel Rwanda premiered in December 2004. A couple of months later *Sometimes in April* aired on HBO on March 19, 2005, while *Shooting Dogs* opened at cinemas on September 11, 2005. These two other films have found themselves in the shadow of *Hotel Rwanda*, but while *Shooting Dogs* has been belittled because of its Eurocentrism, *Sometimes in April* has often been hailed as a better historical film than *Hotel Rwanda*. Why is that, and in what ways do these two productions contribute to the global historical consciousness relating to the genocide against the Tutsi?

Linda Melvern rejects *Shooting Dogs* because it "shows a shocking disregard for the historical record [. . .] there is no doubting the genuine and intense feeling of the filmmakers, nor that they will generate a keener awareness of the brutal truth of the genocide. But because of this, they have a heavy responsibility to tell the truth." Melvern aims three blows against the historical accuracy of this film, co-produced by the BBC: (1) that there was no BBC film crew at École Technique Officielle (ETO), (2) that BBC news misreported the genocide as "tribal factions" in 1994, and (3) that UN peacekeepers are portrayed as "brutish and uncaring," omitting the later bravery of volunteer peacekeepers.[60]

Still, most of the reviewers had an entirely different view on what constituted the truthfulness of *Shooting Dogs*. In *The Austin Chronicle*, for instance, Marc Savlov claims that this is a "horrifically authentic film [. . .] shot on the actual locations of the events depicted, employed a number of survivors in both crew and acting positions, and it was produced and co-written by BBC cameraman David Belton, who witnessed the slow, agonizing death of hope firsthand."[61] In Swedish newspaper *Expressen*, the reviewer wrote: "The fact that the main roles are white and that the story behind the genocide is hardly touched upon sometimes becomes a weakness. But this is well offset by intrusive images, thin-skinned actors, and that the reality-based story was filmed on location where it took place."[62] The UK Holocaust Memorial Day Trust recommend the film "as a way to explore the events of the genocide in Rwanda."[63]

As can be seen, the fact that *Shooting Dogs* was filmed on location in Rwanda had a great impact on its historical credibility among audiences, thus avoiding the criticism that *Hotel Rwanda* had to endure since the latter was shot in South Africa. However, as many critics accepted the "based on a true story" text at the beginning of the film, others still seemed ignorant to the workings of cinematic history. Dauge-Roth accuses *Shooting Dogs* of "pseudo authenticity whose value is purely rhetorical—if not commercial—and no longer referential,"[64] while Swedish reviewer Jenny Richardson claims that "the story behind the genocide is hardly touched upon."[65] So, does *Shooting Dogs* tell a revisionist story about the Rwandan genocide and does the film not even touch upon the pre-history of the genocide?

Shooting Dogs is a British feature film on the genocide against the Tutsi in Rwanda in which John Hurt plays a Catholic priest who is caught up in the first week's events of the genocide. The action is loosely based on the real-life Catholic priest Vjeko Curic's actions as he helped both Hutu and Tutsi victims, earning the nickname the "Croatian Oscar Schindler."[66] The setting of the film is the École Technique Officielle in Kigali where over 2,000 mostly Tutsis were murdered by the Rwandan military and Interahamwe militia on April 11, 1994, after Belgian UN peacekeeping troops had abandoned them. At the end of the film, the Catholic priest sacrifices himself to save four of the schoolchildren, a scene which is played out with an overt connotation of Christ's sacrifice on the cross, as Father Christopher tells his killers that he has only love in his heart just before he is gunned down. However, the development of the early stages of the genocide is seen through a young and idealistic English teacher, Joe Conner—a stand-in for Western audiences as Jack was in *Hotel Rwanda*—who has to learn about the futility of himself, as he abandons Father Christopher, the school, the (platonic) love interest for Tutsi girl Maria, and, not least, Rwanda—as most Westerners did in April of 1994.

Piotr A. Cieplak asserts that the choice of a Catholic priest in the lead role "seems bizarre in the light of the existing evidence of the involvement of the Catholic Church in the genocide and the fact that no whites stayed at the

ETO in 1994."[67] In fact, according to Cieplak "[a]ll the events befalling African characters in the film are projected through Joe and Father Christopher."[68] There is no need to argue about the existence of a Eurocentric perspective in *Shooting Dogs*, but is that perspective totalitarian and does it actually hinder audiences from learning about the genocide? Here we will look at how the Eurocentric perspective affects the storytelling, the display of violence, and the presence of religion as a historic and narrative tool.

The opening of *Shooting Dogs* contains an explanatory text that mainly focuses on the fact that the Hutu majority had persecuted the Tutsi minority for thirty years. This is followed by two flash-forward clips: one of a black girl who is running through the night and one of a Western troop convoy that passes an Interahamwe roadblock outside ETO, before the film's main titles appear. Then we see the same legs running as before, but now in daylight, and a superimposed text: "École Technique Officielle/Kigali, Rwanda/5th April 1994." Soon Joe is introduced as a likable and lighthearted character as he commentates on the running girl, Marie, like a sports commentator on television to amuse the schoolchildren. At one point, Joe runs up to his friend François, the gardener, and asks him about the race in a humorous manner, thus including the Rwandans in the fun.

While Marie, the platonic love interest, functions as an emotional attachment that generates the (Western) guilty consciousness, François has an entirely different role to play in the film. Jokey and likable, he and Joe take the truck for a supply run, detouring home to François's father who offers some homemade *Urwagwa* (banana beer), which Joe drinks despite François's humorous warnings. When they continue their trip, they come to a roadblock manned by the military. François reaches for his identity card in the breast pocket and Joe snatches it away, reading teasingly from it: "François Nikuze. Length: Five foot ten. Sex: Male. Ethnicity: Hutu. Appalling photograph . . .," before a noticeably upset François takes it back and gives it to the soldier.

At this moment, the filmmakers use subtle and intriguing audiovisual hints to reveal the ethnic tensions and to show the expatriates' lack of awareness. As the soldier takes the identity card, he looks stern but when he sees François's ethnic identity, he smiles, gives the card back and greats François in Kinyarwanda: "Amakuru?" (How are you?) As François continues the small talk in Kinyarwanda, Joe looks out the front window and takes notice of how the soldiers at the roadblock roughly search a car, while treating the car owners harshly. We cut back to François and the soldier, who explains the activities with a single word: "Inyenzi" (cockroach) and then waves the truck through, while François laughs. When they drive away, Joe asks: "Who are they?" and François answers: "They are Tutsi," which is an answer the ignorant Joe accepts.

Here the coming genocide is hinted at by the ethnic connection between the soldiers at the roadblock and François, a seemingly average and likable guy who sympathizes with the Hutu extremists, most certainly fueled by the hate propaganda from RTLM radio broadcasts, which are heard throughout the film. Joe, who does not speak Kinyarwanda, is left outside although he (and the watching audience) is aware that something is not quite right.

Further on in the film, when the genocide has started and people are fleeing to "safe havens" such as ETO, Joe tries to talk to an elderly Tutsi refugee couple. When he fails to understand them, he calls François over to translate. Suddenly the couple become suspicious, looking down at their feet, clamping up in the presence of François, who in turn becomes annoyed with them. Joe, once again, senses the tension and guides the couple to a UN soldier instead. Thereafter he confronts his friend François:

Joe: What was that about?
François: "I am Hutu, Joe. The Tutsi hate all Hutu."
J: Half of the kids here are Tutsi, they don't hate you.
F: Joe, you don't understand.
J: So, tell me. Make me understand.
F: The Tutsi wants to become our masters again. To them we are just slaves.
J: That just propaganda . . .
F: It's true, Joe! Them they cannot make slaves; they will kill inside their beds.
J: You don't believe that shit?
F: If they can shoot our president, no Hutu is safe. Hutu must protect themselves or die. I have to go.
J: Will you be safe?
F: I'll go to my father's house.

The line: "Make me understand" is key here, but instead of delivering a brief history lesson on the relations between Hutus and Tutsis, François *reacts* emotionally with a fear that, to Joe (and audiences), seems to be irrational, based on propaganda as it is. However, this scene gives an insight into the power of propaganda (it is *true* for François) and how it affected ordinary people in Rwanda. Once again, Joe fails to realize the seriousness of the situation, caught as he is in a Eurocentric worldview that contains little and/or skewed knowledge about Africa. Nonetheless, he is about to learn the hard way.

A week into the genocide, Joe takes the truck and goes looking for François at his father's home. Eventually he teams up with two journalists, who become interested and join Joe when he tells them that there are, in addition to the

500 Tutsis, forty Europeans hiding at the ETO. On the way back to the school, they are stopped at a roadblock, littered with dead bodies. Threatened with kalashnikovs the three Europeans are violently pulled out of the car and forced down on their knees. To the right of Joe, a beaten-up Tutsi man whimpers on his knees. Two men from the roadblock suddenly drag the man off to the bush, where he is killed by several machete blows, while Joe watches in horror. Then, unexpectedly, a smiling François shows up, wearing rubber boats, blood-soaked pants, and carrying a bloody machete. When asked in Kinyarwanda, François admits that he knows the Europeans, and they are set free. For a moment, Joe's and François's eyes meet, and François makes a gesture with a finger to his head, telling Joe that the others at the roadblock are crazy. However, as they drive away, the camera zooms in on François's blood-soaked pants and machete, telling Joe and the audience that François must be as crazy as the others. On their way back to the school, they make another stop so the journalists can film murdered children lying by the road, all while the camera zooms in to a close-up of Joe's distressed face.

The display of violence is both recurrent and more explicit in *Shooting Dogs* than in *Hotel Rwanda*, as exemplified by the scenes described above but also by additional expositions of violence. For example, only one of the emblematic images is used, "Corpses by the Road," but the filmmakers, director Michael Caton-Jones and the screenwriting team, Richard Alwyn, David Belton, and David Wolstencroft, have extended a couple of the emblematic images in order to enhance the emotional, and perhaps the cognitive, impact among audiences. "Corpses by the Road" is frequently used but the characters do not just observe (or ignore) them but interact with them as well. This is the case with the journalists who stopped to film murdered children by the road, with one saying: "They are never going to show this," while the other laconically responds, "Just

Figure 4.5 An enhanced version of the emblematic image "Corpses by the Road" in *Shooting Dogs* (2005)

get it on tape, Mark." Another example is a scene in which dogs actually eat the corpses, hence the film's title.

Another more elaborate outcome is an extension of "The KPH Images," as a group of Tutsis are trying to escape the school premises before the Belgian UN troops will abandon them and they are overrun by the Interahamwe, who violently kill the refugees with machetes in front of Joe and the UN troops. A minor character, Edda, hides in the grass with her newborn baby but is discovered and killed by machete blows in full view of the camera, as is her baby, although off-camera. This is a brutal visualization of what happed after the refugees were abandoned by the world community at the KPH and the ETO.

The threat of violence is thus realized on a completely different level than in *Hotel Rwanda*, and this violence does not just concern the white expatriates as indifferent onlookers as the criticism would have it. That the Catholic priest Father Christopher sacrifices himself by the end of the film has been interpreted as a Eurocentric ploy that steals the limelight, and suffering, from the real victims. However, the presence of religion as a historic and narrative tool stands out in *Shooting Dogs* in comparison to other fictionalizations of the genocide against the Tutsi in Rwanda. Throughout the film, the meaning of Christianity is discussed and put to the test (often on the losing side) as Christopher and his congregation face the harsh realities of the genocide. Cieplak criticizes a scene that is part of the introduction to Father Christopher, as he is visiting a convent where "two African nuns follow him around, hysterically and uncritically laughing at his jokes, as though this was the only response they are capable of mustering."[69] What Cieplak fails to mention is, first, that this scene shows the humanity of Father Christopher as well as that of the Rwandan nuns, and, second, that this scene works to set up and as payoff for a later scene in which Father Christopher returns to the convent after the genocide has begun, only to find the nuns violently raped and murdered—showing that no one is safe, not even the servants of Christ.

You could argue that Christianity as a religion is transnational, at the same time as it is possible to argue that Christianity in Africa is a colonial construct. Nevertheless, the fact is that Rwanda is one of the most religious countries in the world, and Christian denominations—Catholic, Protestant Evangelical, Seventh Day Adventist—have for a long time dominated the worldview of the average Rwandan. A gruesome statistic underlining this strong faith is the fact that it is estimated that 11 percent of all victims of the 1994 genocide were killed inside churches in which they had sought refuge.[70]

Many academic critics, including Dauge-Roth, Cieplak, and Melvern, seem to have overlooked this transnational use of religion in *Shooting Dogs*. In secular Sweden, for example, the openness towards religion in *Shooting Dogs* is interpreted negatively:

Moviegoers are usually not stupid and do not choose films at random. They probably have some idea of what a film is about, also about this subject. That is precisely what makes the redundant transparency of this film somewhat annoying, both in its images but also concerning the dialogue. Occasionally the moralities in the form of philosophical one-liners become a bit too much.[71]

In America, on the other hand, *Shooting Dogs* has been hailed by many critics precisely because of its handling of religion. Ruthe Stein calls the film's conversations about the role of religion in times of crisis "extraordinary,"[72] and on the Christian website HollywoodJesus.com, the review concludes with the judgment:

> As good as Hotel Rwanda and various documentaries on the Rwandan genocide have been, Beyond the Gates [the US release title] is an important addition to the body of work on that atrocity because it begins to plumb the depth of the spiritual dimension—both good and bad. It helps us consider the ways our choices—our keys—open the door to heaven, or to hell.[73]

Shooting Dogs's way of telling its story is pedagogical, is very effective, and is accomplished with artistic means that differ from the objective methods that characterize historical studies. Instead, it is characterized by a poetic license to tell the truth, and that truth does not just concern itself with getting the all the historical facts right. This poetic license strives, in addition, to depict truthfully basic events and emotions that happen in everyone's lives.[74] Dauge-Roth's accusation against the filmmakers for creating a "pseudo authenticity" for commercial reasons is quite unfair, if not distasteful.

At first glance, *Sometimes in April* has been hailed as a better historical film than *Hotel Rwanda* and *Shooting Dogs*. Dauge-Roth analyzes the three films side by side and concludes that *Sometimes in April* is more original, a statement which rests on an analysis of director Raoul Peck's refusal to use realism in order to "erase the distance between the cinematic mediation and the actual events." That is, according to Dauge-Roth, audiences "cannot feel relieved of its responsibility and guilt" since Peck's film "forbid[s] us from believing in the possibility of our innocence."[75] Comparative literature scholar Urther Rwafa concludes that *Sometimes in April* provides a "much-needed historical and class dimension to the genocide narrative. Further, the film is credible because it complicates human relations in its depiction of the Rwandan genocide."[76] Finally, educational bodies such as the Irish Centre for Global Education recommend the film with the motivation that it "certainly leaves the viewer with a desire to learn more about the situation in Rwanda, and provides additional benefits as a resource for development education."[77]

In contrast, reviews written by film critics and other experts on the moving image give an entirely different view of the same film that could be summed up as important but boring. In *Variety*, it is described as "thuddingly didactic" and "clumsily executed,"[78] while a Swedish film critic wrote, "Indeed, the pedagogical ambitions are very impressive, although it seems to overshadow the film as a drama. We get so many statistics and history thrown into the lap during the first minutes that it feels like you are sitting on a school bench."[79] In *Senses of Cinema*, film director Jon Jost trashes *Sometimes in April* after watching it at the Berlinale in 2005:

> Story wise, it commences with a didactic entry, a bit of history superimposed over a painfully slow zoom into an old map of Africa, finally settling in on Rwanda; then old news reels and films, a quick sketch of the Belgian colonial past, the pitting of ethnic sectors against one another for imperial purposes, the cold war, etc. This is all delivered with a slightly leaden and academic hand, which I think is Peck's manner. He has a political tale to tell, and you are going to get it. Period.[80]

As can be detected in the reception there is a schism between academically inclined readings and more dramaturgically inclined readings of *Sometimes in April*. While the first group appreciates the historical facts delivered and Peck's "objective" interpretations of them, the latter group criticizes this historical drama for being too stiff, or plainly for being too historical. This is the result of two superficially incompatible views concerning history versus cinematic history where the first group believes that the mere presence/presentation of historical facts is enough for a historical film to be successful, while the other group believes that the same presence/presentation can obstruct the interest and/or the learning outcome for audiences. As has been argued about *Hotel Rwanda* and *Shooting Dogs*, both are dramas with the capacity to draw and to keep audiences' attention and, thereby, to teach them something about the genocide against the Tutsi in Rwanda. *Sometimes in April* does also take advantage of a fictionalized human interest story and, hence, the argument between the two factions seemingly revolves around the issues of, exactly, what history is taught and how that history is presented. Here we will take a closer look at a few of Peck's aesthetic and factual choices, and how they supposedly have affected the historical consciousness.

Sometimes in April is an HBO-produced television film, but it breaks the limitations for televisions films when it comes to production values and sheer length with its 140 minutes. The television film typically employs smaller crews, depends on smaller casts, and seldom features costly special effects. The format is often 90 minutes and tied to network-scheduled slots, which means that screenplays are written to reach regular semi-cliffhangers in order for commercials to appear. In recent years premium cable networks such as HBO and Netflix have transformed the television series format, and in doing so the television film has had a much-needed aesthetic upswing, although not on the same level as the television series has.[81] The budget for *Sometimes in April* is unknown, but it is much higher than average and according to Sara L. Rubin, Peck had to make the concession of making the film largely in English to please HBO as the costs mounted.[82] According to Peck, he spent eighteen months in Rwanda and Tanzania, gathering interview material and researching the genocide, and the film is made on location in Rwanda.[83]

The film takes place in 2004 and uses lengthy flashbacks to uncover two major storylines in 1994. The first one is the human interest story about two brothers, Augustin and Honoré, and their troubled relationship, which functions as a dramatized but educational peephole into the Rwandan conflict and the genocide. The brothers are Hutu, but Augustin is married to a Tutsi woman. However, he is also an officer in the Rwandan army, and personally trains the militia, Interahamwe, though without knowing for what. His brother works for RTLM radio, spewing out hate, and is consequently an active part of the murder regime in 1994. However, in 2004 Augustin works as a modest schoolteacher, having lost his family during the genocide—which seemingly exonerates him morally—while Honoré is imprisoned at Arusha, waiting to be tried by the ICTR. The conflict lines are thus both personal and morally intertwined, most likely to display the not always black-and-white circumstances of the genocide. Augustin takes a (somewhat forced) stand during the genocide in order to save his family, while Honoré too tries to take a stand as he attempts, and fails, to save Augustin's wife and children at a roadblock. These failures could be interpreted as the futility of a single person's actions in the midst of genocidal madness, which in turn do free the perpetrators (and spectators) despite Dauge-Roth's idealistic interpretation of the film.

The second set of flashbacks is an inside/outside overview of the work, and utter failure, of the UN and the US state department. Here Peck relentlessly attack the West, from an apparently higher moral ground, for the lack of intervention, among other things using the infamous television footage of US State Department spokesperson Christine Shelley's use of the words "genocidal acts" during a press conference. Nonetheless, Peck still uses a fictional version of the real-life character Prudence Bushnell, Deputy Assistant Secretary of State for African Affairs, to counterbalance the neglect and ignorance, highlighting Bushnell's futile attempts to stop the genocide by threatening Colonel Théoneste Bagosora over the phone as heroic.[84]

Initially, and especially during the second storyline, the film employs documentary aesthetics. That is, Peck imitates the historical documentary, even mixing archival footage with simulated documentary footage without drawing attention to the joints in a similar way that Oliver Stone did, and was criticized for, in *JFK* (1991).[85] In the historical introduction, described as heavy-handed by its critics, the camera zooms in on an ancient map of Africa at the same time as a text keeps on rolling over the screen. French composer Bruno Coulais's eerie and doomful score is applied to establish gravity and to anticipate the gruesomeness to come. At the same time, the music gives authenticity to the informative text, which lays the blame for the ethnic tension and the genocide in Rwanda solely on the Belgian colonialists, skipping over the actual Hutu rule and oppression of the Tutsi from 1959 to 1994. The introduction ends with the apologetic speech President Bill Clinton made in Rwanda in March 1998, which, it turns out, is shown on a small television set by Augustin for his pupils as part of their education. The Clinton speech thus confirm a timeline of (post-)colonial guilt. This creative way of delivering "facts" is why *Sometimes in April* is believed to prevent its audiences from being freed of "responsibility and guilt."[86] This is also why the film, posing as a "documentary," does not leave much room for redemption and afterthought.

However, the one person who does not seem to be driven by a guilty conscience, in this story where everybody is guilty, is the director and screenwriter Raoul Peck. The guilty conscience which constitutes the *mea culpa* for the production of numerous documentary films and feature films about the Rwandan genocide does not seem to apply to him. Why is that, and how does this influence the reception of the film?

The only major complaint raised against *Sometimes in April* is that it is too didactic and thus boring. Yet, the same boringness is what powers a preconceived notion about authenticity, which could in this case be summarized by two choices that Peck has made. The first one is obvious, namely the choice to place the production in Rwanda, using local talent as extras and for simpler film crew assignments. In an interview for the BBC, in connection with a screening of the film in Kigali a couple of months before its official release, Peck proclaimed, "Making a film here meant making a film with the Rwandan people. I just consider myself the medium for them to express their own story."[87] The second choice is the perspective, which is more muddled. While the majority of all films and documentaries have been made by Canadian, European, and American production companies, and certainly often have a Eurocentric understanding of the genocide, *Sometimes in April* has been perceived as a film that takes the Rwandan perspective, irrespective of the fact that it's an American/French production. All principal roles are played by non-Rwandans, including Augustin and Honoré, who are played by the then minor British actors Idris Elba and Fraser James, respectively, although Elba afterwards has since risen to stardom with films like *Pacific Rim* (2013), *Mandela: Long Walk to Freedom* (2013), and *Thor: Love and Thunder* (2022). This means that "blackness" is perceived, and connotes, nationality, in this case Rwandan nationality. Raoul Peck himself is Haitian and was for a short period even Haiti's Minister of Culture, but he was educated in the USA, France, and Germany, which are also the countries he has been active in during his career as a filmmaker. The perspective in *Sometimes in April* is, because of these choices, perceived as a non-Eurocentric one, but this film is just as Eurocentric in its storytelling as *Hotel Rwanda* and *Shooting Dogs*.

This leaves us with the question of whether *Sometimes in April* teaches us something new or different about the genocide in Rwanda that has not already been done in previous film and documentaries. Is there something to provoke audiences into thinking outside the Eurocentric norms that will affect the historical consciousness? The answer is no, with one notable exception—the calculator that counts the number of dead during the genocide, placed in the corner of the television screen as a reminder of how fast and effective the "work" was carried out by ordinary Rwandan citizens.[88]

5

Telling the Truth: Documentary Films and Public Consciousness

While the three normative feature films discussed most certainly have had a significant impact on the global public historical consciousness of the genocide against the Tutsi, they are nevertheless placed in a subordinate position in comparison with the documentary genre vis-à-vis the criteria of authenticity and historical truth. The suspicion in the reception of, for instance, *Shooting Dogs*, is in the reception of the documentary genre replaced by a more trustful attitude towards the filmmaker's aesthetical choices. However, this trust is not always transferred to the choices that are made about the content or the perspective in the films. Here the three nominal feature-length documentaries—*Ghosts of Rwanda*, *Rwanda: Do Scars Ever Fade?*, and *Shake Hands with the Devil: The Journey of Roméo Dallaire*, all released in 2004—will be analyzed side by side because of their numerous similarities, thus consolidating the creation of a dominant transnational historical media memory of the genocide against the Tutsi in Rwanda. These similarities can be summarized by the choice of perspective, the historical explanations that are exploited, the use of emblematic images, and the fact that these three documentaries are executed in expository mode.

According to American documentary film theorist Bill Nichols, the expository mode is characterized by an omnipresent, omniscient, and seemingly objective narrator that addresses audiences directly. In this way, the image—whether it be archival footage, talking heads, titles, or devices such as maps—is subordinated to this "voice-of-God." When documentary aesthetics developed in the interwar years this gave rise to evidentiary editing, a practice where images not only illustrated, illuminated, evoked, or acted in counterpoint to what was said, but where the editing served to maintain the continuity of the spoken argument. As a result, audiences came to understand the image as evidence.[1] More importantly, the expository mode continues to be the dominant one that audiences around the world identify as the documentary genre.

Because of these films' status as television documentaries, reviews are more infrequent than for the three high-profile feature films. Still, the existing reviews have only praise to deliver. *Shake Hands with the Devil* is called "unflinching"[2] and a "gripping and moving film,"[3] while *Ghosts of Rwanda* is seen as "enlightening"[4] and "one of the most in-depth and graphic documentaries [that] accurately describes the Rwandan Genocide and the events leading up to it."[5] The emphasis on the graphic violence is a constantly recurring theme in the reviews. The news footage, most of it originally filmed and aired during the genocide in 1994, thus serves as "proof" of these documentaries' historical authenticity and, at the same time, this use legitimized a never-again understanding of these images. A circumstance explicitly expressed by William Thomas in *Empire Magazine*: "There are graphic images—notorious footage of roadside machete killings in the middle distance of a hidden camera's wide frame is used, which should absolutely be seen (perhaps then it will stick in people's minds and prevent us from ignoring the next genocide attempt)."[6]

All three documentaries have a distinct Western perspective on the events in Rwanda, characterized by a guilty conscience over the abandonment. That is, the main blame for the conditions provided for the genocide is to be found among the Western powers: the UN, the US, France, and Belgium. This is underlined by the fact that the documentaries virtually parade an endless string of European and American talking heads—witnesses, politicians, historians—while the only recurrent African who is interviewed is RPF leader Paul Kagame; the exception being *Rwanda: Do Scars Ever Fade?* which features a miniature reconciliation theme with average Rwandans, perpetrators, and victims. All other Africans are made up either of dead bodies, or of anonymous black faces.

Figure 5.1 The use of Western talking heads. US State Department spokesperson Christine Shelley's reluctance to define what was going on in Rwanda as genocide at a press briefing on April 28, 1994, in *Ghosts of Rwanda* (2004)

110 HISTORICAL MEDIA MEMORIES OF THE RWANDAN GENOCIDE

The use of an omniscient anonymous male narrator is the norm, except for *Shake Hands with the Devil* where the omniscient presence is delivered via informative and determinative texts about the genocide and its background, while the voiceover is that of Dallaire, retelling his personal story of his experiences as commander of the UN peacekeeping force UNAMIR. Furthermore, the normative use of voiceover is integrated with the Western perspective and its concentration on violence and dead African bodies as "evidence." Setting the tone, all three documentaries start with a strong focus on emblematic images, especially several versions of "Corpses by the Road" that are authorized

Figures 5.2 and 5.3 Two variants of "Corpses by the Road" in *Ghosts of Rwanda* (2004) and *Shake Hands with the Devil: The Journey of Roméo Dallaire* (2004), respectively

by suggestive interpretations: "Ten years ago in the small East-African country Rwanda, 800,000 people were slaughtered by their own government" (*Ghosts of Rwanda*); and, "It took just 100 days . . ." (*Rwanda: Do Scars Ever Fade?*), which is a suggestive account underlined by a first talking head's—Samantha Power, author of *A Problem from Hell: America and the Age of Genocide* (2002)—comment: "800,000 single individuals murdered to death."

Typically, these documentaries use television exposition, that is, a short preview at the beginning of the program aimed at drawing in audiences and making them stay in front of their television sets. *Rwanda: Do Scars Ever Fade?* stands out here by using a mix of emblematic images and confirmative talking heads that, within the first minute, exploit four versions of "Corpses by the Road" and, in addition, "The River of Corpses," "Bloated Corpses in the River," and "The Man with a Machete," finishing off with the "The Nick Hughes Footage." It is quite telling that violence is used as the pull factor, and *Rwanda: Do Scars Ever Fade?* begins with a viewers' discretion warning: "This program contains graphic description and imagery of the consequences of war and genocide. Viewer discretion is advised."

In fact, all three documentaries use the emblematic images repeatedly. Both *Ghosts of Rwanda* and *Shake Hands with the Devil* uses all seven emblematic images, while *Rwanda: Do Scars Ever Fade?* uses six of the seven emblematic images on repeat.[7] Although previous documentaries applied a strong Eurocentric perspective on the Rwandan genocide, the use of violent emblematic images was more infrequent. Even *The Triumph of Evil* only used four of the seven images, and not on repeat. This could be compared with the excess of violent emblematic images in *Ghosts of Rwanda*, where director Greg Barker claimed not to have seen any of the previous films before making his own, which seems a bit odd since both *The Triumph of Evil* and *Ghosts of Rwanda* are part of the same Frontline series on PBS.[8] The two films are more or less identical when it comes to perspective, narrative, and the use of the same interview clips of Western talking heads. Even *Shake Hands with the Devil* stands out in this excess, being the only documentary to use all three of the only known live action sequences of actual killings during the genocide.[9]

As previously discussed, in relation to *Hotel Rwanda*, the difference between guilt and shame to evoke a historical consciousness on an emotional level, here it is more appropriate to discuss the different aspects of guilt and disgust in relation to learning and the effect that this potentially has on historical consciousness among audiences. Media and communication scholars Heather L. LaMarre and Kristen D. Landreville have made a tentative, but thought-provoking, study about the influence documentaries have on learning compared to historical feature films. While previous research into emotional psychology and political science has shown a negative effect for interest

Figures 5.4, 5.5 and 5.6 The emblematic images "Bloated Corpses in the River," "The River of Corpses," and "The Man with a Machete" in *Shake Hands with the Devil: The Journey of Roméo Dallaire* (2004) and *Ghosts of Rwanda* (2004), respectively

and learning, LaMarre and Landreville make a distinction where negative emotions such as guilt and disgust were higher, when measuring them, for those who watched documentaries, leading to the conclusion that "it appears that negative affect led to stronger interest in genocide. Interestingly, disgust increased learning and guilt decreased learning."[10] Whereas guilt tentatively cultivated division, distance, and feelings of helplessness, disgust could arouse attention and incite "a desire to create a plan of action to deflect, undermine, or destroy the aversive target. Thus, stronger feelings of disgust will predict knowledge gain."[11] According to this interpretation, the excess of violent and repulsive emblematic images could have a "positive" effect since this excessive use, potentially, could influence public opinion. However, it should be noted that the films used in this tentative study are *Hotel Rwanda* and *The Triumph of Evil*, that is, two films that do not come close in excess and disgust in comparison to *Ghosts of Rwanda*, *Rwanda: Do Scars Ever Fade?*, and *Shake Hands with the Devil: The Journey of Roméo Dallaire*. Moreover, all five films are characterized by a Western perspective riddled by guilty conscience that counteracts the "positive" effect that the excessive use of dead African bodies might have. Paradoxically, the most sensationalistic documentary, The History Channel's *Rwanda: Do Scars Ever Fade?*, is the only one of the three nominal documentaries which, for a moment, detours from the Eurocentric perspective in order to observe the Gacaca court system, which is part of the reconciliation process that has been the Rwandan government's continuous attempt to achieve peace and unity after the genocide. This segment is roughly one-fifth of the documentary's 68 minutes and features interviews with several average Rwandans—victims and perpetrators—as well as official representatives such as Paul Kagame. The two who receive most time are Ezekiel, a Hutu perpetrator, but now a born-again Christian, Bible in hand, and Pierre, a Tutsi victim. Stereotypically, the all-knowing voiceover introduces them with a focus on the violence, pointing out that it was "chillingly intimate," after which the two men get more than three minutes of screen time to—in detail and dubbed into English—describe the atrocities committed. After an overall explanation of the Gacaca court system, the pair return for another three minutes, now explaining how they have forgiven each other. This is a "happy ending" which, nonetheless, is disturbed by the fact that Pierre admits that a "part of the reason that I forgave him, is that I am still afraid of him." Thus, the violence, and the threat of violence, is still the *raison d'être* of the documentary. This in stark contrast to another and lesser known Christian themed documentary on the genocide which was produced in the same year, *Rwanda: Living Forgiveness* (2004), in which Ezekiel and Pierre return and in which the threat of violence is almost entirely replaced by the reconciliation theme in the interviews with the two men.[12]

These three films are probably the most seen documentaries on the Rwanda genocide, all made in connection to the ten-year commemoration of the genocide, and all made in a way that enhances their authenticity and credibility among both critics and general audiences. In *Empire Magazine*, a reviewer wrote the following revealing confirmation about the "neutral" authenticity of *Shake Hands with the Devil*: "Perhaps what's most commendable is the restraint on display. There's no agenda, and there's certainly no Moore-aganda antics."[13] Another verification of the trustworthiness of these documentaries is the many awards they have received. *Rwanda: Do Scars Ever Fade?* was, for example, rewarded with the prestigious Peabody Award, in order to "honor the most powerful, enlightening, and invigorating stories in television, radio, and online media." In the acceptance speech, producer Bill Brummel devoted two sentences to Rwanda: "The heart of our story emanates from many Rwandans who shared their *continuing* personal nightmare with us. I am indebted forever to them," while the rest of the speech is just a long thank you list.[14]

This is not to say that these documentaries are false, but they are certainly one-sided in their perspective, in their choice of identical talking heads who repeat the same stories, and not least in their choice of archival footage with its immense focus on violence and dead bodies. It is perhaps not out of the ordinary to choose to use these emblematic images to portray a genocide, but as social science scholar Frank Möller makes clear, "[n]either images of actual killings nor images of dead bodies explain the killings. Both often leave their audiences momentarily horrified but largely ignorant."[15] In addition, Stanley Cohen's term moral distance, the notion that the repetition of images of suffering increases their remoteness, comes to mind.[16] Compared to the previous documentaries on the Rwandan genocide, this troika of documentaries does not introduce any new insights but instead repeats the dominant "West's Do Nothing strategy"[17] prevalent in the original television news broadcasts and early documentaries, thereby confirming and strengthening an already dominant historical media memory. In fact, thanks to their status as documentaries, and documentaries made in the persuasive and familiar expository mode, they consolidate that historical media memory on a global level.

A final word about these nominal documentaries is that in fact they are less nuanced than the often-scolded feature films, especially in comparison with *Hotel Rwanda* and *Shooting Dogs*, where filmmakers with artistic means were able to create emotional awareness and empathy that also worked on a pedagogical level. These documentaries, of course, only dealt with "historical facts" in the form of talking heads and archival footage but they nevertheless created a specific history of the past. This history re-established a sense of overall Western guilt but also a lasting impression of gruesomeness and otherness for television audiences around the world. To try to change or go against the storytelling and cinematic history in a quintessential film such as *Hotel Rwanda*, or the dominant transnational historical media memory in these documentaries, could therefore be very hard. Part three will analyze films and documentaries that have maintained the dominant historical media memory of the genocide against the Tutsi in Rwanda, but also how this media memory has been extended, developed, and revised due to the vast international production of short films, feature films, and documentary films that commenced in 2004.

Part Three

To Maintain a Historical Media Memory on a Global Level, 2004–2021

6

The Difficulties of Maintaining a Historical Media Memory in Feature Films

While television news and early documentaries laid the groundwork for the memorialization of the Rwandan genocide, quintessential films like *Hotel Rwanda*, *Ghosts of Rwanda*, and *Shake Hands with the Devil* most certainly transformed those often-dissented histories and created what could be labeled as an official historical media memory of the genocide with global reach. As we shall see, this official historical media memory was often maintained in the subsequent production of films and documentaries on the Rwandan genocide. However, the ten-year commemoration of the genocide against Tutsi marked a surge in the production of films that has continued to this day, significantly with peaks in connection to the fifteenth and twentieth commemorations in 2009 and 2014, when eighteen and twenty-nine films were released respectively. Altogether, another 150 films have been produced in the wake of the surge in 2004. This vast global production has not only maintained the official historical media memory but also—almost unavoidably due to the diverse nature of film and television and the creating process involved in cinematic history—extended, developed, and even revised the historical media memory of the Rwandan genocide.

The purpose of this third part is to create an overview of the films that have maintained the official historical media memory of the Rwandan genocide while, at the same time, acknowledge, contextualize, and explicate the competing historical memories that likewise have emerged within this substantial production of cinematic history. This part of the book is therefore divided into five chapters. The first two chapters will commence with a discussion of the international production of feature films and documentary films, respectively, on the Rwandan genocide, partly because the feature film and the documentary film potentially have the opportunity to spread globally, and partly because the majority of these films tends to uphold the official historical media memory. These two chapters are then followed by three chapters concentrating on three specific themes that have crystallized out of the large body of films in comparison to the official historical media memory, namely women, reconciliation, and revision.

Maintenance: Western Guilt, Emblematic Images, and The White Savior Complex

Between 2005 and 2021, eighteen international feature and short films were produced that are about or touch upon the Rwandan genocide, and these films range from the American amateur production of *Angel of Hate* (2005) to the crowdfunded Italian film *Rwanda* (2019) and the Netflix distributed melodrama *Trees of Peace* (2021). The former tells the story of an African-American teenager who is the product of a rape, and of his search for his biological mother. Used as a juxtaposition, a stereotype of an African refugee from Rwanda tells his story of how his family had to flee because of the "fighting between Rwanda and Burundi, where many women were raped." This ignorant mixing up of countries and ethnicities is perhaps excusable due to the amateurish qualities of the production but the fact that this film was produced in 2005 is nevertheless telling, as it becomes an example of the impact that, indeed, films like *Hotel Rwanda* and *Ghosts of Rwanda* had on an American public in creating a historical consciousness of the Rwandan genocide.

Closer to the present day we have the Italian production *Rwanda*. This film stands out since it is crowdfunded and, according to its director, Riccardo Salvetti, the film was produced for less than 100,000 EUR and, on that budget, they had to reproduce "Rwanda" in Italy.[1] Essentially, *Rwanda* is a theater play that has been turned into a film that mixes the original theatrical performance with topnotch mise-en-scène arrangements of the genocide in Rwanda, although everybody still speaks Italian. Based on a true story, the focus is on Augustin, a Hutu, and Cecile, a Tutsi. Augustin refuses to kill Cecile and they flee together through a devastated country, all while two Italian theater actors narrate and interpret their struggles from the stage. Thus, according to the film's homepage:

> [t]he Rwandan Genocide then becomes only a "historical" pretext for telling a story that can actually be set wherever genocide has taken place or is being consumed. From Kosovo to Cambodia, from Bosnia to Congo, the story of Augustin and Cecile, the two protagonists of the film, overcomes the barriers of time and space to become a story-symbol of the values of peace, integration and resistance, an accusation cry against all past and present human rights violations everywhere in the world.[2]

Just like the amateur film, *Angel of Hate*, *Rwanda* uses the Rwandan genocide for aesthetical and educational purposes to tell a bigger story of how hate, mass murder, and rape are morally wrong. However praiseworthy this might be, the fact remains that in both these films the entire concept of "Rwanda" simply equates to genocide, that is, the crime of crimes.[3] This in turn teaches us of the lingering influence that cinematic history can and does have on a historical consciousness mediated on a global scale. From a post-colonial standpoint this ongoing procedure—where Africa and Rwanda are interchangeable entities and where Rwanda connotes genocide—is highly problematic.[4] Nonetheless, this Eurocentric and reductive outlook structures a persistent theme in the narrative film production on the Rwandan genocide and includes films such as the Canadian fictionalization of Roméo Dallaire's autobiography with the same name, *Shake Hands with the Devil* (2007), directed by Roger Spottiswoode who, among many other films, directed the James Bond film, *Tomorrow Never Dies* (1997). Just like the documentary of the same name, *Shake Hands with the Devil* portrays the official story of the genocide, here literally littered with an abundance of emblematic images that include several versions of "The River of Corpses," "Corpses by the Road," "Piles of Corpses," and "Bloated Corpses in the River," all carefully and gorily recreated, and told via flashbacks from Dallaire's therapy sessions. Still, the historical credibility is amplified by the fact that all recreations were made at the actual locations in Rwanda. In *Variety*, reviewer Scott Foundas believes that the film is "unnecessary," because so many films had already been produced on the genocide by that time, but he gave credit to Spottiswoode for "making a film that emphasizes the death and destruction of Rwanda, rather than those incongruous stories of triumph and survival (a la 'Hotel Rwanda')."[5]

Figure 6.1 The fictive Roméo Dallaire (Roy Dupuis) interacts with "Corpses by the Road" in *Shake Hands with the Devil* (2007)

Film theorists Robert Stam and Louise Spence argue that the film apparatus, in its most inclusive sense, can in some ways be said to advocate European colonialism. "It produces us as subjects, transforming us into armchair conquistadors, affirming our sense of power while making the inhabitants of the Third World objects of spectacle for the First World's voyeuristic gaze."[6] To this media perspective, cultural theorist Stuart Hall adds the fact that colonialism functions as the outer layer of capitalism since the historical colonization enabled Europe to globalize the capitalist mode of production by establishing networks and power relationships between and across national borders, and in the process creating unequal dependencies between the former colonies and the Western world.[7]

Other international films which uphold the official historical media memory in this unequal post-colonial sense, frequently based on a guilty Western consciousness, are the Canadian feature film *Un dimanche à Kigali* (*A Sunday in Kigali*, 2006), the two French televisions films, *Opération Turquoise* (2007) and *Lignes de front* (*Black Out*, 2009), the Swedish short film *Den sista hunden i Rwanda* (*The Last Dog in Rwanda*, 2006), the Danish film *Ibrahim* (2007), and the Polish feature film *Ptaki spiewaja w Kigali* (*Birds are Singing in Kigali*, 2017). Even though these films, at first sight, display an impressive diversity in terms of the national origin of the production, Rwanda and the genocide are still treated as concepts that are processed through a thoroughly Eurocentric worldview.

A common feature which exemplifies the unequal perspective in these films is the narrative focus on a Western protagonist who is helpless in the face of "African madness" and the Western powers' indifference towards the genocide. In this way, the protagonist crosses the boundary between self-conscious bystander and active "hero," thus by definition acting as a stand-in for predominantly Western audiences in theirs "conquistador armchairs."

The two French films are cases in point. *Opération Turquoise* narrate the first fifteen days of the real French-led military operation in Rwanda under UN mandate in June 1994. Being a typical *Platoon*-esque war film we get to follow a group of soldiers from the French Special Forces as they arrive in Rwanda, prepared for a humanitarian mission. They are hailed as liberators by Rwandans, that is Hutus waving the tricolor, as they drive through the village streets. Soon enough though, the young and innocently portrayed soldiers discover "the crazy hateful madness" that still reigns in Rwanda, illustrated by, among many other recreated images, several variants of the emblematic "Corpses by the Road." The French soldiers are represented as helpless and as having no clue about the distinction between Hutus and Tutsis, and thus no understanding of the ongoing violence between the two ethnic groups, which just appears to be irrational. The parallels with the young and ignorant American soldiers in the average Vietnam War film are obvious, in which the distinction between the

North and the South Vietnamese is always portrayed as impossible to understand, and thus used as an excuse for the soldiers' actions within the cinematic narrative as well as in real life.[8] Furthermore, the soldiers have to remain neutral in the midst of genocide. Even so, *Opération Turquoise* incorporates criticism of the French involvement, as the soldiers meet leaders of the genocide, part of the Rwandan Armed Forces (FAR), whom they trained when they were there as military instructors before the genocide began.

The other French film, *Black Out*, is directed by journalist Jean-Christophe Klotz. Klotz was stationed as a war reporter in Rwanda in 1994 and had previously directed the documentary feature *Kigali, des images contre un massacre* ("Kigali, Images against a Massacre," 2006), another film with a characteristic Western outlook on the genocide that poses the question of how the genocide was portrayed in the media from a political viewpoint. *Black Out* is likewise critical of the French involvement in Rwanda, where the French government, led by President François Mitterrand, supported the Hutu government of Juvénal Habyarimana against the RPF. Already in 1990, as the Rwandan civil war began, France sent 600 paratroopers to assist the Hutu government against the RPF, and this military support to the *génocidaires* continued up until the commencement of Opération Turquoise late in June 1994.[9] *Opération Turquoise* and *Black Out*, together with a handful of mainly French documentaries that scrutinize France's role in the Rwandan genocide, such as *Tuez-les tous! Rwanda: historie d'un génocide sans importance* (*Kill Them All! Rwanda: The Story of an Unimportant Genocide*, 2004), thus form their own subgenre that highlights the French guilty consciousness within the larger theme of Western guilt.

Black Out follows the young French television journalist Antoine as he ventures into Rwanda at the start of the genocide. At the beginning of the film, he travels with Clement, a Hutu student whose Tutsi girlfriend has disappeared in Rwanda. In documentary fashion, *Black Out* begins with archive footage of "Corpses by the Road" and "The Man with a Machete." The film then continues to use pretend old-school documentary aesthetics as the color scheme changes from color to black-and-white whenever Antoine starts to film with his large camera to document the genocide, which includes several recreations of "Corpses by the Road."

As Clement suddenly disappears from the narrative, Antoine is left to himself to make sense of the situation, and through a series of very slowly paced sequences we are presented with a repeating mix of massacres, hiding refugees, and UN troops—with Roméo Dallaire thinly disguised as General Hillarie—doing nothing to prevent the genocide. There is no intention in the film to explain or to historicize the genocide, rather the opposite as Klotz places the focus on Antione's anguish, resulting in self-harming behavior as he returns to Paris. As Argentinian film scholars Fernando Gabriel Pagnoni Berns and

Juan Ignacio Juvé remark, Antoine does not understand the horrors that his camera registers and, ultimately, he "turn his back and stop[s] narrating on events that are beyond his comprehension."[10]

The Swedish short film *The Last Dog in Rwanda*, a winner at both the Tribeca Film Festival and the Clermont-Ferrand International Short Film Festival, has the same focus on war journalists as does *Black Out*. Here two Swedish journalists venture into Rwanda to document the genocide, but the genocide merely acts as a backdrop to a story of white masculinity and war. We are not given any factual information on the genocide but instead we are presented with parts of the journalistic folklore that has arisen around the genocide, such as slipping on rotting corpses[11] and recreated emblematic images such as "Bloated Corpses in the River" and machetes covered with dried blood. *The Last Dog in Rwanda* is mainly concerned with the male fascination for violence, posing questions about how this fascination is connected to the mechanisms underlying bullying in general, which then, on an even more problematic level, is compared and even equated to genocidal violence. The director, Jens Assur, who previously worked as a war photographer in Bosnia, Somalia, and Rwanda, repeated this idea in interviews in connection with the film's premiere, stating that, "What separates serious acts of violence committed in war from bullying in Sweden is only a question of which legal and moral norms prevail at the moment."[12] This pop-psychoanalytical attempt to explain the genocide, by creating a bridge between the recognizable and the unfamiliar, is perhaps in some ways noteworthy although it is made, yet again, from an extreme Eurocentric perspective. Despite this, *The Last Dog in Rwanda* is widely used as an educational film on the Rwandan genocide in Sweden.[13]

The Danish short *Ibrahim* and the Polish feature film, *Birds are Singing in Kigali*, have the white savior complex as their centerpiece. Films with this white savior theme are often supposedly based on a true story. They feature a nonwhite person(s) in dire conditions, often in conflict with another group that is particularly dangerous or threatening, and the white savior enters the story and through their own sacrifices is able to save the non-white person(s) by the end of the film.[14] In *Ibrahim* the genocide is used as a backdrop or a MacGuffin to set the story in motion. A young refugee from Rwanda, Ibrahim, is about to be sent back, and he runs away because "Rwanda is terrible," which is all the information that audiences receive about the genocide. There are no details about how he came to Denmark, whether he is a Hutu or Tutsi, nor about the contemporary state of Rwanda in 2007, when the film was produced. Instead, we get a Nordic quirky feel-good film in which a white Danish man tries to save Ibrahim from an uncertain fate in Rwanda.[15] Although not a comedy, this is perhaps the most lighthearted film where the Rwandan genocide is part of the story.

Birds are Singing in Kigali is a multiple awarded film about a Polish ornithologist, Anna, who saves Claudine, a Tutsi girl in Rwanda in 1994, and then takes her back to Poland where she grows up. The alienating refugee/immigrant theme is the main storyline for the first half of the film. However, in order to repair their relationship, the couple revisit Rwanda on an emotional journey full of painful memories that are staged in stylistic, but illusive, flashbacks through which we gradually understand that both women are suffering from post-traumatic stress disorder (PTSD) due their experiences in 1994. Here the white savior complex becomes quite paradoxical as the focus shifts from Claudine to Anna, and where Anna's suffering (witnessing a black friend being killed at a roadblock) is compared to Claudine's (who is gang-raped and whose family is murdered), and where Anna's suffering thus equals her (white) sacrifice.

A film which manages to stand out, despite the presence of a white savior complex, is the Canadian production *A Sunday in Kigali* where we yet again see a narrative driven by the journalist-turned-into-hero trope. The film is based on journalist Gil Courtemanche's novel, *Un dimanche à la piscine à Kigali* (*A Sunday at the Pool in Kigali*, 2000) and revolves around Bernard Valcourt, a middle-aged Canadian documentary filmmaker who is shooting a documentary about AIDS in Rwanda. The narrative begins on 15 July, 1994, when Valcourt returns to Kigali after the genocide, and continues partly to be told through flashbacks as he searches for his love Gentille, a young Hutu woman, who is often mistaken for a Tutsi. In fact, in the novel Gentille has a secret. For several generations her Hutu family, tall and pale-skinned, have pretend to be Tutsis, taking advantage of this superior position.[16] Now, as the genocide commences in both the novel and in the adaptation, the tables are turned and Gentille's features are turned against her. As Gentille's life is threatened, Valcourt marries her in an effort to save her. However, they are separated at a roadblock as Valcourt is knocked unconscious by an Interahamwe man, and then involuntarily evacuated with the rest of the expatriates, while Gentille's fate remains unknown until the end of the film.

On the surface, the white savior trope constitutes a strong narrative ingredient, and in accordance with this, and due to the fact that it is an adaptation from a novel, social scientist Lior Zylberman has identified *A Sunday in Kigali* as part of the canon of films on the Rwandan genocide.[17] However, that the film is based on a novel is in itself not a sign of canonization, and the fact that *A Sunday in Kigali* is virtually unknown outside of Canada further undermines Zylberman's claim. Dauge-Roth, on the other hand, has issues with the historiographical qualities, reducing the four-line explanatory text at the beginning of the film to the only historical knowledge in the film worthy of discussion.[18] The main cause of the criticism is that the summary does not address the victims' ethnic identities, but the explanatory text does in fact state, "The majority of the 800,000 victims were of Tutsi ethnic origin." Dauge-Roth claims that audiences must be given more information about Hutus and Twas in order to make sense of the Tutsi identity in a relational context.[19] However, is that really a feature film's first and foremost duty? To teach historical facts? There is no doubt that *A Sunday in Kigali* follows the lead of several of its predecessors, reiterating the official historical media memory of the genocide via the white savior trope, but there are several important differences where the film strays away from the "canon." While Zylberman claims that the attempt to save Gentille is an "attempt to save all in Rwanda,"[20] Dauge-Roth interprets the failed rescue attempt to "symbolically capture the literal and figurative journalistic blackout of the West during the genocide."[21] However, the film is not about saving all Rwandans, nor about the white savior's burden, as in *Birds are Singing in Kigali*. Instead, we get a narrative where Valcourt (and the audience) learns about the mechanisms of the genocide against Tutsi in retrospect as he searches for Gentille.

Valcourt is a man who obliviously take advantage of his status as a white expatriate, staying at the luxurious Hôtel des Mille Collines that happened to be the main center, together with Hotel Intercontinental, for political gossip and business in Kigali, up until the assassination of President Habyarimana. He is only interested in finishing his "important" film on AIDS in Rwanda, and then getting out of there. Valcourt deliberately turns a blind eye to the preludes of the genocide, despite the fact that one of his HIV-infected informants literally tells him that he "should film the hatred that is worse than AIDS." His white savior *savoir vivre* is displayed in a scene where Valcourt declines to be called "boss" by his Rwandan driver, who symptomatically continues to call him boss. The driver turns out to be a Hutu and later in the film he takes revenge on his "boss" at the roadblock. Valcourt is in other words oblivious to the ethnic identities of Hutu and Tutsi before the genocide, a circumstance that in fact reflected the actual situation of most expatriates in Rwanda at the time of the genocide. To insist, as Dauge-Roth does, that a film like *A Sunday in Kigali* ought to correct its historical memory is an afterthought that flies in the face of historical reality.

In addition to the detail that the antagonist is ignorant, the white savior complex is undermined by the fact that Valcourt is not successful in his saving efforts. Rather the opposite. Gentille is repeatedly harassed at the hotel and on the streets due to her "Tutsi looks," and due to her keeping company with a white man, thus doubling the aggressions that a woman in general and a Tutsi woman in particular were subjected to before and during the genocide. The rape of Tutsi women was a very common weapon and it is estimated that at least 250,000 girls and women were raped.[22] In addition, it should be noted that the use of rape in times of conflict is not a by-product, but a pre-planned and deliberate military strategy that was especially prevalent in Rwanda during the genocide.[23] Hence, the utter failure of Valcourt becomes the first narrative feature on the Rwandan genocide that prominently displays the use of rape as a weapon, a subject that we will return to more in depth in connection with the documentaries on the Rwandan genocide.

Besides being harassed because of her features, Gentille is kidnapped at a roadblock and turned into a sex slave for the Hutu extremists. These experiences are "imagined" by Valcourt as he traces Gentille through the genocide, thus learning about the significance of ethnic identities for the genocide and its consequences. When he finally locates Gentille, he "imaginatively and empathically 'relives' Gentille's rape through the traces left behind in the room where she was sequestered and tortured," as Dague-Roth describes it, claiming that "Gentille's martyrdom is only shown through the spectral and mediated artfulness of shadow puppetry."[24] On the contrary, this sequence is carefully intercut with the marriage, the evacuation of expatriates at Milles des Collines, and Valcourt's failure at the roadblock. Of the three intercut scenes with the trapped Gentille, only the first one is staged as "shadow puppetry" but this includes the sound of rape on the soundtrack: fear, crying, and the threatening slurs of the rapists. The other two scenes are filmed in near darkness but the first one focus on Gentille's face during the rape while shadows hide any display of a sexualized female body. Finally, in the third scene, Gentille is raped with a broken bottle, and then scarred in the face by the same bottle, thus again with the focus on her expressive face. Together with the portrayal of harassment and the story of Gentille and her family which comes to life during Valcourt's search, this forms a powerful story of the Rwandan genocide that tends to be overlooked, especially in the potentially more widely spread narrative feature film.

In this way, *A Sunday in Kigali* has something more than mere "historical facts" to teach its audiences. With the exception of two short recreations of the emblematic "Corpses by the Road" and a scene where Valcourt find his Tutsi AIDS informant murdered, the violence is low-key up until the rape sequence, thus putting emphasis on the latter subject as well as the relationship between Valcourt and Gentille.

The Netflix-distributed *Trees of Peace*, directed by American Alanna Brown, and partly funded through Kickstarter, is most definitely a part of the official historical media memory of the Rwandan genocide. However, *Trees of Peace* is the first melodrama on the Rwandan genocide and, in that context, it breaks away from the two totally dominant genres—the serious drama and the factual documentary—that have been employed to portray the Rwandan genocide.

The film begins with the text: "Inspired by true events," which is followed by archival footage of several emblematic images, including, "The Man with a

Machete," "Piles of Corpses," "The River of Corpses," and "The Nick Hughes Footage," that are intercut by further texts explaining that this was the "peak pf a violent history between Hutus and Tutsis, instigated by Belgian colonizers." After that the entire film plays out as a dialogue-driven chamber play in a small basement where four women with different backgrounds hide for eighty-one days of the genocide. These women—a pregnant moderate Hutu, a Tutsi nun, an American NGO, and a Tutsi woman who has been raped—have different stories, told at the beginning, and then they solidify into four stereotypes, there to fulfill the conventions of the melodrama formula.

Modern melodramas usually aspire to achieve a strong emotional appeal, concentrating on bombastic and sentimental dialogue rather than on action—often with challenges from the outside—and *Trees of Peace* is no exception. Taking place in a small, boxed-in space, the genocide is relayed in four ways. First, at the beginning of the film, the women witness the genocide through a small window in two scenes in which a boy is forced to participate in the killing' and then they see a woman being raped and killed, which takes place off-screen. Second, on the diegetic soundtrack, the sounds of the genocide (gunfire, screams) are constantly heard. Third, the four women deliver information in a heavy-handed way through dialogue, and, four, the husband of the moderate Hutu delivers food and water to the women and at the same time gives them the latest news about the genocide. The melodramatic formula thus maintains the official historical media memory of Rwandan genocide and delivers knowledge of the genocide against the Tutsi, but this is still delivered through an extreme Western viewpoint.

Figure 6.2 Witnessing the genocide through a small window in the Netflix melodrama *Trees of Peace* (2021)

In interviews, the director Alanna Brown stated that "I couldn't possibly direct this film had I never been to Rwanda. That feels almost disrespectful, and so that was a big part of it for me."[25] Nonetheless, *Trees of Peace* is filmed entirely in Los Angeles, and only one of the actors is Rwandan, Eliane Umuhire, who plays the moderate Hutu and who also played the daughter in *Birds Are Singing in Kigali*. Furthermore, besides the explicit use of emblematic images, Brown repeatedly refers to familiar points of reference to cinematic history pertaining to the genocide, that is for predominantly Western audiences, such as *Shooting Dogs* and *Hotel Rwanda*. In the first case, dogs eat corpses outside of the basement window, only heard on the soundtrack. In the second case, the husband repeatedly tells the women that they must go to the Hôtel des Mille Collines—that is, "Hotel Rwanda"—since it is the only safe place for Tutsis. This is obviously a historical reference solely based on the cinematic history in *Hotel Rwanda*, and not on the highly problematical relationship of this film, and its hero, Paul Rusesabagina, to Rwanda's own history of the genocide. However, what stands out as the most idealizing Western element in this melodramatic context is the presence of Peyton, the white American NGO. Peyton has the chance to leave the basement and evacuate with the other expatriates in the first half of the film but chooses to stay to make atonement. In an otherwise highly appreciative review in *Afrocritik*, Blessing Chinwendu Nwankwo brings this up:

> the insistence on the character of Peyton and her refusal to be rescued by the UN, which serves the purpose of portraying the discriminatory aid rendered by the UN during the genocide and also the idea of loyalty between the women, stands the risk of being interpreted as a need to present the message in a way that's more palatable to its white audience. For almost every black civil war, there is a white missionary, as if to say that no portrayal of African history can work without a "white" feature.[26]

Deviations: A "Rwandan" Perspective and the Use of Violence for Verisimilitude

Six international films that deviate from the white savior perspective are *Munyurangabo* (2007), *Waramutsebo* (2009), *Le jour où Dieu est parti en voyage* (*The Day God Walked Away*, 2009), *Kinyarwanda* (2011), *'94 Terror* (2018), and *Petit pays* (*Small Country: An African Childhood*, 2020). These six films were made by foreign directors, two Americans, one Belgian, one Cameroonian, one French, and one Ugandan, but the films nevertheless have close ties to Rwanda through their locations, actors, film crews, and not least through the different stories' perspective. Four of these films figured on a top ten list of the best film about the 1994 genocide against the Tutsi, published in connection to the twenty-fifth commemoration week in *The New Times*, Rwanda's biggest newspaper.[27] *The New Times* has the status of an officially sanctioned newspaper in Rwanda, and Human Rights Watch describes *The New Times* as a state-owned newspaper.[28] The list is therefore "approved" in accordance with the official view of the genocide in Rwanda.

Munyurangabo is directed by American Lee Isaac Chung, who later made the highly acclaimed autobiographical drama *Minari* (2020). *Munyurangabo* was made on a shoestring budget in eleven days and the film stands out in two ways. First, the film takes place several years after the genocide and thus deals with the aftermath of the genocide; that is, with feelings of grief, intolerance, and revenge still present in the country. The film tells the story of two boys, the Tutsi Munyurangabo, and the Hutu Sangwa, who leave Kigali to return to their village. Munyurangabo, who has stolen a machete, seeks justice for his parents, who were killed in the genocide, while Sangwa just wants to return home. Their friendship is tested because the parents of Sangwa distrust Munyurangabo and warn their son that Hutus and Tutsis are supposed to be enemies. Munyurangabo eventually seeks out the murderer who killed his parents, only to find him dying of AIDS. The man asks for water and the next day Munyurangabo returns to his house and fills a cup of water. Here the film presents its audience with an open ending as we never get to see if he brings the water to the man, thus paving the way for the second way in which this film deviates, namely that the theme of reconciliation—so clearly present in future film production as we shall see in Chapter 9—is rejected as we are denied a "happy" ending.

According to an interview with Chung, the decision to make a film about the aftermath came because he wanted to make a film for Rwandans, and not another film that evoked the guilt in the West over its inaction during the genocide. Chung also directed the documentary feature, *I Have Seen My Last Born* (2015), which is about the reconciliation process in Rwanda. According to Chung, the eight year gap between the two films mirrored an actual change from prejudice and intolerance to a country where the rapid economic development covered over much of the past, especially for the younger generations.[29]

The long and slow takes, the antiquated camera equipment, and the use of Rwandan amateur actors give *Munyurangabo* a documentary feeling. A. O. Scott in *The New York Times* compared it to Italian neo-realism,[30] and Roger Ebert, who hailed the film for its beauty, claimed that its simple story was "the best way to approach a subject of bewildering complexity."[31]

Waramutsebo, *The Day God Walked Away*, and *Kinyarwanda*, on the other hand, take place during the genocide. *Waramutsebo* is a short film directed by Cameroonian Kouemo Auguste Bernard and it is about two Rwandan students in France during the genocide. We get to follow the entire conflict via phone conversations with relatives in Rwanda and through the television news, thus blending the traumatizing experiences for Rwandans who were abroad with the Western onlooker perspective of the genocide against the Tutsi. This juxtaposition creates a bleak contrast and criticism aimed at the Eurocentric view of "Africa."

The Day God Walked Away tells the story of a young Tutsi maid at the outbreak of the genocide. As her Belgian employers are evacuated, she finds her children brutally murdered and she runs away and hides in the jungle. There she meets an injured man who also has escaped from the slaughter. This then essentially turns into a hide-and-seek survivor film where the violence mostly is depicted at a distance or off-screen—although there are two recreations of emblematic images such as "Corpses by the Road" and "Bloated Corpses in the River"—but with effective use of the sound of violence and death.

The Belgium director, Phillippe Van Leeuw, chose to narrate the horror of the genocide based on the fate of one person, played by Rwandan pop singer Ruth Nirere, who witnessed the genocide first-hand, which was a very important factor for the director when casting her.[32] The credibility in other words is based on an association to genocide by proximity, as audiences tend to interpret that sort of nearness as sincerity. A review on Indiewire.com confirms this notion, as the reviewer first complains that "[c]inema has proven wholly inadequate as a substitute for memory in telling the story of the murderous rampage that took place in Rwanda," but then points out that "The Day God Walked Away takes a massive step forward in using the language of cinema to convey the horror of the genocide." This view is solely based on the proximity factor at the expense of "a pretext for grand statements about personal responsibility or the cultural and tribal conflicts that drove the Hutu majority to murder their Tutsi neighbors en masse."[33]

Kinyarwanda, another shoestring budgeted film shot in sixteen days and directed by Jamaican-American Alrick Brown, tells the story of the genocide from six different perspectives during the genocide as well as through flashbacks, which all are woven together in a credible way. According to the director, the different stories are inspired by true events from the genocide.[34] The film is centered around the Grand Mosque of Kigali, well known for being a place of safety for Muslims as well as Christian Hutus and Tutsis during the genocide.[35] There is a love story between a young Tutsi woman and a young Hutu man amidst the chaos; stories about the Mufti of Rwanda as well as a Catholic priest, a woman RPF soldier, a small boy named Ishmael, and a story from a re-education camp in 2004. Mostly, this film conveys the official history of the genocide whereby Belgian colonialism is responsible, the RPF saves the day, and where the manager at "Hotel Rwanda" "is only taking Tutsis with money."

Figure 6.3 Emmanuel (Edouard Bamporiki) at a re-education camp for Hutu perpetrators in *Kinyarwanda* (2011)

However, there are no white people involved in the stories and the UN is hardly seen at all. Instead, Rwandans commit the murders, suffer from the violence, recover, reconcile, and repent. In fact, *Kinyarwanda* was marketed as the first feature film produced by Rwandans, which is not entirely true due to the existence of films like *100 Days* and *Munyurangabo*.[36] In addition, almost everybody speaks English instead of Kinyarwanda in the film, which is somewhat ironic and undermines the "Rwandan-ness."

Nonetheless, the focus on Rwandan stories told from a Rwandan perspective with Rwandan actors made *Kinyarwanda* a unique historical film in 2011, although its uniqueness is strongly questioned in relation to a "how-the-Rwandan-genocide-should-be-portrayed" perspective. A review in *The Hollywood Reporter* slammed it for "resort[ing] to static discussion and explication" that undermines the "importance of the subject matter" as "the power of the film [is] mitigated by numerous talking-heads discussions of the country's complex history, cultures and religion."[37] Likewise, Robert Koehler in *Variety* called the film "doubly disappointing" due to the fact that the sheer number of stories hampered the films "pace and dramatic momentum," while also pointing to the failure to "convincingly re-create the violent 1994 events."[38] Furthermore, comparative literature scholar Dianne R. Portfleet dismisses *Kinyarwanda* as a film that "barely present[s] the horrors and the unimaginable brutalities of the genocide."[39]

Once again, we have negative responses to the lack of a historical overview and historical facts, as well as the discussion about the significance of whether to depict explicit violence to understand the genocide. It is safe to say that *Kinyarwanda* strays away from how previous films have portrayed the official historical media memory of the Rwanda genocide. However, is an understanding of the genocide possible without a display of explicit violence?

Returning to Zylberman's discussion of a canon of films on the Rwandan genocide, he identifies several films, including *Munyurangabo*, *The Day God Walked Away*, and *Kinyarwanda*, which constitute an archive of films that are not a actively remembered due to their lack of commercial success and scholarly attention. According to Zylberman, these films are characterized by a focus on the effects and consequences of the genocide, by turning women into the main characters, and for not offering a history lesson to their audiences.[40]

These alternative histories of the genocide against the Tutsi had already begun to be produced but predominately in the documentary genre, as we shall see later, where individual stories gradually replaced a more comprehensive historical perspective, and where the documentary proximity factor guaranteed a truthfulness in a way that did not apply to fictional narratives such as the one in *Kinyarwanda*. Consequently, the recurrent use of emblematic and violent images in documentaries on the genocide, as well as the numerous recreations of those same images in the feature film, had by around 2011 affected the historical memory to such an extent that the absence of these images undermined the historical credibility among audiences and critics who associated the genocide to horrors and unimaginable brutalities.

One recently internationally produced film about the genocide which avoids the white savior perspective but retains the "Rwandan" perspective is *'94 Terror*, directed by Ugandan Richard Mulindwa. The film features Ugandan actors and is based on true events, as it highlights the genocide memorial in Kasensero, Uganda, where 2,875 victims of the genocide, fished out of the Akagera river on the border with Rwanda, are buried. The film centers on Keza, a Tutsi survivor who retells her story in lengthy flashbacks of what happened in the 1994 Rwandan genocide. Like *The Day God Walked Away*, it is an action filled survivor film but unlike other similar feature films *'94 Terror* lives up to its title as it is extremely and explicitly gory and violent. We get to follow Keze, and three other women, through a nightmarish escape, starting with the brutal loss of her family and entire village in a massacre committed by Hutu militia gone mad, and this scenario continues with one act of violence after another. For instance, at roadblocks the Interahamwe act entirely out of control and shoot indiscriminately into the queues of people, massacring Tutsis and supposedly Hutus alike. Mulindwa skips over the most common emblematic images and repeatedly stages a more uncommon one, namely "The River of Corpses," showing a panorama of corpses that covers the entire frame, while sentimental music plays on the soundtrack.

The film plays with the audiences' expectations and uses the hero trope in unexpected ways. During the escape, Keze and the other women stumble upon a man hiding in the woods, and they flee with him, expecting to get

Figure 6.4 Recreation of the emblematic image "The River of Corpses" in '94 *Terror* (2018)

some protection. However, it turns out that he is a Hutu and quite incapable of protecting anyone. He leaves them to get help, and during his absence the women hide in a shed. One of the women is nine months pregnant and when her labor contractions begin, another woman tries to silence her screams; in the process, she suffocates the laboring woman, killing both the woman and the infant. And all this is in vain, as they are still discovered, captured, and taken as sex slaves. The first rape is committed off-screen, but with diegetic sound, while the camera lingers on a terrified Keza. Then it is Keza's turn, and now the camera follows and stays in the room where the Hutu militiamen drag her to be raped. However, the director Mulindwa chooses to shoot this scene from Keza's perspective, showing the rapists' faces rather than Keza's body. Eventually, the militiamen kill all the women, but somehow Keza manages to survive and emerges from a pile of corpses. Outside, wandering through a river of corpses, she once again come across the male "hero." He promises her that he can take her through the roadblock because he is Hutu, but instead he is brutally executed for helping a Tutsi. Keza flees and manages miraculously to cross the river to safety in Uganda.

Regionally, '94 *Terror* generated a lot of appreciation, winning the Best Viewers' Choice Movie Award at the Uganda Film Festival, and receiving eighteen nominations, winning no less than seven awards, at the prestigious Golden Movie Award Africa in Ghana in 2019.[41] The film was also awarded for best costume design at The African Film Festival in Dallas in 2019.[42] This success, and its historical verisimilitude, was not least due to Shakira Kibirige, costume designer and make-up artist who recreated this explicit and gory version of the Rwandan genocide. Kibirige also won accolades for the Rwandan-Belgian-French film *The Mercy of the Jungle* (2018), about the Second Congo War, and with Rwandan Joël Karekezi as director, winning for both make-up and costume at the Africa Movie Academy Awards in 2019, the African equivalent to the Academy Awards.[43]

In many ways, you could claim that *'94 Terror* is Hollywood-esque in its approach to its subject, being a gory action-filled thriller, rather than a solemn drama. But just like *The Day God Walked Away* and *Kinyarwanda*, audiences are not served a complete history lesson filled with facts of perpetrator and victims, failed international organizations, or white saviors for that matter. In this way these films stray from the official historical media memory of the Rwandan genocide. The near absence of explicit violence, and the use of the emblematic images, is another way these films deviate. The exception being, of course, *'94 Terror* with its strong focus on the violence and terror of the genocide. It is noteworthy that *The Day God Walked Away* and *Kinyarwanda* were subject to disapproval due to their lack of violence, much in the same way that, for example, *Hotel Rwanda* faced the same criticism. *'94 Terror* was instead, at least on a regional level, rewarded for its explicit use of violence in a way that can be interpreted as historical verisimilitude. In addition, the explicit visualization of rape stands out, especially in comparison with the much more subtle rape scenes in *A Sunday in Kigali*, although both these films stand out with regard to this particular aspect of the Rwandan genocide.

The final film which deviates from the official historical media memory of the Rwandan geocide is *Small County: An African Childhood*, based on French-Rwandan Gaël Faye's semi-autobiographical teenage years' experience of the war in Burundi.[44] Consequently, the genocide against the Tutsi in Rwanda is, as in *Waramutsebo*, almost entirely mediated through news media. Nevertheless, *Small Country* distinguishes itself in two ways. First, the film, as well as the novel, is one of the few that tells the story of the Rwandan genocide entirely from a child's perspective. The boy, ten-year-old Gabriel, and his sister live with their French father and Rwandan mother in Bujumbura, the capital of Burundi. Hence, the genocidal violence in both Burundi in 1993 and Rwanda in 1994 become the setting for this coming-of-age story, in which Gabriel must tackle the question of whether he is French or Tutsi, and how Tutsis are related to Hutus, as the tension starts with the 1993 election in Burundi—all depicted through his and his friends' eyes. The family's existence is quickly turned upside down as violence comes ever closer to their home. The narrative choice to portray the frightening behavior of the adults from the eyes of the children makes *Small Country* an effective vehicle for the portrayal of the genocide. The adults' violence and prejudice seeps into the innocent young lives like poison, and the more the conflict escalates, the more the children are drawn into the events surrounding them.

There are two powerful examples of this. First, Gabriel's Rwandan mother travels back to Rwanda as the genocide against the Tutsi starts and when she returns, after being missing, she suffers from PTSD and mental illness, which affects her children, who are subjected to severe mental and physical torture. Second, the underlying question of ethnicity, which is playfully dismissed by the children at the beginning of the film, eventually becomes a cruel reality as Gabriel is forced to kill a man to prove loyalty to "his" ethnicity. The latter display of violence is also connected to the second deviation, namely that the violence depicted in *Small Country* is foremost committed by Tutsis against the Hutus—which gives an upside-down picture of the genocide in neighboring Rwanda.[45]

Pertaining to Zylberman's archive of films that are not part of an active part of memory, these films fulfill that criteria in terms of their weak presentation of historical facts at the expense of the effects and consequences of the genocide, especially with a strong focus on women. But that does not mean that these films are not an active part of memory. These are alternative memories that found their principal outlet in the documentary genre, and when these audio-visual recollections appeared in the narrative film, they often bumped their head against the wall of the official historiography, a wall defended by mainly Western reviewers, it should be added.

7

Emblematic Images and the Maintenance of a Historical Media Memory in Documentaries

Documentaries which uphold the official historical media memory of the Rwandan genocide are plentiful. A majority of these films constitute a continuation of the three nominal feature films—*Ghosts of Rwanda*, *Rwanda: Do Scars Ever Fade?*, and *Shake Hands with the Devil: The Journey of Roméo Dallaire*—for example, the French film *Kill Them All! Rwanda: The Story of an Unimportant Genocide* from 2004 which focuses on the French involvement in the genocide and uses an abundance of emblematic images, especially "The Nick Hughes Footage" and "Corpses by the Road," that repeatedly are employed to explain the inexplicable violence with images of violence.

It is also *Kill Them All!*, together with the documentary version of *Shake Hands with the Devil*, which familiarizes audiences with the eighth emblematic image of the genocide, "Skeletons and Clothes," in which footage of decomposed bodies turned into skeletons, often with their clothes still on, and filmed

Figure 7.1 A variant of the emblematic image "Skeletons and Clothes" in *Kill Them All! Rwanda: The Story of an Unimportant Genocide* (2004)

at the end of the genocide, testifies to the grim consequences of the genocide against the Tutsi. An often-used variant of "Skeletons and Clothes" consists of newly taken footage of preserved bones, skulls, and clothes displayed at one of the six official genocide memorials in Rwanda. Hence, this footage lacks a sense of now-ness that the other seven emblematic images exhibit. Therefore, this footage has more of an archival function—especially the newly taken footage—of silent artifacts that are used to promote an educational never-again-memory, according to British anthropologist Pat Caplan.[1] In other words, in cinematic history, the use of the eighth emblematic image signals that the genocide is over, while, in comparison, the other seven emblematic images have a sense of urgency to them. When employed in the official historical media memory, these seven images promote the failure of the Western powers in Rwanda in an active sense—we must do something—while the eighth image is able to perform several functions, such as archival, educational, promotional, and nation-building, as we will see further on.[2]

Two French television documentaries which follow in the historical footsteps of *Kill Them All!* are *Kigali, des images contre un massacre* ("Kigali, Images against a Massacre," 2006) directed by Jean-Christophe Klotz, who later directed the feature film *Black Out*, and *7 jours à Kigali, la semaine où le Rwanda a basculé* ("7 days in Kigali: The Week That Led to the Genocide," 2014) which reconstructs the first seven days of the genocide. American versions of the official historical media memory of the genocide can be seen in *On Our Watch* (2007), part of the Frontline series at PBS and a follow-up to *Ghosts of Rwanda*, as well as in the documentary short *I'm Not Leaving* (2014), which focus on American Carl Wilkens, head of the Adventist Development and Relief Agency International in Rwanda during the genocide, and known as the "only American who stayed."[3]

Other international documentary films which deal with the Western guilt theme coupled with the white savior trope are the Italian *La lista del console* ("The Console's List," 2010) about the Italian Pierantonio Costa, the Italian consul in Rwanda during the genocide, who saved Western as well as Rwandan lives during the killings. The title of the film is unmistakably an homage to *Schindler's List* and sometimes this documentary is referred to as *Costa's List*. Norwegian-produced television documentary *Telling Truths in Arusha* (2010) focuses on the choices that a Norwegian judge makes at an ICTR trial against a Catholic priest accused of genocide, while Roméo Dallaire's work to end the use of child soldiers is the focus of the Canadian documentary *Fight Like Soldiers, Die Like Children* (2012), but in which the Rwandan genocide inevitably figures in the background.

Furthermore, the Argentinian documentary *Los 100 días que no conmovieron al mundo* (*The 100 Days That Didn't Shake the World*, 2009) focuses on another

ICTR judge, Ines Wienberg Roca, who was the only representative from Latin America in the ICTR. As the Norwegian *Telling Truths in Arusha, The 100 Days That Didn't Shake the World* has an outside perspective on the Rwandan genocide and during the first half of the film, this perspective is filtered through Weinberg Roca's point of view. We get an insight into the widespread use of rape as a strategy of the genocide, but the film simplifies the genocide by the short-cut use of emblematic images such as "Corpses by the Road," "The Man with a Machete," and "Skeletons and Clothes" as some of the ICTR judges tour the country. The external perspective can be explained in part by what could be called a reverse transnationalism as the second half of the film drifts away from its initial purpose to tell the truth about the genocide. Instead, as Pagnoni and Ignacio Juvé point out, the film not only narrates its historical truth via the Argentinian judge, but the locality of the film tends to spill over to the actual situation in Argentina, that is, "violation of human rights and historical reparation" in Argentina.[4] Within this interpretation, *The 100 Days That Didn't Shake the World* only exploits the Rwandan genocide in order to, indirectly, speak to the political situation in Argentina during the time the film was produced.

On one occasion, *The 100 Days That Didn't Shake the World* slips as audiences are informed—via excerpts from the actual trials against Simon Bikindi, a musician, and Protais Zigiranyirazo, a Hutu business man and politician, also suspected of the murder of Dian Fossey in 1985—that the trust between the ethnic groups is even worse since the genocide, and that the only thing stopping further violence is a fear of the police. This is a deviation from the official historical media memory since it implies that the genocide, or at least its underlying causes, are not yet solved and that the violence could flare up again.

In the Canadian *Triage: Dr James Orbinski's Humanitarian Dilemma* (2007) yet another white man "serves as a bridge to African pain," as Zylberman effortlessly dismisses this film.[5] But what does this bridge to African pain entail? First, it serves as a comparison between African countries, different conflicts, and time gone by as the main character, James Orbinski, former President of the International Council for Médecins Sans Frontières (MSF, Doctors without Borders), returns to Somalia and Rwanda where he was stationed as a field medical doctor in 1993 and 1994, respectively. Second, this comparison functions as a historical explanation to the West's—that is, the US's—reluctance to intervene in Rwanda after the military debacle in The Battle of Mogadishu October 3-4, 1993, in which eighteen American soldiers died (together with some 300 Somali casualties). Third, although this documentary uses short glimpses of "Corpses by the Road" and "The Man with the Machete," the latter incorreltly in the segment on Somalia, the main source of information pertaining to the genocidal violence does not come from images but from Orbinski's verbal testimony. This testimony differs from the hundreds of testimonies that are included in the documentary films on the Rwanda genocide as it is given by a medical doctor with expert medical knowledge.

In one particular scene, taking place at the King Faisel Hospital in Kigali where MSF was stationed during the genocide, Orbinski discusses the boundary between being an objective doctor and being a human being. Here, the director Patrick Reed lets the camera linger on Orbinski, using cut-ins to his hands as he explains, and then a steady close-up of his face as he describes, the injuries inflicted on a woman. At one point, Orbinski stops talking, visually shaken, but the camera stays in close-up and his testimony mercilessly continues on the soundtrack, edited together from several takes:

> It was one woman, who had been macheted; you know many [were], but this particular woman . . . You know with that presence of mind, I looked at her and I could see she had, that she was slowly bleeding to death. So, I immediately started surgery. At one point my forceps . . . the teeth of the forceps . . . I took too much skin, and it pinched her, it hurt her, and . . . she touched my arm, and . . . just moaning, and I . . . just looked up from her abdomen, and I looked at her, and she, you know, had both of her ears cut off, both of her breasts had been cut off . . . the Achilles tendons of both feet had been . . . slashed . . . and she had a pattern cut into her face by a machete; very carefully cut. Somebody took some time to do this, you know. And she had dried semen on her thighs, and . . . the objectivity is gone. This was not a series of stiches, multiple lacerations that had slow bleeding arteries that needed nine or ten stitches, and I just . . . it was a woman . . . I just turned away and I vomited, and . . . it wasn't the blood, it was just . . . [Silence] It is easy to live your whole life with this kind of illusion, that "I am only a doctor," and what is my role? Is it simply to be technically perfect? Scientifically perfect? Or is that part of something else?

At this moment, the superficial white savior perspective crumbles, and a humanitarian connection is made in a way that the endless reuse of the violent and anonymous emblematic images is more difficult to achieve. Largely, *Triage* stays away from political analysis and concentrates on the subjective impressions and imperfect wisdom of one individual. This choice of focus is valuable, in comparison to for example the larger political picture that Roméo Dallaire's recollections insert into in the documentary version of *Shake Hands with the Devil*, as the intimacy of the hand movements and facial expressions actually becomes a bridge to "African pain."

Another three films use the pedagogical tool of comparison. *Screamers* (2006) follows American rock band System of a Down on tour as the film explores the question of why genocides still occur today. The focus is on the

Figure 7.2 The personal and at the same time professional testimony of Dr. James Orbinski, which acts as a human bridge to African pain in *Triage: Dr James Orbinski's Humanitarian Dilemma* (2007)

Armenian genocide, since several of the band members, including lead vocalist Serj Tankian, are decedents of genocide survivors of the Armenian genocide, but the Rwandan genocide is used as a comparative example, notably by the use of emblematic images such as "Corpses by the Road" and "The Nick Hughes Footage" as short-cuts to illustrate the genocide. American short television documentary *Massacre at Murambi* (2007) uses a comparison with the then current genocide in Darfur to criticize Western racism directed at Africa. Another more artistic comparison is *Tour* (2014), a video installation which "embarks on a global journey contemplating former genocide sites, provoking the question of how we can sustain the memory of that which has become invisible."[6] This video installation uses four cases of genocide that are toured and memorialized: Murambi in Rwanda, Wounded Knee in USA, Choeung Ek in Cambodia, and Treblinka in Poland.

Finally, there are a number of international documentaries produced and directed by Americans and Europeans which maintain the official history but which attempt to shift focus from a Western perspective to a Rwandan perspective, although in the end it is the Western perception that ultimately prevails. One example is *Wounded Healers* (2009), an American Christian themed documentary with the tagline: "How Do You Forgive the Unforgivable?" This documentary chronicles the personal stories of five Rwandans in a post-genocide journey towards healing. However, these testimonies, in comparison to that of Orbinski's, are heavily dramatized with wall-to-wall music on the soundtrack and through editing. The Western narrator even narrates the main subjects' stories, instead of using subtitles, thus creating unnecessary distance that is wrapped into a thin historical explanation in line with the official historical media memory of the genocide to obtain credibility. For instance, this is executed through the heavy-handed use of docudrama recreations, and by turning the color scale to black-and-white to mark that these scenes take place in the past.

In *Après–Un voyage dans le Rwanda* ("After–A trip to Rwanda," 2004), French documentary filmmaker Denis Gheerbrant travels alone to Rwanda with his camera equipment with the intention of understanding the genocide through certain random survivors' stories. However, the emphasis in this documentary is mostly on Gheerbrant's filmmaking and reflections "to understand," rather than giving some sort of comprehensive overview of the genocide. Stylistically, Gheerbrant's whispering voiceover, glimpses of unexplained reconciliation ceremonies, and an aberrant focus on orphans who practice traditional Rwandan dances, filmed with a neo-colonial exotic understanding, point to the filmmaker's artistic ambitions. Gheerbrant nevertheless comments that he was "seeking to put aside what differentiated us," "us" being Europeans and Africans.[7] In agreement with this interpretation, French film critic Oliver Barlet argues that "the entire film is [. . .] based on the dialectic between seeing and understanding," claiming that the images are there "in order to get to know and to understand," while the voiceover is superfluous.[8] However, the reliance on the images coupled with a "philosophical" voiceover is just what generates a very Eurocentric outlook on the genocide.

The television documentary *Killers* (2004) is a "return-to-Rwanda" narrative made by Irish foreign correspondent with BBC News, Fergal Keane, who also made *Journey into Darkness* in 1994. In *Killers* he travels back to Nyarubuye to interview victims and perpetrator of the Nyarubuye massacre, committed on April 15, 1994, during which some 35,000 people were killed at Nyarubuye Roman Catholic Church. As with several other documentaries produced in 2004, *Killers* follows the dominant path of the official historical media memory of the Rwandan genocide, richly illustrated with emblematic images such as "Nick Hughes Footage," "The KPH Images," and no less than five different versions of the "Corpses by the Road" image. Reenactments are used as well as interviews, both filmed in 1994 and new versions, in an effort to understand how the genocide could happen. Although *Killers* try to present a Rwandan perspective, it is still the negative Western outlook that prevails, or as Keane stated in an article published in connection to the airing of his documentary, "The official line is that the country is on the road to reconciliation, but I have serious doubts. Having witnessed part of the genocide and returning here on several occasions over the past ten years, I sense a society still haunted. I am not convinced by the official line that Rwanda is on the road to reconciliation."[9]

American documentary *Earth Made of Glass* (2010), directed by Deborah Scranton, is a film that investigates the French connection to the genocide, prompted by a Rwandan investigation into the genocide. With an almost CSI-inspired outlook on the genocide, garnished with extensive use of emblematic images as well as images of French troops in Rwanda, the documentary follows a Tutsi survivor who is looking for the remains of his father. However, the filmmakers had access to President Kagame, who gives his view on the French involvement but also on the reconciliation process in contemporary Rwanda. Kagame endorsed the film and was even present at *Earth Made of Glass*'s premiere at the Tribeca film festival. At the Q and A, he said that the film told the truth, "that is our history" but he also said that "if you want reconciliation and justice at the same time, they tend to conflict. [However,] we move on, we don't become hostage of this very difficult past."[10]

Yet another film that scrutinizes the French complicity in the genocide against the Tutsi in Rwanda is *Justice Seekers* (2014), an Al Jazeera-produced documentary that centers on Franco-Rwandan couple Alain and Dafroza Gauthier and their quest to bring to justice Pascal Simbikangwa, a former spy chief in Rwanda and a top shareholder in RTLM. The narrative motivation is that this is the first court case concerning the Rwandan genocide conducted in France, to where several high-ranking *génocidaires* fled in the aftermath of the genocide, and where they were protected by the French regimes of François Mitterrand and Jacques Chirac. The film recapitulates the official history of the genocide, garnered with an abundance of emblematic images such as "Corpses by the Road" and "The Man with a Machete," and according to an interview with the director, Antonio Rui Ribeiro, the documentary was formed this way to fit into Al Jazeera's format.[11]

When *Justice Seekers* was aired as part of Al Jazeera's current affairs series, Witness, in connection to the twenty-year commemoration of the genocide in April 2014, the documentary was promoted as being a part of an effort to teach the Rwandan genocide, as the genocide risked "fading from the West's collective consciousness."[12] In addition, the Western perspective shines through as *Justice Seekers* audaciously juxtapositions the Holocaust and the Rwandan genocide. According to Ribeiro, this juxtaposition came about as a historical comparison, "While the Holocaust is now firmly embedded in public consciousness as the Holocaust of the Jews, it took almost 20 years for it to be recognised as such, mainly after the trial of Adolf Eichemann [sic] in Israel. It has taken France a similar length of time to recognise the genocide of the Tutsis of Rwanda."[13] We will return to Ribeiro's filmmaking as he directed a longer version of *Justice Seekers* called *Arrows of Truth* (2018) which will be discussed in Chapter 10, on historical revisionism.

Finally, more recent documentaries have begun to appear which build on and expand the official historical media memory of the genocide against the Tutsi in a specific way, namely, to hail the RPF as the heroes who stopped the genocide. The RPF, and foremost Rwandan President Paul Kagame, have of course figured in many documentaries as part of the official historical media memory, but in Belgium-French documentary *Inkotanyi* (2017) and American documentary *The 600: The Solidier's Story* (2019) the focus is solely on the RPF as heroes and liberators. At first sight this constitutes a much-needed Rwandan perspective but both films are clearly Western productions. Whereas both productions use Rwandan talking heads as witnesses, the Belgian-French production employs an abundance of emblematic images such as "Skeletons and Clothes," The Man with a Machete," and "Piles of Corpses" in tandem with criticism of the French involvement. Likewise, the American production is characterized by a pumping soundtrack, a heavy-handed voice-of-God narration (e.g., "one of the worst genocides in history began"/"hundreds of thousands of ethnic minority Tutsi and moderate Hutu were slaughtered by their Hutu countrymen in a sweeping, preplanned wave of murders"), and emotional reenactments in order to tell the heroic story of the battalion of 600 Tutsi men and women that was stationed in Kigali at the start of the genocide as part of the Arusha Peace Agreement. In effect, the Rwandan perspective is narrowed down to that of the winners (the RPF) in the form of what could be labeled as survivor nationalism, a blurring of "Tutsi" with "survivor" in official Rwandan language and decrees.[14]

Both of these films have been endorsed officially by Rwanda as important historical films. In Rwanda's *The New Times*, *The 600: The Soldier's Story* is named as "the best produced movie on the fight for Kigali," with the writer proclaiming: "I remember watching the movie and feeling so very proud of those young men. Not only did I feel proud of them, but I felt represented by them. This movie not only further cemented my personal bond with the uniformed men of then, but also the uniformed men and women of today."[15] And after the premiere of *Inkotanyi* in Kigali—attended by First Lady Jeannette Kagame—the then defense minister of Rwanda, James Kabarebe, said: "What the youth can take from this is that they have no reason to fail to build on from what has been done and sustain progress. The hard work was already done by the Inkotanyi Generation. If they fail, they will have betrayed the country, themselves and those who sacrificed their lives for the country."[16]

This is a case in point of how historical consciousness can work, as people need historical notions of the past to be able to interpret the present and, with the help of these stories, use them to form a perspective on the future. The historical culture of Rwanda is dependent on and intertwined with the transnational historical media memory of the genocide against the Tutsi, and these two films are examples of how cinematic history is used to create experiences and knowledge located in the historical culture that precondition contemporary interpretations of the audiovisual rendering of the past. However, before we venture further into the historical culture of Rwanda, we will first turn to a number of films that deviate from the official historical media memory of the Rwandan genocide since they place Rwandan women at the center of their stories.

8
Women, AIDS, and Rape

While women undoubtedly are part of the cinematic depiction of the official historical media memory of the Rwandan genocide, they nevertheless mostly feature in the background, behind prominent male political actors such as Roméo Dallaire, Paul Kagame, and Carl Wilkens. This is especially true for Rwandan women, who are almost solely featured as victims, while Rwandan men are featured as both victims and perpetrators. Exceptions to this are found in the three feature films, *A Sunday in Kigali*, *'94 Terror*, and *Trees of Peace*, which prominently focus on rape, women victims, and survivors respectively. However, films and television documentaries which retell the official history of the Rwandan genocide create a collective memory that is dominant in relation to these alterative versions of the same memory.

Historically, wartime sexual violence has foremost been aimed at women, with rape frequently used as a means of psychological warfare in order to humiliate the enemy. However, sexual violence does not just constitute rape, it also includes sexual mutilation with the genocidal intent of destroying women's reproductive capabilities, and sexual slavery, something that occurred on a regular basis during the genocide and is exposed, for example, in *'94 Terror*.[1]

One story which is surprisingly absent in the official historical media memory is precisely the one about all the rapes committed as part of the genocide. Another somewhat ironic absence—seen in relation to the story in *A Sunday in Kigali* where the white protagonist makes a documentary about AIDS, while being ignorant about the imminent genocide—is the story of HIV/AIDS as one of the dire consequences of genocidal rape. A third is the story about all "war babies" that were a result of the endless rapes. All these stories are typically not part of the male-oriented official historical media memory of the Rwandan genocide, and this is in spite of the fact that it is estimated that somewhere between 250,000 and 500,000 girls and women were raped—that is, nearly all surviving Tutsi women—and that the Rwandan genocide was the first genocide in which rape was officially declared to be a war crime by an international court.² In 1998, the ICTR handed down the landmark judgment in the case of Jean-Paul Akayesu, a Hutu mayor of Taba commune in Gitarama prefecture during the genocide, who was sentenced to imprisonment for life for genocide and crimes against humanity, including the acts of extermination, murder, torture, rape, and other inhumane acts with the intent to destroy a group.³ The legal work leading up to the trial and the trial itself is detailed in the American feature-length documentary *The Uncondemned* (2015).

About ten documentary films deal with these stories of rape and its aftermath and which largely are missing from the official historical media memory of the Rwandan genocide. Unlike the focus on women as passive victims, these documentaries have a different approach as they look at women as survivors, that is, as active agents of their own destiny. The structure of these films is also different as usually they are divided into a *before* and a *now*, and where the before consists of a brief historicization of the genocide primarily built upon short introductory texts as well as interviews with women and Rwandan officials and to a lesser extent on recreations and emblematic images—and when the latter do appear they almost solely consist of "Skeletons and Clothes" images. The exception here is the American and Academy Award-nominated documentary short *God Sleeps in Rwanda* (2005), in which the filmmakers use "Corpses by the Road" and "The River of Corpses" to quickly establish what they say "culminated in one of the worst crimes against humanity."

However, the "now" consists of interviews and footage of everyday life where the filmmakers without exception keep themselves out of the image and instead let the women and the girls tell their stories in their own words. The now stories are survivors' stories about the struggle to live and to get by in a patriarchal society in which women are undervalued, where Tutsi women are still threatened, and where raped women with "war babies" and/or AIDS are shunned and stigmatized.⁴ Hence, while the before constitutes the starting point, where horrendous testimonies about rape and violence are told, it does not become a means-to-an-end to tell yet another horrific story of the genocide as in the official historical media memory. This is perhaps why the male reviewer in *The New York Times* easily dismissed *God Sleeps in Rwanda* as "heartening but [it] has a girl-power sheen to it."⁵

In addition to *God Sleeps in Rwanda*, Canadian documentary *Mothers Courage, Thriving Survivors* (2005) uses archival material to establish the history of the genocide before turning to interviews with raped Rwandan women with AIDS who, somewhat paradoxically according to the director and narrator Léo Kalinda, subsequently had the opportunity to become full citizens in post-genocide Rwanda. In the Norwegian *Duhozanye: The Widows of Rwanda* (2011) we get to follow several women who started an association called Duhozanye for Tutsi and Hutu widows who used to be married to Tutsi men. *Duhozanye* shows association members helping female victims of rape and HIV/AIDS to run small businesses and to start classes in gender violence prevention. In connection to the twenty-year commemoration, the Belgian full-length documentary *Rwanda, la vie après–Paroles de méres* (*Rwanda, Life Goes On*, 2014) tell the stories of six Tutsi women who were raped during the genocide, which resulted in pregnancy, childbirth, and a complex life for what UNICEF representative Marie-Consolee Mukangendo has termed "children of hate."[6] In the documentary short *Intended Consequences: Rwandan Children Born of Rape* (2008) Israeli photographer Jonathan Torgovnik uses photographs as a catalyst for thirty-one Rwandan women to tell their stories. Those photographs, together with the interviews, were also compiled as the exhibition "Intended Consequences: Rwandan Children Born of Rape" that was shown at photographic and art museums around the world.[7]

In Canadian twin documentary films, *A Women's Story* (2015) and *A Women's Place* (2018), the director Azra Rashid uses historical juxtaposition as a tool to tell women's stories in relation genocides. The first film explores survivor stories told by three women who experienced the Holocaust, the genocide in Bangladesh in 1971, and the Rwandan genocide in 1994, respectively. While *A Woman's Story* examines the survival process through a female perspective, *A Woman's Place* continues this discussion on a global-political level with another juxtaposition, namely between surviving women in Rwanda, Cambodia, and the Indigenous communities in Canada. *A Women's Place* has a special focus on food and food crises in the wake of genocide whereby women must learn new skills in order to survive, which included starting new businesses where food, in this case, became a statement of resistance. Likewise, American short documentary *Mama Rwanda* (2016) follows two Rwandan mothers who become entrepreneurs to overcome extreme poverty.

One of the most interesting projects about surviving Tutsi women in Rwanda is the Swedish trilogy of television documentaries that began in 1995 with *Blodsarvet*, a film that recorded the aftermath of the genocide in refugee camps inside and outside of Rwanda. Interviews are conducted with child refugees, Hutu prisoners, and political leaders from MRND who are allowed to deny the genocide without being confronted. Nevertheless, Swedish filmmakers Maria and Peter Rinaldo returned to Rwanda to make the two sequels, *Blodsbarn* ("Blood Children," 2001) and *Mothers of War* (2009), and in-between they produced a fourth documentary about the role of religion in the genocide, *I Guds namn* ("In the Name of God," 2004).

In *Blodsbarn* and *Mother of War* the filmmakers reconnect with Marianna and her extended family. Marianna, eight years old at the time, was one of the orphans originally interviewed in *Blodsarvet*, where she showed the filmmakers around and, among other things, pointed out the corpses of her parents.

WOMEN, AIDS, AND RAPE   149

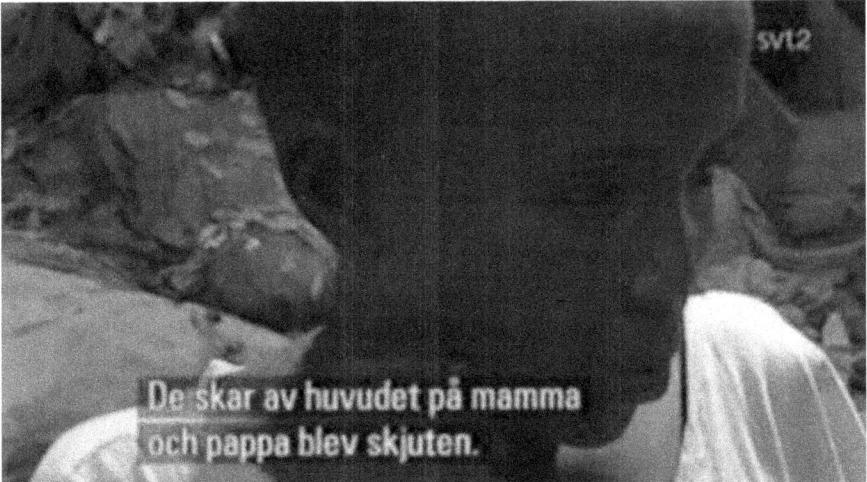

Figure 8.1 Eight-year-old Marianna points out the corpses of her parents in *Blodsarvet* (1995). The caption reads: "They cut off mom's head and dad was shot"

The follow-up, *Blodsbarn*, is a psychological documentary—stylistic and more artistic in its editing and in transitions, made without commentary from the filmmaker—about children with war trauma. Audiences get to follow Marianna, now thirteen years old, as she goes to school, waking up with nightmares and afraid of dying, trying to handle a severe case of PTSD. Her adopted parents, Beate and Bernedette, beat her, finding it difficult to navigate her teenage angst combined with her PTSD, but eventually Marianna gets the opportunity to visit a trauma therapist for treatment. Here she is counseled to write letters to her dead mother, something that the filmmakers visually make use of as Marianna's narrative voice throughout the film. Marianna is also sent to boarding school in Butare to get away from the destructive environment in Nyamata.

Paralleling Marianna's narrative is the story of Beate, who is sick, believing it to be malaria. However, reluctantly visiting the doctor, it transpires that she has AIDS, having been raped by three Interahamwe men during the genocide. Beate hides the disease from Marianna and secretively seeks help, becoming a member of an organization for women with AIDS. She visits an insurance company where she tries to buy an insurance policy to be able to pay for the expensive medicine, but to no avail; the insurance is too expensive and does not cover diseases such as HIV. The film ends as Marianna is called back from boarding school when Beate becomes seriously ill. In the last letter, Marianna writes, "When she dies, I will lose my second mother."

Mothers of War continues the narrative eight years later and now Marianna herself is a young single mother to a boy. This documentary has a different approach than the earlier two, moving from an intended observational mode to a more participatory mode, to use Bill Nichols's terminology.[8] The narrator, that is, the director Maria Rinaldo, comments on what is happening, historicizing Rwandan society from a women's perspective as well as the genocide, but it is not the voice of God we hear on the soundtrack. For example, many reconciliation documentaries unproblematically refer to the fact that the Rwandan parliament has the highest representation of women in the world as a measurement of success, but that figure does not always compute with the lived reality of women in Rwanda, as Rinaldo notes. The film begins with a recap of the two earlier films, and here Rinaldo immediately admits that the filmmakers bought antiretroviral drugs for Beate, but that it was too late and she died—two circumstances that were knowingly omitted from *Blodsbarn*. This "confession" is a typical example of the filmmaker's participatory engagement with the subjects in the film.

As in the earlier films, interviews are intercut with images of a lived reality in which Marianna quit school, preferring instead to hang around with boys in Kigali. Bernadette, her third mother, is a devout Catholic, and as the filmmakers make clear, this symbolically parallels the highly problematic relationship between the Catholic Church and the RPF in Rwanda.[9] Bernadette is therefore in a constant fight with Marianna about her late nights and the fear that she will end up like Beate, that is to say, infected with HIV due to sin. Bernadette supports the family financially by operating a bar in her home, which provides a few scenes in which Rwandan men (always Tutsis as it turns out) are sitting outside in the shade getting drunk and chatting while the women work. This is then intercut with interviews with Marianna and Bernadette where they state that men are not to be trusted as "they just drink and do other stupid things." This in turn is intercut with Marianna's former therapist, now operating out of Kigali, who notes that alcohol does not help with trauma; and that it only has a temporary and superficial effect. This in turn is supported by the narrator who comments that work at home, pregnancy, and childcare are women's sole responsibility in Rwanda—especially if you are a single mother—which in turn is supported by interviews with Marianna and Bernadette and, naturally, with images of another group of men getting drunk in the shade of Bernadette's house.

The theme of children's trauma due to the genocide is followed up in *Mothers of War*, as Marianna discusses the subject in relation to her own behavior and her son, who clearly has forced her out of her shell. Bernadette and Marianna and her son also visit the Ntarama Genocide Memorial Centre, located in the former Catholic Church in which 5,000 Tutsis were killed on April 15, 1994, including both of Marianna's parents. "We often visit the place where my parents were massacred," Marianna says as she carries her boy around the shelves

Figure 8.2 Marianna and her son at the Ntarama Genocide Memorial in *Mothers of War* (2009)

with the remains of victims. The boy mistakes the bones for firewood, trying to play with the skulls, totally unaware of their significance, and Marianna becomes visually upset.

A scene towards the end of the film takes up the question of memory of the genocide. Marianna has no intention of telling her son about the genocide because she is afraid that he will feel hatred and will want revenge. Then an elderly Tutsi man puts pressure on her:

Man: If you don't want to tell others about their lost fathers, mothers, aunts … What do you do for your country? Nothing. You have to tell them that so that they know about it! Why do you refuse?
Marianna: It is important to me, I was there. He wasn't.
Man: He still needs to know! How could you have a good life if you do not tell the children what happened? Well, what are you going to do?
Marianna: Okay, I'll tell him.

But this is just lip service; Marianna still has no intention of talking about the genocide with her son.

In addition to the "Skeletons and Clothes" images that the filmmakers filmed at the Catholic Church in Ntarama in 1994, and the newly taken footage of Marianna's visits to the Genocide Memorial Center in *Blodsbarn* and *Mothers of War*, there are no other violent images used to explain the genocide. Instead, we gradually learn about the genocide and its long-time consequences in the form of PTSD, AIDS, and women's vulnerability in a patriarchal society through the stories told by Marianna, Beate, and Bernadette over a time span of fifteen years. In this way, *Blodsbarn* and *Mothers of War* constitute—along with other documentaries with a focus on women's experiences and survivor stories—alternative versions of the dominant official historical media memory of the genocide. We will turn now to another variation of the documentary on the Rwandan genocide, namely the large body of reconciliation documentaries.

9

Reconciliation and Gacaca Documentaries

Alongside the feature films, short films, and feature-length documentaries that uphold the officially historical media memory of the Rwandan genocide is a large group of related documentary films belonging to what could be referred to as the reconciliation documentary. Around sixty short and feature-length documentary films have been produced in this subgenre, starting with Anne Aghion's nominal film *Gacaca: Living Together Again in Rwanda?* (2002) and then continuing with a steady stream of releases, with surges in connection to the tenth, fifteenth, and twentieth commemorations of the genocide against the Tutsi.

The reconciliation documentary is characterized by an international interest in the aftermath of the genocide in Rwanda. In short, how is it possible for a society to transition from genocide to become a society where mutual respect and a sense of security can prevail? The reconciliation documentary generally includes a short historicization of the genocide, often with the aid of graphic emblematic images such as "Corpses by the Road" as a short-cut, seen for example in American films *Back Home* (2006), *Rising from Ashes* (2012), and *From Trauma to Peace* (2014). However, history is not at the center of these documentaries and notably the most commonly used emblematic image is "Skeletons and Clothes," often filmed contemporarily at the different genocide memorials in Rwanda. Lisa Fruchtman, director of *Sweet Dreams* (2012), for instance is very explicit in this use of "Skeleton and Clothes" images as a way for Western audiences "to get a grasp of the reality of what it was [. . .] We wanted people to know enough to understand the degree of trauma that exists in the country. But we didn't want to go deeply into the history."[1] Otherwise, the horrors of the genocide are retold via short information texts at the beginning of the reconciliation documentary and/or through survivor testimonies, and to a lesser degree via confessions made by the perpetrators.

Instead of history, the reconciliation documentary focuses on the different forms of reconciliation present in Rwanda after the genocide, mainly consisting of a range of communal and cultural projects that bring together Hutus and Tutsis, for example in *Eyes on Rwanda* (2010, a school for the deaf), *Rwanda, Take Two* (2010, filmmaking), *One Drop* (2010, clean water), *Poetry of Resilience* (2011, surviving poets), *Sweet Dreams* (the first ice-cream store in Rwanda), *Rising from Ashes* (cycling), *Finding Hillywood* (2013, filmmaking), *A Place for Everyone* (2014, love between young Rwandans), and *Rwanda & Juliet* (2016, the staging of Shakespeare's play in Kigali). In addition, there is a strong focus on Gacaca trials as a way to understand the Rwandan reconciliation process from an outsider's position, for example in *In the Tall Grass: Inside Gacaca* (2006), *Gacaca Justice* (2009), and *As We Forgive* (2010).

Generally, the reconciliation documentary can be divided into two main approaches: those films which describe post-genocide Rwanda's development as a success story, which comprise the great majority of productions; and those films which in different ways portray the same development as false or as a failure, and which make up a minority of the films.

All the documentaries listed above belong to the success stories that rush over the history of the genocide in order to talk about the positive connoted aftermath. Nevertheless, the history is seldom entirely ignored, but usually is just skimmed over. History is there mainly as a dark past and as something that the filmmakers can rely on to supply a strong contrast to the positive changes taking place in their films, most often leading to an upbeat ending. The successful reconciliation story can in turn be divided into two main areas: forgiveness, frequently connected to religion; and a focus on survivors' stories in connection to the reconciliation process, always seen through an outsider, Western perspective.

A typical example of the success story is the American *As We Forgive*, winner of the Student Academy Awards for Best Documentary for its director Laura Waters Hinson. In the film, we get to follow two Rwandan women, Rosaria and Chantale, as they come face-to-face with the men who killed their family members during the genocide, in order to answer the questions: "Can survivors truly forgive the killers who destroyed their families? And can the Church, which failed at moral leadership during the genocide, fit into the process of reconciliation today?"[2] *As We Forgive* uses several emblematic images, "Corpses by the Road," "The Nick Hughes Footage," "Bloated Corpses in the River," and the actor Mia Farrow as narrator, with the intention to create a contrast between genocidal violence and forgiveness. In an interview, Waters Hinson justifies her use of this imagery: "I think it is hard to understand the sacrifice of forgiveness without seeing a bit of the horror that people experienced."[3] Once again, history takes a back seat to an exploration of the "impossible" act of forgiveness. Waters Hinson says that she got her inspiration for the documentary on hearing a story that astonished her "even more than the nation's devastating

1994 genocide"; that being the Rwandan government's release of thousands of genocide perpetrators who had confessed their crimes from prison. "I wondered, 'can this even be true?' Is it possible for survivors of genocide to forgive their killers?'"[4]

Certainly, Waters Hinson, and many other predominately American filmmakers in films like *The Diary of Immaculée* (2006), *Rwanda Rising* (2007), *Wounded Healers, If Only We Had Listened* (2011), and *Through the Valley* (2013) for instance, find common ground in religion, more specifically Christianity, as way to explain the "inexplicable" process of forgiveness.[5] In fact, within the reconciliation documentary there exists a whole subgenre of films that exploit the Rwandan genocide in order to promote Christianity, both in Rwanda—which is ironic given that Rwanda is one of the most religious countries in the world—and in the West, predominantly in the USA. In films like *Rwanda: Living Forgiveness* (2005), *Hunting My Husband's Killers* (2005), and *If Only We Had Listened* forgiveness is seen as a divine act, and historical explanations are ignored at the expense of black-and-white rationalizations grounded in good and evil, God and the Devil. These documentary films are therefore

Figure 9.1 Forgiveness as a "divine" act. An already convicted perpetrator is forgiven by a white Christian woman whom he has never met before in *Hunting My Husband's Killers* (2005), one of several Christian reconciliation films on the Rwandan genocide

part of the fight for Christian souls between different Evangelical denominations and the Catholic Church, both in Rwanda where the Catholic Church has lost followers because of the Church's involvement in the genocide, as well as in the US where audiences are made up of Evangelical and Catholic denominations.[6]

This black-and-white rationalization is part of the narrative in *As We Forgive*, as one of the perpetrators claims that "The Devil did it," which in turn is reflected in a review in the conservative *National Review* that highlights this particular dualistic perspective, "What touched me was the unexpected beauty of forgiveness, the victory of love over evil, the bursting of light into darkness."[7]

To achieve this "divine" forgiveness, *As We Forgive* uses, among other techniques, interviews and reenactments, in order to build towards "the film's tension-filled climax" according to Waters Hinson, where Chantale meets her father's murderer.[8] However, this is obviously a staged meeting which has been forced on Chantale, as she refuses to forgive the murderer, and yet he is "revealed" and plans to visit her once a week! One could question the uniqueness of this event as, for instance, Water Hinson uses individuals, in this case a perpetrator named Pascal, who is also featured in *Wounded Healers* where he reenacts the same "role." This rehashing of the Rwandan victim/perpetrator pairing is not uncommon in the reconciliation documentary and occurs, for example, in *Rwanda: Living Forgiveness* and *Rwanda: Do Scars Ever Fade?* Another example is the series of particularly blue-eyed short films that Peace Works Travel produced: *Playing a Part* (2014), *I Am Kizito* (2014), *The Rhythm of Healing* (2014), *Children of the Genocide* (2014), and *Cut the Tall Trees: The Killing Power of Words* (2014).

The relationship between the success of the forgiveness theme and the grim history of the Rwandan genocide is complex. Some documentaries, such as *Flower in the Gun Barrel* (2008), narrated by Hollywood actor Martin Sheen, rely heavily on the official historical media memory with colonial explanations, while others, *Reconciling Rwanda* (2007), *Rwanda: Hope Rises* (2009), *The Courage of Neighbors: Stories from the Rwandan Genocide* (2010), and *Let the Devil Sleep* (2014), rely on approved Rwandan information, verging on propaganda, as can be detected by the participation of Rwandan officials in the film, most notably President Paul Kagame, or in that the victims talk about "my fellow Rwandans" instead of Hutus and Tutsis. In the German *My Globe is Broken in Ruanda* (*My Globe is Broken in Rwanda*, 2010) it is even claimed that the words Hutu and Tutsi have been erased from the official Rwandan language, Kinyarwanda. Hence, the explanations for the outbreak of genocidal violence become simplified, whether they come in the guise of dualistic spiritualized accounts and rationalizations or whether they are channeled through the official historical media memory. In any case, forgiveness becomes a *fait accompli*, that is, the long and hard process for victims to actually forgive perpetrators, who have raped, tortured, and killed family members, and for perpetrators to confess and ask for forgiveness, is something that the filmmakers only get in hindsight as it has already happened long before they arrived in Rwanda.

American Phillip A. Cantrell II, who specializes in East Central African history, admits that *As We Forgive* is "emotional and inspiring," and that the Anglican Church is paramount to promoting "reconciliation through the lens of Christian love and forgiveness." However, the message of Christian reconciliation and the act of divine forgiveness dims any "criticism leveled at the Gacaca court system." For instance, Cantrell II points to the fact that the Gacaca courts did not provide a forum for "those victimized by RPF and Tutsi crimes against Hutus."[9] Since *As We Forgive*—and many other reconciliation documentaries focusing on survivors without being overtly religious, such as *Flores de Ruanda* (*Flowers of Rwanda*, 2008), *Rwanda, je me souviens* ("Rwanda, I Remember," 2009), *You Must Be Something* (2010), *Sydämeni taakka* (*Burden of My Heart*, 2011), *When I Was Young I Said I Would Be Happy* (2014), *Coexist* (2014), and *Unversöhnt* (*Unforgiven*, 2014), to name a few—never touches upon this subject, there is an imbalance in the forgiveness and reconciliation processes. To use Cantrell II's words:

> *As We Forgive* can also be placed within a larger narrative meant for the outside world about post-genocide Rwanda. Promoted by the ruling party and endorsed by most in the church apparatus, this narrative posits Rwanda as a model of reconciliation and unity under the auspices of its post-genocide government, yet with little historical balance and framework.[10]

A similar critique can be aimed at *In the Tall Grass: Inside Gacaca*, a reconciliation documentary that vividly employs emblematic images and focuses on a Gacaca trial initiated by a Rwandan woman, whose husband and four children were killed during the genocide. *In the Tall Grass* is widely circulated as educational media and hailed as a "powerful film" that is recommended "to both academic and public libraries for a human perspective on the genocide."[11] However, film scholar John J. Michalczyk sees things differently, posing the question of whether the Gacaca court system as shown in the film can work, "when killers threaten a victim's family or show no remorse."[12] Michalczyk quotes a prosecutor at the ICTR, Christopher J. Mon, who maintains that the system is fraught with inadequacies: "Ultimately, then, the *gacaca* courts likely will be unable to achieve their stated goals of psychologically rebuilding Rwanda, establishing a historical record of the genocide, avoiding impunity, showing that justice is being done, and reintegrating hundreds of thousands of perpetrators into their communities without provoking retributive violence."[13]

A minority of the reconciliation documentaries expose this criticism in various ways within the narrative. One example is *Rwanda, les collines parlent* (*Rwanda: The Hills Speak Out*, 2006) in which Belgian director Bernard Bellefroid interviews perpetrators and victims before and after the first Gacaca trials in 2005. The focus is on three perpetrators who show no remorse and who even use the Gacaca as a cynical strategy to be released, thus invoking a culture of impunity. The image of the Gacaca is also undermined in the film by the fact that several members of the preceding court are themselves accused. In this way *Rwanda: The Hills Speak* weaves a portrait of a society still at war with the ever-present ideology of genocide, thus undermining the ideal image of the Gacaca.

The most renowned of the reconciliation documentaries is French-American documentary filmmaker Anne Aghion's acclaimed Gacaca trilogy, *Gacaca: Living Together Again in Rwanda?*, *Au Rwanda on dit . . . La familie qui ne parle pas meurt* (*In Rwanda We Say . . . The Family That Does Not Speak Dies*, 2004)—awarded an Emmy in 2005—and *Les Cahiers de la Mémoire* (*The Notebooks of Memory*, 2009). In addition, a feature-length documentary, *Mon tueur Mon voisin* (*My Neighbor, My Killer*), covering the whole period of the trilogy, was released in 2009.

The Gacaca court system was a result of the Rwandan government trying to re-establish the traditional grassroots community of the Gacaca in order to relieve pressure on the ordinary courts that had approximately 130,000 suspected *génocidaires* awaiting trial in prison. Consolidating in 2004 and being fully operational between 2005 and 2012, 12,103 Gacaca Courts tried 1.2 million cases throughout the country.[14] The Gacaca court system had five goals: (1) establish the truth about what happened; (2) accelerate the legal proceedings for those accused of genocide crimes; (3) eradicate the culture of impunity; (4) reconcile Rwandans and reinforce their unity; and (5) use the capacities of Rwandan society to deal with its problems through a justice based on Rwandan custom.[15] Out of these five goals, goal number four—to reconcile Rwandans and reinforce their unity—constitutes the main, if not the only, theme in the reconciliation documentary, thus leaving out any inconveniences with the purpose of establishing the success of the reconciliation process in the narrative.

Conversely, political anthropologist Bert Ingelaere points to three thought-provoking discrepancies in the Gacaca court system. First, that "the difference between the old and the new Gacaca is not one of degree but a difference in kind." The new Gacaca was installed by the state with specific rules, while the traditional Gacaca "was much more straightforward in its functioning and objective. The idea was to bring people together, talk about the problem or conflict in order to restore harmonious relations, and prevent hatred lingering on between families." However, in the new Gacaca court system, the element of reconciliation is no longer at the center of the institution.[16]

Second, initially the *inyagamugayo* (local judges) consisted of "wise and old men," as tradition had it, but soon no less than 26,752 (or 15.7 percent) of the judges "had to be replaced because they were accused in the Gacaca themselves." They were replaced by women, younger people, and genocide survivors, thus undermining the tradition. Furthermore, the Gacaca courts often consisted of a mix of survivors (Tutsi) and so-called non-survivors (Hutu), and according to Ingelaere the ethnic composition of the court was "seen as a means to get a viewpoint passed."[17]

Third, the Gacaca court system is "a form of unpopular participatory justice. Attendance is compulsory. The large crowds that attend are physically present but psychologically absent or unsupportive of the activities."[18]

Although Aghion adopts an observational fly-on-the-wall style of documentary filmmaking, the Gacaca trilogy is far from neutral in its approach to the reconciliation process. Aghion filmed periodically for nearly ten years in the small hillside community of Gafumba in Northern Rwanda, collecting a huge amount of material which then was edited to tell the story of the Gacaca processes in Rwanda for the outside world. And it is not a straightforward success story that Aghion delivers.

The first film, *Gacaca: Living Together Again in Rwanda?*, details the preparations for the introduction of the Gacaca system. Instead of the usual introduction of the official historical media memory, supported by interviews with Rwandan officials, audiences get to follow two stories simultaneously. On the one hand, Aghion gives voice to the alleged perpetrators, showing the dire conditions of the prisons and lengthy interrogations with the prisoners, as well as shooting interviews with the accused killers. On the other hand, the focus is also on the survivors and their often outright rejection of the Gacaca system as they try to wrap their heads around the reality that tens of thousands of these killers are to be released. The traditional idea of Gacaca—that is, to bring people together to talk about problems in order to prevent hatred—seems remote as Aghion lays bare the lingering mistrust between the two ethnic groups as well as the seeming randomness of the local proto-Gacaca trials in Gafumba with indeterminate witnesses and swift trial procedures. In this way, Aghion does not only question the fourth goal of the Gacaca system, to reconcile Rwandans and reinforce their unity, but she also succeeds in obtaining a certain degree of perceived objectivity. However, this objectivity comes at a price since the editing comes off as arbitrary, or as the reviewer in *Time Out* puts it: "Powerful material, of course, but it's stitched [sic] together with no very apparent organising principle."[19] In other words, to achieve "documentary objectivity" by just presenting the unaltered testimonies and the procedures at a few of the proto-trials, Aghion loses track of what these experiences and events signify on a political and a historical level, at least for audiences with no prior knowledge.

Figure 9.2 Rwandans preparing for Gacaca in *Gacaca: Living Together Again in Rwanda?* (2002)

The process is simply left unexplained, thus leaving plenty of room for interpretation.

This interpretative vacuum becomes apparent, for example, in *Variety*'s review which dwells on irrelevant details, while centering in on the violence: "Rwanda is renowned for its beauty: Even the mass graveyards and sites of wholesale slayings look green and peaceful. The lush pastoral scenery forms an incongruous backdrop to tales of unthinkable atrocities as the survivors, mainly women (the prisoners are mainly men) relate how their entire families were exterminated."[20] Once again, the inexplicable violence (seemingly even more so in such a beautiful environment) becomes the outcome as a *fait accompli* due to Aghion's stylistic choices.

The follow-up film, *In Rwanda We Say . . . The Family That Does Not Speak Dies*, opens in January 2003 when President Paul Kagame announced that 16,000 *génocidaires*—who had confessed their crimes in terms appropriate to the upcoming Gacaca process, and who had already served the maximum sentence—were provisionally to be released back to their communities. Set in the same hillside community as in the first film, Gafumba, the film mainly focuses on one of the prisoners who featured in the first film, Abraham Rwamfizi, and consequently on the process of accepting his presence as a murderer among his close neighbors.

As the Gacaca trials are yet to be properly implemented, the narrative in this second documentary film becomes scattered, especially in relation to the five goals of the Gacaca court system that Ingelaere highlighted. First, the delays of the actual court proceedings in combination with the release of already punished Hutu perpetrators does not accelerate the legal proceedings in an acceptable way—for the Tutsis anyway—thus undermining the reconciliations process. However, what is most poignant about *In Rwanda We Say . . .* is the collapse of the first goal—to establish the truth about what happened—as the film gives voice to the deep-rooted suspicion among the Tutsi towards this governmentally forced development. In interviews with victims and survivors, they express fear and resentment: "our killers have returned"; "let them take what's left of me"; "we don't have the stamina for vengeance"; "they outnumber us"; and "they don't even bother to ask for forgiveness." This, in combination with the fact that the main character, Rwamfizi, avoids speaking clearly about what happened, as it would incriminate him, creates a hesitation around the reconciliation process in Aghion's film. One of the reasons for this is that Aghion moves from taking a supposedly objective fly-on-the-wall approach in the first film to a more interactive mode because the villagers asked Aghion to bring them together. Aghion then decided to become more personally involved, unlike in the first film where "she remained at a distance and was more unobtrusive."[21] In other words, while this more interactive mode still keeps audiences away from a historical truth of what actually happened, at the same time it brings the same audiences close to the real fears and concerns present in Rwanda as the ten-year commemoration approached. As cultural studies scholar Roger Bromley puts it: "One of the great strengths of the film is that it enables this pain to be articulated without, as in some of the other films produced, trying to make a simplistic claim about healing."[22]

The reviewer in *Variety* is, in accordance with this, also confused by *In Rwanda We Say . . .*, as the documentary "unfortunately cannot tie things up for a dramatically satisfying ending. No real justice is administered, no trial is held, no verdict given, and the remaining Tutsis are left so much poorer and alone."[23] As in the first film, *Gacaca: Living Together Again in Rwanda?*, the narrative thus seems to become almost too objective, especially in relation to a historical truth that is never delivered.

Finally, the third film in the Gacaca trilogy, *The Notebooks of Memory*, shot over three years, focuses on the actual Gacaca trials themselves, and in particular the case against Léonard Kanyamugara, the older brother of Rwamfizi and one of the local leaders of the genocide in Gafumba. If *In Rwanda We Say . . .* switched to an interactive mode, *The Notebooks of Memory* firmly returns to the observational and supposedly objective mode of the first film in the trilogy. Aghion therefore, once again, leaves audiences with little historical explanation, but gives them many images of lush Rwandan hillsides, and a camera that observes the trials, often from a distance. From an outside perspective, the proceedings therefore become somewhat incomprehensible since the organization, the testimonies, and the judgments appear to be random, mostly given the fact that audiences are not given enough historical context to be able to interpret what is happening.

Consequently, words like exoticism and orientalism come to mind, but that is perhaps a rather unfair accusation given the time and effort put into this thirteen-year project. However, these are not run-of-the-mill reconciliation documentaries. Instead, they most definitely belong to the canon of films on the Rwandan genocide.[24] They are also framed and marketed as educational films in a way that separates them from other reconciliation documentaries, primarily aimed at "researchers, students and specialists who are drawn to the anthropological and historical value of this work."[25]

While Dauge-Roth has pointed out that Aghion's documentary films have shown that "Kagame's primary concern was not the fate of the direct victims and survivors of the genocide," Bromley is more suspicious as he suspects that the RPF's narrative has influenced these documentary films insofar as the themes of national unity, ethnicity, and divisionism have been adjusted according to the RPF's politics.[26] However, the fact of the matter is that Aghion's trilogy does expose the Gacaca court system to criticism, but it is a criticism that is formulated solely via its "objective" and observational mode, laying bare the apparent shortcomings of the Gacaca court system in relation to its five official goals, most clearly the goal to reconcile Rwanda and reinforce national unity.

Yet again, the canonization of the trilogy and its educational purposes stand in stark contrast to Aghion's aesthetic choices since these films come without the necessary historical explanations. Audiences are therefore dependent on prior knowledge of the Rwandan genocide and its aftermath in order to fully grasp the intricate proceedings that concern the Gacaca trials and their surrounding context. This historical absence could thus be precarious since the "objective" and observational mode leaves the field open for varied interpretations—of the origin and the execution of the genocide, of the political purposes of the Gacacas, and not least how Western audiences are supposed to understand the often-complete randomness of the judgments delivered in the Gacaca trials, as portrayed in Aghion's overtly "objective" Gacaca trilogy.

One final reconciliation documentary that shows the shortcomings of the reconciliation process, rather than portraying it as an uncritical success, is the rarely noticed *Life after Death* (2014) by American independent filmmaker Joe Callander. *Life after Death* is a documentary which follows the twenty-something-year-old young man Kwasa and his friend Flis, who grew up as street children in Kigali in the aftermath of the genocide. The film is produced by Saddleback Leather Company and Love 41, sister companies owned and operated by American husband and wife team Dave and Suzette Munson. While the former company is a commercial leather manufacturer located in Texas, the latter is a Christian Evangelical charity organization that focuses its charity work on financing day care centers for children, Women's Center Vocational Schools, and child sponsorship for orphans and street children in Rwanda.[27] However, unlike the subgenre of Christian documentaries discussed above in which different Evangelical denominations and the Catholic Church fought over Christian souls in Rwanda, *Life after Death* is primarily produced to promote Saddleback Leather and Love 41 rather than to spread the word of the Bible.

Joe Callander functioned as the filmmaker in residence for Saddleback Leather and Love 41 for a couple of years, directing ads and shorts for both companies. This work took him to Rwanda, where he filmed two shorts, *Tina Delivers a Goat* (2013) and *Tim and Susan Have Matching Handguns* (2013), where the former got a nod on twitter by renowned documentary filmmaker Joshua Oppenheimer, director of the Oscar nominated *The Act of Killing* (2012), while the latter was nominated for best short documentary at the Sundance Film Festival.[28]

Life after Death was filmed during three trips to Rwanda on Love 41 business. Callander was then left to his own devices to portray the evangelistic relationship between the sponsored subject Kwasa and the sponsors Dave and Suzette Munson.[29] However, although this "evangelical relationship" is part of the documentary it never overtakes the portrayal of Kwasa. Rather, the evangelical relationship with its colonial implications is used as a juxtaposition between a white savior complex and the actual hardships of Kwasa's everyday struggles to get by and to handle a very troubled juvenescence due to the history of the genocide.

Callander employs an observational fly-on-the-wall mode in order to observe Kwasa's lived experience seemingly spontaneously. Yet, it is evident that Kwasa and the other participants are well aware of the camera, and that "spontaneous" situations in which Kwasa hangs out with Flis or in which Suzette is trying to talk sense to him are staged or at least arranged. Initially, the composition of the film seems to be for the benefit of Love 41 in order to highlight the Christian deeds of the Munsons in a sort of self-promotional endeavor. However, this dual perspective, this juxtaposition, gives way to a closer understanding of Kwasa as his problematic backstory is gradually revealed. During this process, the Munsons' intentions, as the de facto producers, tend to diminish and the complex history of the genocide and its aftermath shines through.

Kwasa is presented as "difficult," that is he is unable to keep the menial jobs he is offered, he is committing crimes, and he has a drinking problem. His situation is then cross-cut with images from the Munsons' comfortable home in San Antonio, Texas, as they are having an online conversation with Kwasa, who calls them his "American parents." In the next scene, Suzette is visiting Kigali, where she takes Kwasa to the dentist, arranges for him to rent a room, and is

Figure 9.3 Kwasa and his "American mommy," Suzette Munson, in *Life after Death* (2014)

called "Mommy," thus peddling the white savior's theme. This angle, however, is gradually turned on its head.

While there is no question that Kwasa and Flis have grown up on the streets as a direct result of the genocide, their ethnic identity is never explicitly mentioned in *Life after Death*. Because of audiences' preconceptions and knowledge of the genocide, we are expected to think of them as Tutsi survivors, and this is supported by a dark testimony that Kwasa gives in the film as he tells the story of how his mother was impaled on an underwater spear trap as she tripped and fell into a river as she fled the genocide with Kwasa on her shoulders. This is then cross-cut with another scene filmed in Texas, this time portraying Tim and Susan, supporters of Love 41, who discuss and mourn Kwasa's awful story—"I can't image that"—taking pity on him as yet another set of American parents. A little later in the film, we get another clue as to this ethnic division as we find out, via a conversation with his sister, that Kwasa's father is in prison for having killed people during the genocide, and that he received a much longer sentence because "the neighbors took bribes to testify against him." It thus transpires that Kwasa's family is in fact Hutu and not Tutsi, the presumed victims of the genocide, and that Kwasa has used this ethnic expectation in order to secure advantages from his American parents who, during the running time of the film at least, seem to be oblivious to the tensions between Hutus and Tutsis, and that they, as a result of this ignorance, are incapable of grasping the full meaning of this division still present in Rwanda.[30]

After these revelations, Callander continues to dig deeper. Following a scene in which Kwasa and Flis kill and eat a chicken in front of the camera—breaking the fourth wall as Kwasa tell Flis: "Don't look at the camera, you idiot" and "White people don't eat the bones, don't embarrass me"—Kwasa confesses that he used to "spill a lot of blood when I was on the street, but I don't want to kill anymore," thus implying that he has killed people as an adolescent in order to survive on the streets of Kigali. This scene is followed by another in which we learn that Kwasa's mother was not impaled on a spear trap but that in fact she died of cholera in a refugee camp in Zaire, as approximately 50,000 Hutus did during their exodus into their neighboring countries in the aftermath of the genocide.[31] It is a fellow refugee and female acquaintance of the mother, who has occasionally taken care of Kwasa and Flis, who gives the details about the mother and lets us know that the boys "were eating dog, whatever they could find. It didn't matter," as street children.

This virtual transformation of Kwasa (and most of the people surrounding him in *Life after Death*) from a presumed Tutsi survivor into a Hutu survivor puts pressure on and even questions the official historical media memory of the genocide, where the stark division between Tutsi survivors and Hutu perpetrators has constituted the norm, both in most of the films discussed here as well as in Rwandan society, leaving little room for an anomaly such as a Hutu child survivor. The fact that Kwasa exploits this ethnic division is, first, a grim confirmation of the impact that the transnational historical media memory has had—especially in relation to how the West, here embodied by the "American parents," has remembered the Rwandan genocide. Second, this revealing upside-down perspective lays bare the problems with national unity and national identity present in Rwanda. The use of the idiom "Rwandan" appears superficial since it cannot even be applied to the young people in society who lived through the genocide and its aftermath on the "wrong" ethnic side. In this sense and through the fact that *Life after Death* quite subtly deals with Hutu survivors, the film is on the verge of being perceived as revisionist because of how it questions the historical media memory and thus the national identity.

In light of this upside-down perspective on the genocide, the evangelical efforts of the "American parents" to save Kwasa and his soul become ill-informed and unqualified. Kwasa, who obviously suffers from mental health problems such as PTSD, is for example constantly lectured by his "American mother" Suzette not to use his cell phone for sexual purposes and to keep away from a girlfriend who is "not good" for him; that is, to practice the form of sexual abstinence that is part of the Evangelical counsels. Due to the performative development of the film, the overlapping colonial and missionary incentives stand in stark contrast to Kwasa's lived reality, and in the process this highlights the distance between well-intentioned Westerners and a Hutu survivor where both adapt their actions according to the official historical media memory of the genocide.

Towards the end of the film, Dave Munson turns up in Rwanda, trying to convince Kwasa to become a carpenter ("as Jesus") by making chess pieces, but Kwasa turns him down, claiming that he "can find a better job than this." The film ends with the intercutting of two emblematic images, "Bloated Corpses in the River" and "The Man with a Machete," with a depressed Kwasa walking in slow motion, presumably with the intent to illustrate the weight of memories that Kwasa carries with him. Of course, this use of emblematic images is quite paradoxical since they depict the genocide against the Tutsi, thus upholding the dichotomy between Tutsi victims and Hutu perpetrators.

The few reviews available of *Life after Death* completely miss the subtle portrayal of ethnicities and how these are connected to the memory of the genocide. Instead, the focus is on Kwasa as an individual and the question of whether he is simply "exploiting the kindness of others for his own personal gain."[32] The reviewer in *Cinema Axis*, Courtney Small, even takes a strictly Western interpretative perspective when he writes, "Frankly, it is questionable if Kwasa is even capable of changing based on the circumstances he lives in. The film hardly touches on the numerous factors that would be needed to truly evoke positive change. We are simply left to feel good that there are individuals like Suzette and Dave, as well as sponsors such as Suzanne and Tim, who are willing to do their part."[33]

10

Historical Revisionism and Historical Negationism

While a film like *Life after Death* problematizes the official historical media memory and thus the creation of national identity in Rwanda, a handful of documentaries and a television series go further and tip over the edge, landing in a gray area where they can be perceived as revisionist.

Historical revisionism is often associated with the Holocaust, more specifically with Holocaust denial.[1] While Holocaust denial certainly can be positioned within a black-or-white area, historical revisionism in general falls more within a gray area. French historian Henry Rousso coined the term "Historical negationism" in a study of the Vichy regime in order to be able to distinguish between historical revisionism and plain denial. He argues that the former usually refers to "a normal phase in the evolution of historical scholarship," while denial of the Holocaust, "is a system of thought, an ideology, and not a scientific or even critical approach of the subject."[2]

As described in Chapter 3, a few documentaries produced in the aftermath of the genocide, for instance *Hand of God, Hand of the Devil* (1995), *Chronicle of a Genocide Foretold* (1996), and *Blodsarvet* (1995), with their strong focus on "innocent" Hutu refugees and Hutu prisoners as "equal" victims, paved the way for an alternative historical media memory of the genocide against the Tutsi—that of the double genocide. This early approach had logistical reasons since the refugees were easier for journalists to access at that time, but as this study overwhelmingly has demonstrated, this alternative perspective was not developed in film and television. The alternative or rather revisionist historical memory of a double genocide was instead foremost upheld by Hutu rebel groups such as Democratic Forces for the Liberation of Rwanda (FDLR),[3] and it would take some twenty years before a type of historical negationism entered media production on the genocide, partly based on the theory of the double genocide.

The theory of the "double genoIide" is that the Tutsi minority, led by the RPF, carried out a so-called counter-genocide on the Hutu majority group during and directly after the recognized genocide against the Tutsi between April and July 1994, which was followed by military action against refugee camps across the border in Zaire in 1995–1996.[4] In 2009, two American political scientists, Christian Davenport and Allan C. Stam, also claimed that the majority of the dead were Hutus rather than Tutsis and that "among other things, it appears that there simply weren't enough Tutsi in Rwanda at the time to account for all the reported deaths,"[5] which are usually reported to have been between 500,000 and 1 million.

However, the theory that the RPF's retaliatory actions would have turned into a legitimate genocide is strongly contested.[6] The RPF admits that some retaliatory actions were carried out and that the perpetrators have been punished, but what further complicates the whole situation is that Rwanda's legislation prohibits "genocide denial" and thus an open discussion of what took place, and that the number of victims that the RPF admits to is only one-tenth of what is sometimes estimated.[7] American political scientist Scott Straus emphasizes that the violence against Hutus was organized in a completely different way than the genocide against the Tutsi. The intention to "destroy" an entire population group was not there, but the motive for what he calls a "mass categorical violence"—large-scale, long-term, group-selective violence against civilians—had the aim of controlling and punishing the Hutu population, not completely eliminating them.[8] Nonetheless, in the First Congo War massacres of Hutu refugees were carried out by the Alliance des Forces Démocratiques pour la Libération du Congo-Zaïre (AFDL), an alliance backed by Rwanda. The death toll for these massacres of both Congolese and Rwandan Hutus varies greatly, depending on who you are talking to, but it is estimated to have been between 10,000 and 200,000.[9]

Evidently, the theory of a double genocide is a complex mixture where RPF retaliation and repression is used to obscure the genocide against the Tutsi. It is thus, according to Rousso, a type of historical revisionism that tends to slip over into historical negationism and even denial. The complexity lies in the fact that the RPF committed transgressions, although it is unclear to what extent, and the ongoing discussion of this could be placed within a normal phase in the evolution of historical scholarship. However, when this discussion is set against the actual genocide against the Tutsi, it tends to diminish the genocide, or in some cases even denies it. Consequently, filmmakers who in different ways deal with the double genocide theory must tread a thin line between historical revisionism and historical negationism.

Three documentaries that balance on this thin line are *D'Arusha à Arusha* (*From Arusha to Arusha*, 2008), the short film *Fractured Lives: The Aftermath of the Rwandan Genocide* (2012), and the already mentioned *The Arrows of Truth* (2018). The title, *From Arusha to Arusha*, directed by French-Canadian filmmaker Christophe Gargot, alludes to an imaginary journey from the peace agreement made in Arusha in 1993, to the ICTR trials in the same Tanzanian city in 2007 and 2008. In the filmography which accompanies the research anthology *The Rwandan Genocide on Film*, which contains the only mention of this film in the scholarship on the Rwandan genocide and media, this documentary is neutrally described as a "[d]ocumentary with archival footage from the International Criminal Tribunal for Rwanda (ICTR), as well as original interviews."[10] However, on the National Film Board of Canada's homepage, the documentary is described as one which "presents conflicting points of view and invites the Rwandan people to re-appropriate their own history."[11] It is these "conflicting views" that are in focus in *From Arusha to Arusha*.

The bulk of the documentary consists of original recordings from the trials in Arusha, and the film revolves around two high-profile perpetrators, accused of genocide, Théoneste Bagosora and Georges Ruggiu, who were sentenced to life imprisonment and twelve years in prison, respectively. Bagosora has been pointed out as the chief orchestrator of the genocide, while Belgian-Italian Ruggiu was a radio presenter who worked for Rwandan radio station RTLM, which had a substantial role as it promoted the genocide against the Tutsi before and during the genocide.[12] These trial recordings are coupled with interviews with a few average Rwandans as well as with Laurien Ntezimana, a Rwandan Catholic theologian and peace activist who protected Tutsis during the genocide.

The documentary begins with three short information texts, which give the impression of a recapitulation of the official history of Rwanda and what led up to the genocide, as in so many other documentaries on the genocide against the Tutsi. However, these texts are far from neutral, and the first one reads: "In 1919, Belgium colonized Rwanda with the support of the reigning Tutsi royal family." The problems with this description are plentiful. First, Belgium took control over Rwanda in 1916, and it was Germany that colonized Rwanda in 1894. Second, the suggestion that Belgium colonized Rwanda with the support of the Tutsi royal family is a highly problematic claim, as the acceptance in that statement puts the blame on the Tutsis. The same rhetoric is used in other historical texts, thus highlighting the Tutsi as a group. This is then followed by silent footage from the Murambi genocide memorial site before the filmmaker gives almost four unedited minutes to Bagosora's defense lawyer Raphaël Constant's opening statement in which he points out the fact that seventy-seven Hutus, and no Tutsis, are on trial, thus questioning the objectivity of the ICTR court but also whether a genocide has been committed at all. Unsurprisingly, Constant is on a mission to exonerate his accused client, but since the director, Gargot, wants to complicate the process by highlighting these "conflicting views," he leaves no room for the other side. For instance,

Gargot includes unedited and uncommented-on footage in which Bagosora is allowed to deliberate at length on the difference between genocide and excessive massacres, ending up in a reasoning that places the blame on the RPF and the Tutsis, and in which the Hutu leadership and Hutus in general are transformed into the victims:

> Yes, there have been excessive massacres. But these massacres, in my opinion, weren't planned in advance. I say that because the massacres were not systematic immediately after the attack on the president's plane. On the morning of the 7th, I saw political assassinations and/or score-settling. So, people were targeted. If there had been the plane attack alone, I think the loss of human lives could have stopped there. The anger seemed to pass. But the war and the pressure from the RPF, which set a million people adrift inside the country . . . Those people alarmed the whole population. A government that runs away, in any case, is no longer credible. Countries like France and Belgium sent units to evacuate their citizens. The town was abandoned to chaos. All this to say, the massacres that spread through the country were carried out amid serious unrest, with no political responsibility. But in my view, we were victims of a poor international policy that did not support our actions.

In fact, all the talking heads in *From Arusha to Arusha* are there with the purpose of questioning the fact that the genocide was planned. One of these witnesses

Figure 10.1 The *génocidaire* Théoneste Bagosora at his ICTR trial in *From Arusha to Arusha* (2008)

is Faustin Twagirmungo, of Hutu origin and Chairman of the Republican Democratic Movement (MDR) before the genocide, and the first prime minister in Rwanda after the genocide between 1994 and 1995. Like several other Hutu moderates, Twagirmungo resigned after the Kibeho massacre in April 1995, thus ending up in opposition to the RPF's political fraction.[13] Although Twagirmungo was on the death lists, he claims that he was not aware of any plan. The same goes for an interview with Ntezimana, who likewise claims that there was no plan for the destruction of the Tutsi population. Instead, he claims that the killing happened in several waves, and that this was due to a combination of fear and greed, which he connects to the Rwandan expression, *Irivuz'umwami*, the King's Order, meaning, you obey, or you are executed. By putting these moderate Hutus on "the witness stand" in the film, Gargot creates an impression of objectivity but at the same time he leaves out the fact that they are not objective, since they were both in opposition to the political power of the RPF.

This false objectivity is further strengthened by the intercutting of interviews with average Rwandans, with a special focus on Jean de Dieu, a remorseful Hutu perpetrator who has been released from prison pending a local Gacaca trial. The filmmaker makes a point about the fact de Dieu does not know who Bagosora is, implying that he could not have planned or ordered the genocide. But in 1994, the primary medium in Rwanda was radio, not television, which explains why de Dieu is not familiar with Bagosora's appearance; in addition, Bagosora was—to the general public—an anonymous army colonel. The one politician with whom the average Rwandan was familiar at the time was the president, Juvénal Habyarimana, due to the personal cult that had built up around him.

Another lengthy and one-sided sequence of the court proceedings is dedicated to the shooting down of the president's plane. Through Anne Lacour's distinct editing, this is absolutely linked to the belief that the side which shot down the plane was morally and factually responsible for the outbreak of the genocide. In *From Arusha to Arusha*, this is clarified through Bagosora's testimony and by a long exposition from Bagosora's defense lawyer, Raphaël Constant, who ridicules the investigations into the event, and, in the process, more than indicates that the RPF fired the missile. This is a form of historical negationism which, regardless of which side shot down the plane, ignores the unequivocal fact that the Hutu majority methodically killed the Tutsi minority, thus undermining and, by extension, denying the genocide against the Tutsi.

In addition, on an emotionally rhetorical level, to end the film Gargot uses an asymmetrical comparison between the Hutu de Dieu and the Belgian-Italian Ruggiu in order to point out the legally precarious context of the court's processing. The remorseful de Dieu is sentenced to thirty years in prison by a local

Gacaca court while the equally remorseful Ruggiu is sentenced to twelve years in prison by the ICTR. By comparing their sentencing in this way, Gargot parallels these two completely different court systems, thus undermining the ICTR's credibility. And through the film's strong focus on de Dieu—uneducated, remorseful, an average Rwandan citizen—Gargot also suggests that the handling of the Hutus in general was unjust, as de Dieu's sentencing seems to be awful and disproportionate, that is, in the context of this film.

To sum up, the "conflicting views" that are presented in *From Arusha to Arusha* do not constitute a "normal phase in the evolution of historical scholarship," in line with Rousso's definition; instead these views slide over to historical negationism. This happens mainly because the filmmakers do not give room for the other side as they present a historical media memory whereby both sides committed massacres, thus sustaining the theory of a double genocide. Symptomatically, Gargot includes Constant's lengthy closing argument, where he states, among other things, "What happened in Rwanda remains unanswered."

From Arusha to Arusha has not received a lot of attention and has a low profile in the filmography of the Rwandan genocide. Still, on release it was awarded with several film festival prizes, for example the Georges de Beauregard Prize at the Festival International de Cinéma de Marseille, and the Amnesty International Award at the IndieLisboa International Independent Film Festival.[14] These awards could most likely be attributed to an ignorance about the genocide against the Tutsi in the West, where even a *génocidaires* like Bagosora could be attributed credibility; probably because he was as unknown to audiences in the West as he was to de Dieu.

Two other equally as unknown films are *Fractured Lives: The Aftermath of the Rwandan Genocide* and *The Arrows of Truth*. *Fractured Lives* is a short still photo essay produced for International Alert, an independent international peacebuilding organization—financed by among other organizations, USAID and Swedish SIDA—which treads the line of historical negationism. The film works as an advertisement for the Dialogue Club, set up by International Alert in order to reconcile Rwandans. However, the film is obviously not aimed at Rwandans, but instead at international contributors, with the objective of receiving financial support.

As with so many of these reconciliation documentaries, *Fractured Lives* starts with a brief historical recollection of the genocide in 1994, followed by a few witness statements from Tutsi survivors claiming to have benefited from the Dialogue Club in order to reconcile with their former perpetrators. However, a few minutes in and these testimonies switch over to Hutu survivors, for instance: "After the genocide war ended, I suffered from grinding poverty and a sense of isolation, being Hutu. I was deeply depressed" (Esperance, survivor).

In itself, this statement is not a problem, were it not for the fact that nine out of the ten following Hutu testimonies portray perpetrators and ex-combatants as innocent, for instance: "I was falsely accused of being part of the killings and hauled into jail without trial. After seven torturous years, I was set free" (Jean-Marie, ex-prisoner). These statements are then concluded by assertions that the Hutu survivors in turn have benefited from the Dialogue Club in order to reconcile with their accusers.

Due to the historical ignorance of the filmmakers and their potential supporters, this approach creates an upside-down view of the genocide, as the overwhelming concentration on innocent Hutu perpetrators and ex-combatants produces an imbalance in the narrative that, although incidentally, tends to support the theory of a double genocide. Audiences with no previous knowledge of the genocide thereby risk receiving an uninformed impression of the genocide since the film diminishes the fact that the genocide was committed against the Tutsi.

The Arrows of Truth is a longer version of the previously discussed documentary *Justice Seekers*, directed by Antonio Rui Ribeiro. Unlike *Justice Seekers*, this film has not been given airtime or distribution. This is probably because *The Arrows of Truth* presents a more complex narrative of the genocide. While *Justice Seekers* upholds the official historical media memory of the genocide, primarily dealing with French complicity in the genocide as it concentrates on Franco-Rwandan couple Alain and Dafroza Gauthier and their quest to bring Pascal Simbikangwa to justice, *The Arrows of Truth* incorporates Simbikangwa's story as well, thus problematizing the notion of what happened in Rwanda in 1994.

In a long and exhaustive interview included in the anthology *The Rwandan Genocide on Film*, Ribeiro is very clear about the fact that a genocide against the Tutsi took place. Nevertheless, when gathering material to produce *Justice Seekers*, he also wanted to engage with one of the perpetrators, but the production company, Al Jazeera, only wanted the Gauthier story.[15] The other side of the story—that is, the Hutu side of the story—was therefore saved and then presented alongside the official history in *The Arrows of Truth*. In a sense, this creates a journalistic balance and is in line with Rousso's definition of historical revisionism as an ongoing discussion of what happened, but the mere fact that people in the film question what really happened makes this film tread the thin line of historical negationism. For instance, Belgian researcher Filip Reyntjens, an international expert on the Great Lakes region of Africa and a fierce critic of Kagame, takes part in *The Arrows of Truth* and challenges Gauthier's story as being too easy and simplistic. However, he was edited out of *Justice Seekers*, in which the official historical media memory was maintained. Another example is the focus on Simbikangwa, who only appears in still images throughout the film, and near the end, on the soundtrack, but who still is humanized with a personal history, among other things by an intimate interview with his sister, Monica Uwizungemariya.

The reason for the differences between the two films is, according to Ribeiro, that *Justice Seekers*, missed "out a huge element, which is that the current regime in Kigali isn't all that we are led to believe, and it misses out the fact that there were huge crimes being committed alongside the genocide."[16] Although Ribeiro does not specifically summon the theory of the double genocide, the fact that he brings up RPF atrocities—for example, the butchering of civilians—as a hidden history alongside that of the recognized genocide has the effect that audiences certainly interpret the history in *The Arrows of Truth* as a double genocide. In the interview, Ribeiro is also quite certain that Paul Kagame ordered the shooting down of the president's plane, which points to Tutsi complicity or even conspiracy.[17]

These three films try, to different degrees, to problematize the history of the genocide in Rwanda in 1994, and in the process they all border on a type of historical negationism that destabilizes the official historical media memory of the genocide against the Tutsi. The theory of a double genocide is lurking in all three films, as RPF atrocities tend to appropriate the official memory at the expense of the recognized genocide. Nevertheless, while *Fractured Lives: The Aftermath of the Rwandan Genocide* and *The Arrows of Truth* clearly recognize the genocide against the Tutsi, *From Arusha to Arusha* questions the genocide, pointing to the fact that massacres were committed on both sides. Moreover, what all three films have in common is that they are relatively unknown since they have not received distribution at any major level, which in part could be explained by their historical revisionism, which is opposed to the official and dominant historical media memory of the genocide in Rwanda.

Rwanda: The Untold Story

A revisionist documentary which received worldwide distribution on the other hand was the BBC's *Rwanda: The Untold Story* (2014). The film aired as part of the This World documentary series on BBC Two on October 1, 2014, and was immediately subject to controversy due to its content and its deviations from the official historical media memory of the Rwandan genocide.

Rwanda: The Untold Story, like for instance *Justice Seekers*, was made for the twentieth commemoration of the genocide, but unlike most documentaries that uphold the official historical media memory of the Rwandan genocide, this documentary tries to negotiate the history of the genocide. The "untold" and thus presumably overlooked component in this story is, once more, RPF atrocities committed before, during, and after the genocide, and as such the documentary becomes a vehicle for the double genocide theory. However, in

Rwanda: The Untold Story this is realized via a primary focus on Paul Kagame and his continuous rule over Rwanda since 1994. The film relentlessly attacks Kagame's leadership, and as the main culprit Rwanda's president becomes a stand-in for both the RPF as well as for the entire Tutsi population. While it certainly falls under the domain of investigative reporting to criticize political leadership, corruption, and repression, it becomes more problematic when these generalizations are exploited to explain the genocide or try to figure out what really happened in Rwanda.

The documentary frames its issue with a short recap, typical of the television documentary format, in which, among other things, the genocide against the Tutsi is questioned ("We think we know the story, but do we?"), and in which the voiceover of reporter Jane Corbin ask the insinuating question "But what kind of man is Paul Kagame?" followed by a soundbite from Filip Reyntjens in which he declares that Kagame is "the most important war criminal in office today." Corbin's preamble is illustrated by the two emblematic images, "Piles of Corpses" and "The Man with a Machete," while Reyntjens's statement is illustrated by "The Nick Hughes Footage." That is, *Rwanda: The Untold Story* exploits archival footage taken during the first week of the genocide showing Hutus killing Tutsis to imply that Kagame, and by extension the RPF and the Tutsi population, were in fact guilty of committing atrocities or even perpetrating a genocide against the Hutus. Regardless of how you frame it, this is a highly unethical use of archival footage that turns the recognized genocide against the Tutsi on its head, particularly as one of the talking heads in the recap explains that Kagame is not just accountable, but that he "enjoys killing his owns citizens." Hence, this revisionist documentary has a lot to prove within its approximately one-hour airtime.

Aside from the recap, *Rwanda: The Untold Story* can be divided into five segments whereby the first segment presents a version of the official historical media memory of the genocide, while the other four segments dispute and pull apart this historical media memory, trying to recreate an "untold truth." Tellingly, in the first segment the official historical media memory is illustrated with, as mentioned, emblematic archival footage but also with images from the feature film *Hotel Rwanda*, which is used as an example of the false memory that has been created about the genocide, especially regarding the trope where the RPF is represented as the organization that stopped the genocide. It is somewhat ironic that *Hotel Rwanda* is used in this way by opponents of Paul Kagame since the RPF and Kagame himself, likewise, despise the film because it positions Paul Rusesabagina as a hero. Nevertheless, due to the status of *Hotel Rwanda* as the quintessential film on the genocide—the film that Western audiences at least know about—it is a well-chosen piece of collective media memory.

However, the factual history that is presented in the introduction of *Rwanda: The Untold Story* is arranged in a way that excludes important parts of the history, for instance the organized massacres of Tutsis in Rwanda before 1994. The intention is to undermine the official historical media memory and to advocate a history where the RPF and the Tutsis are responsible for the outbreak of the genocide. This is accomplished with a rhetoric whereby Tutsis were "favored by history," where the Tutsis that fled to Uganda and other neighboring countries did so out of guilt (and not because they were massacred), and that this then, according to Reyntjens, created a "timebomb," resulting in the guerilla war that started in 1990. Reyntjens then presents what he sees as the sinister intentions of Kagame, as the scholar claims that the only purpose of this war was to allow the RPF to "take power by the bullet." One outcome of the film's negationism vis-à-vis the official historical media memory is that Hutus, throughout history, had been afraid of the Tutsi, which becomes a rationalization whereby the genocide against the Tutsi is justified as self-defense.

What follows then are four segments in which the official historical media memory is not just revised but negotiated, based on the documentary's historical introduction that portrays Kagame and the Tutsis as the bad guys. The first of these segments is about the 1994 plane crash, and here the filmmakers use the same moral logic as we could see in revisionist films such as *From Arusha to Arusha* and *The Arrows of Truths*. That is, the side that shot down the president's plane is morally responsible for triggering the genocide, based on the "logic" that if the plane had not been shot down, the genocide would not have taken place.

The segment is based foremost on interviews with Theogene Rudasingwa, Kagame's former chief of staff, Luc Marchal, Commander of the Belgian UN-troop to Rwanda, and the former RPF Lieutenant-General and chief of staff of the army, Kayumba Nyamwasa, who all claim that Kagame was behind the assassination, but without presenting any actual evidence for this claim that is not plain hearsay.[18] In addition, the filmmakers refer to an investigation conducted by French judge Jean-Louis Bruguière. The report was based on interviews and concluded that the assassination had been ordered by Kagame.[19] In 2006, Bruguière issued arrest warrants for nine of Kagame's aides, including Nyamwasa, with the result that Rwanda broke diplomatic relations with France. What the filmmakers fail to mention is that the Bruguière report is only one of nine different investigations carried out between 1994 and 2012. Four of these reports—among them the so called Mutsinzi report that concluded that the missile was fired by FAR from the Kanombe camp, near the presidential residence—point to Hutu extremists with government and army ties.[20] Two reports indicate that the RPF was behind the assassination, while three international investigations conducted by Belgium, France, and the Organisation of African Unity (OAU), respectively, were inconclusive.[21] By only highlighting the Bruguière report, and ignoring the other eight investigations that existed when the documentary was produced, the filmmakers present a narrow and skewed image of what happened.

It is also of interest how this is presented audiovisually. The segment is mainly illustrated with three kinds of images. First, there is contemporary footage of the reporter Jane Corbin as she walks around the crash site, where debris from the plane still lies around in President Habyarimana's backyard. This provides a feeling of nearness for audiences, but does not in any way provide evidence for the claim. These images were also taken under the false pretense that the film was made in connection to the twentieth commemoration of the genocide.[22] Second, the filmmakers exploit archival footage of Paul Kagame in military uniform, but they run the images in slow motion coupled with ominous music on the soundtrack to clearly pinpoint who the real culprit is. Third, the segment is illustrated with emblematic images such as "Corpses by the Road," "Piles of Corpses," "The Man with a Machete," and "The Nick Hughes Footage." That is, once more images of Hutus killing Tutsis are used to "prove" the opposite.

The second segment is even more problematic as it centers on two American academics, Allan Stam and Christian Davenport, and their claim that the figures of the genocide do not add up. They visited Rwanda in 1998, and ten years later they presented a model with troop movements in Rwanda during

Figure 10.2 BBC reporter Jane Corbin walks around the crash site, where debris from the plane that carried Rwandan President Juvénal Habyarimana still lies around in the backyard of the former presidential residence in *Rwanda: The Untold Story* (2014)

1994 which literally turned the genocide on its head as they claimed that only 200,000 Tutsis had been killed while approximately 800,000 Hutus had been killed by advancing RPF troops and other related causes.[23] This "untold truth" is presented as unabridged evidence with talking head interviews, still images from Rwanda, and a display of scientific-looking statistics of troop movements on a screen as the two academics assert that Kagame and the RPF did not stop the violence but in fact orchestrated it for their own ends. Yet again, the filmmakers exploit emblematic images of dead Tutsis killed by Hutus to drive home this point, but they also use images of refugees. Of course, no competing voices are allowed to counter this rather bold statement, which doubtless transgresses into historical negationism, especially given that the researchers' results have not been accepted for publication.[24] Furthermore, their conclusions go against the research in the field, and even Filip Reyntjens, who participated in the documentary and who is a well-known adversary of Kagame, clearly distances himself from Stam and Davenport's claims in an article that responds to criticism of the documentary.[25]

The third and fourth segments are connected as they concentrate on the period after the genocide, that is, after July 1994. The third segment begins with Corbin's voiceover stating: "The killing did not stop," and then audiences are told the story of the Kibeho massacre where the Rwandan Patriotic Army (RPA) most likely killed between 4,000 and 5,000 returning Hutus in a refugee camp on April 22, 1995,[26] as already described in the documentary *Sitting on a Volcano* that was made in the same year as the massacre. *Rwanda: The Untold Story* then continues to explore the aftermath, which unbeknownst to uninformed audiences slides over to the events of the First Congo War, which in this way becomes a prolongation of the genocide and thus supports the theory of the double genocide. This in turn is maintained by statements from Reyntjens where he concludes, among other things, that: "[the] RPF has committed crimes against humanity and war crimes in a massive scale"; and by an interview with Carla del Ponte, one of the chief prosecutors of the ICTR, who tried to investigate RPF war crimes. In a meeting with Kagame, she claims that he yelled at her: "'How dare you continue madame prosecutor, how dare you persist with these investigations'; He said, 'You are finished being prosecutor'." This scene is illustrated by footage of del Ponte at one of the genocide memorials where she examines the clothes and skulls of what are presumably dead Tutsis, thus invoking the emblematic image of "Skeletons and Clothes." The segment ends with archival footage of refugee camps in Zaire, taken circa 1995/1996, to where around 2 million Hutus had fled, which is coupled with one witness interview with "Marie," a Hutu survivor, while the filmmakers make the double claim that "hundreds of thousands" of refugees were killed in such camps located in Congo and that "The international community knew about the slaughter."

The remark about the international community is the cue for the fourth and final segment, which circles around the question of how it is possible for Kagame to continue his rule over Rwanda, despite the RPF's atrocities, and despite leading a repressive regime with rigged elections. This segment primarily consists of archival footage of Kagame at ceremonies and together with world leaders such as Tony Blair and Bill Clinton, which is complemented with talking head interviews, foremost with Rudasingwa, Nyamwasa, and Reyntjens. Together, these opponents of Kagame make it very clear that Kagame's crimes have been overlooked by Western world leaders, who "see him as a strong leader that prevents further ethnic violence." This endorsement has in turn emboldened Kagame to invade Congo, fix elections, and to continue the repression of ethnic Hutus in Rwanda, despite all the regime's talk about reconciliation—and all while Rwanda continues to receive foreign aid on a massive scale.[27]

Being a BBC production, Tony Blair, who declined to take part in the documentary, is specifically designated as "the British man who actually sided with a dictator," and Reyntjens's statement from the recap is reiterated: "Their [Blair, Clinton, and other world leaders] closeness is a closeness with, what I call, the most important war criminal in office today." In other words, in the final segment the filmmakers turn the spotlight on the leaders of the West, who become collaborators with a repressive regime that is even accused of genocide. In this vein the relationship between Kagame and the West is juxtaposed with other murky relationships between the West and "strong and successful" leaders such as Muammar Gaddafi and Saddam Hussein.

Rwanda: The Untold Story ends with the prediction that Rwanda cannot reconcile without the truth coming out. But as long as genocide ideology governs what Rwanda's citizens are allowed to say and write, trouble will brew like a volcano about to explode in yet another cataclysm of ethnic killings.

The primary objective of this documentary is to discredit Kagame and, in the process, the international community that allows him to continue his repressive rule over Rwanda. While parts of the criticism that concerns RPF repression and civil rights could be deemed as legitimate, as can be observed by international rankings on democracy, freedom, and human rights in which Rwanda persistently appears at the bottom,[28] the parts that question the official historical media memory are more problematic as they literally turn the genocide upside down without any other evidence than the questionable work of Stam and Davenport. The focus instead is on Kagame and the RPF's activities before, during, and after the officially recognized genocide against the Tutsi. Put together, these activities build a narrative whereby Tutsis in general had an already clear objective from 1962, that is, to "take power by the bullet," and whereby they did not even shy away from planning—according to the documentary's interpretation on the assassination of Habyarimana—and committing a genocide against the Hutu population. This of course is a narrative lifted directly from Hutu extremist propaganda before and during the genocide where the elimination of the Tutsi "cockroaches" (*inyenzi* in Kinyarwanda) was described in terms of self-defense.[29] The *raison d'etre* is that the genocide made Kagame, and if the "untold truth" is presented, it would unmake or dethrone him.

The complications with this narrative are multiple. First, the narrative is unambiguously one-sided, as the ethnic cleansing and massacres of Tutsis in 1959–1962, 1973, and 1990 are not even mentioned. In addition, without exception, all the participants in the documentary, especially the former top RPF officials Rudasingwa and Nyamwasa, are adversaries of Kagame and are therefore biased. The other side does not have a say at all, and for obvious reasons Kagame declined to be part of the documentary. Instead, the filmmakers exploit archival footage of Kagame to fill this gap, but this footage is edited, and manipulated audiovisually, to make him appear in a bad light. Furthermore, Rudasingwa and Nyamwasa, who belonged to the RPF elite until 2004 and 2010 respectively, have nothing to say about their own activities or responsibilities as chief of staff to Kagame and chief of staff of the Rwandan Army/Head of Rwandan intelligence in relation to RPF atrocities and the alleged double genocide. According to their uncontested testimonies, everything is Kagame's fault.

Second, the story of RPF atrocities is not new but has played a part (albeit a minor one) in the oeuvre of films on the Rwandan genocide since 1994. What is new is that these atrocities are not related to the recognized genocide against the Tutsi, but instead are interpreted as a genocide in itself. Furthermore, the disputes about these RPF atrocities have always been a part of the international academic discussion on the history of the genocide and therefore are nothing new. However, from the filmmakers' point of view, what they present is probably seen as novel in relation to what they perceive is the official historical media memory of the genocide, especially considering the Western audiences targeted. Hence, that is why the use of *Hotel Rwanda* is significant as it has become a symbol for the official historical media memory of the genocide for general audiences, even though both sides of this historical conflict loathe this particular film. Nonetheless, despite what Corbin claims there is no new evidence presented in *Rwanda: The Untold Story*, but rather a different narrative that, quite ironically, is illustrated with excessive use of emblematic images of dead Tutsis and Hutus killing Tutsis—the opposite of the documentary's narrative. The use of archival footage could be seen as lazy, but in fact it could also be interpreted as plain racist, as black, African bodies are interchangeable according to the logic of the filmmakers.

Rwanda: The Untold Story was met with massive criticism after it aired, foremost by academics. Andrew Wallis, a journalist and researcher specializing in

Central and East Africa, pointed out the fact that the documentary "totally reattributes the historical reality of a genocide in a mere one hour," putting aside twenty years of scholarly research as well as "thousands of witness interviews for the ICTR."[30] Another scholar, Marijke Verpoorten, questioned the documentary's use of Christian Davenport and Allan Stam and their controversial claim that 200,000 Tutsi were killed during the genocide, as this figure was based on a census made in 1952, and not the 1991 census, "thereby seriously compromienocide quality of the extrapolation." Furthermore, in the 1991 census the number of Tutsi was underreported "because the Habyarimana government wanted to minimize the importance of Tutsi in the population."[31] And as mentioned, even Reyntjens disqualified Davenport and Stam's research.

The filmmaker Nick Hughes, who filmed the infamous emblematic images "The Nick Hughes Footage" in 1994, said in an interview that he "was deeply upset" by *Rwanda: The Untold Story*, and that "there is something deeply rotten at the heart of BBC"; comparing it to the unthinkable event of the BBC making a film that denied the Holocaust.[32]

Several articles and editorials in Rwanda's *The New Times* criticized the documentary for not keeping up with editorial standards, wondering why the BBC had engaged a list of "who is who in terms of Rwanda's sworn enemies, criminal convicts, disgruntled political figures and revoked Genocide deniers."[33] The National Commission for the Fight Against Genocide (CNLG) even proposed the theme for the 2015 commemoration to be "about fighting Genocide denial beyond the Rwandan borders," as a direct result of the blatant genocide denial in *Rwanda: The Untold Story*.[34]

Nonetheless, many critics and non-experts of the genocide did notice the controversy but saw it just as another layer in the historical research on the genocide in Rwanda; that is, as a revision of the history rather than as a historical negationism. For instance, Gerard O'Donovan in *The Telegraph* called the film "intense" and "mind boggling" and ended his review with the statement that it was "deeply concerning" that the UK continued to help to keep Kagame in power with foreign aid.[35] In 2016, *Rwanda: The Untold Story* was even used as evidence by the defense at the appeal trial of Pascal Simbikangwa, the convicted war criminal who appeared in *Justice Seekers* and *Arrows of Truth*.[36]

Perhaps unsurprisingly, the BBC defended *Rwanda: The Untold Story*, stating that they "had a duty" to make the film and that "We believe this programme, which was produced by a BBC current affairs team in London and broadcast in the UK, made a valuable contribution to the understanding of the tragic history of the country and the region."[37] Furthermore, a spokeswoman said that the BBC regretted calls for sanctions against the documentary and criticized the "threat of direct measures against an independent broadcaster," describing it as "inappropriate."[38]

These inappropriate measures consisted of Rwanda suspending BBC broadcasts in the Kinyarwanda language with immediate effect because the Rwanda Utilities Regulatory Agency (RURA) had received complaints from the public of incitement, hatred, revisionism, and genocide denial due to the content of the documentary.[39] These complaints consisted of, among other things, an open letter from Ibuka (Rwanda's umbrella association for survivor groups) directed to the Director General of the BBC, in which Ibuka claimed that the documentary "seems intent on reopening our wounds." The letter expressed disappointment with BBC, known for its "reputation for integrity and fairness," and for providing a platform to "politicise the Genocide and deny the planned and systematic killing of over one million people," thus ignoring evidence and research from "local, national and UN court records and from scholars and academics." But above all, Ibuka pointed out the fact that the filmmakers did not reach out "to a single survivor or survivor organization" when researching the documentary.[40]

Rwanda: The Untold Story, although sanctioned and defended by the BBC, had no decisive effect on the official historical media memory of the Rwandan genocide, as no other documentaries followed it that tried to develop the theory of a double genocide. However, a few years later, a television series with even greater international distribution would pick up the theme.

Black Earth Rising

In the spring of 2019, *The New Times*, Rwanda's largest daily newspaper, reported that Netflix's drama series, *Black Earth Rising* (2018), had been criticized by a Rwandan audience on social media for being fictional and misleading. Wilson Misago, a screenwriter and producer at Afrifame Pictures, said it would be better for Rwandans to tell their own stories and share them on different platforms:

> As a Rwandan content creator, I'm sure that we are the ones who are in a better place to tell our own stories. Black Earth Rising, as well as many other films, which were made by the West, about Rwanda, are biased and shallow and they are told in the perspective of the West, which sometimes does not respect our own culture and ownership of our own stories.[41]

Here two aspects of the historical media memory about Rwanda and the genocide against the Tutsi are formulated. First, the perception that Western representations are misleading and superficial, and that this story is stolen from Rwanda and its people. Second, the notion that history can be owned by someone or something, such as a nation. However, history—and especially a genocide with so many international components and repercussions such as the Rwandan genocide—cannot by definition belong to a nation. Nonetheless, *Black Earth Rising* opened the can of worms that is historical revisionism. Therefore, in addition to discussing the television series, here the focus will be on the international reception as well as the Rwandan reception of *Black Earth Rising*. By analyzing the international reception, the divide between what is considered historical revisionism and historical negationism is laid bare, since the international reception displays an example of a historical revision in full swing.

Black Earth Rising is a co-production between BBC Two and Netflix. It revolves around Kate Ashby, a legal investigator with roots in Rwanda who works for the lawyer Michel Ennis in London. When Ashby's adoptive mother takes a case against a Congolese militia leader, a series of events unfolds that take place with the Rwandan genocide as a historical background. During the series, Ashby's identity and thus also the official historical media memory of the genocide are questioned as *Black Earth Rising* concentrates its suspenseful "mystery" around a massacre of Hutu refugees in Zaire, thus blending the final phase of the genocide with the First Congo War. It should be mentioned from the off that *Black Earth Rising* does not concentrate its story on the genocide against the Tutsi or its causes; instead the series relates only to the genocide through a series of imaginative and somewhat abstract animations.

The series is written and directed by Hugo Blick, who made the acclaimed miniseries *The Honorable Woman* (2014), which also deals with a complex subject, the Israel-Palestine conflict. The initial international reception of these historical television series is very similar in that a long line of critics praised the two series from the perspective that these were complex television series on very complex topics.[42]

A common denominator in their reception is that the tribute to their "complexity" did not include a discussion of the historical events portrayed in the two television series. In fact, it seems that the complex narrative with a focus on "relationships and the human psyche" suggests that the spectator "does not have to be politically savvy or overly interested in the conflict."[43] That is, the fact that history serves as a backdrop against which the drama takes place has no consequences for the history portrayed, according to the series' receptions. The artistic freedom thus trumps reality, but nevertheless many of the reviewers emphasize how important these series are in maintaining a historical memory, for example of the Rwandan genocide. In the Danish *Soundvenue*, the reviewer writes that "'Black Earth Rising' is a patient but well-told story about a dark chapter in recent world history,"[44] and in the *Los Angeles Times* it is emphasized that this "exciting but uneven drama tells of the worst genocide in modern history."[45]

The homage to the artistic complexity equals historical truth for most critics, while the subject itself, the Rwandan genocide, guarantees that the story is in line with the truth. In other words, there is a slippage between, on the one hand, a poetic truth and, on the other hand, a historical truth. The poetic truth denotes a human drama that everybody can identify with, that is, that the dramatization in *Black Earth Rising* is so realistically portrayed that it obtains value in itself, but at the same time this fictional reality tends to affect the historical representation.

This poetic perspective only works if the historical portrayal does not relativize a generally accepted historical truth, or alternatively that the historical truth is not sufficiently known for any relativizations to be noticed. While the Israel-Palestine conflict has existed in Western historical consciousness since the UN voted on the partition of Palestine in 1947, the genocide in Rwanda, and not least its aftermath, has at best been on the fringes of the same historical consciousness. It can thus be argued that the historical ignorance among international reviewers is sometimes offset using words such as "complex" and "mysterious."[46]

This historical ignorance of the genocide against the Tutsi in Rwanda thus has the effect that critics often accept the poetic truth as historical reality. *The Sydney Morning Herald*, for example, praised *Black Earth Rising* as an "engrossing limited series [that] shines light on a lot of things," including the "unthinkable atrocities and the protection of their perpetrators."[47] The statement that the perpetrators were protected is in a way not wrong if the reviewer is referring to the vengeful actions that the military part of the RPF carried out in the aftermath of the genocide, when nearly 2 million Hutus fled Rwanda, including the entire Rwandan army and the Interahamwe militia. However, the claim becomes problematic in that it is linked to the genocide in which the main "perpetrators" were solely the latter army and militia. Further, *The Gulf News* in the United Arab Emirates described the genocide as "the worst genocide in modern history," but also called it a "civil war,"[48] which is a problematic term according to the journalist Linda Melvern, also a consultant for the prosecution at the ICTR. Melvern points out that the term "civil war" was used synonymously with "tribal war" during the ongoing genocide in 1994, which resulted in the genocide being dismissed as an internal African matter.[49] In other words, there is a revisionist tone present in the international reception which supports the theory of the double genocide, which could be interpreted as a direct result of historical ignorance coupled with Blick's attempt to complicate the history of the Rwandan genocide.

In Rwanda, much of the public opinion is driven by blogs and bloggers who are sanctioned in various ways, either officially by the government or unofficially, by blog posts being shared on prominent people's social media, thus legitimizing the content. The blogs can be located both in Rwanda and abroad, but the writers are usually Rwandan. One such post was shared by Eric Kabera, CEO of The Kwetu Film Institute. In it, the blogger Jessica Gérondal Mwiza launches a fierce attack on *Black Earth Rising* as a neo-colonial production, characterized by it not being filmed in Rwanda (but in Ghana) and without any Rwandan participation, but also by a "white privilege" whereby Blick assumes the right to "take a traumatic story, change it, deform it and exoticize it" with the sole purpose of "making a lot of money."

> If I seem to write this review in a mocking tone, like many Rwandans I was rather deeply hurt by watching these few hours of revision of the history of the genocide against the Tutsi. This promotion of the infamous double genocide theory is intolerable. There were no "bastards against other bastards," our story is very precise: there are culprits, there are active collaborations, passive collaborations, there are victims. Nothing is vague or mysterious.[50]

Hence, there is only one truth and nothing mysterious, because *Black Earth Rising* "is neither reality nor an acceptable or an excusable fiction." Despite this, this fiction is spread on a massive scale via Netflix, and Gérondal Mwiza concludes her post by rhetorically asking the question of what significance this has for young people who watch the series and then refer to it as Rwanda's history.[51] Another Rwandan blogger believes that Blick does not make "a complex history less complex; instead he trivializes it" by "promot[ing] ambiguity where there is historical clarity: that a genocide against the Tutsi happened is a fact that stands alone without the need to qualify it with the unintelligible 'but' whose use only serves to promote the double genocide theory."[52]

Another critic, Central and East African specialist Laetitia Tran Ngoc, attacks the miniseries' lack of historical context:

> *Black Earth Rising* constantly blurs the boundaries between reality and fiction. This version of Rwanda is governed by a leadership straight out of Blick's imagination, while the chronology is voluntarily left vague [. . .] The alleged crimes of the RPF that inspired the story's biggest twist are not particularly new, contrary to what the show makes it look like. In fact, much of the storyline gives the feeling that Hugo Blick stumbled upon a Wikipedia page about the genocide in Rwanda and, electrified by what he discovered, gave free rein to his imagination.[53]

Evidently, geographical closeness to and historical knowledge of the subject tends to debunk the poetic truth presented in *Black Earth Rising*, a critique that is further fueled by the fact that the television series with its thriller intrigue deviates from the two main genres in which the Rwandan genocide has generally been depicted, namely the factual documentary and the solemn drama.

In a global perspective, Blick's attempt to complicate the history of the Rwandan genocide can be interpreted as a way to avoid criticism, as it is obviously a fiction and not a documentation, while from a Rwandan perspective the same approach becomes a verification that Blick "freed himself from the constraints of reality to enjoy all the liberties fiction can offer, while still presenting its work as a reliable comment on Rwanda's recent history. But artistic freedom is not an absolute right; viewers, on their part, deserve honesty. If an artist chooses to tell the story of others, a little due diligence should be a minimum requirement."[54] In other words, *Black Earth Rising* is opened up to the same kind of criticism that *Hotel Rwanda* has been subjected to in Rwanda, where this quintessential film is seen as a pure falsification of history, shot as it is in South Africa and with fictional characters.[55]

In several interviews, however, Hugo Blick and Michaela Coel, who played the lead role as Kate Ashby, both presented a historical-didactic approach to the series and its content. Coel rhetorically wonders, "Why weren't we taught this at school?"[56] and admits that her participation in *Black Earth Rising* has been an eye-opener. Blick believes that the "unfamiliarity of the story is both the strength of the show and the hill it has to climb":

> Sometimes when you write a project of this size, you absolutely know your destination, you know what you're going to hit. But on this occasion, I found that the destination changed due to both the experience of research, writing and filming [. . .] It takes away this idea that we're there to instruct, which is A: incredibly contentious, on a massive geopolitical scale, but B: just not very true, because so many societies now in Africa don't need to be instructed in the way that we think they do. It is my hope that this drama will open people's eyes, both to the past and to the current situation, which, as the show demonstrates, is not black and white.[57]

Apparently, both Blick and Coel want to draw attention to an overlooked history, but by complicating it they simultaneously create a new story about the Rwandan genocide. What happens then when a historical memory that is repressed or even non-existent is replaced by a newly created (and more exciting) historical memory—not least since *Black Earth Rising* does not to any great extent address the genocide against the Tutsi and its causes other than through rather abstract and non-informative animations? Even though the international reception claims that *Black Earth Rising* is a television series about the Rwandan genocide, the emphasis of the story is undeniably on events that take place after the genocide. This is in line with the celebration of the series' "complex-

Figure 10.3 The use of animations to circumvent the use of real imagery of the genocide against the Tutsi in *Black Earth Rising* (2018)

ity" which did not include any questioning of the historical content, probably because these elements were perceived as poetic truths. In several interviews Blick justified the use of animations to portray the actual genocide:

> The animation reminds viewers that the graphic scenes they've become accustomed to about the Rwandan Genocide are real human beings. Ironically, withholding the real imagery, helped maintain the characters [sic] the character's humanity. It proved to be a unique way of processing trauma without re-traumatizing those who've experienced genocide and avoiding violence as a plot device.[58]

Once again, the didactic approach is emphasized, which here becomes somewhat contradictory because, on the one hand, *Black Earth Rising* is marketed as a way of combating ignorance of the genocide, but, on the other hand, the audience apparently already knows the graphic and emblematic images of the same genocide. What, then, is the difference between using animations and graphically documented imagery without adequate contextualization? In the international reception, the lack of a historical perspective is evident as "complex" and "mysterious" become signal words for a reception that is based on Blick's intricate narrative twists, but which above all points to a consistent historical ignorance of Africa in in general and Rwanda and the genocide in particular.

The Rwandan concern that a dramatized television series like *Black Earth Rising* will spread like wildfire around the world shows a strong awareness that "based-on-a-true-story" film and television productions are more widespread, and thus have a greater potential impact on a historical media memory than has a documentary or a book. In connection to the commemoration week of the genocide in April 2019, *The New Times* published a list of the ten best films that portrayed the genocide against the Tutsi and, symptomatically, eight of these were international feature films while only two were documentaries.[59] And in connection to the commemoration week the year before, the CEO of the Kwetu Film Institute, Eric Kabera, was interviewed, and he emphasized that the Film Institute encouraged young people to embrace the film medium in their storytelling:

> Film has a powerful message to change the mindset and perspective of a people['s] perception [and] to have the memory preserved for future generations [. . .] Film and media in general are very good tools of education and sensitisation for the people to unite and look at things in a positive light. The reverse is also very true.[60]

We therefore now leave the global level, returning to the national level in order to discuss how the genocide against the Tutsi is portrayed in Rwandan film and televisions productions, focusing on how Rwanda, as a nation, creates its own images of the genocide and how these are incorporated into a new national identity.

Part Four

The Use of Historical Media Memories in Rwanda, 2001–2021

11

The Genocide against the Tutsi in Rwandan Film and Television

In 1994, radio and newspapers were the dominant mass media outlets in Rwanda.[1] A government-owned television channel, Télévision Nationale Rwandaise, had existed since 1992, but only those few who belonged to the elite could afford the cost of a television set at that time.[2] Equally, there were no proper Rwandan cinemas other than a few *cinés* in Kigali and in the university city of Butare. These cinés screened imported films, mostly on VHS, for local paying audiences, and some of them still exist but they are now primarily offering broadcasts of sport events such as the Champions League. Nonetheless, an audiovisual culture has developed in Rwanda over the last few decades with no less than twelve television channels of which eleven are privately owned while the dominant one, Rwanda Television (RTV), is state-owned and run by the Rwandan Broadcasting Agency (RBA) that provides news and entertainment for the Rwandan public in three languages, Kinyarwanda, English, and French.[3] In 2011, a multiplex cinema, Century Cinema, opened as part of the prestige building Kigali City Tower in the central business district of Kigali, with four screens, including a 4D film screen, which regularly screens Hollywood, Bollywood, and some African films. There is also a two-screen cinema in Nyamirambo, Star Cinema. However, ownership of televisions sets and visits to the cinema remain modest, and are in fact a luxury for most Rwandans, and instead the main source for consuming audiovisual media is the cell phone.[4] In this chapter, the main focus will be on Rwandan film production, and to a lesser degree on television programming, although these two sometimes overlap.

Rwanda's film industry has expended rapidly over the last twenty years, but it is a development that started from nothing, and the local film industry is still miniscule in comparison to Hollywood or the closer New Nigerian cinema or "Nollywood" as it is often carelessly called. The Rwandan film industry even has its own epithet, Hillywood, an analogy to Rwanda being identified as the land of a thousand hills. Filmmaker and CEO of The Kwetu Film Institute,

Eric Kabera, has stated that this development started with the production of *100 Days* (2001), a British-Rwandan co-production that became the first narrative feature film on the Rwandan genocide and predated *Hotel Rwanda* by three years.⁵ It was directed and written by Nick Hughes, but virtually all film crew and actors are Rwandan, and Eric Kabera produced the film. It is thus a film that could be identified as international as well as Rwandan, and there are several films in this chapter that tread this thin transnational line, and where the financing especially originates from a plethora of international organizations, NGOs, and film companies. However, what makes these films "Rwandan" despite the international involvement is that they take a distinctive Rwandan perspective on the genocide, that they are filmed in Rwanda, and that there is a strong local involvement through the participation of a Rwandan film crew and Rwandan actors.

With his experiences from the production of *100 Days*, Kabera started the Rwanda Cinema Center in 2003 with two goals being to start an international film festival and to initiate the For Youth by Youth program in order to train Rwandan youth in filmmaking. The Rwanda Film Festival was initiated in 2004 and held its first annual festival in Kigali in 2005. The film festival is not confined to Kigali, it travels throughout the county, screening films on large inflatable screens in rural areas as a way to promote the medium of film.⁶ Simultaneously, Kabera started the Rwanda Film Institute as a stand-alone unit in 2003, which offered intensive courses in filmmaking and received support from several Rwandan governmental ministries.⁷ In 2010 the Rwanda Film Institute transferred its operations more directly to the private sector when Kabera started the Kwetu Film Institute, a film school with offices, premises for film production, and screening possibilities in the "Kwetu House," located in the posh area of Kimihurura in Kigali. Kwetu Film Institute primarily offers, for a fee, a range of practical and theoretical filmmaking and film producing courses that range from three months to two years, and they regularly use invited pro bono international filmmakers as teachers. One of the main goals is that the "graduates in film and digital media production are self-employed and employ others hence boosting the Rwandan Economy." Another ambition is to let "Rwandans tell their own story and share it with other people worldwide."⁸

The Rwanda Film Institute and, subsequently, the Kwetu Film Institute, had and still has a dominant position in Rwandan film culture with its educational monopoly and by the fact that it has produced a number a graduation films, mainly short films and short documentaries. As young as the Rwandan film industry is, there is already a division between the semi-officially approved films of the film institutes which are deemed as "quality" or "educational" films and a plethora of small film companies which often produce only one film, often feature films aimed at the direct-to-DVD/VOD market.⁹ This division can also be distinguished by the different subjects that these films cover. Films produced by the two institutes have to a great extent consisted of films that in different ways deal with the genocide against the Tutsi, while independently funded feature films to a far lesser extent deal with the subject of genocide. Examples of the latter are *Umutoma* (2012), a romantic drama; *Mu Buzima* (2014), a film about a singing competition and moving to the big city; *Amahano I Bwami* ("The Tragedy," 2014), a historical drama set before the colonization; and *I Bwiza* (*Tenacity*, 2021), a coming-of-age story and a film about the importance of art.

In 2018 Kabera stated that the "genocide against the Tutsi has been a stepping stone for the new Rwandan narrative about our recent past. Today, we speak of the Rwandan film industry based on the actual fact that many films have been made on the subject."[10] However, the international and the national involvement, mainly through financing, have doubtlessly influenced the choice of subjects. Films about subjects like the genocide, AIDS/HIV, or the position of women in Africa are of course important subjects but they are also *considered* to be more important than a film about ancient kingdoms, a comedy, or juxtapositions between the countryside and the city, thus being able to source funding from various bodies such as US AID, the Swedish Film Institute, the Goethe Institute, the Rwanda Development Board (RDB), and the Rwandan National AIDS Commission.[11]

The dual ambition to create a film industry and to promote the film (and television) medium for an audiovisual uneducated Rwandan audience has therefore been a process intertwined with an educational ambition to teach the historical memory of the genocide. Or as Kabare says, "We are also humbled to have contributed to the education process on the Genocide against the Tutsi, positively inside Rwanda and around the world."[12] In a similar way, John Kwezi, the President of the Rwanda Film Federation, hailed Rwandan filmmakers for their contribution in "showing the world the truth about what the country went through [. . .] Our part is to produce true stories because we are part of the country's history and we are in the right position to tell our own stories and our vision."[13]

Nevertheless, the creation of a specific Rwandan historical media memory of the genocide against the Tutsi has not been realized in a political, cultural, or an aesthetical vacuum. International influencing through financing does not only mean that the choice of the films' subjects is affected, but also how these subjects, such as the genocide, are introduced, communicated, and contextualized. In addition, the significant influence of the dominant transnational historical media memory of the genocide, chiefly via the large international production of documentaries with their abundant use of emblematic images, has inevitably affected Rwandan film production about the genocide—and thus the memory of the genocide.

Having said that, it must be emphasized that the genocide in its audiovisual form still constitutes a small part of the collective memory of the genocide in Rwanda. Fighting genocide ideology and commemorating the genocide against the Tutsi constitute cornerstones in Rwandan nationalism and thus in Rwandan propaganda. In 2003, the Rwandan government adopted the official policy of ethnic non-recognition—outlawing the use of the ethnic markers Hutu, Tutsi, and Twa—and in 2008 the government outlawed genocide ideology and denial.[14] The implementation of a new Rwandan nationalism aimed to create a unified national identity far from the previous ethnical divisions is foremost achieved via the school curriculum, newspapers and radio, the use of genocide memorials, and official ceremonies in connection to what is known as Kwibuka ("to remember"), the annual commemoration of the genocide against the Tutsi. Under the motto, "Remember-Unite-Renew," Kwibuka is an event which in different ways highlights the genocide against the Tutsi, foremost during the seven-day commemoration with televised national ceremonies, but also with daily local meetings all around the country where survivors and perpetrators testify about the atrocities, and which is combined with proclamations and information about Rwanda's road to resilience and its progress in areas such as health, education, agriculture, trade, and economy. The main motivation is to unite the country by promoting a vision of hope, dignity, and prosperity for the people of Rwanda.[15] The commemoration week is followed by a 100-day mourning period during which the genocide, although given a lower profile, is constantly present in newspaper articles, radio broadcasts, and on television, where, for example, the Kwibuka logo for many years was visible during the 100-day period as a constant reminder of the genocide. As international scholars have remarked, the Kwibuka period goes against the adopted ethnic non-recognition in Rwanda as Tutsis as survivors are explicitly and implicitly pitted against Hutu perpetrators for those 100 days.[16]

The constant presence of the genocide and its use to promote Rwandan nationalism through reconciliation affects the memory of the genocide in Rwanda and, furthermore, the memory that is presented in Rwandan films; especially considering that these productions are semi-officially sanctioned by the film institutes. However, these national and international influences do not mean that the audiovisual memory is predetermined; it is more accurate to analyze it as a progression but it's a progression that seldom or never transgresses the official historical media memory of the genocide.

As noted, the consumption of film and other audiovisual media is low, especially in theaters, and television programs about the genocide are relatively few and do not feature among the most watched.[17] The exception is the annual

Figure 11.1 Commemoration meeting during commemoration week in Kigali in April 2015. Photo: Taliah Pollack

commemoration week when all programming on RTV is about the genocide, mostly consisting of different commemoration events, such as the presidential lighting of the flame at the Kigali Genocide Memorial, but also pre-produced material with human interest stories about survivors and how they are getting along. According to Arthur Asiimwe, Director General at RBA, television is seen and used as a form of education. And in around 2012, a policy was accepted by RTV to "move away from the use of graphic images of corpses, machetes, and violence, and instead promote unity as a way to move forward as one nation, using uplifting stories."[18] Nonetheless, although there are no available ratings, a search on RTV's YouTube channel, with more than 17,000 uploaded videos, reveals that the genocide is not a priority subject among viewers. Instead, other items are much more popular, such as official speeches by President Paul Kagame, state visits, sporting events like football and cycling, and the Miss Rwanda contest. Far down the list of the most clicked videos you will find some genocide related items such as Bishop Constantin Niyomwungere's testimony at the Paul Rusesabagina trail (149,764 views), the official ceremony of Kwibuka28 (81,445 views), and the hearing of Paul Rusesabagina (73,332 views). The most viewed news item on the genocide *per se* are even further down the list, for example the arrest of *génocidaire* Félicien Kabuga in Paris in 2020 (41,445 views).[19]

Likewise, the number of genocide-related Rwandan films and documentaries have decreased in a similar way as international productions on the Rwandan genocide have steadily decreased since the peak was reached in conjunction with the twenty-year commemoration of the genocide in 2014. The are several reasons for this decline in interest, and one is that filmmakers and audiences alike have lost interest due to overproduction; in Rwanda another reason is that people would like to move on.[20] As will be discussed in this chapter, this decline could also be subject to a changed approach towards the genocide, whereby the focus shifts from historical lessons (or memories) to contemporary reconciliations.

The Beginning: *100 Days*

100 Days is a low-budget film, and according to Nick Hughes and Eric Kabera filming started without a proper budget in place, relying more on continued support from financiers and on Rwandan goodwill, both local and governmental—borrowing trucks, houses, catering, mobile phones, and hotel stays as they went along. It was Kabera who had suggested this set-up, saying "people will only believe that we *will* make this film when we are actually making it." The whole process took about a year, which included three months to train the Rwandan amateur actors and two months of shooting.[21]

100 Days is an independent film production and much of its credibility as a genuine and truthful adaptation of the genocide relies on that fact. The use of amateur actors in all roles, and the decision to place the story in the small town of Kibuye instead of Kigali, and especially the use of St. Jean Catholic Church where thousands of Tutsis had been murdered, were conscious decisions based on three reasons: (1) it was cheaper to film in Kibuye than in Kigali, (2) Kibuye was accessible and "the landscape added enormously to the film," and (3) Kibuye had been one of the epicenters of the killings in 1994.[22]

Unlike its much better-known successor, *Hotel Rwanda*, *100 Days* never received a wide release. The film circulated at about fifty film festivals in 2001 and 2002, always to critical acclaim, but nobody picked it up and only a small number of DVDs were sold.[23] In addition, *100 Days* holds fifth place on the top ten list of the best films about the genocide that the government organ *The New Times* published in 2019, thus endorsing its status as an officially sanctioned feature about the genocide.[24] Also unlike its successor, *100 Days* has been unambiguously hailed in scholarship as the "best cinematic representation of the genocide,"[25] a celebration which can be broken down into five determining factors: (1) the film's Rwandan perspective with no Western heroes, (2) that it is filmed in Rwanda with amateur Rwandan actors, (3) that the film includes material on the failure of the West and the Catholic Church, (4) the feeling that it was based on historical facts, and (5) that it has an educational value.[26]

Three (2, 4, 5) out of these five factors align *100 Days* with the documentary genre, rather than with the based-on-a-true-story feature film. Amateur actors, even if trained, have added an impression of reality and credibility since the inception of Italian neo-realism, and the use of actual locations constitutes in itself a kind of guarantee of the truth as well as a kindship with the documentary genre.[27] Dauge-Roth, for example, consistently compares *100 Days* with the later feature films on the Rwandan genocide, claiming that *100 Days* is a film that "rejects the abuse of the memory that *Hotel Rwanda*, *Shooting Dogs*, and *Shake Hands with the Devil* uphold in valuing a realistic aesthetics that seeks to hide the crafted elements of their portrayals," that is, "pretending to mediate an unmediated reality."[28] Seemingly then, according to Dauge-Roth, *100 Days* is able to display its created elements in an almost Brechtian manner—that is with a distancing, *Verfremdungseffekt*—that treads the line of direct cinema with its aspiration to capture and represent reality truthfully. What is more, Dauge-Roth points to the film's pedagogical benefits, as *100 Days* manages to "call the audience's attention to the behind-the-scenes institutional work that went into planning the genocide," thereby deconstructing the "casual perception" that the genocide of the Tutsi was a spontaneous act following President Habyarimana's assassination.[29]

The perceived similarity to the documentary genre and documentary truth, which singles it out as superior to the future feature films about the Rwandan genocide, is noteworthy since *100 Days* was produced several years before these films premiered and thus had no previous precedent. This historical juxtaposition with feature films therefore becomes a bit skewed, and instead *100 Days* should be understood in relation to the production of previous documentary films and their use of emblematic images, but also in relation to Rwandan nationalism, based as it is on the genocide.

As discussed in Chapter 3, the focus on emblematic images in documentaries and the recreation of the same emblematic images in feature films generated a moral distance—the notion that a repetition of images of suffering led to increased remoteness.[30] And while principal feature films like *Hotel Rwanda* and *Shooting Dogs* contributed to create a public consciousness about the genocide on a global scale, they never aimed to individualize the victims of the genocide. Director Nick Hughes, who was involved as a cameraman in the production of several documentaries on the Rwandan genocide, such as *People of the Apocalypse* (1994), *UN Blues* (1995), and *Rwanda: The Bloody Tricolour* (1995), felt that "the documentaries weren't direct enough and angry enough," because they did not expose the guilt of the perpetrators or the guilt of the international community, especially the involvement of the French and the involvement of the Catholic Church. The intention with a feature film was to raise awareness in a way that was more immediate and sympathetic to the victims, thus transforming the images of corpses and alienating numbers to actual individuals.[31] The emphasis on Tutsi victims and survivors in *100 Days* will therefore be analyzed in tandem with the formation of a new Rwandan nationalism, focusing on those historical explanations that are highlighted and used to explain the genocide in this early production.

In *100 Days*, Hughes and Kabera tells the story of the genocide against the Tutsi in Rwanda on two narrative levels. The first one includes a critical, and at the same time observational, perspective that exposes the structure and the mechanisms behind the genocide. This is mainly achieved using several tableaux-like scenes with Catholic priests and local Hutu officials where the genocide is not so much explained but where the genocide against the Tutsi is portrayed as a planned state project and not as an ethnic war that suddenly erupted—which of course is a reaction to previous portrayals in Western media and news reporting of the Rwandan genocide as an African tribal war. These scenes also include accusatory portrayals of the Catholic Church and of the French involvement, whereby those characters are represented as one dimensional and solely evil caricatures. For example, the film starts with a sequence that intercuts between Hutu officials discussing "the work" to be done and a dinner with one of the said Hutu officials, where a white Catholic priest argues that during the Second World War the Germans committed terrible crimes and that the Americans also committed war crimes, "but we don't remember them, because the Americans won." However, the Hutu official is still doubtful about the killing, to which the priest replies: "Killing is wrong, but you are entitled to defend yourself," thus legitimizing the genocide according to the notion that the Tutsis and the RPF were the aggressors. Another rather blunt example is when the French leave Rwanda in the hands in the Interahamwe, and a French officer jokes: "Next time I come back, not so many dead bodies."[32]

The second narrative level includes the Rwandan perspective, which in this case is equivalent to the Tutsi victim/survivor perspective with a personal story that focuses on the relationship of two young Tutsis—Josette and Baptiste—whose lives are destroyed by the genocide. Josette's brother is murdered, while Baptiste's entire family is slaughtered in their house. The two young lovers are separated. Josette and her family flee the Interahamwe and seek shelter in a church, which is protected by the UN, and Baptiste manages to escape and hides in the forest, where he stays hidden until the end of the genocide when he is recruited by advancing RPF forces. At the church, the Hutu Catholic priest, Kennedy, betrays Josette's family, who are massacred along with all the other Tutsi refugees. The priest only agrees to spare Josette's life if she submits to him. She is then repeatedly raped, and by the time Josette is reunited with Baptiste neither of them can face the brutal reality of their situation. Josette is pregnant with the priest's child, something that Baptiste is unable to accept, and he abandons her. After Josette gives birth to the child, she in turn immediately abandons it at the bank of the river, which symbolically turns red.

The first narrative level of *100 Days* has a more Western than Rwandan perspective, as it consists of Hughes's predicaments and frustration with the media image of the Rwandan genocide, where the trope of Western guilt and thus denial had been launched during and after the genocide. This historical media memory would be firmly established later with the production of principal films such as *Hotel Rwanda* and *Ghosts of Rwanda*. In *100 Days*, this guilt is obliviated as the focus instead is on Western culpability, but the film also sheds light on the indifference of the West as the UN and white journalists are portrayed as useless and clueless. The film includes a reference to "The KPH Images" when the UN abandoned the church where the Tutsis had taken shelter. The UN soldiers shoot into the air to keep the refuges from entering the lorries, and then they drive away. In addition, there is a scene with an almost absurd quality in which Baptiste's brother has just discovered his massacred family. Shaken, he leaves the house, and two Western television journalists approach him out of nowhere, bombarding him with questions about what is going on. The scene demonstrates the western insensibility towards the whole situation and, according to Hughes, this scene illustrated the incomprehensible meeting of Western journalists on the ground in Rwanda and those who lived through the genocide.[33]

The composition of the first narrative level, although predominantly Western, still supports a Rwandan perspective and thus the particular brand of Rwandan nationalism connected to the genocide against the Tutsi that was under development as *100 Days* was being produced. The fierce attacks on France and the Catholic Church are in line with the RPF's historical perspective on the genocide. For instance, the Rwandan Catholic Church was involved in the genocide at a level where several individual priests participated in the genocide, as is represented in *100 Days*. In addition, the Catholic Church, with its close ties to the Hutu-based Mouvement Révolutionnaire National pour le Développement (MRND) regime, has also been accused of aiding the genocide morally with its official support of the interim government.[34] The National Commission for the Fight against Genocide (CNLG) and the umbrella of genocide survivors associations, Ibuka, have both demanded that the Catholic Church officially apologizes for its involvement.[35] This apology came in November 2016, but it has not been accepted, since it is believed that the Catholic Church still resists efforts by the government and groups of survivors to acknowledge the Church's complicity in mass murder, saying that those church officials who committed crimes acted individually.[36] This sanctioned animosity against the Catholic Church is connected to two other developments: the fact that many Tutsi returnees brought their Evangelical faith back with them to Rwanda, combined with an intensification of missionary work in Rwanda performed by Evangelical and Fundamental denominations, which has greatly reduced the number of Catholic parishioners, who traditionally have been made up of Hutus.[37]

However, one important historical component of Rwandan nationalism that is excluded from the narrative of *100 Days* is the impact of colonialism on the genocide. Dauge-Roth believes this omission to be strange and even relativizing,[38] not least since the Rwandan government's formation of a new Rwandan identity relies to a certain extent on the idea that pre-colonial Rwanda was harmonious and without ethnic markers. According to American anthropologist Annalisa Bolin, the RPF considers this pre-colonial past as part of the nation-building project and, consequently, as a "kind of 'golden era' interrupted by colonialism."[39] However, during the production of *100 Days* the colonial component of Rwandan nationalism was still under development and thus not yet the vital part of Rwandan identity that it would become during the first decade of the new millennium, which eventually would be incorporated into Rwandan film production.

The second narrative level of *100 Days* is connected to the personal stories of, foremost, Josette and Baptiste and their respective families. This personal viewpoint thus equals the Rwandan perspective that is acknowledged as one of *100 Days*' novel and educational factors. In addition, the use of exclusively amateur actors as well as actual locations for the killings in the film strengthens the feeling that this film is based on historical facts.[40] In *Variety*'s review, for instance, *100 Days* is tellingly described as "docudrama filmmaking at its finest"[41] rather than as a historical drama based on true events, the difference being that the docudrama is comprised of reenactments of real events while the historical drama frequently incorporates wholly fictionalized events set in historical locations and/or against the backdrop of historical events.

To be clear, *100 Days* is not a docudrama but a historical dramatization. Nevertheless, the personal level is the entry into the genocide that Hughes and Kabera use to tell their story, and the reason for this is Western audiences' ignorance of African history. Hughes states that he believes in the idea of a collective memory and that film could be a part of that memory. At the same time, he notes that although Western historical films are educational, Western films about Africa can only teach their audiences about "the character, that particular character's experience, not about the history of the time" because "[Western audiences] don't understand what's going on."[42] In other words, the personal level and the individual characters function as a gateway to the truth, and the connotations to docudrama and the documentary strengthen this belief.

However, cinematic history is always subjected to narrative and stylistic choices, and in *100 Days* one of those choices is the focus on the Tutsi couple, the families, and their experiences. Dauge-Roth highlight this narrative choice as novel in comparison to Western feature films about the genocide, claiming that "most movies depict mixed couples—Tutsi-Hutu, Tutsi-Muzungu, or Hutu-Muzungu," thereby underrepresenting Tutsi victims.[43] What scholars like Dauge-Roth do not seem to consider is the fact that the equaling of the Rwandan perspective with the personal viewpoint of the film simultaneously equals the Rwandan perspective with that of the Tutsi survivor's. Although this perspective could be perceived as novel in an international context, in a Rwandan context (and in the continuing Rwandan film production) it is connected to what peace and conflict scholar Gretchen Baldwin has termed *survivor nationalism*, a conscious blurring of "Tutsi" with "survivor" in official Rwandan language and decrees that pass down survivor identity to Tutsi youth at the same time as non-Tutsis, in a dichotomy, "are being held responsible for survivors' trauma without having their own war-related trauma positioned within the 'new Rwanda' rhetoric."[44] Baldwin sets up four conditions that survivor nationalism relies on:

(1) the genocide must exist in a historical vacuum, without a fuller recognition of the conditions of civil war; (2) ethnic recognition needs to be annually revived for a limited, controlled time; (3) Rwandans who were not alive during the genocide but nevertheless identify as survivors need to participate in Kwibuka programming; (4) the population must be publicly reminded both that the RPF is the reason for peace and prosperity and that Tutsi were victimised in 1994.[45]

For Tutsi victims to be victimized a perpetrator is needed, and on the other side of the dichotomy are the Hutus, portrayed as one-dimensional caricatures throughout the narrative of *100 Days*, regardless of whether they are officials, villagers, or Interahamwe. Not even the Catholic priest, Kennedy, gets a proper character development despite the fact that he has quite a lot of screen time. At the beginning of the film, he is quietly introduced standing beside the village prefect as he makes a fiery speech to the townsfolk about the need for the Hutus to defend themselves against the Tutsi invasion. Dressed in his clerical collar and with a giant cross around his neck, the symbolic connection between the Catholic Church and the *génocidaires* could not be any stronger. The priest then pretends to be neutral as the killing starts when he warns Josette's family, urging them to take shelter in the church. But this is just a scheme for him to get close to and take control of Josette, whom he lusts for. Kennedy assists the Interahamwe in their massacre of the Tutsis in his own church, but he keeps Josette as his sex slave, thus violating the clerical discipline of celibacy. The breaking of the fifth and tenth commandments could have been used to create character development in scenes in which the priest questions his faith and his role in the genocide, as a dramatized attempt to explain the genocide, but the only explanation given for his (and indirectly for the Catholic Church's) behavior and choices is individual lust and the urge for power. Hence, the shallow treatment of the antagonists in *100 Days* has, among other things, the paradoxical effect that the film's attack on the Catholic Church for its complicity in the genocide ends up at the same causal explanation that the Rwandan Catholic Church has defended itself with; that the genocide comprised individual events and that only individuals participated, not the Catholic Church as an organization.

As seen in Chapter 8, the subjects of rape and war babies were unusual in international film production on the genocide, and in Rwandan film production on the genocide rape and its consequences, war babies, are all but absent. *100 Days* appears to be the exception that proves the rule. This can be explained partly by the Western perspective gaining the upper hand for a while, allowing this suppressed perspective to be dramatized. Hughes says that the intention was to portray the unimaginable trauma wherein women gave birth to children of rape; partly because it was an ignored memory of the genocide, and partly because Hughes felt that the we-can-all-live-together narrative was something that the international community tried to impose on Rwanda.[46]

Although nearly all surviving Tutsi women had been raped during the genocide according to the UN, this particular victimization of Tutsi women has not been made part of the survivor nationalism narrative.[47] Its absence depends on a cultural and ethnic custom noticeable in Rwandan society whereby mothers' ethnic identities are still subordinate to the fathers' ethnic identities, thus justifying their social exclusion from their maternal ethnic group. According to political scientist Marie-Eve Hamel's fieldwork in Rwanda, "women who had children born out of rape were finding it difficult to see their children as anything but the son/daughter of a killer." By extension this has led to a situation where mothers are unable to imagine a future for their child, because cultural assimilation to the mother's and well as the father's group is near impossible, thus excluding war babies from the community. For example, for children to be entitled to receive assistance as survivors, they had to have been born before December 31, 1994, meaning that "children born out of rape are excluded from this assistance and from being designated as of survivors since they were born in 1995";[48] in short, because there were thought to be Hutus due to their father's background. Hence, Baptiste's inability to accept a "Hutu" child, and Josette's abandonment of her child at the end of *100 Days*, are thus representations of a lived reality, but it is a memory that is not incorporated into either Rwandan or survivor nationalism.

Finally, the most obvious expression of victimization in *100 Days* is the portrayal of genocidal violence. Released several years before the other fictionalized feature films, *100 Days* sets a precedent, but it is a precedent that is dependent on the previous production of documentary films with their abundant use of emblematic images. Hughes is the cameraman behind the perhaps best-known of the emblematic images, "The Nick Hughes Footage," and his first-hand experiences of the genocide have affected the use of violence in *100 Days*, but not in a straightforward way that peppers the film with scenes that emulate the emblematic images from news reporting and documentaries. In fact, the only instance when an emblematic image is used is a short recreation of "Bloated Corpses in the River." Otherwise, explicit genocidal violence is, although realistically portrayed in a bleak way, limited to five scenes and sequences, in addition to the already discussed rape scene. However, there is a constant threat of violence looming over the Tutsi characters in *100 Days* which permeates the film. Hughes has commented that "as long as the film is as miserable, as true to life as the genocide was," this constitutes the real story because in a story of the genocide "there is no hope."[49]

The five scenes with genocidal violence could be said to recreate this hopeless reality behind the media image of the Rwandan genocide. The first scene is when Josette's brother Pierre finds Baptiste's family murdered in their house and audiences have to adopt his shocked viewpoint (fear, confusion) as he finds the bloodied bodies (intentionally blocked by the filmmakers)—bodies that have been alive and part of the narrative but for whom the filmmakers chose not the include their violent murders in the film. The second scene takes place at a roadblock, where Josette's father is humiliated and physically abused but not murdered, yet again reinforcing the sense of threat rather than putting on a sensationalist display of explicit killings. Hughes has remarked that the roadblock scene "was not acting" since the amateur actors "knew what they were doing [. . .] their behavior was real"[50]—thus reinforcing this sense of reality. The third scene too recreates a reality behind the images in the news reporting. It is here that the bloated bodies are glimpsed as Baptiste and Pierre stumble over them in the river as they are hunted by an armed anonymous Hutu mob. Baptiste manages to get away while Pierre drowns in the streamy river and thus literally turns into one of the anonymous bloated bodies that were shown on the television news around the world in 1994.

The intense emotional build-up culminates in two horrific scenes that explicitly display the magnitude of the genocide. The first of these scenes comes in the middle of the film after the UN, the expatriates, and Western paratroopers have left Rwanda. At the town square people have gathered as the prefect orders all Tutsi schoolboys to be handed over and locked into a gas station. The screaming boys are dragged and lifted into the building as the mass of Hutu onlookers watch passively. Then gasoline is poured over and into the building and a torch is lit, but the man holding the torch hesitates, which gives time for a few images of the boys passively crying in the gas station to be shown, before the prefect takes the matter into his own hands and throws the torch at the building, creating an explosive fire. At that moment, Hughes cuts to a long shot showing hundreds of Hutu inhabitants backing off from the burning building, and the shot lingers on the building as black smoke rises to the sky—with obvious connotations to church and synagogue burnings during the Second World War, but also to the smoking chimneys at Nazis death camps.

This is a scene in which Hughes uses the power of poetic license since this event never took place in Rwanda during the genocide; instead, a similar event took place in Burundi eight months before, something which Hughes witnessed the aftermath of. Originally, Hughes planned to include another scene of genocidal mass violence in which a Hutu Catholic priest bulldozed his own church in which his own congregation had hidden, shooting those who tried to escape from the rubble, but due to the lean budget of *100 Days*, that scene became impossible to produce.[51]

As mentioned, financial reasons were one of the motivations, together with historical authenticity, for choosing Kibuye and the church there to portray the genocide. The fifth and last scene is the Hutu militia's nighttime attack on the church, which is shot in near darkness and in which both the attackers and the victims are mere shadows, although brief close-ups allow audiences to identify individuals such as Josette's father and little brother, who are slain, and one of the nameless leaders of the local Interahamwe, who has been glimpsed in previous scenes, as he enters the church. Otherwise, both killers and victims are seen as an anonymous mass of people. This interchangeability is underscored by the fact that Hutus played Tutsis and Tutsis played Hutus in the film.[52] The scene of the church massacre is short and brutal, executed as chaotic, with explosions and smoke as the killers wreak havoc on the parishioners.

Film scholar and filmmaker Piotr A. Cieplak has noted that *100 Days* relies on the dynamic of "othering," but not the othering of people. Instead, he claims that it is an othering "of the experience, that is associated—at least in the western tradition—with the supernatural and with that which cannot be logically explained." That is, the display of genocidal violence and of numerous anonymous corpses is a trope employed to convey the scale of the atrocity, but the effect, according to Cieplak, is a display "without any particular point of view—a gaze with no narrative agency."[53]

However, *100 Days* is characterized by both a Western as well as a Rwandan perspective, where especially the latter perspective is equated with survivor nationalism through the personalization of Tutsi victims and the anonymization of Hutu perpetrators. Although the promotion of survivor nationalism was most probably not on the agenda for either Hughes or Kabera, their creative choices nevertheless laid the foundation for future audiovisual depictions of the genocide against the Tutsi in which, as we shall see, the lines between survivor nationalism and Rwandan nationalism continue to be indistinct.

The Films of Eric Kabera

Eric Kabera's contributions to Rwandan cinema have been indispensable. Via the Rwandan Film Institute and the Kwetu Film Institute he has been involved in many Rwandan film productions as producer, script producer, consultant, translator, location manager, art director, and as an extra. In addition to *100 Days*, he has also worked on several international productions such as *Sometimes in April*, *Africa United* (2010), and *Finding Hillywood*. As director, co-director, screenwriter, and producer Kabera has in his own right influenced and shaped the historical media memory of the genocide in fundamental ways, not least for a Rwandan audience through the traveling Rwandan film festival and television screenings of his documentaries.

Kabera's directorial debut was *Gardiens de la mémoire* (*Keepers of Memory*, 2004), released in Kinyarwanda and with dubbings in French and English, thus aimed at both national and international audiences. This documentary is about Tutsi survivors who became guards and guides at the genocide memorials in Ntarama, Murambi, and Nyarubuye, and the film is built around their highly emotional testimonies about the events that took place during the genocide but also how these survivors are coping with the past. The film includes testimonies from Hutu perpetrators, who in very matter-of-fact tones recount the atrocities they have committed. The contrast between the survivors' perspective and the perspective of the perpetrators could not have been more obvious and the bifurcated ethnicities are explicitly expressed in this film, even though Rwanda's official policy of ethnic non-recognition was already in place.

Some scholars have highlighted *Keepers of Memory* as novel and even as "remarkable" in the subgenre of films about the genocide, pointing to the Rwandan perspective as a "measure of autonomy and subjectivity for the Rwandans in the film."[54] However, documentaries including survivor and/or perpetrator testimonies were nothing new at the time of the release of *Keepers of Memory*. Likewise, the structure of the film, which intercuts between testimonies and archival footage, is a traditional documentary technique; usually supported by a God-like voiceover, in this case it is the voice of Kabera that explains and recounts, for instance, Hutu politics over images of Interahamwe training and burial sites. Occasionally, survivor testimonies function as the explanatory voice when testimonies continue on the soundtrack as the film cuts to the archival footage consisting of images of expatriates being evacuated, of UN vehicles in Kigali, and of roadblocks in Kigali, but more often than not this footage is "silent." That is, it is accompanied by low-key, sad, and sometimes ominous music, particularly when Kabera uses an abundance of emblematic images, many filmed by Nick Hughes in 1994, consisting of several versions of "The Man with a Machete," "The Nick Hughes Footage," "Corpses by the Road," and "Piles of Corpses." The one exception with original sound is the 1998 Clinton speech in which the US President acknowledged the genocide.

Doubtless, *Keepers of Memory* does have a Rwandan perspective, but the Rwandan voices in it, including Kabera's, do not depart in any significant way from the official historical media memory of the genocide created in previous documentaries. The act of collecting and preserving these memories is, of course, of utmost importance, and one of the most extraordinary sequences is the excavation of dead bodies, where relatives of the victims testify to the horrific events when men, women, and children were thrown into an empty well, where they suffocated from the pressure of all the other people on top of them.

Nevertheless, it must be noted that Kabera's film simultaneously contributes to the creation of survivor nationalism, particularly pertaining to Gretchen Baldwin's fourth condition for perpetuating Rwandan nationalism, namely that the genocide must exist in a historical vacuum, without recognition of the conditions of civil war. The historical explanations are slim, and the narrative essentially stays within the 100 days of the genocide. The film starts with two captions, the first explaining that the genocide was initiated by the shooting down of President Habyarimana's plane and that it is "believed" that Hutu extremists were behind the attack; something that is substantiated later in the film when Kabera's voiceover explains the Interahamwe's role in the genocide. However, the second caption deviates from the official historiography on two points and simply reads: "Although disease and more killings claimed additional lives in the refugee camps, the genocide is over by Mid July 1994. An estimated 800,000 Rwandans have been killed in 100 days." The first sentence includes the mass deaths in the refugee camps, which mainly involved fleeing Hutus, while the second sentence mentions the number of 800,000, which is the UN's estimated number, and which differs from Rwanda's official estimate of 1,000,000 dead Rwandans. Interestingly enough, this number is later adjusted to "over one million people" in the voiceover account. This temporary inclusion of Hutus as victims is one of a few examples which show that the official Rwandan historical media memory had not been set yet.

The abundant use of emblematic images in *Keepers of Memory* is dependent on the international production of documentaries on the Rwandan genocide and could be contributed to Kabera's relationship with Nick Hughes, who provided much of the archival footage for the film. However, there is another connection to be made here pertaining to Rwandan audiovisual culture, or more correctly, the lack of such a culture in 2004. In that same year, the permanent

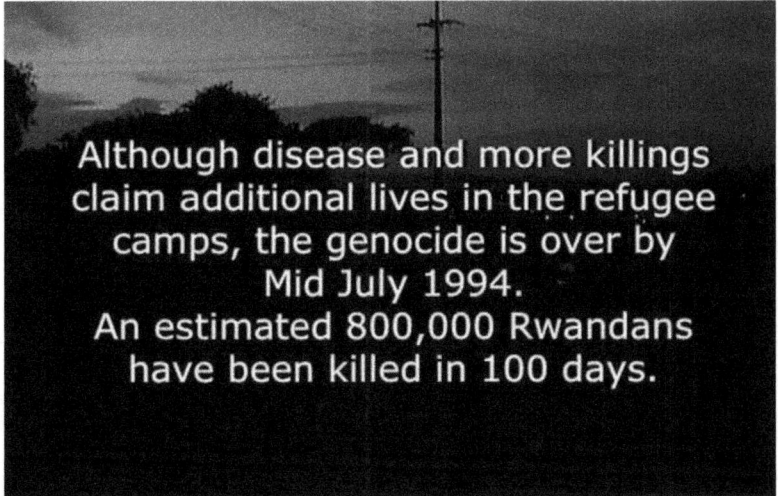

Figure 11.2 One of the captions at the beginning of *Keepers of Memory* (2004) which deviates from the official historical media memory of the genocide in Rwanda

exhibition at The Kigali Genocide Memorial, located in Gisozi in Kigali, was inaugurated. The memorial is the biggest in Rwanda and is the burial ground for some 250,000 people. The visitor center was commissioned by the CNLG and is managed by the Aegis Trust, an UK-based international organization working to prevent genocide that also produced the permanent exhibition.[55] The ground floor is devoted to the genocide against the Tutsi and consists of four rooms. The first room explains the historical background to the genocide, with the Belgian colonization as the basis of the explanation. The second room reveals what happened during the genocide. The third room focuses on the resistance to the genocide, while the fourth, circular, room contains only photographs of people who were killed, something which is depicted in the documentary *The Faces We Lost* (2017). As British anthropologist Pat Caplan has noted, the fourth room appears somewhat paradoxical because all the photos show the victims as "happy and smiling" since they are "taken on celebratory occasions like graduations, weddings, birthdays."[56]

The first three rooms are composed of exhibition texts, maps, and photographs, but each room also has a television set showing short films in Kinyarwanda, where the visitor can choose between English or French subtitles. The first two of these short films are of interest because, although a large part of the visitor base is international, many survivors but also Rwandan school groups regularly visit the memorial, something that has contributed to an audiovisual culture in Rwanda pertaining to the genocide—although this influence was of course greater in 2004 than it is today.

Figure 11.3 The television set in the first room of the Kigali Genocide Memorial, where visitors can watch a three-minute film about the history of Rwanda, with a focus on the colonial influence of Belgium. Photo: Tommy Gustafsson

The first film is just over three minutes long and deals with the history of Rwanda; and above all with a focus on Belgium's colonial influence which is illustrated with reenactments of the Tutsi royal family, skull measurements, archival still photographs, and statements that the Belgians "befriended the Tutsi, and used them in controlling the country." This in turn, the film explains, aroused hatred against the Tutsi and when the 1959 revolution occurred, "limited violence took place," which sowed deep distrust among Rwandans. When the Belgians left in 1962, the voiceover explains that Rwanda had "lost its values. It misapprehended its future but forgot its history. It gained a national pride, but one social group was offered."

The second film is in the room that demonstrates what happened during the genocide. It lasts only 1 minute and 23 seconds, but it consists of nineteen separate film clips made up almost entirely of different variations of seven emblematic images shown in slow-motion.[57] What is added are six short clips of five wounded and crying children, and one adult, showing horrific injuries from machetes. This second film is entirely silent, which makes it all the more brutal. Undoubtedly, it is influenced by international documentaries about the genocide against the Tutsi and their use of emblematic images, thus contributing to the official historical media memory. However, the images of wounded children, although they appear here and there as single shorts in the oeuvre of international documentaries, have not become part of the same media memory.

Together, these two films place an emphasis on colonial influences as an outside force on the genocide—in 2004 not yet part of the official historical media memory in Rwanda as they eventually would be—and thus on a historiography which partly relieves Rwandans of responsibility. In tandem with this, the second film with its silent emblematic images shows only the gruesome result of the genocide and not explicitly who was responsible. Nonetheless, the permanent exhibition, which has not been changed since 2004, clearly highlights the two, in Rwanda, forbidden ethnicities, thus portraying the Hutus as a group as perpetrators and the Tutsis as the victims.[58]

This development of a stronger focus on colonialism as an explanation for the genocide, the problem of dealing with the two forbidden ethnicities, and the use of emblematic images to illustrate the genocide continues in three films that Kabera was heavily involved in: *Through My Eyes: A Film about Rwandan Youth* (2004), *We are all Rwandans* (2008), and *Iseta: Behind the Roadblock* (2008).

Through My Eyes is a short documentary about Rwandan youths as they express themselves ten years after the genocide, and thereby deals with the genocide through theater, dance, poetry, music, and painting. The film is often wrongly credited to Kabera, who produced and scripted the film together with its Kenyan-Rwandan director, Kavila Matu.[59] Many of the participating youngsters were orphaned in the genocide. One such is the young artist Aimable, who lost his mother during the genocide, and now paints abstract art to express his inner feelings. As with *Keepers of Memory*, the film includes survivor testimonies and crying children, but the overall outlook is much more hopeful as the narrative is aimed at the future where young people, constituting over 50 percent of the population, are the ones with the responsibility of uniting Rwanda beyond its old ethnicities. In accordance with this, no emblematic images are used in the film. However, unlike *Keepers of Memory*, the colonial perspective is clearly present. At the beginning of the film, the voiceover states, over stunning images of Rwandan landscapes, "Rwanda, a beautiful land set in a thousand hills. For centuries its people lived together there in peace. But this suddenly changed!" A cut is made to the Butare Art Festival, where a theater play is being performed, and in Kinyarwanda one of the actors narrates: "Colonial masters manipulated history . . . They introduced lots of divisions . . . This was taught as our history, and we foolishly believed it."

The words "Hutu" and "Tutsi" are used sparingly in the documentary as it strives to use the demonym "Rwandan." Interestingly, as a substitute for Hutu extremists and *génocidaires*, the word "politician" is used. Likewise, in all the sequences where the young Rwandan artists collaborate their ethnicities are not highlighted nor even mentioned. Nonetheless, due to the population distribution in Rwanda, it is obvious that the majority must actually be Hutus. Even so, it is only Tutsi survivors who are interviewed and whose art is displayed in the film, thus supporting survivor nationalism rather than Rwandan nationalism.

However, halfway through the film a crack appears in the united front as the film team, for some unknown reason, runs into and starts talking to a group of young orphaned street boys in ragged clothing—the antithesis of the film's display of national unity, reconciliation, and progress. Although it is never explicitly expressed, these children are most probably either Hutu survivors or "Hutu" war babies by designation of a Hutu father raping a Tutsi woman during the genocide, thus justifying their social exclusion from their maternal ethnic group. The boys talk concisely about their backgrounds; one has escaped from a drunk and abusive mother, another's parents died when he was born. One boy says sarcastically, "I wish I could go to school. I'll end up as minister or as the President of the Republic . . . leading the country," while another boy is utterly serious as he analyzes Rwanda's and his own situation: "The country has lost a lot, but we have bad people everywhere. Rwanda should help us to go to school and not return on the streets. You grow up on the streets, can't even write or read your death sentence on the billboard." Director/editor Matu

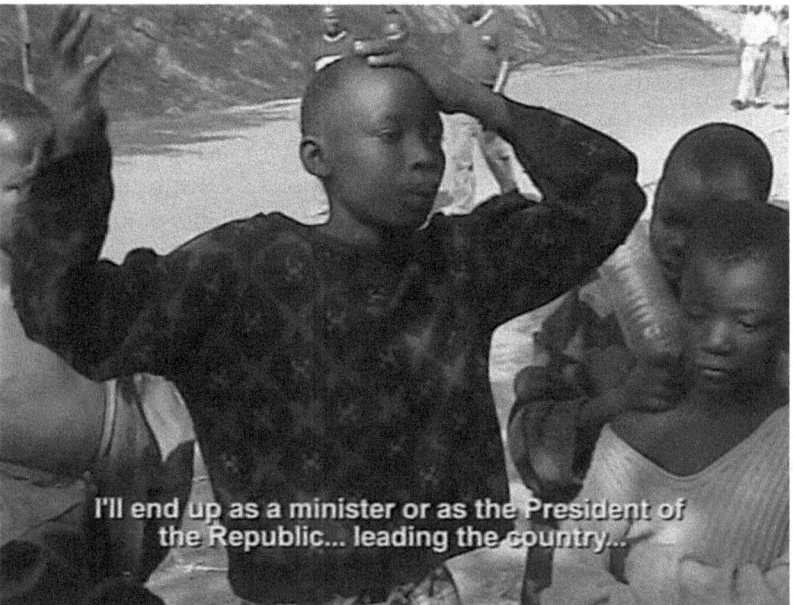

Figure 11.4 The Hutu street boys in *Through My Eyes: A Film about Rwandan Youth* (2004)

then cuts directly to Chantal, a poor Tutsi girl, and the art of pot making, a sequence which features dancing and singing, thus creating a stark contrast to the glue-sniffing Hutu street boys, who are not included in the community and therefore stick out like a sore thumb in the film's narrative.

Kabera was also the producer of the short docudrama *We are all Rwandans*, directed by the British director Debs Gardner-Paterson, who later would direct the feel-good film *Africa United*. The screenplay was written by Rwandan filmmaker Ayuub Kasasa Mago in collaboration with Gardner-Paterson. As the title reveals, *We are all Rwandans* is the inspirational based-on-a-true-story about an attack by ex-FAR/Interahamwe Hutu insurgents on Nyange secondary school on March 19, 1997. In the reenactment, the students are portrayed as ideal citizens. In the film and in real life, the students are asked to separate into their ethnic groups during the attack, and when they refuse, six of them are brutally murdered. This courageous refusal to reveal their ethnicities, and the call of "Twese turi abanyarwanda" ("We are all Rwandans"), as one schoolgirl declares before being shoot, have become part of a national heroic myth of Rwandan nationalism, celebrated every year in connection to the public holiday, National Heroes Day, on February 1. An editorial in *The New Times* addresses the importance of Rwanda's youth for its unity and future, which is idealized in films like *We are all Rwandans* and *Through My Eyes*:

> These children-cum-heroes did what many elderly Rwandans failed to do whenever they would be confronted with the same situations [. . .] But while the spirits of the slaughtered Nyange students rest silent, we should all be inspired by their bravery and sense of unity. They chose unity over disunity, Rwandan identity over ethnic differences. Today, they are our heroes and so will they be for many generations to come [. . .] Their sacrifices should never be in vain. And we can only pay them back if we furthered their dream of one great nation, one united people; freedom for everyone; and education and prosperity for all.[60]

American film and television scholar Andrew Phillip Young has problematized the ubiquitous use of mantras like "forgive, but don't forget" and "we are all Rwandans," uttered on television, radio, and in classrooms across the country, and points to the problem that "they gloss over the serious socio-cultural cracks that remain in contemporary Rwanda," asking how if "the latent practice of linking ethnic identity to responsibility for the genocide (the perpetrator/victim dynamic) persists in Rwanda's cultural consciousness, then are all Rwandans actually as equal as the mantra suggests?"[61]

Iseta: Behind the Roadblock revolves around survivor testimonies with a heavy focus on emblematic images, foremost the "Nick Hughes Footage," but also variations of "Corpses by the Road" and "The Man with a Machete" which are shown five and three times, respectively. However, what makes this documentary unique among other documentaries about the genocide is its behind-the-scenes approach as the filmmakers track down and identify the victims, survivors, killers, and witnesses to the footage that Nick Hughes took from the roof of the French school in Kigali in April 1994. Once again, this is a cooperation between Kabera and Hughes in which both produced as well as acted in front of the camera, while a Finnish film student, Juan Reina, directed the film. However, here opinions differ because Hughes states that Kabera essentially directed the film while Reina edited it.[62] Kabera, on the other hand, states that Reina indeed directed the film, helping to give it a fresh eye.[63]

Despite the Rwandan perspective—*Iseta: Behind the Roadblock* is an obvious continuation of *Keepers of Memory*'s thematic of survivor testimonies—the story is foremost mediated through Nick Hughes's personal recollections and explanations of the genocide. These function as the driving narrative throughout the film, exemplified via Hughes's recurring conversations with Kabera: "Nobody in Europe or America has any possibility of having any compassion for someone like you [Kabera] because you are not European, you are not American, you are an African so they can't sympathize with any emotions that you have"; or as in the closing words of the film: "Anybody who was in Rwanda, anybody who even comes after, and is touched by the genocide is a lesser human being. You cannot have any experience with the genocide without being reduced."

This international perspective on the genocide, with a focus on the failures of France and the UN, is closely related to that of *100 Days*, the exception being the addition of a colonial perspective as an imperative explanation. Noticeably, this new perspective is firmly introduced from the top in a talking-head interview with Domitilla Mukantaganzwa, then Executive Secretary for National Gacaca Jurisdiction, who states that, "from 1959 Rwanda has been governed on the basis of ethnicity, specifically from colonial time people of Rwanda have been divided."[64]

In accordance with this, the perspective of survivor nationalism is fulfilled in scenes where Hughes and Kabera search for and eventually identify the victims in "The Nick Hughes Footage," Justine and Gabriel. However, *Iseta: Behind the Roadblock* ends with two quite exploitative sequences in the then novel genre of the reaction video, as survivors first are showed the footage while the filmmakers film their horrified reactions, something that Kabera thought was "unbearable." "It must have been atrocious for them to watch the footage."[65] Then five Hutu prisoners are summoned to the local Gacaca court to watch the footage and thus expose their guilt, and yet again their reactions are filmed. They all deny any involvement, leading a survivor to stand up and say that "We aren't here for revenge. This is reconciliation." Even so, at the end of the film viewers are informed that five have been sentenced to long prison terms; one of them with the footage as evidence.

Clearly, there is a development from 100 Days to Iseta: Behind the Roadblock regarding the stronger focus on colonialism as an explanation for the genocide, which follows the development of the official historical memory of Rwandan nationalism. In addition, the extensive use of emblematic images mirrors the international production of documentaries on the Rwandan genocide, but in particular this could be attributed to the close cooperation between Kabera and Hughes. Nevertheless, survivor nationalism, with its strong Tutsi perspective and survivor testimonies, undoubtedly overshadows the perspective of Rwandan nationalism and its aspiration of unity for all Rwandans.

Nevertheless, in Kabera's latest directing effort to date, Intore (2014), efforts are made to achieve a more complete and inclusive nationalism based on the memory of the genocide. As with Through My Eyes, the focus is on Rwandan youth and Rwandan culture as a unifying factor, beyond divided ethnicities. Kabera interviews several cultural workers and artists repeatedly throughout the film—musicians, singers, songwriters, dancers, composers, poets, language teachers, and historians; among them singer/songwriter Corneille Nyungura, who at once states that his father was Tutsi, and his mother was Hutu, thereby highlighting the issue of dual ethnicities existing in one person and thus in one country. These interviews are not merely survivor testimonies as in previous films. Instead, the different artists draw on their experiences to analyze the genocide and its causes on a personal level, using this then, in a second step, to analyze how Rwanda can move forward. During these interviews Kabera inserts black-and-white flashes of emblematic images such as "Corpses by the Road, "The Nick Hughes Footage," and The Man with a Machete" in order to visualize the difference between the past and the future, which in turn is richly illustrated with sequences about Rwandan traditional dance, classroom teaching, and the music festival Kigali Up—cultural events that feature participants from both ethnicities, although this is never mentioned as it would go against Intore's idea of one national identity. Even brief flashbacks from Gacaca trials are reproduced in black and white to show that Rwanda has now moved on.

This outlook is hopeful, but it is also dependent on an analysis of the past and the genocide as something foreign, or as one artist explains, "the whole genocide was not Rwandan at all, and it was because Rwanda had lost its own culture." That is to say, European colonialism destroyed a deeply rooted Rwandan culture which must now be revived through the use of the arts as a way to move forward, both drawing on ancient traditions of dance as well as modern expressions such as rap music. Or as another young artist expresses it, "1994 does not define what we are as people."

However, what complicates the issue with *Intore* and its aim for national unity is its connection to the old military institution of Itorero and the pre-colonial kingdom's Tutsi elite warriors, Intore (translated to "the chosen ones"). In 2007 the Rwandan government introduced Itorero ry'Igihugu, a nation-building and development program that was implemented country-wide in 2012 with the intention to rehabilitate the nation by using a new interpretation of this old, Tutsi, military tradition, whose war dances are the same as the traditional dances that occurs in *Intore*. German anthropologist and conflict studies scholar Erika Dahlmanns has raised concerns about how the Itorero tradition can "support an integration of all segments of the population into a nation, a shared sense of citizenship and belonging?"[66] Dahlmanns's conclusion is largely positive:

> However, the Government's founding narrative of a culture-based, moral, united and strong pre-colonial nation and its cultural decline seems to serve nation-rebuilding. By defining all Rwandans as victims of a loss of culture and simultaneously as heroic promoters of a cultural and moral revolution for the return to a "Golden Age" like state, this narrative of national recreation externalizes guilt by making the colonizers responsible for social tensions and bridges social divides by providing a positive, heroic collective self-image, derived from the familiar figure of the Intore.[67]

The artists' different interpretations of Intore are also explicitly connected to a Rwandan identity in *Intore*: "a man of integrity," "stand up to the challenge," "great moral integrity," "a hero," "somebody who would die for their country," "to love the culture of your country." In that way, Kabera succeeds in neutralizing the Tutsi connoted expression Intore into a more inclusive outlet for Rwandan nationalism.

The Rwandan Reconciliation Film

The films of Eric Kabera, his production work within the Kwetu Film Institute, as well as official Rwandan policies and laws on ethnicities and genocide denial all contribute to, and set a frame for Rwandan filmmakers who want to make a film about the genocide. As mentioned, the genocide against the Tutsi was the dominant—but not the only—theme in Rwandan film production from 2004, and for approximately ten years after that. Unlike Kabera's feature-length films, most of these productions consist of short films and short documentaries, often in the form of graduation films from the Rwandan Film Institute and the Kwetu Film Institute. Considering these combined circumstances, it is hardly surprising that the reconciliation film is a recurring theme.

While the international reconciliation documentary is characterized by an outside-looking-in interest in the aftermath of the genocide in Rwanda—often containing brief historicizations illustrated with graphic emblematic images—the Rwandan reconciliation film is characterized by an inside-looking-in perspective devoid of emblematic images, although not entirely of violence. Explicit historical explanations are often absent, meaning that the different implications of colonialism are not employed as rationalizations, and in their place Christianity's dualistic worldview of good and evil sometimes serves as an explanatory model. The genocide, if portrayed at all, often comes in the form of flashbacks, as in *Lyzia* (2011), a short film dealing with a young girl's traumatic memory of her parents' death, where the film shifts to black and white when the genocide is recalled. This means that the narrative and the actions of the Rwandan reconciliation film take place in the present, which in turn points to a future of reconciliation. The past is therefore "self-evident" and something that does not need to be explained in the same way for Rwandan audiences as for international audiences. Here there is a parallel to how RTV handles the genocide as either a historical moment to be remembered once a year in the present, or as a social dilemma seen through the lens of legislative reforms of the present but which aims for the future.[68]

Another difference between the international reconciliation documentary and the Rwandan reconciliation film is that the international documentary focuses to a greater extent on activities, measures, and organizations, while the Rwandan reconciliation film is more interested in the conflict between the personal trauma and how this might be overcome for the benefit of reconciliation—and by extension, national unity. For instance, there are hardly any documentaries about the Gacaca system in Rwanda, the only exception being the documentary short *The Power of Gacaca* (2010). Another example that typifies this transnational difference is *Icyizere: Hope* (2009), directed by American-Kenyan Patrick Mureithi, which is a feature-length documentary centered around a three-day Healing and Rebuilding Our Communities (HROC) workshop in Gisenyi where ten survivors and ten perpetrators meet.[69] Although this documentary could have qualified as "Rwandan" due to its proximity, there is nevertheless a clear outside-looking-in perspective present. The colonial history is used to explain the genocide and the shorthand use of emblematic images, such as "Corpses by the Road," is there to illustrate and "explain" the genocide. What is more, due to the presence of a camera and a Western film crew, the conversations in the workshop come across as arranged in order to follow the model for national reconciliation.[70]

This is not to say that some Rwandan reconciliation films aren't pure message films, bordering on propaganda, as in the short film *Charcoal* (*Ikara*, 2009), in which a gang of Tutsi boys takes revenge on a Hutu boy, Ndahiro, for the crimes—never dramatized—that his father has committed during the genocide. However, the family against whom the father committed the crimes takes in Ndahiro, proclaiming: "We need to look forward to the future. We need to remember the past to build our Rwanda today and for tomorrow." Ndahiro then reunites his father with the father of the Tutsi family, who forgives him.

Personal trauma beyond survivor testimonies can be found in a handful of productions, for example in the short documentary *Behind of Full of Sorrow* (2010), in which Tutsi survivors search for their dead relatives in a village they share with Hutu perpetrators. After fourteen years, the dead bodies are found and can be buried with dignity, and some kind of reconciliation is achieved. Another three reconciliation films which portray the personal trauma in diverse ways are *Crossing Lines* (2014), *Hutsi–Akaliza Keza* (2014), and *The Invincible* (2014). The first two are short fictionalizations and the last one is a short documentary about prominent Rwandan singer/songwriter Jean-Paul Samputu's journey to forgive his childhood friend Vincent, responsible for killing Samputu's father. All three films were finalists in a screenwriting competition on the theme of "Rethinking Reconciliation," commissioned in connection to the twenty-year commemoration of the genocide against the Tutsi in 2014.[71]

While *The Invincible*, the winner of the competition, gives an idealized image of reconciliation, *Hutsi–Akaliza Keza* and *Crossing Lines* dig deeper into the personal trauma. *Hutsi–Akaliza Keza* revolves around a young Tutsi survivor girl whose life is shattered when she gets pregnant and learns that her fiancé is in fact Hutu. Having lost her father in the genocide, and while her only brother is suffering from brain damage inflicted by her father's killers, she cannot marry or love a Hutu. She calls off the wedding and sets off on a journey of self-destruction, even considering an abortion as the child would become "Hutu" according to Rwandan social traditions. The trauma of having a baby with "the enemy" is thus a conflict that symbolizes the lingering ethnic conflict, which must be and eventually is resolved in the name of reconciliation. The parallel to the issue with Rwandan war babies is unmistakable but, as has been made clear, this memory has not been incorporated into the historical media memory on which Rwandan nationalism is based.

In *Crossing Lines*, directed by Samuel Ishimwe, the trauma is presented doubly, which is rare. The film centers on genocide survivor Kayihura, a young doctor who lives with depression as a drug and alcohol abuser because he cannot forget the sight of his mother being raped and killed in the genocide, visualized in flashbacks. During the twenty-year commemoration period, a desperate man, just released after fifteen years in prison for the murder of a twelve-year-old Tutsi boy, tries to kill himself and is brought to the doctor's house, clutching a suicide letter. Although never explicitly identified as a Hutu in the film, the unnamed man also has flashbacks, in his case of the bloodied body of the boy that he killed.

Their meeting is not characterized by the programmatic reconciliation that typifies much of Rwandan film. Instead, Ishimwe dramatizes this as a chance encounter between two human beings. Kayihura dutifully bandages the man and when he wakes up, Kayihura says laconically, "Welcome to the world of the living dead," then he takes drugs again to escape the memory of the genocide, falling asleep. In the meantime, we get to take part in the wounded man's backstory, who tells us that, "I have been freed but my heart is still full of fear," which is why he cannot return to his home village and instead attempts suicide. However, he repairs a cassette radio that Kayihura has failed to repair and accidentally leaves the confessional suicide letter on the table next to it. When Kayihura wakes up, he discovers the letter and violently confronts the man, who says he is already dead and belongs in hell. The only difference between them, the man points out, is that Kayihura is killing himself slowly instead of quickly. Kayihura leaves the room in anger but returns when the man plays the cassette tape, with a recording of Kayihura's mother playing guitar, which was the reason why Kayihura wanted to fix the cassette radio in the first place. When Kayihura hears the music, he is finally able to replace the memory of his mother being brutally murdered with a memory of his mother playing the guitar and smiling. The man pulls back the curtains and symbolically lets in the light before he disappears out the door. Kayihura reconciles with himself, but the film leaves open whether the Hutu man can forgive himself. In either case, the process of reconciliation is not made easy, which perhaps is why *Crossing Lines* did not win the competition.

Finally, two Rwandan reconciliations films which received attention on the international festival circuit are the two versions of *The Pardon*, first made as a short in 2009 and then expanded into the feature film *Imbabazi: The Pardon* (2013).[72] What stands out about these two reconciliation films is the use of explicit violence. The films are directed by Joël Karekezi, who went on to direct *The Mercy of the Jungle* (2018), a war film that takes place during the Second Congo War.

Both versions of *The Pardon* follow the same contemporary storyline and use flashbacks to portray events before and during the genocide. Two good friends from the same village, Karemera and Manzi, find themselves on opposing sides during the 1994 genocide. Manzi, unable to withstand the peer pressure, joins the local Interahamwe and kills Karemera's younger brother (and his family in the longer version), an event that in both versions is showed explicitly viciously and gorily in a way that sets these films apart in comparison to most Rwandan films on the genocide. When Manzi is released from prison after fifteen years, Karemera, who has a new life in the city with a family, wants revenge. He tries

Figure 11.5 The explicit use of violence in the reconciliation film *The Pardon* (2009)

the legal route without success because, as his lawyer points out, "He was an executor, not a planner, he can't stay in prison for ever," which is a narrative that problematizes the substantial release of genocide prisoners in Rwanda in 2003.

The film then splits into two narratives. Karemera's details his obsession, to the extent of neglecting his family, as he returns to the village to gather evidence against his former friend. When Karemera confront Manzi, he flees. Manzi, in turn, is depressed and tries to drown his bad memories with alcohol. However, during a conversation with a former Interahamwe collaborator, also released from prison, he has an insight: "We need to speak about what we did. It's our responsibility to educate the people." His friend wonders if he is crazy, saying, "people are trying to forget." Nevertheless, Manzi sets out on his mission to educate, ending up (in the short version) at Karemera's son's school where once again he is confronted by Karemera. Manzi asks what he can do to earn Karemera's forgiveness, but Karemera coldly says, "Bring me back my brother!"

In the short version, Manzi hands over a confessional letter to Karemera, asking him to do whatever he wants with it. In a daydream-flashback, Karemera remembers how he and Manzi played football, and when he wakes up, he sees his son fighting with another boy over a football, threatening to kill him. In a state of self-awareness, he tears up the letter and the film ends with an image of two hands being shaken. The long version has a more action-filled climax, where Manzi saves Karemera from drowning. That film ends with the two friends building a house together.

The Pardon, especially the longer more fleshed-out version, portrays how national and personal catastrophes concerning both ethnic sides could happen and how the population can learn to deal with this burden. A German reviewer points out the film's message as radical and important for a German audience, in comparison with the Holocaust, because in the Rwandan genocide it was not strangers who killed, but actual best friends and even family members. However, the same reviewer is critical of the fact that Karakezi does not include any colonial explanations for the genocide in the film, even schooling him about the German and Belgian influences, claiming that "the whole problem of the film [is that it] looks like a quintessentially African one [when] it is a typically European one."[73]

This adoption of an outside-looking-in perspective is rather typical for the European reception and is similar to Dauge-Roth's reaction to the absence of colonial perspectives in *100 Days*.[74] However, the Rwandan reconciliation film is characterized by an inside-looking-in perspective where the conflict between the personal trauma and how this might be overcome for the benefit of reconciliation and national unity is emphasized, thus more often than not leaving out historicizations, the use of emblematic images, and colonialist rationalizations.

The Memory Film: Generational and Personal Perspectives

While the reconciliation film aimed inwards and towards the future, there are several related films, similar to the reconciliation film, that deal foremost with the memory of the genocide without necessarily having reconciliation as the goal. These memory films consist of feature films, short films, as well as documentaries, and they are diverse by nature. Although memory is a tool for remembering the past, the act of remembering is both individual and collective; the latter especially in relation to the film medium where the very motivation for its creation is that the finished product is exhibited and, by extension, that it influences many more than the individual director, on whose memories it is usually based. Hence, an inherently collective memory such as the historical media memory of the genocide against the Tutsi cannot by definition be characterized as individual without considering the surrounding context. The Rwandan memory film can be divided into two categories, whereby the first one deals with the generational aspects of the genocide while the second uses personal experience as a starting point to create historical media memories of the genocide.

The generational aspects take different expressions, but they can all be linked to a problematization of one of Baldwin's conditions for survivor nationalism, namely the fact that a large number of Rwanda's population were infants or were not alive during the genocide, and therefore must relate to it as a memory, without lived experience. This happens, for example, in the short film *Fora* (2009), in which a single father raises two sons and teaches them to stick together, one of whom has clear psychological problems because his mother was killed in the genocide, something that is only hinted at in the film.

Another take on this is the post-genocide film which explores the seldom examined family relations that surround the genocide by focusing on young adult survivors and the predicament of having no first-hand memory of the killings. This theme appears in short films like *Shema* (2011) and *Ishimwa: From Bloodshed to Grace* (2017) and it is further developed in Samuel Ishimwe's short film *Imfura* (2017), which was the first Rwandan film to enter the Berlin International Film Festival, winning the category of best short film in 2018. *Imfura* tells the story of a young university student who lost his mother during the genocide, and when he returns to his village finds himself in the middle of an inheritance dispute regarding the land that his family owned and on which the ruins of the family's former house stand as a "memorial" to the genocide. Should he sell the property, or should he preserve the memory of his mother, and thus of the genocide of which he remembers nothing?

This use of materialism as a way to remember is employed in an intricate way in the feature film *Long Coat* (2009), in which Rugamba, an uneducated chicken farmer and son of a perpetrator, finds a coat in the attic. The coat becomes the catalyst for a story where memory and the history of the genocide merge. Rugamba's mother tells him that it is his grandfather's coat and that his father has probably kept it to remember him by. On his way to visit his father in prison he catches a lift, and receives a lecture from the driver, who tells him that the avoidance of history will lead to history repeating itself—and that Rwanda must be built "on the foundation of love" to become the "first ranked country in the world." This is pure propaganda, and *Long Coat*'s director, Edouard Bamporiki, who got his start as an actor in Lee Isaac Chung's *Munyurangabo* (2007), eventually went on to become a Member of the Rwandan Parliament, and in 2019 was appointed States Minister in the Ministry of Youth and Culture.[75] This idealized view of reconciliation and a belief in the power of education are also recurring themes in the editorials of *The New Times* during commemoration week.[76]

Nonetheless, Bamporiki does not stop at propaganda platitudes but continues to drill into this as a generational issue, mainly from a Hutu perspective, which is unusual. While in the car, Rugamba meets Claire, a young Tutsi survivor whom he befriends, and she points out the generational issue by saying: "Don't you think we share the consequences of the genocide?," thus including the young Hutus who had nothing to do with the atrocities. Later, in prison, his father not only distances himself from the coat—"it has a bad history around

Figure 11.6 Rugamba (Edouard Bamporiki) visits his father in prison in *Long Coat* (2009)

it which can affect our family"—but he also orders Rugamba to hide it. His father then tries to change the topic of conversation, but when Rugamba talks appreciatively about the preparations of the upcoming commemoration week, this produces an outburst from the father: "Remembering what . . . with whom are you remembering?" When Rugamba says that this concerns all Rwandans, the father accuses him of siding with the enemy, claiming to be innocent. And when Rugamba later confronts his mother, she too distances herself from the commemoration ceremony, saying: "How can you know history when you know nothing about it?"

However, Rugamba defies his mother and is thrown out of the house as a result. By standing up for himself (and thus for Rwanda), Rugamba sets out on a personal journey where the family's memories are challenged by Claire's survivor memories, but also by other Tutsis who reject his approaches as well as his friendship with Claire. Wearing the coat, Rugamba turns up at the commemoration ceremony, and there he is hit by a repressed childhood memory: of his father beheading the owner of the coat, which he then steals. It turns out that the owner of the coat is Claire's father, who in this way finds peace of mind and can move on with her life. With *Long Coat*, Bamporiki symbolically shows that the memory of the genocide is not only opposed by Rugamba's own family but also by the memories of the survivors—and ultimately that it is with the next generation that the responsibility lies for creating a united Rwanda.

The individual's fate as a stand-in for the greater history of the genocide is of course a common narrative in narrative feature films, but personal experiences also serve as a starting point for documentaries about the memory of the genocide. In Gilbert Ndahayo's trilogy of documentary films on the genocide, audiences are taken on a journey that starts with the personal experience of surviving, continuing with the trauma of confronting the perpetrators, and eventually reaching a perspective where the genocide is explained and understood historically. This memory journey is in a sense paralleled by Ndahayo's personal and professional development.

Ndahayo made his debut with the Kabera-produced short *Scars of My Day* (2006), a film about two friends who leave the countryside for the big city where they are taken in by a street gang and end up in despair as one is infected by HIV. Ndahayo then directed his first feature documentary film, *Behind this Convent* (2008), about the massacre at the convent in the town of Astrida (Butare) on April 10, 1994, where Interahamwe killed 153 Tutsis and dumped their bodies in a pit behind the building. Among the victims were Ndahayo's parents, and he himself narrowly managed to escape.[77] Using his own as well as eyewitness survivor testimonies, this documentary is quite conventional and is rather in line with a survivor documentary such as *Keepers of Memory*, were it not for the lack of emblematic images (there are images of the excavation of corpses), the lack of historical contextualization—although it is framed by the 1998 Clinton speech and a closing text that blames the UN—and the fact that the film does not end as other reconciliation films. Andrew Phillip Young highlights this ending as a problem, saying that the "film poses, without ever actually answering it [. . .] how forgiveness can work when every day is a reminder of a singular shared trauma."[78] However, the focus of the film is on the personal experiences, and the consequences that the survivors had to endure as Ndahayo sets out to investigate the murders of his family, and in that way he leaves the question of reconciliation open.

Behind this Convent won two prizes at the Zanzibar International Film Festival in 2008. That same year Ndahayo moved to the USA, where he made his second film, *Rwanda: Beyond the Deadly Pit* (2009), also a multiple award-winning documentary film, including a nomination from the African Movie Academy Awards.[79] This feature documentary moves on from the survivors to the perpetrators of the convent massacre. Reusing material from *Behind the Convent*, Ndahayo continues to explore the genocide by confronting his parents' killers during a Gacaca trial. At the same time the film widens its context by including archive material such as the 1998 Clinton speech—but no emblematic images—as well as interviews with expatriates and survivors who now expand their testimonials with accusations aimed at the Rwandan Catholic Church as well as the Western powers, foremost the involvement of the French.

Accordingly, the personal approach to the memory of the genocide is expanded in *Rwanda: Beyond the Deadly Pit*, something which certainly has international influences but also elements of Rwandan nationalism as we have seen in the films of Kabera, including tackling the theme of reconciliation.

In *Rwanda: Beyond the Deadly Pit*, the killer of Ndahayo's parents ask for forgiveness and Ndahayo reluctantly gives it to him, thus fulfilling that particular theme of Rwandan nationalism, as well as international expectations according to the international reconciliation film. However, by intercutting survivors questioning the perpetrators at the Gacaca court with filmed images of himself expressing doubt, Ndahayo maintains the personal perspective, and thereby complicates the conflict between personal trauma and the benefit of reconciliation and national unity.

The third documentary feature, *The Rwandan Night* (2013), grew out of the first two films, reusing interview material from both, but now a historical and a chronological perspective is introduced whereby colonialism serves as an explanation for the genocide. According to Ndahayo, *The Rwandan Night* is more research-based than the previous two films, which were more emotionally driven.[80] Still, *The Rwandan Night* is largely driven by the emotional aspects of four interrelated and intercut subjects: survivor testimonies, this time given by survivors in the diaspora, like Ndahayo himself; the 2006 commemoration ceremony at Nyamirambo stadium; expert interviews made at the third international conference on genocide at Sacramento State University in 2011; and, finally, "the longest monologue in the recorded history of survivors in Rwanda."[81]

It is this continuous poetic monologue, performed by the oldest survivor of the genocide, Fidele Sakindi, in combination with the use of original Rwandan music for the commemoration ceremony, which helps to define this film as an "ethno-documentary."[82] Paradoxically, it is Sakindi's poetic narration that contributes to the historicization of the genocide—starting with the haunting memories of the 1959 Rwandan Revolution where thousands of Tutsis were killed and some 336,000 fled the country[83]—thus combining poetic and factual elements in a similar way as with Michel Bouquet's poetic narration of Holocaust survivor Jean Cayrol's script in *Night and Fog* (1956).

In the press material for *The Rwandan Night*, Ndahayo clarifies the reasons for the inclusion of this monologue. It is not there just to give room to a Rwandan perspective. According to Ndahayo the voiceover in Western documentaries about the genocide is "useful when the filmmaker does not have enough footage nor understand [the] subject. Voiceovers oversimplify the narratives and create distance between the audience and the characters even when the shots are close-ups."[84] Hence, Western documentaries about the genocide against the Tutsi are singled out as uninformed and oversimplified—thus justifying the Rwandan drive to correct this historical memory. As a director Ndahayo retains his unique personal perspective—in *The Rwandan Night* through Sakindi's monologue—but as he becomes more critical of the international historical media memory of the genocide, his films increasingly meet more and more criteria for survivor nationalism. Hence, the diaspora seems to create a critical distance to filmmaking and the historical memory at the same time as the diaspora seems to generate increased proximity in relation to the nationalist perspective.[85]

Deviations from Survivor Nationalism: Films with a Hutu Perspective

Survivor nationalism in the guise of Rwandan nationalism dominates Rwandan film production on the genocide. This means that the historical media memory of the genocide is based on the experiences of Tutsis, rather than on the experience of Hutus. This is not a surprising development since a perpetrator's perspective is rather unusual in genocide dramas, especially at an early stage when the genocide in question is only a decade or so old.[86] In addition, the Rwandan development is dependent on the legal issues surrounding the genocide and where the gray zone of "genocide denial" constitutes an impediment for depictions other than those in line with official historical memory. Historical revisionism or historical negationism is therefore non-existent in Rwandan film production, and in alignment with this, a Hutu perspective of any kind has been severely downplayed as potentially it could be interpreted as "genocide denial"—which does not correspond well with the inclusive ideal of Rwandan nationalism.

Nonetheless, there are a handful of Rwandan films that tread the thin line of "genocide denial" by including a more distinctive Hutu perspective. The tactics and outcomes are different, but the focus is essentially on either a younger generation of Hutus born after the genocide or on the perpetrators. *Long Coat*, with its strong generational and reconciliation themes and its focus on the young, uneducated chicken farmer Rugamba, the innocent son of a perpetrator, belongs in the first category.

Another film in this category is *Maibobo* (2010), a short fictionalization portraying the lives of a gang of street kids, scornfully called "maibobo," who live on the fringes of society. These children lost their parents during the genocide and its aftermath and although it is never explicitly mentioned in the film, they are of Hutu origin, either survivors or Hutu war babies, and thus shut out of any survivor benefits. These are the same type of street kids that are glimpsed as an anomaly in *Through My Eyes*, or as Kwasa, the Hutu boy in *Life after Death* who pretended to be Tutsi in order secure support from his American "saviors."

In *Maibobo*, the director Yves Montand Niyongabo, who later made *The Invincible* with its idealized image of reconciliation, tells the story of a young country boy searching for a better future in the city. However, instead of being greeted by an inclusive Rwandan nationalism he encounters hostility and hypocrisy, thus ending up in the company of other equally shunned street kids who must fend for themselves. Directed in a realistic way with amateur child actors and real-life settings, Niyongabo provides a voice for these forgotten children but also a subtle criticism of the prevailing order of things. In a scene reminiscent of one in *Through My Eyes*, where the street kids sarcastically joke about becoming president, one of the children in *Moibobo* says, "If you vote for me [for president], I will organize less meetings and more action"—which constitutes a clear criticism of the endless public meetings held throughout Rwanda during commemoration week. *Maibobo* therefore functions as a contra-narrative to the one-sided media image in Rwanda, where a bright future is proclaimed for all young people.

A third film that takes a different approach is *A Love Letter to My Country* (2006), directed by Thierry Dushimirimana. This film was released after the implementation of the official policy of ethnic non-recognition, but before the laws on genocide ideology, a fact that probably contributed to its unusually strong Hutu perspective. This short film could be characterized as a reconciliation film, and it is produced by Kabera, but in some ways it strays from the dominant mode of survivor nationalism. The film is about a young couple who falls in love, Martha a young Tutsi survivor whose parents were killed in the genocide, and Rukundo, a young Hutu male. As they announce their plan to get married, they encounter fierce resistance from their relatives and friends who accuse the other side of being murderers and unreliable "cockroaches," respectively. However, unlike other idealized reconciliation films, the dilemma of two separate ethnic identities is not so easily solved and the film ends with the two of them eloping, without the blessing from their respective families.

The alternative Hutu perspective is displayed on two narrative and intricately interwoven levels, one from Martha's point of view and the other from Rukundo's point of view. The film starts with a flashback of images in black-and-white of a young man who flees through the jungle, and via previous films on the genocide the obvious connotation is that it is a Tutsi boy running from his assailants. A text then tells us that ten years has gone by, and the next scene is a history lesson at a university. The lecturer asks the students what they know about Rwandan history and one young man delivers the official answer with colonial connotations: "Before the arrival of the whites in Rwanda, people lived in peace without any discrimination. They were governed by a king, the father of the nation." However, another student raises his hand, countering the first one's answer: "I don't think the king was the father of the nation as my colleague has just said, as I've never heard of a Hutu who became a king, and at that time, Tutsis were given more opportunities while the majority mainly made of Hutus was oppressed."

This answer, of course, complicates the official history by highlighting a Hutu perspective on Rwandan history, and it is accepted by the lecturer without further discussion. But for the narrative of the film, the importance lies in the fact that Martha attends this history class. During the discussion Dushimirimana cuts several times to her face, thus emphasizing that she absorbs this alternative way of thinking about the role of the Hutus, which then implicitly facilitates the coming love story.

As the young couple gets to know each other, they tell each other their respective stories. However, when Rukundo tells his story—prompted by Martha's questions: "Where were you? Were you with the killers?"—we get a lengthy black-and-white flashback that further nuances the Hutu involvement in the genocide. It turns out that Rukundo's father was a local leader during the genocide and that the family received military training and weapons. As the genocide starts, the father first forces Rukundo's brother to kill his Tutsi wife, and then the father tries to coerce the young Rukundo to kill a woman with a machete at a roadblock. When Rukundo refuses, the father prepares to kill his own son, but he is saved by his brother, who tells him to flee—thus leading to the scene at the beginning of the film where he runs through a jungle full of dead bodies.

By focusing on a young and, during the genocide, innocent Hutu boy, *A Love Letter to My Country* not only complicates the official Rwandan history of the genocide—without ever denying what happened—but the film also delivers a fierce critique of the official policy of ethnic non-recognition as something quite impossible, at least on a family level where the memories of the genocide and ethnicity continue to cast long shadows into the future.

As seen in the international film production on the genocide against the Tutsi a focus on perpetrators was not uncommon; first in the earliest documentaries produced immediately after the genocide in which the perpetrators often were portrayed as equal victims, and second in the plethora of reconciliation films in which the perpetrators' graphic testimonies were used to establish, from a Western perspective, the seemingly impossible path to reconciliation. In Rwandan documentary film production this second practice of using perpetrators' testimonies occurs in films like *Keepers of Memory* to create a contrast between the survivor's perspective and the perspective of the perpetrators. However, there are three films that depart from the portrayal of perpetrators as embodiments of pure evil.

In the short film *Confession* (2008), the debut film of Kivu Ruhorahoza, directed under the name "Daddy" Ruhorahoza, the point of view is that of a Hutu family man in Rwanda who suffers from a guilty conscience as he is unable to forget the young woman he raped and left for dead during the genocide thirteen years earlier. This is an ultra-low-budget film, but despite that it is a film full of symbolism—principally religious symbolism—as the man is of the Catholic faith. It is also the Sacrament of Penance that in some sense releases him in the end. The fact that the film is about rape during the genocide and that it is mainly told through the eyes of the rapist make it stand out, bordering as it does on "genocide denial." During a screening of the film at Centro de Información Naciones Unidas Mexico (United Nations Information Center Mexico) in 2009, Ruhorahoza explained this particular point of view in *Confession*, saying that "there is always some humanity left in every criminal"—a standpoint that brought the film international praise (*Confession* was screened at the Venice Film Festival and was rewarded at the Milan, African, Asian, and Latin American Film Festivals) but also criticism in Rwanda where he was accused of sympathizing with the rapist, and thus with the "enemy."[87]

Better In Than Out (2008) is a short documentary film which follows a group of genocide convicts, freed by Kagame's presidential amnesty, on the eve of their release from a prison on the outskirts of Kigali. It is not a straightforward film about Hutu perpetrators confessing their crimes. Instead, the film observes how the prisoners make plans for their re-entry into society. One prisoner wants to buy some land, while others dream of a new cell phone. When released the next day, there are tearful reunions: wives hugging husbands, fathers greeting children, with rising music on the soundtrack and close-ups filmed in slow motion. In short, the Hutu perpetrators are shown as human beings. However, the twist is that the filmmaker then juxtaposes them with one prisoner, seemingly the only one who feels remorse about his crimes, thus pointing to the possible problems of releasing these prisoners. With this set-up, the film turns into a critique of Rwanda's chosen path to reconciliation, thus straying from the official narrative.

The third film with a Hutu perspective, *Matière Grise* (*Grey Matter*, 2011), is a feature film directed by Kivu Ruhorahoza. *Grey Matter* not only stands out among Rwandan films about the genocide. With its unique artistic expression—taking clear inspiration from the European Art Cinema tradition—the film stands out in relation to the international film production on the genocide, where the solemn drama and the factual documentary totally dominated output. In accordance with this, *Grey Matter* received attention on the international film festival circuit, winning awards at both the Tribeca Film Festival and the Warsaw Film Festival in 2011.[88]

Grey Matter is comprised of three interrelated narratives. The first is a circular meta-narrative where we follow a director, Balthazar, as he struggles to finance a feature film about the genocide called "Le cycle du cafard" ("The Cycle of the Cockroach"), and whose efforts are dismissed as his story is deemed to be irrelevant by a government representative. Instead, he is encouraged to make a film with a clear message on either HIV prevention or gender-based violence.

Despite this setback, Balthazar pushes on with the production of the film, and in what are seemingly imagined scenes we get to see realizations of the two parts of "The Cycle of the Cockroach." The first part portrays the Madman, a Hutu perpetrator who is locked up in an asylum where he listens to (imagined) broadcasts of hate radio where the announcer rails against "cockroaches." The Madman catches a cockroach in a glass, and verbally attacks and finally "rapes" it. The second part of "The Cycle of the Cockroach" tells the story of two traumatized Tutsi siblings, Yvan and Justine, who have locked themselves into a compound where they try to rebuild their lives.

Ruhorahoza deliberately dissolves both time and space in *Grey Matter*. The circular meta-narrative takes place in an undisclosed African country, although the context and the origin of the actual director, Ruhorahoza, unavoidably places it in Rwanda, with the genocide against the Tutsi as its logical focal point. Yet, at the same time, the two narratives of "The Cycle of the Cockroach" are not as easily located. The Madman's narrative could take place both before and after the genocide; while the narrative with the siblings could take place after the genocide, indicated in the film by the fact that they arrived in the undisclosed country after the genocide, but also during the genocide as they, when leaving the safe comfort of the compound, are attacked by the machete wielding Madman.

Grey Matter could be interpreted as a continuation of the short film *Confession*, where the perpetrator Hutu theme was nuanced according to the principle that there is always some humanity left in every criminal. In *Grey Matter* this view is expanded to include the difficulty of collective memory and remembrance in the meta-narrative, but also the question of individual versus collective guilt and trauma in the two parts of "The Cycle of the Cockroach." That is, what is often seen as a black-and-white narrative of the genocide turns into grayer areas in *Grey Matter*. One of the reasons for the narrative's dissolution, and the use of an undisclosed country instead of a specified one, is that Ruhorahoza tries to discuss and thus portray these issues on a more general, human level.[89] In an interview, Ruhorahoza clarified this position: "Unfortunately, most politicians are too cynical to try and understand the context in which citizens become perpetrators of mass atrocities. Perpetrators (or villains) are certainly victims of systems—that is all. And survivors are victims of the perpetrators, just to avoid labeling people with the same adjective."[90]

A central sequence in the narrative about the Madman which exemplifies this thinking, while simultaneously criticizing the use of colonialism in the official historical Rwandan memory on the genocide, comes when the Madman receives different objects through his barred window (beer, pills, marijuana, and finally a machete), passed through by black hands. When he is intoxicated, a video is projected onto the wall, showing white hands making a cockroach

Figure 11.7 The Madman (Jp Uwayezu) in *Grey Matter* (2011)

omelet, assisted by black hands. Finally, the Madman is handed a key to his cell by a white hand. This preparation and manipulation of the Madman does not deliver him from personal guilt, but at the same time it offers a deeper understanding of how perpetrators became victims of a system that was run by Hutu extremists (black hands) and substantiated by colonialist involvement (white hands, foremost symbolizing the French).

Grey Matter is one of a few Rwandan films to have received academic attention, and the interpretations of the film differ, which perhaps can be seen as a positive result of the film's complex narrative. Social scientist Lior Zylberman points out that *Grey Matter* "enables audiences to get to know the genocidal violence without recreating or exhibiting corpses," while media analyst Mick Broderick interprets the film as a critique of Rwanda's national project of reconciliation.[91] Film scholar and filmmaker Piotr Cieplak takes a more elaborate view, stating that the complex story with multiple narratives in *Grey Matter* is an indication of "the irrelevance of historical objectivity when confronted with the subjectivity of experience and personal trauma." According to Cieplak, Ruhorahoza manages to avoid national and political positions, thus succeeding in "retaining the overwhelming and invasive intimacy of recollection, recurrence and presence."[92]

Cieplak's interpretation is right on point, but the question remains: is it even possible to avoid the national, and, thereby, the official history of the genocide? Obviously, this is what Ruhorahoza does in *Grey Matter* when the history of the genocide turns into subjective histories of the same event, which also include a Hutu perspective that in some ways complicates the presentation of the perpetrator as a sort of victim. However, none of the scholars discusses *Grey Matter* with its reception in mind, begging the question: who is the intended audience? For instance, Cieplak concludes that *Grey Matter*, both "formally and in terms of the plot, work[s] against history, against knowledge but not against understanding."[93] But whose understanding does this apply to? Ruhorahoza himself is very clear about his ambition and the different audience receptions:

> I didn't think much about the audience because I knew the film would end up being seen by very few individuals in several cities across the world. I am very much aware that movies such as mine are watched by hardcore cinephiles and some other curious individuals who have a connection to the story depicted. What I realized is that when I screened the film abroad, I had audiences understanding the approach and methodology but not getting the story. In Rwanda on the other hand, I had audiences understanding the story but being confused by the approach and methodology.[94]

This presumes that Western audiences were or are ready for a novel, more artistic approach towards the Rwandan genocide, while Rwandan audiences were/are not. Although winning several international prizes, *Grey Matter* was not received without criticism by Western reviewers. In *The New York Times*, the lukewarm review positioned *Grey Matter* as an "acutely probing (if somewhat static and indulgent) film,"[95] while Howard Feinstein found no redeeming qualities in the film's narration, writing that "you could interpret it as the fickleness of the mind, especially in its engagement with the creative process. Perhaps both . . . here Ruhorahoza appears to want it both ways, which make for a silty cake that has failed to rise."[96] This kind of reception can easily be interpreted as Ruhorahoza unnecessarily complicating such an important subject as the genocide by making it too artistic.

There are no regular Rwandan reviews of *Grey Matter* but the film was nevertheless a recurrent news item due to the international attention it received. in addition to reporting on the different prizes, two striking similarities occur in these articles. First, the reporters, when referring to the story and the narrative, confess to not understanding the film. Second, the conspicuous Hutu narrative in *Grey Matter* is either downplayed or most often is not even mentioned, in comparison to the Tutsi perspective which is always mentioned.[97] The one time the Madman story is mentioned, it is from an accusatory standpoint: "The second story is about a man locked up in an asylum, haunted by the atrocities he committed during the Genocide."[98] But as the dissolution of time and space in *Grey Matter* has revealed, the second storyline could just as easily have taken place before the genocide. Obviously, such a grayish storytelling does not correspond well with such a black-and-white subject as the genocide in Rwanda.

The Everyday Use of the Genocide in Rwandan Film and Future Goals

Doubtless, the genocide and, above all, the memory of the genocide have greatly affected the development of the Rwandan film industry, both in terms of international influence and, more concretely, on a material level via the different international film productions that have been located in Rwanda, from *100 Days* to *Small Country: An African Childhood* (2020). This has contributed to professional know-how and thematic as well as visual inspiration. In addition, foreign involvement has come via the funding of the Rwandan Film Institute and the Kwetu Film Institute, where specific topics, such as the genocide, have generated financial support. A side effect of this development is that the Rwandan film industry has expanded over the last twenty years, but these international influences have also been combined with national policies and regulations regarding how the genocide is portrayed and remembered. Foremost this has resulted in narrative and documentary films that are characterized by survivor nationalism. However, another outcome of these restrictions on artistic freedom is that the number of genocide films has decreased over the years—a decline probably connected to a loss of interest among filmmakers and audiences, and a desire to move on, not least among Hutu audiences. Already in 2009, Eric Kabera expressed a wish to move away from the genocide theme and into more lighthearted projects, which eventually resulted in comedies such as *Africa United* and *Karani Ngufu* (2019), on which he acted as executive producer. In the same interview Kabera stated that "young filmmakers in Rwanda don't necessarily relate to the genocide," instead focusing on other subjects.[99]

Although the genocide theme has lost some of its power as a major subject of Rwandan film, the genocide against the Tutsi still affects the films produced, in various ways, both directly and indirectly. For instance, in *Umurabyo* ("Flash," 2015), an action/drama film about trafficking set in Kigali, the genocide is used in a normalized way. That is, the genocide is not part of the main plot. Instead, it is used to develop the main character, Prince, and this is achieved in two scenes. The first scene is short and shows Prince having a nightmare, which is illustrated with just two seconds-long clips of "Corpses by the Road" and "The Nick Hughes Footage," thus immediately establishing Prince not only as a survivor but also as a young man with psychological problems due to the genocide. Later, Prince has a conversation with his love interest of film, Zubeda, during which he informs her that his parents were killed in the genocide. Besides this, the genocide is not mentioned; it is just there, thus becoming an everyday part of Rwandan society in the narrative.

Even though the genocide is part of *Umurabyo*, the ethnicities of Hutu and Tutsi are never mentioned in the film; perhaps seemingly obvious for a Rwandan

Figure 11.8 "The Nick Hughes Footage" used as a nightmare in *Umurabyo* (2015)

audience, but also dependent on the official policy of ethnic non-recognition in Rwanda, implemented by the Rwanda Development Board (RDB) that issues a "Registration Certificate of Artistic Work." This non-recognition of ethnicities occurs in several films, for example in the short film *JFJ* (2009) in which a soldier (evidently a Tutsi) is sent to the front to fight the enemy (the Hutus). An even more conspicuous use of this non-recognition occurs in *Amahano I Bwami*, a historical drama about the taboo of incest within the royal family set at the turn of the century in 1900, when Rwanda was under the rule of Tutsi kings. Although filled to the brim with folklore, dances, historical costumes, and historical characters, the Tutsi ethnicity is not mentioned once in the film.

HIV/AIDS is another subject that could have been more closely associated with the genocide, as rape was used as a weapon on a massive scale against Tutsi women in 1994. HIV/AIDS is also a recurring theme in Rwandan film production, supported financially by both national and international organizations, and resulting in short films such as *Scars of My Day* (2006), *Graduation Day* (2006), and *Hey Mr DJ* (2007). However, as has been discussed already, the devastating effects of AIDS due to war rape never became part of the survivor nationalism narrative. The subject is not even touched upon in the documentary *Through My Eyes*, where the problems associated with AIDS form a large part of the narrative. The only exception where this connection is hinted at is in the short film *Strength in Fear* (2012), directed by Ella Mutuyimana.

Strength in Fear is about a young schoolgirl Isekere, whose mother is dying of AIDS. It soon becomes noticeable that Isekere too is sick, and when she shows symptoms, she is shunned and made fun of in school, where the other pupils, and even some of the teachers, imply that she has been infected by having sex, and thus has only herself to blame. However, Isekere has been infected by her mother during pregnancy, and it turns out that her mother in turn has been raped, thus becoming infected with HIV. However, this is only implied, and there is never any explicit connection to the genocide, or to ethnicities in the film, other than as a subtext, thus allowing Muruyimana to tell a story about war rape and AIDS without getting into trouble with the government.

While it is true that the genocide theme has given way to other subjects in Rwanda, a film like *Umurabyo* shows that the genocide is and continues to be a distinctive part of Rwandan collective memory. On the other hand, prolific and acclaimed filmmakers such as Kivu Ruhorahoza, Gilbert Ndahayo, and Joël Karekezi have moved on, literally to other countries, but also to other subjects. However, as the Rwandan debate about *Black Earth Rising* showed, there is awareness and an aspiration for Rwandan filmmakers to tell their own stories about the genocide, and thus to create their own media memories of the killings, often in contrast to the transnational historical media memory of the Rwandan genocide. This struggle seemingly stands between who owns the story of the genocide and what the true story is, but also how a story about the genocide ought to be portrayed, narratively and aesthetically.

Nonetheless, an underlying issue in this debate concerns the question of how the memory of the genocide is disseminated and what possible impact this has on the collective local as well as global memory. A Hollywood film or a Netflix series can, only by virtue of its size and distribution methods, appropriate an almost total monopoly on the historical media memory. But this is not a black-and-white issue. Kivu Ruhorahoza, for example, sets this up as a dichotomy between the global media perspective and the local media perspective:

> *Hotel Rwanda* and *Shooting Dogs* were designed like mainstream products supposed to make money with simplistic narratives. *Hotel Rwanda* succeeded very well but *Shooting Dogs* was just so bad. We live in a world where it is never the most honest and the most erudite whose messages get communicated. The loudest, the smartest and the most strategic are competing for attention and winning.[100]

Conversely, there exists a vision to make a Rwandan big-budget film about the genocide against the Tutsi that can compete with the international productions and, at the same time, correct the transnational historical media memory of the genocide. Here the focus above all is on Hollywood's production of cinematic history as an example to follow, since films like *Malcolm X* (1992) and *Judas and the Black Messiah* (2021) have "not only kept the memories of the heroes [. . .] alive, [they have] also ingrained in young American minds a respect for, and willingness to, commit acts of heroism as well. Acts of heroism, in their psyche, have become almost as American as apple pie."[101] To be able to accomplish this, the film in question must reach and touch audiences dramatically. In the documentary *My Globe is Broken in Rwanda* (2010) there is a scene in which Alice Kayisire, a co-worker at the Rwandan Film Festival, watches *Shooting Dogs*, and comments on what Rwandan films on the genocide are lacking:

> The films of Rwanda, I don't think they are so powerful as the films about the Holocaust. Sometimes when you watch films about the Holocaust, through the stories of the Jews you're watching the story of Rwanda. When you watch a film about Rwanda it feels empty. Films about the Holocaust convey what happened in the Rwandan genocide. If you watch films about the Rwandan genocide, they don't touch you.

This perceived emptiness can probably be linked to the restrictions that Rwandan film production regarding the genocide is subjected to but also to the financial situation with consistently low budgets.

Nevertheless, according to Eric Kabera, the said big-budget film on the genocide is in the works and has been for quite some time.[102] The working title is "Inkotanyi" and it will tell "the story of the liberators, the ones who stopped the Genocide."[103] In Kinyarwanda, inkotany means to fight without delay, to never to give up, but it is also the official name of the RPF. Presumably, it will be a historical film with nationalist overtones, told from the winning perspective. However, the question is if yet another Rwandan film made from a survivor/winner perspective will satisfy the local as well as the transnational historical media memory of the genocide against the Tutsi, especially considering Rwanda's official policy that all citizens are equally Rwandans. However, that is a question for the future.

Notes

Chapter 1

1. See, for example, "Recommended History VIDEO," Active History, https://www.activehistory.co.uk/library/index-VIDEO.php; "Teaching Schindler's List," Facing History, https://www.facinghistory.org/resource-library/teaching-schindlers-list; "Home Page," Teach with Movies, https://teachwithmovies.org/; "Schindler's List as an Educational Tool," Yad Vashem, https://www.yadvashem.org/education/educational-materials/lesson-plans/schindlers-activities.html; "Teacher's Notes," Film Education, http://www.filmeducation.org/pdf/film/schindler.pdf; "Schindler's List 2019," Swedish Film Institute, https://www.filminstitutet.se/sv/fa-kunskap-om-film/filmpedagogik/filmhandledningar/schindlers-list-2019/; "Companion Resource to Using Schindler's List in the Classroom," Echoes and Reflections, https://echoesandreflections.org/wp-content/uploads/2019/01/Companion_Resource_to_Schindlers_List_Bios.pdf; "Teaching Schindler," Southern Institute, https://southerninstitute.info/teaching-schindler/; "'Mój dziadek by mnie zastrzelił'. Zwierzenia ciemnoskórej wnuczki nazistowskiego zbrodniarza," DW, http://www.dw.de/m%C3%B3j-dziadek-by-mnie-zastrzeli%C5%82-zwierzenia-ciemnosk%C3%B3rej-wnuczki-nazistowskiego-zbrodniarza/a-17114326, all accessed March 14, 2023.
2. Sophia Wood, "Film and Atrocity: The Holocaust as Spectacle," in *Film & Genocide*, Kristi M. Wilson and Tomás F. Crowder-Taraborrelli, eds. (Madison and London: The University of Wisconsin Press 2012), 26–33. See also, *Spielberg's Holocaust. Critical Perspectives on Schindler's List*, Yosefa Loshitzky, ed. (Bloomington and Indianapolis: Indiana University Press 1997) and Liel Leibovitz, "Steven Spielberg's Schindler's List is both a Moral and an Aesthetic Disaster, an Embodiment of Much that is Wrong with American-Jewish Life," *Tablet Magazine*, December 13, 2011, http://tabletmag.com/jewish-arts-and-culture/85945/list less, accessed March 14, 2023.
3. "Steven Spielberg," Box Office Mojo, http://www.boxofficemojo.com/people/chart/?view=Director&id=stevenspielberg.htm&sort=gross&order=DESC&p=.htm, accessed March 14, 2023.

4 "Home Page," USC Shoah Foundation, https://sfi.usc.edu/, accessed March 14, 2023.
5 "Schindler's List Awards," IMDb, https://www.imdb.com/title/tt0108052/awards/?ref_=tt_awd, accessed March 14, 2023. Sara Horowitz, "But Is It Good for the Jews? Spielberg's Schindler and the Aesthetics of Atrocity," in *Spielberg's Holocaust: Critical Perspectives on Schindler's List*, Yosefa Loshitzky, ed. (Bloomington and Indianapolis: Indiana University Press 1997), 119–139.
6 Wood, "Film and Atrocity," 37–39. See also, Joshua Hirsch, *AfterImage: Film, Trauma, and the Holocaust* (Philadelphia, PA: Temple University Press 2004), 3.
7 Ty Burr, "Hotel Rwanda Movie Review: Cheadle Brings Quiet Power to 'Rwanda'," *The Boston Globe*, January 7, 2005; Madelaine Hron, "Genres of 'Yet An Other Genocide': Cinematic Representations of Rwanda," in *Film & Genocide*, Kristi M. Wilson and Tomás F. Crowder-Taraborrelli, eds. (Madison and London: The University of Wisconsin Press 2012), 140; Philip French, "Schindler in Rwanda," *The Observer*, February 27, 2005.
8 Mick LaSalle, "Amid a Massacre, an Ordinary Man Stands Tall to Protect Others," *San Francisco Chronicle*, January 7, 2005. See also Roger Ebert, "Hotel Rwanda," *Chicago Sun Times*, December 21, 2004.
9 See, for example, "Material didáctico (abierto). 'Hotel Rwanda'," Proyecto DeCine, https://proyectodecine.wordpress.com/2009/09/08/material-didactico-abierto-hotel-ruanda/; "Comprehension and Discussion Activities for the Movie Hotel Rwanda," Curriculum Project, http://curriculumproject.org/wp-content/uploads/Hotel%20Rwanda.pdf; "Hotel Rwanda," Film Education, http://www.filmeducation.org/pdf/film/HotelRwanda.pdf; "Hotel Rwanda and Sometimes in April," Teach with Movies, https://teachwithmovies.org/hotel-rwanda/; "Der Völkermord in Ruanda im Film," Lernen aus der geschichte, http://lernen-aus-der-geschichte.de/Lernen-und-Lehren/content/2616/2009-10-10-Der-Voelkermord-Ruanda-im-Film; "Hotel Rwanda," Enseignons, http://www.enseignons.be/upload/secondaire/histoire/Rwanda-edu-FR-LR.pdf; "Hotell Rwanda", Swedish Film Institute, https://www.filminstitutet.se/sv/fa-kunskap-om-film/filmpedagogik/filmhandledningar/hotell-rwanda/; "Filmer til bruk i undervisningen," HL-senteret, http://www.hlsenteret.no/undervisning/materiell/7filmer-til-bruk-i-undervisningen.html, all accessed March 14, 2023.
10 Urther Rwafa, "Film Representations of the Rwandan Genocide," *African Identities* 8:4 (2010), 389–408; Jonathan D. Glover, "Genocide, Human Rights, and the Politics of Memorialization: 'Hotel Rwanda' and Africa's World War," *South Atlantic Review* 75:2 (2010), 102; F. Alex von Tunzelmann, "Hotel Rwanda: History with a Hollywood Ending," *The Guardian*, August 7, 2014. "Hotel Rwanda," Box Office Mojo, http://www.boxofficemojo.com/movies/?id=hotelrwanda.htm, accessed March 14, 2023.
11 Glover, "Genocide, Human Rights, and the Politics of Memorialization," 96.
12 Nyasha Mboti, "Song and Genocide: Investigating the Function of Yvonne Chaka Chaka's 'Umqombothi' in Hotel Rwanda," *Critical Arts: A South-North Journal of Cultural & Media Studies* 26:5 (2012), 728–744.

13 Tanja Sakota-Kokot, "When the Past Talks to the Present: Fiction Narrative and the 'Other' in Hotel Rwanda," *Critical Arts: A South-North Journal of Cultural & Media Studies* 27:2 (2013), 221.
14 Mohamed Adhikari, "Hotel Rwanda: Too Much Heroism, Too Little History—or Horror?," in *Black and White in Colour: Africa's History on Screen*, Vivian Bickford-Smith and Richard Mendelsohn, eds. (Athens: Ohio University Press 2006), 290-291.
15 Argentina, Austria, Bangladesh, Belgium, Bosnia and Herzegovina, Cambodia, Cameroon, Canada, Czech Republic, Congo, Denmark, Ethiopia, Finland, France, Georgia, Germany, Iraq, Ireland, Israel, Italy, Japan, Kenya, Morocco Netherlands, Norway, Palestine, Poland, Russia, Rwanda, Serbia and Montenegro, Slovakia, South Africa, Spain, Sweden, Switzerland, Uganda, the UK, the USA, Zambia.
16 Tommy Gustafsson, *Det var en gång: historia för barn i svensk television under det långa 1970-talet* (Malmö: Roos & Tegnér/Universus Academic Press 2014), 18-38.
17 Tommy Gustafsson and Klara Arnberg, *Moralpanik och lågkultur: genus- och mediehistoriska analyser 1900-2012* (Stockholm: Atlas Akademi 2013). See also, *Silencing Cinema: Film Censorship around the World*, Daniel Biltereyst and Roel Vande Winkel, eds. (London and New York: Palgrave Macmillan 2013).
18 See, for example, Robert A. Rosenstone, *History on Film/Film on History* (Harlow: Pearson Education Ltd 2006), 3; Alan S. Marcus and Thomas H. Levine, "Exploring the Past with Feature Film," in *Celluloid Blackboard. Teaching History with Film*, Alan S. Marcus, ed. (Charlotte, NC: Information Age Publishing 2006), 3; Ulf Zander, *Clio på bio: Om amerikansk film, historia och identitet* (Lund: Historiska media 2006), 14; Robert Brent Toplin, *Reel History: In Defense of Hollywood* (Lawrence: University Press of Kansas 2002), 60-61.
19 Tommy Gustafsson, "Filmen som historisk källa. Historiografi, pluralism, representativitet," *Historisk tidskrift* 126:3 (2006), 471-479. Toplin, *Reel History*, 17-19; Aaron Kerner, *Film and the Holocaust: New Perspectives on Dramas, Documentaries, and Experimental Films* (New York: Continuum 2011), 1.
20 See, for example, the discussions in Alexander MacGregor, "Gladiator," *Filmhäftet* 29:2 (2001), 7-12, and Rosenstone, *History on Film/Film on History*, 1-16.
21 Mats Jönsson, *Film och historia: historisk hollywoodfilm 1960-2000* (Lund: KFS 2004), 4-5, 8-9.
22 Hayden White, *Metahistory: The Historical Imagination in Nineteenth-Century Europe* (Baltimore, MD and London: The Johns Hopkins University Press 1975).
23 Keith Jenkins, "Modernist Disavowals and Postmodern Reminders of the Condition of History Today: On Jean François Lyotard," *Rethinking History* 8:3 (2004), 367-368.
24 Ian Traynor, "Irving Jailed for Denying Holocaust," *The Guardian*, February 21, 2006; D. D. Guttenplan, *The Holocaust on Trial: Justice and the David Irving Libel Case* (New York and London: W. W. Norton & Company 2002); Négationnisme, "Robert Faurisson condamné à trois mois avec sursis," *L'Humanité*, October 4, 2006.

25 Klas-Göran Karlsson, "The Holocaust as a Problem of Historical Culture," in *Echos of the Holocaust: Historical Cultures in Contemporary Europe*, Klas-Göran Karlsson and Ulf Zander, eds. (Lund: Nordic Academic Press 2003), 30-38.
26 Rosenstone, *History on Film/Film on History*, 163.
27 There are a few exceptions to this rule, where European historical films are discussed. See, for example, *Perspectives on European Film and History*, Leen Engelen and Roel Vande Winkel, eds. (Gent: Academia Press 2007) and Ib Bondebjerg, *Screening Twentieth Century Europe: Television, History, Memory* (London: Palgrave Macmillan 2020).
28 Rosenstone, *History on Film/Film on History*; Toplin, *Reel History*; Andrew Higson, *English Heritage, English Cinema: Costume Drama Since 1980* (Oxford and New York: Oxford University Press 2003). See also, Mike Chopra-Gant, *Cinema and History: The Telling of Stories* (London and New York: Wallflower Press 2008); Trevor McCrisken and Andrew Pepper, *American History and Contemporary Hollywood Film* (New Brunswick, NJ: Rutgers University Press 2005).
29 See, for example, Jönsson, *Film och historia*, 1.
30 *The Persistence of History: Cinema, Television and the Modern Event*, Vivian Sobchack, ed. (London and New York: AFI and Routledge 1996); Christian Metz, *The Imaginary Signifier: Psychoanalysis and the Cinema* (Bloomington and Indianapolis: Indiana University Press 1986).
31 See, for example, Hirsch, *Afterimage*.
32 Kerner, *Film and the Holocaust*, 6, 21.
33 Zander, *Clio på bio*, 16-20.
34 David Ludvigsson, *The Historian-Filmmaker's Dilemma. Historical Documentaries in Sweden in the Era of Häger and Villius* (Uppsala: Acta Universitatis Upsaliensis 2003), passim.
35 Rosenstone, *History on Film/Film on History*, 111-133; Toplin, *Reel History*, passim.
36 Ludvigsson, *The Historian-Filmmaker's Dilemma*, 13-19.
37 Kerner, *Film and the Holocaust*, passim.
38 See, for example, Rwafa, "Film Representations of the Rwandan Genocide"; Glover, "Genocide, Human Rights, and the Politics of Memorialization"; Duncan Fisher and Jolyon Mitchell, "Portraying Forgiveness through Documentary Film," *Studies in World Christianity* 18:2 (2012), 154-168; Frank Möller, "Rwanda Revisualized: Genocide, Photography, and the Era of the Witness," *Alternatives* 35:2 (2010), 113-136; Heather L. LaMarre and Kristen D. Landreville, "When is Fiction as Good as Fact? Comparing the Influence of Documentary and Historical Reenactment Films on Engagement, Affect, Issue Interest, and Learning," *Mass Communication and Society* 12:4 (2009), 537-555; Roger Bromley, "After Such Knowledge, What Forgiveness? Cultural Representations of Reconciliation in Rwanda," *French Cultural Studies* 20:2 (2008), 181-197.
39 See, for example, LaMarre and Landreville, "When is Fiction as Good as Fact?," 543; Sakota-Kokot, "When the Past Talks to the Present," 225; Hron, "Genres of 'Yet an Other Genocide'," 139.
40 For further history of the blockbuster film, see Justin Wyatt, *High Concept: Movies*

and Marketing in Hollywood (Austin: University of Texas Press 1994) and *Blockbuster Movies*, Julian Stringer, ed. (London and New York: Routledge 2003).
41 "Hotel Rwanda," IMDb, http://www.imdb.com/title/tt0395169/, accessed March 14, 2023.
42 Richard O'Connell, "Interview with Greg Barker, Director of *Ghost of Rwanda* (2004)," in *Film & Genocide*, Kristi M. Wilson and Tomás F. Crowder-Taraborrelli, eds. (Madison and London: The University of Wisconsin Press 2012), 210.
43 "Censorship Card 93,125" Swedish Board of Film Censorship's Archive at The National Archives (1958).
44 Ulf Zander, "Holocaust at the Limits: Historical Culture and the Nazi Genocide in the Television Era," in *Echoes of the Holocaust. Historical Cultures in Contemporary Europe*, Klas-Göran Karlsson and Ulf Zander, eds. (Lund: Nordic Academic Press 2003), 261–263.
45 Yosefa Loshitsky, "Introduction," in *Spielberg's Holocaust. Critical Perspectives on Schindler's List*, Yosefa Loshitzky, ed. (Bloomington and Indianapolis: Indiana University Press 1997), 2.
46 Miriam Bratu Hansen, "*Schindler's List* Is Not Shoah: Second Commandment, Popular Modernism, and Public Memory," in *Spielberg's Holocaust. Critical Perspectives on Schindler's List*, Yosefa Loshitzky, ed. (Bloomington and Indianapolis: Indiana University Press 1997), 80–85.
47 Stanley Cohen, *States of Denial: Knowing about Atrocities and Suffering* (Cambridge: Polity Press 2007), 185.
48 See, for example the dissertation in Anthropology, Anna Hedlund, *Exile Warriors: Violence and Community among Hutu Rebels in the Eastern Congo* (Lund: Lund University 2014).
49 Toplin, *Reel History*, 60–61.
50 Hannah Arendt, *Eichmann in Jerusalem: A Report on the Banality of Evil* (London: Penguin Books 1996).
51 Piotr A. Cieplak, "Nick Hughes, Director of *100 Days* (2001), interviewed by," in *Film & Genocide*, Kristi M. Wilson and Tomás F. Crowder-Taraborrelli, eds. (Madison and London: The University of Wisconsin Press 2012), 221.
52 Piotr A. Cieplak, "The Rwandan Genocide and the Bestiality of Representation in *100 Days* (2001) and *Shooting Dogs* (2005)," *Journal of African Cinemas* 2:1 (2010), 57.
53 Bratu Hansen, "*Schindler's List* is Not Shoah," 98.
54 Kerner, *Film and the Holocaust*, 28.
55 See, for example, Tomas Sniegon, *Den försvunna historien. Förintelsen i tjeckisk och slovakisk historiekultur* (Lund: Lund University 2008), 173–211.
56 Tommy Gustafsson, "Swedish Television News Coverage and the Historical Media Memory of the Rwandan Genocide," *Scandia* 76:2 (2010), 80–98.
57 Cieplak, "The Rwandan Genocide and the Bestiality of Representation in *100 Days* (2001) and *Shooting Dogs* (2005)," 53–54.
58 Kobi Lev Niv, *Life is Beautiful, But not for Jews: Another View of the Film by Benigni* (New York: Scarecrow Press 2003).

59 Tommy Gustafsson, "*The Last Dog in Rwanda*: Swedish Educational Films and Film Teaching Guides on the History of Genocide," in *Regional Aesthetics: Locating Swedish Media*, Erik Hedling, Olof Hedling and Mats Jönsson, eds. (Stockholm: National Library of Sweden 2010), 43-62.

60 For valuable overviews of global/transnational history, see Akira Iriye, *Global and Transnational History: The Past, Present, and Future* (London: Palgrave Pivot 2013); Sebastian Conrad, *What Is Global History?* (Princeton, NJ: Princeton University Press 2017); Fiona Paisley and Pamela Scully, *Writing Transnational History* (London and New York: Bloomsbury 2019).

61 David L. Ransel, "Reflections on Transnational and World History in the USA and its Applications," *Historisk tidskrift* 127:4 (2007), 628.

62 See, for example, Anthony D. Smith, *Nations and Nationalism in a Global Era* (Oxford: Polity Press 1995) and George L. Mosse, *Fallen Soldiers: Reshaping the Memory of the World Wars* (Oxford and New York: Oxford University Press 1990).

63 Elisabeth Ezra and Terry Rowden, "General Introduction," in *Transnational Cinema. The Reader*, Elisabeth Ezra and Terry Rowden, eds. (London and New York: Routledge 2006), 1.

64 Ezra and Rowden, "General Introduction," 3.

65 See, for example, Ella Shohat and Robert Stam, *Unthinking Eurocentrism: Multiculturalism and the Media* (London and New York: Routledge 2014).

66 Toplin, *Reel History*, 60-61.

67 For a wider discussion of *Shoah*'s construction, see for example, Stella Bruzzi, *New Documentary* (London and New York: Routledge 2006), 98-109.

68 General Assembly Resolution 260, "Convention on the Prevention and Punishment of the Crime of Genocide." Adopted by the General Assembly of the United Nations on December, 9, 1948, http://un-documents.net/a3r260.htm, accessed March 14, 2023.

69 Ransel, "Reflections on Transnational and World History in the USA and its Applications," 630.

70 Mamadou Diawara, Bernard Lategan and Jörn Rüsen, "Introduction," in *Historical Memory in Africa: Dealing with the Past, Researching for the Future in an Intercultural Context*, Mamadou Diawara, Bernard Lategan and Jörn Rüsen, eds. (New York and Oxford: Berghahn 2013), 3.

71 Meeting with Jean Damascène Bizimana, Executive Secretary of The National Commission for the Fight against Genocide (CNLG), Kigali, March 12, 2015.

72 United Nations Security Council, Resolution 2150. Adopted by the Security Council at its 7155th meeting, on April 16, 2014, 2, https://digitallibrary.un.org/record/769207?ln=zh_CN, accessed March 14, 2023.

73 Catharine Newbury, *The Cohesion of Oppression. Clientship and Ethnicity in Rwanda, 1860-1960* (New York: Columbia University Press 1988), 229. See also, Erin Jessee and Sarah E. Watkins, "Good Kings, Bloody Tyrants, and Everything In Between: Representations of the Monarchy in Post-Genocide Rwanda," *History in Africa* 41 (2014), 35-62.

74 Newbury, *The Cohesion of Oppression*, 53-61, 152.

75 Newbury, *The Cohesion of Oppression*, 14. See also, Mamadou Diawara, "Remembering the Past, Reaching for the Future: Aspects of African Historical Memory in an International Context," in *Historical Memory in Africa: Dealing with the Past, Researching for the Future in a Intercultural Context*, Mamadou Diawara, Bernard Lategan and Jörn Rüsen, eds. (New York and Oxford: Berghahn 2013), 90-91.
76 Newbury, *The Cohesion of Oppression*, 213.
77 Newbury, *The Cohesion of Oppression*, 38-52.
78 Newbury, *The Cohesion of Oppression*, 52, 115-117.
79 Roméo Dallaire (with Brent Beardsley), *Shake Hands with the Devil. The Failure of Humanity in Rwanda* (New York: Carroll & Graf Publishers 2005), 279-280.
80 Newbury, *The Cohesion of Oppression*, 179.
81 Newbury, *The Cohesion of Oppression*, 114, 190-199.
82 Newbury, *The Cohesion of Oppression*, 191.
83 Mahmood Mamdani, *When Victims Become Killers. Colonialism, Nativism, and the Genocide in Rwanda* (Princeton, NJ: Princeton University Press 2001), 14.
84 Mamdani, *When Victims Become Killers*, 34-36.
85 Gérard Prunier, *The Rwanda Crisis: History of a Genocide* (Kampala: Fountain Publishers Limited 1999), 188. Linda Melvern, *Conspiracy to Murder: The Rwandan Genocide* (London and New York: Verso 2004). 49.
86 Linda Melvern, *Att förråda ett folk. Västmakterna och folkmordet i Rwanda* (Stockholm: Ordfront 2003), 31, 39.
87 Melvern, *Conspiracy to Murder*, 40.
88 Melvern, *Att förråda ett folk*, 66-67.
89 Security Council S/1999/1257. *Report of the Independent Inquiry into the Actions of the United Nations during the 1994 Genocide in Rwanda*, (United Nations: New York 1999), 8, 66, https://www.securitycouncilreport.org/atf/cf/%7B65BFCF9B-6D27-4E9C-8CD3-CF6E4FF96FF9%7D/POC%20S19991257.pdf, accessed March 14, 2023.
90 Jean-Pierre Chrétien, "RTLM Propaganda: The Democratic Alibi," in *The Media and the Rwanda Genocide*, Allan Thompson, ed. (London and Ann Arbor, MI: Pluto Press 2007), 55-61.
91 Thierry Lévêque, "French Probe Exonerates Rwanda Leader in Genocide," *Reuters*, January 10, 2012; Linda Melvern, "Rwanda: At Last We Know the Truth," *The Guardian*, January 10, 2012.
92 Prunier, *The Rwanda Crisis*, 182, 243; Melvern, *Conspiracy to Murder*, 20, 56; Melvern, *Att förråda ett folk*, 31-32, 79-80, 88-90; Dallaire, *Shake Hands with the Devil*, 255-256, 258.
93 The original fax can be found here: "The Rwanda 'Genocide Fax' Deconstructed," unredacted, https://nsarchive.wordpress.com/2014/01/09/genocidefaxdeconstructed/, accessed March 14, 2023.
94 Prunier, *The Rwanda Crisis*, 169.
95 "Brief History of Rwanda," Republic of Rwanda, https://rwandacg.org.au/home/about-rwanda/history-of-rwanda/; "Background of the Genocide against the

Tutsi," The National Commission for the Fight Against Genocide, https://www.cnlg.gov.rw/index.php?id=80, both sites accessed March 14, 2023.
96 United Nations, "The International Day of Reflection on the 1994 Genocide in Rwanda," http://www.un.org/events/rwanda/backgrounder.html, accessed April 23, 2015; Alison Des Forges, *"Leave None to Tell the Story": Genocide in Rwanda* (New York: Human Rights Watch 1999), 15.
97 See, for example, Pierre Péan, *Noires fureurs, blancs menteurs: Rwanda 1990–1994* (Paris: Hachette Pluriel 2014); Edward S. Herman and David Peterson, *Enduring Lies: The Rwandan Genocide in the Propaganda System, 20 Years Later* (The Real New Books 2014); Barrie Collins, *Rwanda 1994: The Myth of the Akazu Genocide Conspiracy and its Consequences* (London and New York: Palgrave Macmillan 2014).
98 "Rwanda: Ten Years After the Genocide," UNICEF, http://www.unicef.org/infobycountry/rwanda_genocide.html, accessed April 23, 2015.
99 Dallaire, *Shake Hands with the Devil*, 232, 245; Prunier, *The Rwanda Crisis*, 230.
100 Melvern, *Conspiracy to Murder*, 137, 197.
101 Dixon Kamukara, *Rwanda Conflict: Its Roots and Regional Implications* (Kampala: Fountain Publishers 1997), 92.
102 Melvern, *Conspiracy to Murder*, 229.
103 Dallaire, *Shake Hands with the Devil*, 275–291; Jared A. Cohen, *One Hundred Days of Silence: America and the Rwanda Genocide* (Lanham, MD and New York: Rowman & Littlefield 2006), 79.
104 Melvern, *Att förråda ett folk*, 206. See also, Anne Chaon, "Who Failed in Rwanda, Journalists or the Media?," in *The Media and the Rwanda Genocide*, Allan Thompson, ed. (London and Ann Arbor, MI: Pluto Press 2007), 162.
105 Charles Mironko, "The Effect of RTLM's Rhetoric of Ethnic Hatred in Rural Rwanda," in *The Media and the Rwanda Genocide*, Allan Thompson, ed. (London and Ann Arbor, MI: Pluto Press 2007), 125–135.
106 Melvern, *Conspiracy to Murder*, 164–165.
107 Prunier, *The Rwanda Crisis*, 236.
108 Melvern, *Conspiracy to Murder*, 169, 195, 209–210.
109 Prunier, *The Rwanda Crisis*, 261.
110 Prunier, *The Rwanda Crisis*, 261.
111 Prunier, *The Rwanda Crisis*, 261.
112 Binaifer Nowrojee, "A Lost Opportunity for Justice: Why Did the ICTR Not Prosecute Gender Propaganda?," in *The Media and the Rwanda Genocide*, Allan Thompson, ed. (London and Ann Arbor, MI: Pluto Press 2007), 362–372; Mark A. Drumbl, "'She Makes Me Ashamed to Be a Woman': The Genocide Conviction of Pauline Nyiramasuhuko, 2011," *Michigan Journal of International Law* 34 (2012), 116; United Nations, *Report on the Situation of Human Rights in Rwanda submitted by Mr. René Degni-Segui, Special Rapporteur on the Commission of Human Rights*, January 29, 1996, 7.
113 Mary Kimani, "RTLM: The Medium that Became a Tool for Mass Murder," in *The Media and the Rwanda Genocide*, Allan Thompson, ed. (London and Ann Arbor, MI: Pluto Press 2007), 120.

114 OAU report: *Rwanda—The Preventable Genocide. The Report Of The International Panel Of Eminent Personalities To Investigate The 1994 Genocide In Rwanda And The Surrounding Events*, Section 10.13; Mark A. Drumbl, *Atrocity, Punishment, and International Law* (Cambridge and New York: Cambridge University Press 2007), 1; "Nyarubuye Memorial," Genocide Archive Rwanda, https://genocidearchiverwanda.org.rw/index.php?title=Nyarubuye_Memorial&gsearch=Nyarubuye, accessed March 14, 2023.

115 James Smith and Carol Rittner, "Churches as Memorial Sites, A Photo Essay," in *Genocide in Rwanda: Complicity of the Churches?*, Carol Rittner, ed. (Newark, NJ: Aegis 2004), 181.

116 Dallaire, *Shake Hands with the Devil*, 264-269; Prunier, *The Rwanda Crisis*, 261.

117 Prunier, *The Rwanda Crisis*, 312; Dallaire, *Shake Hands with the Devil*, 336.

118 Mark Doyle, "Reporting the Genocide," in *The Media and the Rwanda Genocide*, Allan Thompson, ed. (London and Ann Arbor, MI: Pluto Press 2007), 145-159. The RPF and the Rwandan Government have never denied these killings, claiming that the perpetrators have been punished for their crimes. However, there are also reports, although disputed, that the RPF committed targeted massacres during and after the genocide aimed at the Hutu elite and population. The infamous, and apparently never completed "Gersony Report," estimated that about 20,000 to 35,000 people were killed by the RPF. Des Forges, *"Leave None to Tell the Story,"* 109.

119 Prunier, *The Rwanda Crisis*, 291-292.

120 Dallaire, *Shake Hands with the Devil*, 459; Prunier, *The Rwanda Crisis*, 298-299.

121 Gérard Prunier, *Africa's World War: Congo, the Rwandan Genocide, and the Making of a Continental Catastrophe* (Oxford and New York: Oxford University Press 2009), 24-25.

122 Dallaire, *Shake Hands with the Devil*, 518-519. See also Prunier, *Africa's World War*.

Chapter 2

1 See, for example, Jo Ellen Fair and Lisa Parks, "Africa on Camera: Television News Coverage and Aerial Imaging of Rwanda Refugees," *Africa Today* 48:2 (2001), 35-57, Melvern, *Att förråda ett folk*, 159, Jared A. Cohen, *One Hundred Days of Silence*, xviii, 65, 157, and Daniel C. Harvey, "The Invisible Genocide: An Analysis of ABC, CBS, and NBC Television News Coverage of the 1994 Genocide in Rwanda" (University of Western Ontario—Electronic Thesis and Dissertation Repository 2012), 110.

2 Cohen, *States of Denial*, 65-69.

3 Virginia de la Guardia, *Genocide in Rwanda. The Role of the Media in Confusing Public Opinion and Encouraging the Killings* (Kindle Digital Edition 2012), 7-10. Barry Glassner, *The Culture of Fear: Why Americans are Afraid of the Wrong Things* (New York: Basic Books 1999).

4 *The Media and the Rwanda Genocide*, Allan Thompson, ed. (London and Ann Arbor, MI: Pluto Press 2007).

5 Doyle, "Reporting the Genocide," 145-159. Lindsay Hilsum, "Reporting Rwanda: The Media and the Aid Agencies," in *The Media and the Rwanda Genocide*, Allan Thompson, ed. (London and Ann Arbor, MI: Pluto Press 2007), 167-187.
6 Linda Melvern, "Missing the Story," in *The Media and the Rwanda Genocide*, Allan Thompson, ed. (London and Ann Arbor, MI: Pluto Press 2007), 198-210.
7 Nick Hughes, "Exhibit 467: The Genocide Through a Lens," in *The Media and the Rwanda Genocide*, Allan Thompson, ed. (London and Ann Arbor, MI: Pluto Press 2007), 231-234, and Tom Giles, "Media Failure over Rwanda's Genocide," in *The Media and the Rwanda Genocide*, Allan Thompson, ed. (London and Ann Arbor, MI: Pluto Press 2007), 235-237.
8 See for example: Melvern, *Att förråda ett folk*, Fred Grunfelt and Anke Huijboom, *The Failure to Prevent Genocide in Rwanda. The Role of Bystanders* (Leiden and Boston, MA: Martinus Nijhoff Publishers 2007), Michael Barnett, *Eyewitness to a Genocide: The United Nations and Rwanda* (New York: Cornell University Press 2003), Jean Hatzfelt, *Machete Season: The Killers in Rwanda Speak* (New York: Picador 2005), and Dallaire, *Shake Hands with the Devil*.
9 Sweden did have a brief colonial past, with three short-lived colonies: The Swedish Gold Coast (Ghana) 1649-1658, 1660-1663; New Sweden (at the Delaware River) 1638-1655; and Saint-Barthélemey (Caribbean) 1785-1878.
10 "FN och Sverige," Government Offices of Sweden, https://regeringen.se/lattlast-information-om-regeringen-och-regeringskansliet/sverige-i-varlden/fn-och-sverige/, accessed March 14, 2023.
11 Stig Hadenius and Lennart Weibull, *Massmedier: En bok om press, radio & TV* (Stockholm: Albert Bonniers förlag 2005), 165, 176.
12 Hadenius and Weibull, *Massmedier*, 234, 241.
13 Hadenius and Weibull, *Massmedier*, 216.
14 Chaon, "Who Failed in Rwanda," 164.
15 Harvey, "The Invisible Genocide," 94.
16 See, for example, Chaon, "Who Failed in Rwanda," 162.
17 Chaon, "Who Failed in Rwanda," 165.
18 Cohen, *States of Denial*, 169, 183-184.
19 Cohen, *States of Denial*, 185 (italics in original).
20 Cohen, *States of Denial*, 5-6.
21 Cohen, *States of Denial*, 187-191.
22 Cohen, *States of Denial*, 8, 137, 173, 194.
23 Cohen, *States of Denial*, 160.
24 Cohen, *States of Denial*, 249.
25 All quotes from Swedish to English have been translated by the author in this chapter. Spoken English in interviews and such has been transcribed to written English.
26 Tommy Gustafsson, "The Visual Re-creation of Black People in a 'White' Country: Oscar Micheaux and Swedish Film Culture in the 1920s," *Cinema Journal* 47:4 (2008), 30-49.
27 *Rapport*, April 10, 1994.

28 *Nyheterna*, April 8, 1994.
29 *Nyheterna*, April 9, 1994. Claude Dusaida is wrongly cited as Paul Dusaida in the interview.
30 *Nyheterna*, April 10, 1994.
31 *Rapport*, April 11, 1994.
32 Chaon, "Who Failed in Rwanda," 162.
33 Hughes, "Exhibit 467," 232-233.
34 *Rapport*, April 11, 1994.
35 *Rapport*, April 12, 1994.
36 Dallaire, *Shake Hands with the Devil*, 291.
37 *Rapport*, April 12, 1994.
38 Susan Moeller, *Compassion Fatigue: How the Media Sell Disease, Famine, War, and Death* (New York: Routledge 1999), 283.
39 Chaon, "Who Failed in Rwanda," 162, and Hilsum, "Reporting Rwanda," 173.
40 Steven Livingston, "Limited Vision: How Both the American Media and Government Failed Rwanda," in *The Media and the Rwanda Genocide*, Allan Thompson, ed. (London and Ann Arbor, MI: Pluto Press 2007), 191.
41 *Rapport*, April 19, 1994.
42 *Rapport*, April 19, 1994.
43 *Rapport*, April 19, 1994.
44 *Nyheterna*, April 23, 1994.
45 *Nyheterna*, April 21, 1994.
46 *Rapport*, May 1, 1994.
47 Cohen, *States of Denial*, 117.
48 Melissa Wall, "An Analysis of News Magazine Coverage of the Rwanda Crisis in the United States," in *The Media and the Rwanda Genocide*, Allan Thompson, ed. (London and Ann Arbor, MI: Pluto Press 2007), 262-263.
49 *Rapport*, May 1, 1994.
50 *Nyheterna*, April 29, 1994.
51 *Nyheterna*, April 29 and May 2, 1994.
52 *Nyheterna*, May 3, 1994.
53 *Rapport*, May 3, 1994.
54 Repeated in *Rapport*, May 1, May 3, May 5, 1994, and *Nyheterna*, May 1, 1994.
55 *Rapport*, May 1, 1994.
56 *Rapport*, May 3, 1994.
57 *Rapport*, May 11, 1994.
58 Fair and Parks, "Africa on Camera," 36, and Hilsum, "Reporting Rwanda," 173.
59 Cohen, *States of Denial*, 68.
60 Prunier, *Africa's World War*, 24-25.
61 See, for example, *Nyheterna*, May 6, 1994.
62 *Rapport*, May 17, 1994.
63 See, for example, *Nyheterna*, May 3 and May 6, 1994.
64 *Nyheterna*, May 8, 1994.

65 *Rapport*, May 14, 1994. Theogene Rudasingwa is wrongly cited as Theogene Ruda in this clip taken from a press conference.
66 Cohen, *States of Denial*, 135.
67 *Rapport*, May 5, 1994.
68 *Nyheterna*, May 6, 1994.
69 Melvern, "Missing the Story," 201-202.
70 For example, *Rapport*, June 5, 1994.
71 *Rapport*, June 24, 1994.
72 *Rapport*, May 14, 1994. Bernard Kouchner is wrongly cited as the former Minister of International Development in the interview.
73 *Rapport*, May 22, 1994.
74 *Rapport*, May 26, 1994.
75 *Rapport*, May 5, 1994.
76 For example, in *Rapport*, May 11, 1994.
77 For example, in Rapport, May 14, 1994.
78 *Nyheterna*, May 3, 1994.
79 *Rapport*, May 17, 1994.
80 *Rapport*, July 4, 1994.
81 Cohen, *States of Denial*, 165. The mission was called the United Nations Assistance Mission to Rwanda II (UNAMIR II).
82 *Rapport*, May 26, 1994.
83 See, for example, *Rapport*, May 22 and May 31, 1994.
84 *Rapport*, June 15, 1994.
85 *Rapport*, June 23, 1994.
86 Quoted in Chaon, "Who Failed in Rwanda," 161.
87 Doyle, "Reporting the Genocide," 155-156.
88 See, for example, *Rapport*, June 7, 1994.
89 See, for example, *Rapport*, April 10, April 24, May 11, June 7, and July 3, 1994.
90 *Rapport*, June 7, 1994.
91 *Rapport*, June 15, 1994.
92 Marika Griehsel and Simon Sandford are a married couple, and Sandford is of South African nationality.
93 *Rapport*, June 23, 1994.
94 *Rapport*, June 23, 1994.
95 *Rapport*, June 24, 1994.
96 *Rapport*, June 25, 1994.
97 *Rapport*, July 3, 1994.
98 *Rapport*, July 4, 1994.
99 *Rapport*, July 14, 1994.
100 Hilsum, "Reporting Rwanda," 167.
101 Referenced in Hilsum, "Reporting Rwanda," 176.

Chapter 3

1 Jeffrey Andrew Barash, *Collective Memory and the Historical Past* (Chicago and London: University of Chicago Press 2016), 40-51.
2 Barash, *Collective Memory and the Historical Past*, 136-164.
3 Argentina, Austria, Bangladesh, Belgium, Bosnia and Herzegovina, Cambodia, Cameroon, Canada, Czech Republic, Congo, Denmark, Ethiopia, Finland, France, Georgia, Germany, Iraq, Ireland, Israel, Italy, Japan, Kenya, Morocco Netherlands, Norway, Palestine, Poland, Russia, Rwanda, Serbia and Montenegro, Slovakia, South Africa, Spain, Sweden, Switzerland, Uganda, the UK, the USA, Zambia.
4 There are a few instances of scholars who briefly mention some of these early documentaries, such as Georgina Holmes, *Women and War in Rwanda: Gender, Media and the Representation of Genocide* (London and New York: I. B.Tauris 2014), who focuses on the BBC's documentaries, and Randall Fegley, *A History of Rwandan Identity and Trauma: The Mythmakers' Victims* (Lanham, MD: Lexington Books 2016). Also, in *The Rwandan Genocide on Film: Critical Essays and Interviews*, Matthew Edwards, ed. (Jefferson, NC: McFarland 2018), there is an interview with journalist Steve Bradshaw, who made The Panorama Trilogy on the Rwandan Genocide, 136-146.
5 See, for example, Giles, "Media Failure over Rwanda's Genocide," 237.
6 Another early documentary which features footage from Nick Hughes is *People of the Apocalypse* (1994), which aired on August 15, 1994, and was part of British ITV's *World in Action* series. This television documentary is foremost about the AIDS epidemic in Rwanda, but it touched briefly upon the genocide. In an interview, Hughes says that the film "glossed over the event, and that was really disgusting in a way." Matthew Edwards, "100 Days: An Interview with Nick Hughes," in *The Rwandan Genocide on Film: Critical Essays and Interviews*, Matthew Edwards, ed. (Jefferson, NC: McFarland 2018), 152.
7 Holmes, *Women and War in Rwanda*, 185.
8 "Television," Steve Bradshaw's homepage, http://steve-bradshaw.com/television.html, accessed March 14, 2023.
9 These images are actually used for the first time in the second part of the three-part series *Chronicle of a Genocide Foretold* (1996), which did not have the same impact as *The Triumph of Evil*.
10 Reuters, "Aid Workers in Rwanda Report 750 Slain at a Mental Hospital," *The New York Times*, October 10, 1994. A similar situation occurred at ETO (École Technique Officielle) in Rwanda where Belgian UN peacekeeping troops abandoned 2,000 Tutsi refugees, of whom 400 were children. *Left To Die at ETO And Nyanza: The Stories of Rwandese Civilians Abandoned by UN Troops on 11 April 1994* (Kigali: African Rights 2001), 47-52.
11 "Resources at a Glance," United States Holocaust Memorial Museum, https://www.ushmm.org/remember/days-of-remembrance/resources, accessed March 14, 2023.
12 Dina Temple-Raston, *Justice on the Grass: Three Rwandan Journalists, Their Trials for War Crimes, and a Nation's Quest for Redemption* (New York and London: Free Press 2005), 109.

13 Thierry Cruvellier and Chari Voss, *Court of Remorse: Inside the International Criminal Tribunal for Rwanda* (Madison: University of Wisconsin Press 2010), 155.
14 "DECEASED–BIZIMANA, Augustin (MICT-13-39)," United Nations, International Residual Mechanism for Criminal Tribunals, https://www.irmct.org/en/cases/mict-13-39, accessed 14 March 2023.
15 Prunier, *Africa's World War*, 41.
16 Fegley, *A History of Rwandan Identity and Trauma*, 47. Fegley refers to an evidently anti-RPF homepage, "Rising Continent," where Marie Madeleine Bicamumpaka, a former polyglot journalist who fled Rwanda after the RPF takeover in 1994, accuses the RPF of censorship, but without actually pointing out exactly who it is that has censored the third part of *Chronicle of a Genocide* and where she has watched the censored version. Marie Madeleine Bicamumpaka, "An Award-Winning Documentary On Rwanda Censored Off By Its Third," The Rising Continent, https://therisingcontinent.com/2012/08/22/an-award-winning-documentary-on-rwanda-censored-off-by-its-third/#more-2617, accessed April 18, 2017.
17 Melvern, *Att förråda ett folk*, 107. ICTR-98-44-A: "Judgement and Sentence," ICTR, https://ucr.irmct.org/LegalRef/CMSDocStore/Public/English/Judgement/NotIndexable/ICTR-98-44/MSC22535R0000565274.PDF, accessed March 14, 2023.
18 Bill Nichols, *Introduction to Documentary* (Bloomington and Indianapolis: Indiana University Press 2010), 127.

Chapter 4

1 "Hotel Rwanda Awards," IMDb, http://www.imdb.com/title/tt0395169/awards?ref_=tt_awd, accessed March 15, 2023.
2 Michael Gray, "Twenty Years On: Finding a Place for the Rwandan Genocide in Education," *Intercultural Education* 25:5 (2014), 401–402. See also, for example, "Hotell Rwanda", Swedish Film Institute, https://www.filminstitutet.se/sv/fa-kunskap-om-film/filmpedagogik/filmhandledningar/hotell-rwanda/, accessed March 15, 2023.
3 Edouard Kayihura and Kerry Zukas, *Inside Hotel Rwanda: The Surprising True Story ... And Why It Matters Today* (Dallas, TX: BenBella Books 2014), xxxiii.
4 *Blood Diamond* and *Gorillas in the Mist*, Box Office Mojo, http://www.boxofficemojo.com/movies/?id=blooddiamond.htm and http://www.boxofficemojo.com/movies/?id=gorillasinthemist.htm, accessed March 15, 2023.
5 "Shooting Dogs", Swedish Film Institute, https://www.filminstitutet.se/sv/fa-kunskap-om-film/filmpedagogik/filmhandledningar/shooting-dogs/, accessed March 15, 2023.
6 "Hotel Rwanda and Sometimes in April," Teach with Film, https://teachwithmovies.org/hotel-rwanda/, accessed March 15, 2023.
7 *Shake Hands with the Devil* won the audience award for the category, World Cinema–Documentary, "Shake Hands with the Devil: The Journey of Roméo Dallaire Awards," IMDb, http://www.imdb.com/title/tt0424435/awards?ref_=tt_awd, accessed March 15, 2023. See also "Time Machine: Rwanda–Do Scars Ever Fade?

Awards," IMDb, http://www.imdb.com/title/tt0444700/awards?ref_=tt_awd, accessed March 15, 2023.
8 Michael Atkins, "Cheadle Survives a Timid Account of the Rwandan Genocide," *The Village Voice*, December 14, 2004. See also, Alexander Dunefors, "Krigsdrama som inte lyckas beröra," Moviezine, January 1, 2008, https://www.moviezine.se/movies/hotell-rwanda, accessed March 15, 2023.
9 See, for example, Mick LaSalle, "Amid a Massacre, an Ordinary Man Stands Tall to Protect Others," *San Francisco Chronicle*, January 7, 2005; Roger Ebert, "Hotel Rwanda," *Chicago Sun Times*, December 21, 2004; Mats Bråstedt, "Hotell Rwanda," *Expressen*, March 17, 2005; Andrew Dembina, "Hotel Rwanda," *South China Morning Post*, April 24, 2005.
10 Karin Lindstedt, "Hotell Rwanda," *Aftonbladet*, March 18, 2005.
11 Johan Bergström, "Hotel Rwanda," Gamereactor.se, July 28, 2005, http://www.gamereactor.se/blu-ray/4612/Hotel+Rwanda/, accessed March 15, 2023.
12 Toplin, *Reel History*, 123.
13 The story of Paul Rusesabagina was first told in 1998, by the American journalist Philip Gourevitch in *We Wish to Inform You That Tomorrow We Will Be Killed with Our Families: Stories from Rwanda* (London: Picador 2000).
14 Ebert, "Hotel Rwanda."
15 See, for example, Philip French, "Schindler in Rwanda," *The Guardian*, February 27, 2005.
16 Alexandre Dauge-Roth, *Writing and Filming the Genocide of the Tutsis in Rwanda: Disremembering and Remembering Traumatic History* (Lanham, MD and Boulder, CO: Lexington Books 2010), 184–185.
17 Theodore W. Adorno and Max Horkheimer, *Dialectic of Enlightenment* (Stanford, CA: Stanford University Press 2002), 94–95.
18 Dauge-Roth, *Writing and Filming the Genocide of the Tutsis in Rwanda*, 199–207.
19 Dauge-Roth, *Writing and Filming the Genocide of the Tutsis in Rwanda*, 200–201.
20 Christina Olin-Scheller, *Såpor istället för Strindberg? Litteraturundervisning i ett nytt medielandskap* (Stockholm: Natur och Kultur 2008), 43–76.
21 Dauge-Roth, *Writing and Filming the Genocide of the Tutsis in Rwanda*, 200. See also Kayihura and Zukas, *Inside Hotel Rwanda*, xxxi.
22 Karlsson, "The Holocaust as a Problem of Historical Culture," 43.
23 Karlsson, "The Holocaust as a Problem of Historical Culture," 45.
24 Jönsson, *Film och historia*, 1, 60–62, 201–214.
25 Paul Rusesabagina (with Tom Zoellner), *An Ordinary Man: An Autobiography* (London: The Penguin Group 2006).
26 Alfred Ndahiro and Privat Rutazibwa, *Hotel Rwanda: Or The Tutsi Genocide as Seen by Hollywood* (Paris: L'Harmattan 2008), 3.
27 Kayihura and Zukas, *Inside Hotel Rwanda*, 226.
28 Kayihura and Zukas, *Inside Hotel Rwanda*, 72, 77, 80.
29 Linda Melvern, "Hotel Rwanda—Without the Hollywood Ending," *The Guardian*, November 17, 2011.
30 Rusesabagina, *An Ordinary Man*, passim; Kayihura and Zukas, *Inside Hotel Rwanda*,

189–219. See also Rusesabagina's Facebook page, Hotel Rwanda Rusesabagina Foundation, https://www.facebook.com/Hotel-Rwanda-Rusesabagina-Foundation-107533569296635/?fref=ts, accessed March 15, 2023.
31 Daniel Howden, "Hero of 'Hotel Rwanda' is Declared Enemy of the State," *The Independent*, October 28, 2010.
32 Kayihura and Zukas, *Inside Hotel Rwanda*, 244.
33 James Munyaneza, "Victims of MRCD-FLN Attacks in Southern Rwanda," *The New Times*, October 2, 2020; Abdi Latif Dahir, Declan Walsh, Matina Stevis-Gridneff, and Ruth Maclean, "How the Hero of 'Hotel Rwanda' Fell Into a Vengeful Strongman's Trap," *The New York Times*, September 18, 2020; "Hotel Rwanda's Hero Given 25-year Sentence in 'Terrorism' Case," Al Jazeera (September 20, 2021), https://www.aljazeera.com/news/2021/9/20/rwanda-court-finds-hotel-rwanda-hero-guilty-in-terrorism-case, accessed February 23, 2023.
34 See, for example, Louise Lagerström, "Hotell Rwanda, filmhandledning," Swedish Film Institute: Stockholm 2005. See also Swedish government's public authority, Forum för levande historia (The Living History Forum), which uses the histories of different genocides as a starting point for reflection and lessons for the future, concerning issues on tolerance, democracy, and human rights. The Living History Forum, http://www.levandehistoria.se/english, accessed March 15, 2023.
35 Dauge-Roth, *Writing and Filming the Genocide of the Tutsis in Rwanda*, 200. David Moshman, "Fighting 'Genocide Ideology' in Rwanda," *Huffington Post*, April 19, 2016, http://www.huffingtonpost.com/david-moshman/fighting-genocide-ideolog_b_9716142.html, accessed March 15, 2023. Moshman claims that the new law (passed in 2008), which criminalized "genocide ideology," is also a law that punishes "thought crime" since people are punished for what they believe, not for what they say. But speech becomes evidence of those beliefs.
36 Dauge-Roth, *Writing and Filming the Genocide of the Tutsis in Rwanda*, 200
37 Zine Magubane, "Saviors and Survivors: Western Passivity, African Resistance, and the Politics of Genocide in Hotel Rwanda (2004)," in *Through a Lens Darkly: Films of Genocide, Ethnic Cleansing, and Atrocities*, John J. Michalczyk and Raymond G. Helmick, Sj., eds. (New York: Peter Lang 2013), 220–224.
38 Toplin, *Reel History*, 17.
39 Toplin, *Reel History*, 18.
40 Toplin, *Reel History*, 18.
41 Wilson Morales, "Hotel Rwanda: An Interview with Director Terry George and Paul Rusesabagina," blackfilms.com, December 2004, http://www.blackfilm.com/20041217/features/terryandpaul.shtml, accessed March 15, 2023. See also, Terry George, "Smearing a Hero," *Washington Post*, May 10, 2006, and Robert Brent Toplin, "Interpreting History on the Screen: An Interview with Terry George," Perspectives on History: The News Magazine of the American Historical Association (April 1999), https://www.historians.org/publications-and-directories/perspectives-on-history/april-1999/interpreting-history-on-the-screen-an-interview-with-terry-george, accessed March 15, 2023.
42 Toplin, *Reel History*, 50.

43 Karlsson, "The Holocaust as a Problem of Historical Culture," 43.
44 Tamara J. Ferguson, Daniel Brugman, Jennifer White, and Heidi L. Eyre, "Shame and Guilt as Morally Warranted Experiences," in *The Self-Conscious Emotions. Theory and Research*, Jessica L. Tracy, Richard W Robins and June Price Tangney, eds. (New York and London: Guilford Press 2007), 345.
45 Gabriele Taylor, *Pride, Shame, and Guilt. Emotions of Self-Assessment* (Oxford: Clarendon Press 1985), 86-97.
46 *Making of Hotel Rwanda*, Extra Features included in the DVD-edition of *Hotel Rwanda* (Scanbox 2005).
47 Adhikari, "Hotel Rwanda," 290-291.
48 Sakota-Kokot, "When the Past Talks to the Present," 221.
49 Vittorio Bufacchi, "Two Concepts of Violence," *Political Studies Review* 3 (2005), 193-204.
50 Bufacchi, "Two Concepts of Violence," 199.
51 See, for example, Erich Goode and Nachman Ben-Yehudea, *Moral Panics. The Social Construction of Deviance* (Malden, MA and Oxford: Wiley-Blackwell 2009), and Gustafsson and Arnberg, *Moralpanik och lågkultur*.
52 Bromley, "After Such Knowledge," 192.
53 Dauge-Roth, *Writing and Filming the Genocide of the Tutsis in Rwanda*, 223-224.
54 Cohen, *States of Denial*, 137, 173, 194.
55 *Report on the Situation of Human Rights in Rwanda submitted by Mr. René Degni-Segui, Special Rapporteur on the Commission of Human Rights*, United Nations, January 29 (1996), 7.
56 Sakota-Kokot, "When the Past Talks to the Present," 225.
57 Kerner, *Film and the Holocaust*, 187-193.
58 Kerner, *Film and the Holocaust*, 187 (italics in original).
59 Hron, "Genres of 'Yet An Other Genocide'," 137. See also Shohini Chaudhuri, *Cinema of the Dark Side: Atrocity and the Ethics of Film Spectatorship* (Edinburgh: Edinburgh University Press 2014), 51.
60 Linda Melvern, "History? This Film is Fiction," *The Guardian*, March 19, 2006. See also Dauge-Roth who mimics Melvern's criticism, Dauge-Roth, *Writing and Filming the Genocide of the Tutsis in Rwanda*, 176.
61 Marc Savlov, "Beyond the Gates," *The Austin Chronicle*, June 1, 2007. See also Jens Peterson, "Shooting Dogs," *Aftonbladet*, April 28, 2006; Ruthe Stein, "Amid Genocide in Rwanda, One Man Stands Tall," *San Francisco Gate*, March 23, 2007; "Shooting Dogs," Holocaust Memorial Trust (2005), http://hmd.org.uk/content/shooting-dogs, accessed July 24, 2017.
62 Jenny Richardson, "Shooting Dogs," *Expressen*, April 26, 2006.
63 "Shooting Dogs," Holocaust Memorial Day Trust (2005).
64 Dauge-Roth, *Writing and Filming the Genocide of the Tutsis in Rwanda*, 176.
65 Richardson, "Shooting Dogs."
66 Jakov Sedlar and Fra Ivo Tadić, "Filming a Long Feature Documentary," Father Vejko Center (October 10, 2008), http://vjeko-rwanda.info/en/news/72-snimanje-dugometraznog-filma.html, accessed March 15, 2023.

67 Cieplak, "The Rwandan Genocide and the Bestiality of Representation in *100 Days* (2001) and *Shooting Dogs* (2005)," 52.
68 Cieplak, "The Rwandan Genocide and the Bestiality of Representation in *100 Days* (2001) and *Shooting Dogs* (2005)," 56.
69 Cieplak, "The Rwandan Genocide and the Bestiality of Representation in *100 Days* (2001) and *Shooting Dogs* (2005)," 56.
70 Andrea Dooley, "Implicated Geographies: Public Memorials and the Topographies of Genocide," *Sightlines* 8 (June, 2010), 34. See also, Tommy Gustafsson, "A Fight over Souls: Documentary Films on the Rwandan Genocide with a Christian Theme," *Journal of Religion and Film* 21:2 (2017), 1–38.
71 Daniel S. Ogalde, "Om detta må ni berätta," Moviezine, January 1, 2008, https://www.moviezine.se/movies/shooting-dogs/, accessed March 15, 2023.
72 Stein, "Amid Genocide in Rwanda."
73 "Beyond the Gates," HollywoodJesus.com, http://www.hollywoodjesus.com/beyond-the-gates-2007/, accessed August 23, 2017.
74 Jönsson, *Film och historia*, 8.
75 Dauge-Roth, *Writing and Filming the Genocide of the Tutsis in Rwanda*, 247–248.
76 Rwafa, "Film Representations of the Rwandan Genocide," 406.
77 Patsy Toland, "Sometimes in April," *Policy & Practice: A Development Education Review* 5 (2007), 108–109.
78 Leslie Felperin, "Review: 'Sometimes in April'," *Variety*, February 18, 2005.
79 Johan Lindahl, "Sometimes in April (2005): Döden utanför hotellet," Russin.nu (2006), http://www.russin.nu/filmview.php?filmid=1518, accessed March 15, 2023.
80 Jon Jost, "Some Notes on 'Political Cinema' Prompted by Seeing Raoul Peck's Sometimes in April in Competition at the Berlin Film Festival," *Senses of Cinema* 35 (April 2005).
81 See, for example, Rebecca Weeks, *History by HBO: Televising the American Past* (Lexington: The University of Kentucky Press 2022).
82 Sara L. Rubin, "Specificity in Genocide Portrayal on Film: *Sometimes in April* (2005)," in *Through a Lens Darkly: Films of Genocide, Ethnic Cleansing, and Atrocities*, John J. Michalczyk and Raymond G. Helmick, eds. (New York: Peter Lang 2013), 226.
83 "'Sometimes in April' looks at Rwandan Genocide," The Associated Press (March 23, 2004), https://www.today.com/popculture/sometimes-april-looks-rwandan-genocide-wbna4586777, accessed March 15, 2023.
84 Charles Stuart Kennedy, "Interview with Ambassador Prudence Bushnell: The Association for Diplomatic Studies and Training Foreign Affairs Oral History Project," Library of Congress (2005), 89, http://lcweb2.loc.gov/service/mss/mfdip/2010/2010bus02/2010bus02.pdf, accessed March 15, 2023.
85 Toplin, *Reel History*, 105.
86 Dauge-Roth, *Writing and Filming the Genocide of the Tutsis in Rwanda*, 247.
87 Robert Walker, "Genocide Movie Premiere in Rwanda," BBC Home, January 25, 2005, http://news.bbc.co.uk/1/hi/world/africa/4202751.stm, accessed March 15, 2023.

88 "Going to Work" was the allegory for the killings of Tutsis during the 100 days of the genocide. See Hatzfeld, *Machete Season*, passim.

Chapter 5

1 Nichols, *Introduction to Documentary*, 167.
2 Joshua Land, "After Two Fictionalized Accounts, an Unflinching Rwanda Doc," *The Village Voice*, May 10, 2005.
3 Peter Bradshaw, "Shake Hands with the Devil," *The Guardian*, August 4, 2005.
4 Virginia Heffernan, "Television Review; Looking Back Across a Decade, With Bloody Regret," *The New York Times*, April 1, 2004.
5 Jett Scrimsher, "Documentary Review: Ghosts of Rwanda," Media Center, April 29, 2016, https://sites.lib.byu.edu/mediacenter/2016/04/29/documentary-review-ghosts-of-rwanda/, accessed March 15, 2023.
6 William Thomas, "Shake Hands with the Devil: The Journey Of Romeo Dallaire Review," *Empire*, August 5, 2005, http://www.empireonline.com/movies/shake-hands-devil-journey-romeo-dallaire/review/, accessed February 24, 2023.
7 The only emblematic image not used in *Rwanda: Do Scars Ever Fade?* is "The KPH Images."
8 O'Connell, "Interview with Greg Barker," 207.
9 Besides "The Nick Hughes Footage," there is a short film by a Reuters cameraman, and one taken by an unknown Rwandan cameraman. See Hughes, "Exhibit 467," 231-235.
10 LaMarre and Landreville, "When is Fiction as Good as Fact?," 540-547.
11 LaMarre and Landreville, "When is Fiction as Good as Fact?," 551-552.
12 For further reading on *Rwanda: Do Scars Ever Fade?* and Christian themed documentaries on the Rwandan genocide, see Bromley, "After Such Knowledge," 187-190 and Gustafsson, "A Fight over Souls," 11-13, respectively.
13 Thomas, "Shake Hands with the Devil."
14 "Rwanda—Do Scars Ever Fade?," Peabody Awards (2004), http://www.peabodyawards.com/award-profile/rwanda-do-scars-ever-fade, accessed March 15, 2023. The pronunciation of "continuing" in the original speech.
15 Möller, "Rwanda Revisualized," 115-116.
16 Cohen, *States of Denial*, 194.
17 Steve Bradshaw's homepage.

Chapter 6

1 "ÉCU 2019 Interviews—RWANDA, Riccardo Salvetti," The European Independent Film Festival, YouTube, April 6, 2019, https://www.youtube.com/watch?v=TgqQUJzmE_A, accessed March 15, 2023.
2 "Rwanda," homepage, http://www.rwandailfilm.it/la-storia/, accessed May 13, 2020.

3 Scott Straus, "The Limits of a Genocide Lens: Violence against Rwandans in the 1990s," *Journal of Genocide Research* 21:4 (2019), 505.
4 Rwafa, "Film Representations of the Rwandan Genocide," 391. See also, Shohat and Stam, *Unthinking Eurocentrism*.
5 Scott Foundas, "Shake Hands with the Devil," *Variety*, September 24, 2007.
6 Robert Stam and Louise Spence, "Colonialism, Racism, and Representation: An Introduction," in *Film Theory and Criticism*, Leo Braudy and Marshall Cohen, eds. (Oxford and New York: Oxford University Press 2009), 754.
7 Stuart Hall, "When was 'The Postcolonial' Thinking at the Limit," in *The Post-Colonial Question: Common Skies, Divided Horizons*, Iain Chambers and Lidia Curtis, eds. (London and New York: Routledge 1996), 250.
8 See, for example, David Desser, "Race and Culture in the Vietnam War Films," in *Inventing Vietnam: The War in Film and Television*, Michael Anderegg, ed. (Philadelphia, PA: Temple University Press 1991), 81–102.
9 Andrew Wallis, *Silent Accomplice: The Untold Story of France's Role in the Rwandan Genocide* (London: I. B. Tauris 2006), 24–25.
10 Pagnoni Berns, Fernando Gabriel, and Juan Ignacio Juvé, "Let Us Speak of Rwanda (and Argentina and France)," in *The Rwandan Genocide on Film: Critical Essays and Interviews*, Matthew Edwards, ed. (Jefferson, NC: McFarland 2018), 130.
11 Niclas Ericsson, "Oss hundar emellan," folder included in *The Last Dog in Rwanda* educational DVD (Swedish Film Institute and Utbildningsradion 2006), 7.
12 Anon., "Jens Assur satsar på filmen," *Svenska Dagbladet*, January 24, 2006.
13 For further reading on educational films and genocide in general, and on *The Last Dog in Rwanda* in particular, see Gustafsson, "*The Last Dog in Rwanda*," 80–98.
14 Matthew Hughey, *The White Savior Film: Content, Critics, and Consumption* (Philadelphia, PA: Temple University Press 2014), passim.
15 For more about the Nordic Quirky Feel-Good, see Ellen Rees, "The Nordic 'Quirky' Feel-Good," in *Nordic Genre Film: Small Nation Film Cultures in the Global Marketplace*, Tommy Gustafsson and Pietari Kääpä, eds. (Edinburgh: Edinburgh University Press 2015), 147–158.
16 Gil Courtmanche, *A Sunday at the Pool in Kigali* (Edinburgh: Canongate 2018), 197–199.
17 Lior Zylberman, "From Invisibility to Recognition: Archive and Cultural Memory of the Rwandan Genocide," in *The Rwandan Genocide on Film: Critical Essays and Interviews*, Matthew Edwards, ed. (Jefferson, NC: McFarland 2018), 83–86.
18 Dauge-Roth, *Writing and Filming the Genocide of the Tutsis in Rwanda*, 207–208.
19 Dauge-Roth, *Writing and Filming the Genocide of the Tutsis in Rwanda*, 208.
20 Zylberman, "From Invisibility to Recognition," 87.
21 Dauge-Roth, *Writing and Filming the Genocide of the Tutsis in Rwanda*, 230.
22 *Report on the Situation of Human Rights in Rwanda*, 7.
23 Lisa Sharlach, "Rape as Genocide: Bangladesh, the Former Yugoslavia, and Rwanda," *New Political Science* 1:22 (2000), 89–102.
24 Dauge-Roth, *Writing and Filming the Genocide of the Tutsis in Rwanda*, 231.
25 See, for example, Ian Spelling, "Trees of Peace Director Alanna Brown on Her

9-Year Journey to Get the Netflix Movie Made and Why the Story of the Women in Rwanda Is Close to Her Heart," Below the Line, August 23, 2022, https://www.btlnews.com/crafts/trees-of-peace-director-alanna-brown-interview/, accessed March 6, 2023.
26. Blessing Chinwendu Nwankwo, "Netflix: 'Trees of Peace' Review: Saved by the Will to Survive," Afrocritik, July 6, 2022, https://www.afrocritik.com/netflixs-trees-of-peace-review/, accessed March 6, 2023.
27. Simon Peter Kaliisa, "Top 10 Movies About the 1994 Genocide against the Tutsi," *The New Times*, April 12, 2019. (1) *The Day God Walked Away*, (2) *Shake Hands with The Devil*, (3) *Sometimes in April*, (4) *Keepers of Memory*, (5) *100 Days*, (6) *Shooting Dogs*, (7) *My Neighbour My Killer*, (8) *'94 Terror*, (9) *Munyurangabo*, (10) *Kinyarwanda*.
28. Georgette Gagnon, "Response to The New Times Article on Rwandan Genocide," Human Rights Watch, March 18, 2009, https://www.hrw.org/news/2009/05/18/response-new-times-article-rwandan-genocide, accessed March 15, 2023.
29. Matthew Edwards, "*Munyurangbo*: An Interview with Director Lee Isaac Chung," in *The Rwandan Genocide on Film: Critical Essays and Interviews*, Matthew Edwards, ed. (Jefferson, NC: McFarland 2018), 171–181.
30. A. O. Scott, "15 Years Later, a Quiet Film about a Still-Traumatized Rwanda," *The New York Times*, May 28, 2009.
31. Roger Ebert, "Two Boys on the Road to Life in a Newly Calm Rwanda," *Chicago Sun Times*, July 22, 2009.
32. Jan-Kees Verschuure, "The Day God Walked Away—Le jour où Dieu est parti en voyage (2009)," Cinemagazine, 2009, https://cinemagazine.nl/the-day-god-walked-away-le-jour-ou-dieu-est-parti-en-voyage-2009-recensie/, accessed March 15, 2023.
33. Twhalliii, "The Day God Walked Away," Indiewire.com, September 11, 2009, https://www.indiewire.com/2009/09/toronto-2009-the-day-god-walked-away-227529/, accessed March 15, 2023.
34. *Kinyarwanda*, "Muceceke! Tangira! (Shut Up! Action!): The Making of Kinyarwanda" (2011), Documentary Featurette, DVD (Breaking Glass Pictures). See also Kinyarwanda Press Kit, downloadable at http://www.kinyarwandamovie.com/, accessed March 15, 2023.
35. Emily Wax, "Islam Attracting Many Survivors of Rwanda Genocide," *Washington Post*, September 23, 2002; Alana Tiemessen, "From Genocide to Jihad: Islam and Ethnicity in Post-Genocide Rwanda," Paper for Presentation at the Annual General Meeting of the Canadian Political Science Association (CPSA) in London, Ontario (June 2–5, 2005), 13, file:///C:/Users/tguhum/Desktop/tiemessen%20from%20genicode%20to%20jihad.pdf, accessed June 10, 2020.
36. See, for example, Duane Bygre, "Sundance Review: Ambitious 'Kinyarwanda' Centers on 1994 Rwandan Genocide," *The Hollywood Reporter*, January 27, 2011.
37. Bygre, "Sundance Review."
38. Robert Koehler, "Kinyarwanda: Awkwardly Patches Together Story Strands Meant to Provide a Panoramic View of War and Reconciliation," *Variety*, January 30, 2011.
39. Dianne R. Portfleet, "The Films of Eric Kabera, the Kwetu Film Institute and

Hillywood," in *The Rwandan Genocide on Film: Critical Essays and Interviews*, Matthew Edwards, ed. (Jefferson, NC: McFarland 2018), 100.
40 Zylberman, "From Invisibility to Recognition," 92–95.
41 Javira Ssebwami, "Excitement as Uganda's 94 Terror Movie Wins Seven Awards at Golden Movies Awards in Ghana," *PML Daily*, August 26, 2019.
42 Gabriel Buule, "Ugandan Film on Rwandan Genocide Bags International Award," Sqoop, July 1, 2019, https://www.sqoop.co.ug/201907/news/events/ugandan-film-on-rwandan-genocide-bags-international-award.html, accessed March 15, 2023.
43 Gabriel Buule, "Kibirige has Branded Herself a Special Effects Make-up Artist," *Daily Monitor*, November 17, 2019.
44 Gaël Faye, *Petit pays* (Paris: Le Livre de poche 2017).
45 A study conducted by the UN's Population Fund in collaboration with the Burundian government in 2002 estimated that the number of people killed from October to December 1993 was 116,059 (of whom 100,000 were killed October). The proportion of Hutu and Tutsi is still unclear, but the violence began with a wave of violence against the Tutsi, which was then followed by a wave of violence unleashed by the Tutsi-led army against the Hutu. Tom Bundervoet, "Livestock, Land and Political Power: The 1993 Killings in Burundi," *Journal of Peace Research* 46:3 (2009), 357–376.

Chapter 7

1 Pat Caplan, "'Never Again': Genocide Memorials in Rwanda," *Anthropology Today* 23:1 (2007), 20–22.
2 See, for example, Annalisa Bolin, "Dignity in Death and Life: Negotiating Agaciro for the Nation in Preservation Practice at Nyamata Genocide Memorial, Rwanda," *Anthropological Quarterly* 92:2 (2019), 345–374.
3 See the PBS documentary *Ghosts of Rwanda* and Carl Wilkens, *I'm not Leaving* (World Outside My Shoes 2011).
4 Pagnoni and Ignacio Juvé, "Let Us Speak of Rwanda," 123–127.
5 Zylberman, "From Invisibility to Recognition," 88.
6 Millie Chen, "Tour," http://www.milliechen.com/tour, accessed March 15, 2023.
7 Quoted in Oliver Barlet, *Contemporary African Cinema* (East Lansing: Michigan State University Press 2016), 192.
8 Barlet, *Contemporary African Cinema*, 192.
9 Fergal Keane, "Reconciliation a Distant Dream in a Haunted Land," *The Irish Times*, April 10, 2004.
10 "President Paul Kagame at 'Earth Made of Glass' Premiere at Tribeca Film Festival," YouTube, 2010, https://www.youtube.com/watch?v=1x3KmYyKVtc, accessed March 15, 2023.
11 Samantha Ashenden, James Brown, and Philip Spencer, "Justice Seekers and The Arrows of Truth: An Interview with Antonio Ribeiro," in *The Rwandan Genocide on Film: Critical Essays and Interviews*, Matthew Edwards, ed. (Jefferson, NC: McFarland 2018), 208.

12 "Justice Seekers: One Couple Hopes to Take Action Against High-profile Rwandan Exiles, Alleged to Have Been Deeply Complicit in Crimes," *Witness*, Al Jazeera, April 13, 2014, https://www.aljazeera.com/programmes/witness/2014/04/justice-seekers-201449105827945155.html, accessed March 15, 2023.
13 Antonio Ribeiro, "Filmmaker's View," *Witness*, Al Jazeera, April 13, 2014, https://www.aljazeera.com/programmes/witness/2014/04/justice-seekers-201449105827945155.html, accessed March 15, 2023.
14 Gretchen Baldwin, "Constructing Identity Through Commemoration: Kwibuka and the Rise of Survivor Nationalism in Post-conflict Rwanda," *Journal of Modern African Studies* 57:3 (2019), 358–359.
15 Sanny Ntayombya, "We Need to Bring our Heroes to Life on Film and Television," *The New Times*, January 31, 2023.
16 Collins Mwai, "Inkotanyi: How a Filmmaker Immortalized the Liberation Struggle," *The New Times*, July 8, 2017.

Chapter 8

1 Carol Rittner, *Rape: Weapon of War and Genocide* (St. Paul, MN: Paragon House 2012); Carol Rittner, "Rape, Religion, and Genocide: An Unholy Silence," in *Confronting Genocide: Judaism, Christianity, Islam*, Steven Leonard Jacobs, ed. (Plymouth: Lexington Books 2009), 291–305.
2 *Report on the Situation of Human Rights in Rwanda*, 7.
3 "Judgement: The Prosecutor vs Jean-Paul Akayesu," Case No. ICTR-96-4-T (September 2, 1998), 179, https://web.archive.org/web/20130611203452/http://www.unictr.org/Portals/0/Case/English/Akayesu/judgement/akay001.pdf, accessed March 15, 2023.
4 For more on the stigmatization of raped Tutsi women, see *The Men Who Killed Me: Rwandan Survivors of Sexual Violence*, Anne-Marie De Brouwer and Sandra Ka Hon Chu, eds. (Vancouver, BC: Douglas & McIntyre 2009).
5 Neil Genzlinger, "A Collection of 'Academy Award-Nominated Documentary Shorts'," *The New York Times*, March 31, 2006.
6 Marie-Consolee Mukangendo, "Caring for Children Born of Rape in Rwanda," in *Born of War: Protecting Children of Sexual Violence Survivors in Conflict Zones*, R. Charli Carpenter, ed. (Bloomfield, CT: Kumarian Press 2007), 40.
7 See, for example, "Jonathan Torgovnik | Intended Consequences" at Fotografiska in Stockhollm (March 8, 2011), https://www.fotografiska.com/sto/en/news/jonathan-torgovnik-intended-consequences/, accessed June 24, 2020.
8 Nichols, *Introduction to Documentary*, 172–194.
9 See, for example, "Rwandan Priest Guilty of Genocide," BBC News, December 13, 2006, http://news.bbc.co.uk/2/hi/africa/6175717.stm, accessed March 15, 2023. See also Melvern, *Conspiracy to Murder*, 189.

Chapter 9

1. Matthew Edwards, "*Sweet Dreams*: An Interview with Director Lisa Fruchtman," in *The Rwandan Genocide on Film: Critical Essays and Interviews*, Matthew Edwards, ed. (Jefferson, NC: McFarland 2018), 229–230.
2. *As We Forgive*, DVD-Cover (MPower Pictures 2010).
3. Matthew Edwards, "As We Forgive: An Interview with Director Laura Waters Hinson," in *The Rwandan Genocide on Film: Critical Essays and Interviews*, Matthew Edwards, ed. (Jefferson, MC: McFarland 2018), 188.
4. Edwards, "*Sweet Dreams*," 183.
5. According to IMDb, there is a feature film titled *91 Nights a Left to Tell Story* (2019) which is, as are the documentaries *The Diary of Immaculée* and *If Only We Had Listened*, based on the experiences of Immaculée Ilibagiza, a Catholic Tutsi survivor, who wrote the publicly noted book, *Left to Tell: Discovering God Amidst the Rwandan Holocaust* (Carlsbad, CA and New York: Hay House 2006). However, besides the information on IMDb, I have not been able to track down any further information on this film, not even a trailer nor a single review. IMDb, https://www.imdb.com/title/tt1528082/, accessed March 7, 2023. For further information on Ilibagiza's religious and commercial exploitation of the genocide, see Gustafsson, "A Fight over Souls," 19–27.
6. For more about this Christian subgenre, see Gustafsson, "A Fight over Souls," 1–38.
7. Frederica Mathewes-Green, "As We Forgive," *National Review*, October 16, 2009.
8. Edwards, "As We Forgive," 184.
9. Phillip A. Cantrell II, "Reconciliation in Post-Genocide Rwanda as Presented in the Film As We Forgive," in *The Rwandan Genocide on Film: Critical Essays and Interviews*, Matthew Edwards, ed. (Jefferson, NC: McFarland 2018), 111–113.
10. Cantrell II, "Reconciliation in Post-Genocide Rwanda," 114.
11. *In the Tall Grass* is, for example, available at Berkeley Library, University of California, https://www.lib.berkeley.edu/mrcvault/videographies/tall-grass-inside-citizen-based-justice-system-gacaca; Brown University Library, https://search.library.brown.edu/catalog/b4103514; and The University of Queensland, Australia https://search.library.uq.edu.au/primo-explore/fulldisplay?docid=61UQ_ALMA21103467300003131&context=L&vid=61UQ&lang=en_US&search_scope=61UQ_All&adaptor=Local%20Search%20Engine&tab=61uq_all&query=any,contains,in%20the%20tall%20grass&offset=0, all accessed March 15, 2023. For the reviews, see Abby Alpert, "In the Tall Grass: Inside the Citizen-Based Justice System Gacaca," *Booklist*, February 1, 2007, and Beth Traylor, "In the Tall Grass: Rwanda's Search for Redemption: Inside the Citizen-Based Justice System Gacaca," *Library Journal*, April 15, 2007
12. John J. Michalczyk, "Village Justice: *In the Tall Grass* (2006)," in *Through a Lens Darkly: Films of Genocide, Ethnic Cleansing, and Atrocities*, John J. Michalczyk and Raymond G. Helmick Sr., eds. (New York: Peter Lang 2013), 234.
13. Christopher J. Mon quoted in Michalczyk, "Village Justice," 235.

14 Bert Ingelaere, "The Gacaca Courts in Rwanda," in *Traditional Justice and Reconciliation after Violent Conflict: Learning from African Experiences*, Luc Huyse and Mark Salter, eds. (Stockholm: International IDEA 2008), 37–41; "The Justice and Reconciliation Process in Rwanda," The United Nations (March 2012), https://www.un.org/en/preventgenocide/rwanda/pdf/bgjustice.pdf, accessed March 15, 2023.
15 Ingelaere, "The Gacaca Courts in Rwanda," 38.
16 Ingelaere, "The Gacaca Courts in Rwanda," 44.
17 Ingelaere, "The Gacaca Courts in Rwanda," 48–49.
18 Ingelaere, "The Gacaca Courts in Rwanda," 49.
19 Anon., "Gacaca, Living Together Again in Rwanda?," *Time Out*, 2003, https://www.timeout.com/london/film/gacaca-living-together-again-in-rwanda, accessed March 15, 2023.
20 Ronnie Scheib, "Gacaca, Living Together in Rwanda?," *Variety*, July 22, 2003.
21 Bromley, "After Such Knowledge," 185.
22 Bromley, "After Such Knowledge," 185.
23 Ronnie Schieb, "Review: 'In Rwanda We Say . . . The Family That Does Not Speak Dies'," *Variety*, March 30, 2004.
24 See for example, Zylberman, "From Invisibility to Recognition," 92–93.
25 Quoted from the booklet included in the DVD box of The Gacaca Trilogy (Gacaca Productions 2012), 3. See also the online store at The Gacaca Film Series, https://gacacafilms.com/store/, accessed March 15, 2023.
26 Dauge-Roth, *Writing and Filming the Genocide of the Tutsis in Rwanda*, 19; Bromley "After Such Knowledge," 182.
27 "The Love 41 Story," The Saddleback/Love 41 homepage, https://saddlebackleather.com/love41/the-love-41-story/, accessed March 15, 2023.
28 Joshua Oppenheimer, Twitter, April 21, 2014, https://twitter.com/joshuaoppenheim/status/458304115370893312, accessed March 15, 2023; "25 New Faces of Independent Film: Joe Callander," *Filmmaker Magazine*, 2014, https://filmmakermagazine.com/people/joe-callander-2/#.YBFAa0-g82y, accessed March 15, 2023.
29 "25 New Faces of Independent Film: Joe Callander."
30 This particular interpretation is also supported by the way the genocide is described on Love 41's homepage, where ethnic identities are not even mentioned once. See "The Love 41 Story," Love 41 homepage, https://saddlebackleather.com/love41/the-love-41-story/, accessed March 15, 2023.
31 John Miaschi, "The Great Lakes Refugee Crisis," WorldAtlas, April 25, 2017, https://www.worldatlas.com/articles/what-happened-during-the-great-lakes-refugee-crisis.html, accessed March 15, 2023. In the Czech documentary, *Circus Rwanda* (2018)—a film portraying an exchange between Czech and Rwandan circus performers—a similar story is told, where a former street kid confesses to murder in order to survive, and whose mother had disappeared in Congo after the genocide.
32 Courtney Small, "Hot Docs Review: Life After Death," Cinema Axis, May 3, 2014, https://cinemaaxis.com/2014/05/03/hot-docs-review-life-after-death/, accessed March 15, 2023. See also Andrew Parker, "Hot Docs 2014: Life After Death

Review," That Self Staff, April 21, 2014, https://thatshelf.com/hot-docs-2014-life-after-death/, accessed March 15, 2023.
33 Small, "Hot Docs Review."

Chapter 10

1 See, for example, Deborah Lipstadt, *Denying the Holocaust: The Growing Assault on Truth and Memory* (New York: Free Press 1993), and Michael Shermer and Alex Grobman, *Denying History: Who Says the Holocaust Never Happened and Why Do They Say It?* (Oakland: University of California Press 2009).
2 Henry Rousso, *The Vichy Syndrome: History and Memory in France since 1944* (Cambridge, MA: Harvard University Press 1991), 151.
3 Hedlund, *Exile Warriors*, passim.
4 See for example, Judi Rever, *In Praise of Blood: The Crimes of the Rwandan Patriotic Front* (Toronto: Penguin Random House 2018); Herman and Peterson, *Enduring Lies*, and Péan, *Noires fureurs, blancs menteurs*.
5 Christian Davenport and Allan C. Stam, "What Really Happened in Rwanda?," *Pacific Standard*, October 6, 2009.
6 Philip Verwimp, "Testing the Double-Genocide Thesis for Central and Southern Rwanda," *The Journal of Conflict Resolution* 47:4 (2003), 435.
7 Straus, "The Limits of a Genocide Lens," 510-511. See also Prunier, *Africa's World War*, 42. The RPF's estimation of these revenge killings is 4,000, but the suppressed and by now almost mythological "Gersony Report" estimates that these killings, mostly taking place in the southern provinces, were systematic and that the number of dead amounted to somewhere between 20,000 and 35,000 for the period late April/May to August 1994. "Prospects for early repatriation of Rwandan refugees currently in Burundi, Tanzania and Zaire" [The Gersony Report], United Nations High Commissioner for Refugees (October 11, 1994), 1-14.
8 Straus, "The Limits of a Genocide Lens," 509, 513.
9 Max Delany, "Rwanda Dismisses UN Report Detailing Possible Hutu Genocide in Congo," *The Christian Science Monitor*, August 27, 2010, https://www.csmonitor.com/World/Africa/2010/0827/Rwanda-dismisses-UN-report-detailing-possible-Hutu-genocide-in-Congo, accessed March 15, 2023; "Democratic Republic of Congo, 1993-2003," United Nation's Digital Library (2010), https://digitallibrary.un.org/record/709895, accessed March 15, 2023.
10 *The Rwandan Genocide on Film*, 249.
11 "From Arusha to Arusha," National Film Board of Canada, https://www.nfb.ca/film/from_arusha_to_arusha/, accessed March 15, 2023.
12 René Lemarchand, "Rwanda: The State of Research," SciencePo, June 25, 2018, https://www.sciencespo.fr/mass-violence-war-massacre-resistance/en/document/rwanda-state-research, accessed March 15, 203.
13 Prunier, *Africa's World War*, 17f.
14 "D'Arusha à Arusha (2008) Awards," IMDb, https://www.imdb.com/title/tt1379642/awards/?ref_=tt_awd, accessed March 15, 2023.

15 Ashenden, Brown, and Spencer, "Justice Seekers and The Arrows of Truth," 204, 215.
16 Ashenden, Brown, and Spencer, "Justice Seekers and The Arrows of Truth," 208.
17 Ashenden, Brown, and Spencer, "Justice Seekers and The Arrows of Truth," 215.
18 For years Nyamwasa claimed to know about the plane, but without presenting any hard evidence, and in October 2018 the investigating magistrates in Paris dismissed his claims as worthless. Linda Melvern, *Intent to Deceive: Denying the Genocide of the Tutsi* (London and New York: Verso 2020), 125.
19 Jean-Louis Bruguière, *Délivrance de mandats d'arret internationaux*, 97.295.2303/0, Tribunal de Grande Instance de Paris, November 17, 2006.
20 *Report of the Investigation into the Causes and Circumstances of and Responsibility for the Attack of 06/04/94 against the Falcon 50 Rwandan Presidential Aeroplane, Registration number 9XR-NN*, Rwanda Government (2010). See also, "Rwanda/Burundi: Turmoil in Rwanda," US Department of State Bureau of Intelligence and Research/SPOT Intelligence Report (April 7, 1994), and "Destruction en vol du Falcon 50," Kigali (Rwanda), Cour d'appel de Paris, Tribunal de grande instance de Paris, Rapport d'expertise (2012).
21 "Report of the Commission d'enquête parlementaire concernant les événements du Rwanda," Section 3.5.1: L'attentat contre l'avion présidentiel, Belgian Senate session of 1997–1998 (1997); "Report of the Information Mission on Rwanda, Section 4: L'Attentat du 6 Avril 1994 Contre L'Avion du Président Juvénal Habyarimana," Assemble nationale (1998), https://www.assemblee-nationale.fr/dossiers/rwanda/r1271.asp#P3515_490312, accessed March 15, 2023; "Rwanda: The Preventable Genocide," Organization of African Unity (2000), https://www.refworld.org/docid/4d1da8752.html, accessed March 15, 2023.
22 John Conroy, "The Making of . . . Rwanda's Untold Story," BBC Two This World (2014), https://www.bbc.co.uk/programmes/articles/4GXplnBCF3RBslndxp1XgTL/the-making-of-rwandas-untold-story, accessed March 15, 2023.
23 See their homepage *GenoDynamics*, https://genodynamics.weebly.com/, accessed March 15, 2023.
24 Later, these researchers toned downed their claims somewhat, claiming to look at "all forms of violence." David A. Armstrong II, Christian Davenport, and Allan Stam, "Casualty Estimates in the Rwandan Genocide," *Journal of Genocide Research* 22:1 (2020), 105.
25 Filip Reyntjens, "'Rwanda: The Untold Story': Facts and Fabrication," Open Democrazy.net, October 26, 2014, https://www.opendemocracy.net/en/rwanda-untold-story-facts-and-fabrication/, accessed March 15, 2023.
26 Prunier, *Africa's World War*, 41.
27 In 2019 Rwanda received US$1,191,000,000 in foreign aid, which approximately comprised 70 percent of the central government expenditure. The World Bank, World Development Indicators: Aid Dependency, Rwanda, http://wdi.worldbank.org/table/6.11, accessed March 15, 2023.
28 "Freedom in the World 2021: Rwanda," Freedom House, https://freedomhouse.org/country/rwanda/freedom-world/2021; "Rwanda," Reporters without Borders,

https://rsf.org/en/rwanda; "Rwanda," Human Rights Watch, https://www.hrw.org/world-report/2019/country-chapters/rwanda#, all accessed March 15, 2023.
29 See, for example, Alison Des Forges, "Call to Genocide: Radio in Rwanda, 1994," in *The Media and the Rwanda Genocide*, Allan Thompson, ed. (London and Ann Arbor, MI: Pluto Press 2007), 41–54, and Doyle, "Reporting the Genocide," 156.
30 Andrew Wallis, "'Rwanda: The Untold Story': Questions for the BBC," Open Democracy, October 6, 2014, https://www.opendemocracy.net/en/rwanda-untold-story-questions-for-bbc, accessed March 15, 2023.
31 Marijke Verpoorten, "Rwanda: Why Claim that 200,000 Tutsi Died in the Genocide is Wrong," African Arguments, October 27, 2014, https://africanarguments.org/2014/10/rwanda-why-davenport-and-stams-calculation-that-200000-tutsi-died-in-the-genocide-is-wrong-by-marijke-verpoorten/, accessed March 15, 2023.
32 Edwards, "*100 Days*," 155.
33 Arthur Asiimwe, "Instead of Being Bullish, the BBC should Eat Humble Pie," *The New Times*, April 22, 2015. See also, for example, Lonzen Rugira, "To the BBC: When in a Hole, the First Rule is to Stop Digging," *The New Times*, March 2, 2015.
34 Edwin Musoni, "Taking on the Fight Against Genocide Denial," *The New Times*, March 3, 2015.
35 Gerard O'Donovan, "This World: Rwanda's Untold Story, BBC Two, Review—'Intense'," *The Telegraph*, October 1, 2014. See also Yaa-Lengi Ngemi, "Controversy Over BBC's 'Rwanda: The Untold Story'," *Huffington Post*, October 30, 2014, and Nicoletta Fagiolo, "Rwanda's Untold Story. A Commentary on the BBC Two Documentary," Reset Dialogues, December 17, 2014, https://www.resetdoc.org/story/rwandas-untold-story-a-commentary-on-the-bbc-two-documentary/, accessed March 15, 2023.
36 Melvern, *Intent to Deceive*, 117.
37 Dugald Baird, "BBC: We Had a 'Duty' to Make Rwandan Genocide Documentary," *The Guardian*, October 24, 2014.
38 Baird, "BBC: We Had a 'Duty' to Make Rwandan Genocide Documentary."
39 "Rwanda Suspends BBC Broadcasts over Genocide Film," BBC News, October 24, 2014, https://www.bbc.com/news/world-africa-29762713, accessed March 15, 2023.
40 Anon., "Survivors Outraged by BBC Genocide Denial Film," *The New Times*, October 5, 2014.
41 Sharon Kantengwa, "Storytelling in the Digital Era: Are Young People Getting the Most From It?," *The New Times*, April 12, 2019.
42 See, for example, Julia Raeside, "The Honourable Woman Review: A Very Human Conclusion to a Gripping Thriller," *The Guardian*, April 22, 2014; Rebecca Unnerud, "Sommarens bortglömda pärla till serie," Moviezine.se, October 17, 2014, https://www.moviezine.se/series/the-honourable-woman, accessed March 15, 2023; Helena Lindblad, "Helena Lindblad om veckans tv-serier," *Dagens Nyheter*, February 8, 2019; Karolina Fjellberg, "'Black Earth Rising'—komplex och krävande thriller om krigsförbrytelser," *Aftonbladet*, February 25, 2019; John Powers, "'Black Earth Risin' Is A Fascinating, If Clunky, Take On The Rwandan Genocide,"

National Public Radio, January 30, 2019, https://www.npr.org/2019/01/30/689892841/black-earth-rising-is-a-fascinating-if-clunky-take-on-the-rwandan-genocide, accessed March 15, 2023.
43 Unnerud, "Sommarens bortglömda pärla till serie."
44 Tyue Løkkegaard, "'Black Earth Rising': Fremragende Netflix-serie om et af de værste folkemord i menneskets historie," Soundvenue, February 26, 2019, http://soundvenue.com/film/2019/02/black-earth-rising-fremragende-netflix-serie-om-et-af-de-vaerste-folkemord-i-menneskets-historie-350231, accessed March 15, 2023.
45 Lorraine Ali, "Review: Netflix's 'Black Earth Rising' Deftly Explores War but Lacks a Personal Connection," *Los Angeles Times*, January 24, 2019.
46 See, for example, Reidar Spigseth, "'Black Earth Rising': Spennende, gripende og mystisk," *Dagsavisen* (Norway), February 7, 2019; Henrik Palle, "Næsten på niveau med 'Natportieren': Fremragende Netflix-serie beskriver en af den nye verdenshistories mest brutale og blodige konflikter," *Politikken* (Denmark), February 22, 2019; A. J. Estrada, "7 Best Netflix Series to Binge Watch Right Now," *Inquirer* (Philippines), February 3, 2019.
47 Brad Newsome, "This Engrossing British TV Drama Comes with a Shocking Twist," *The Sydney Morning Herald*, February 7, 2019.
48 Lorraine Ali, "'Black Earth Rising' Review: Dark Lesson in History," *Gulf News*, January 26, 2019.
49 Melvern, "Missing the Story," 198–200.
50 Jessica Gérondal Mwiza, "À propos de la série 'Black Earth Rising'," Blog: Le blog de jessica gérondal mwiza, *Mediapart*, January 29, 2019, https://blogs.mediapart.fr/jessica-gerondal/blog/290119/propos-de-la-serie-black-earth-rising?utm_source=twitter&utm_medium=social&utm_campaign=Sharing&xtor=CS3-67&fbclid=IwAR3jCPCngLKrl52amUa0hdw-FvgPp3LJrbHPlS8SB43UigQ7Ei3MLQUQla0, accessed March 15, 2023.
51 Gérondal Mwiza, "À propos de la série 'Black Earth Rising'."
52 Nelson Gashagaza, "The Recently Concluded BBC series Black Earth Rising is, for Lack of Better Words, a Disturbing Show," Medium, November 10, 2018, https://medium.com/@gashagaza/the-recently-concluded-bbc-series-black-earth-rising-is-for-lack-of-better-words-a-disturbing-5033597d9443, accessed March 15, 2023.
53 Leatitia Tran Ngoc, "Adding Insult to Injury: 'Black Earth Rising' and the Rwandan Genocide," International Policy Digest, February 12, 2019, https://intpolicydigest.org/2019/02/12/adding-insult-to-injury-black-earth-rising-and-the-rwandan-genocide/, accessed March 15, 2023.
54 Tran Ngoc, "Adding Insult to Injury."
55 See, for example, Kayihura and Zukus, *Inside Hotel Rwanda*.
56 Nosheen Iqbal, "'Why Weren't We Taught This at School?' Asks Star of Rwanda Drama," *The Observer*, September 16, 2018.
57 Ben Allen, "Rwanda, Genocide and the ICC: Hugo Blick Explains the True Story Behind Black Earth Rising," *Radio Times*, September 2018, https://www.radiotimes.com/news/tv/2019-06-10/black-earth-rising-bbc2-real-political-history-rwandan-genocide-international-criminal-court/, accessed March 15, 2023.

58 Kathleen Anaza, "'Black Earth Rising' Imagines A Catharsis For Rwandans Decades After Genocide," Shadow and Act, May 14, 2019, https://shadowandact.com/black-earth-rising-imagines-a-catharsis-for-rwandans-decades-after-genocide, accessed March 15, 2023. For a further discussion about the use of animations, see Danielle Turchiano, "'Black Earth Rising' Team Talks Animating a Tragedy," *Variety*, May 30, 2019; "Black Earth Rising—Using Animation Where Words Fail," BBC Writers Room, September 28, 2018, https://www.bbc.co.uk/blogs/writersroom/entries/bf5734ca-ff6e-4ade-86ca-2715ed43bb63, accessed March 15, 2023; Robert Goldrich, "Hugo Blick Discusses Challenges Of, His Hopes For 'Black Earth Rising'," Shoot, June 27, 2019, https://www.shootonline.com/news/hugo-blick-discusses-challenges-his-hopes-black-earth-rising, accessed March 15, 2023.
59 Kaliisa, "Top 10 Movies About the 1994 Genocide Against the Tutsi."
60 Anon., "Kabera on Impact of Movies in Telling the Rwandan Story," *The New Times*, April 20, 2018.

Chapter 11

1 Jean-Marie Vianney Higiro, "Rwandan Private Print Media on the Eve of the Genocide," in *The Media and the Rwanda Genocide*, Allan Thompson, ed. (London and Ann Arbor, MI: Pluto Press 2007), 73–89.
2 Thomas Kamilindi, "Journalism in a Time of Hate Media," in *The Media and the Rwanda Genocide*, Allan Thompson, ed. (London and Ann Arbor, MI: Pluto Press 2007), 136. Andrew Phillip Young, *"We are all Rwandans": Imagining the Post-Genocidal Nation Across Media*, unpublished dissertation (Los Angeles: University of California 2016), 176–177, https://escholarship.org/uc/item/18v9b19c, accessed March 15, 2023.
3 "Television Stations in Rwanda," Media High Council, http://www.mhc.gov.rw/index.php?id=60, accessed March 15, 2023.
4 The latest figure for television ownership in Rwanda is 8 percent according to the fourth Rwanda Population and Housing Census, *Fourth Population and Housing Census, Rwanda, 2012*, Census Atlas (National Institute of Statistics of Rwanda 2014), 79, which can be compared to the number of subscribers to RTV's YouTube channel, 384,000, which corresponds to approximately 3.0 percent of Rwanda's population as of March 2023. "Rwanda TV," YouTube, https://www.youtube.com/c/RwandanTVRBAHafiYawe/videos?view=0&sort=p&flow=grid, accessed March 15, 2023. See also, Quartz, "As Smartphones and Internet Connections Rise in Africa, so does Entertainment Streaming," *The New Times*, December 28, 2018. Also, in Jean Hatzfelt's interview book, *Pappas blod* ([original title: *Un papa de sung*] Stockholm: Weyler bokförlag 2015), most of the interviewees say that they never, or perhaps once, had visited a cinema, and that the main sources for audio-visual recollections of the genocide are through Internet sites like YouTube and television, the latter especially during the annual commemoration week (pp. 57, 88, 98, 106–107, 178).
5 Madelaine Hron, "Interview with Film Producer Eric Kabera," in *The Rwandan*

Genocide on Film: Critical Essays and Interviews, Matthew Edwards, ed. (Jefferson, NC: McFarland 2018), 169.
6 "About," Rwanda Cinema Center, September 17, 2008, https://rwandacinemacenter.wordpress.com/about/, accessed March 15, 2023. Hron, "Interview with Film Producer Eric Kabera," 167–168.
7 The Rwanda Film Institute is supported by the Rwandan Ministry of Education, the Rwandan Ministry of Youth, Sports and Culture, and the Rwandan Ministry of Science, Technology, Scientific Research and Information Communication Technologies. "Partners" and "About," Rwanda Film Institute, https://rwandafilminstitute.wordpress.com/partners/ and https://rwandafilminstitute.wordpress.com/about/, respectively, both accessed March 15, 2023.
8 "About Us," Kwetu Film Institute, https://kwetu.rw/about, accessed March 15, 2023.
9 This division was expressed by Eric Kabera in an interview, where he would not recognize the existence of the then (2015) viable online site rwandancinema.com (now closed) where approximately 100 films were for sale (direct-to-DVD), and where the majority were not about the genocide. Interview with Eric Kabera, conducted in Kigali by the author, April 21, 2015.
10 Anon., "Kabera on Impact of Movies in Telling the Rwandan Story."
11 These funding bodies have financed Rwandan films such as *Graduation Day* (2006), *Scars of My Day* (2006), *Hey Mr DJ* (2007), *Long Coat* (2009), and *Strength in Fear* (2012).
12 Anon., "Kabera on Impact of Movies in Telling the Rwandan Story."
13 Eddie Nsabimana, "Kwibohora25: How Local Film Industry Has Helped in Telling True Stories about Rwanda," *The New Times*, July 3, 2019.
14 Baldwin, "Constructing Identity Through Commemoration," 358–363; Bolin, "Dignity in Death and Life," 348.
15 See, for example, the official government site for Kwibuka, https://www.kwibuka.rw/, accessed March 15, 2023.
16 See, for example, Baldwin, "Constructing Identity Through Commemoration," 355–375; Terrence Lyons, "The Importance of Winning: Victorious Insurgent Groups and Authoritarian Politics," *Comparative Politics* 38:2 (2016), 167–184; Bert Ingelaere, "Do We Understand Life after Genocide? Center and Periphery in the Construction of Knowledge in Postgenocide Rwanda," *African Studies Review* 53:1 (2010), 41–59.
17 In 2018, it was reported that Zacu TV, a web-based video streaming channel accessible through subscription, would be launched. The platform would host Rwandan films, documentaries, and locally produced television series such as *Seburikoko* (2105–2017) and *City Maid* (2015–2016), both originally aired by RTV. Zacu TV started in 2019, but as of 2022 their site is reported to be "under construction." Instead, Zacu TV is presently active on YouTube, where productions that have to do with the genocide are virtually non-existent. Moses Opobo, "Zacu TV, Rwanda's First Subscription-based Video Platform is Here," *The New Times*, December 4, 2018; "Start page," Zacu TV, https://zacutv.com/, accessed March

15, 2023; Zacu TV on YouTube, https://www.youtube.com/c/ZACUTV/featured, accessed March 15, 2023. See also Nsabimana, "Kwibohora25."
18. Meeting with Arthur Asiimwe, Director General at Rwanda Broadcasting Agency (RBA), Kigali, May 26, 2015.
19. RTV on YouTube, videos sorted by popularity, https://www.youtube.com/c/RwandanTVRBAHafiYawe/videos?view=0&sort=p&flow=grid, accessed March 15, 2023.
20. Already in 2008, Eric Kabera expressed this view as he was interviewed in connection to the 2008 Rwanda Film Festival. Signature APF, "Don't Mention the Genocide: Rwanda Film Industry Moves On," ABC News (March 17, 2008), https://www.abc.net.au/news/2008-03-28/dont-mention-the-genocide-rwanda-film-industry/2385270, accessed March 15, 2023.
21. Edwards, "*100 Days*," 153-154.
22. Cieplak, "Nick Hughes," 221-222. It's estimated that 59,050 Tutsis were killed in the Kibuye prefecture, corresponding to 82.9 percent of the Tutsi population before the genocide. Philip Verwimp, A *Quantitative Analysis of Genocide in Kibuye Prefecture, Rwanda* (Leuven: Catholic University of Leuven 2001), 8.
23. Cieplak, "Nick Hughes," 219; Edwards, "*100 Days*," 161.
24. Kaliisa, "Top 10 Movies About the 1994 Genocide Against the Tutsi."
25. Edwards, "*100 Days*," 148.
26. See, for example, Edwards, "*100 Days*," 148-152; Cieplak, "Nick Hughes," 217-219; Dauge-Roth, *Writing and Filming the Genocide of the Tutsis in Rwanda*, 184, 211; Zylberman, "From Invisibility to Recognition," 92-94.
27. Nichols, *Introduction to Documentary*, 144-145.
28. Dauge-Roth, *Writing and Filming the Genocide of the Tutsis in Rwanda*, 174.
29. Dauge-Roth, *Writing and Filming the Genocide of the Tutsis in Rwanda*, 211.
30. Cohen, *States of Denial*, 194.
31. Cieplak, "Nick Hughes," 222-223; Edwards, "*100 Days*," 152-153.
32. According to Nick Hughes, this was an exact recreation of a situation he had encountered during the genocide. Cieplak, "Nick Hughes," 226.
33. Cieplak, "Nick Hughes," 225-226.
34. See, for example, "Rwandan Priest Guilty of Genocide," BBC News, December 13, 2006, http://news.bbc.co.uk/2/hi/africa/6175717.stm, accessed March 15, 2023. See also Melvern, *Conspiracy to Murder*, 189.
35. Jean Mugabo, "Genocide: Church to Apologise for Role 'Soon'," *The New Times*, May 4, 2015.
36. Angela Mutoni, "Catholic Church Apology Ambiguous: Vatican Deafeningly Silent," *Rwanda Dispatch* 60 (January 2017), 12-15.
37. Philip A. Cantrell II, "'We Were a Chosen People': The East African Revival and Its Return to Post-Genocide Rwanda," *Church History* 83:3 (2014), 422, 437. For an in-depth discussion of the importance of religion in Rwanda and how religion has been used in documentary films about the genocide, see Gustafsson, "A Fight over Souls," 1-38.
38. Dauge-Roth, *Writing and Filming the Genocide of the Tutsis in Rwanda*, 212.

39 Bolin, "Dignity in Death and Life," 349.
40 See, for example, Edwards, "*100 Days*," 150.
41 Dennis Harvey, "'100 Days' (Rwanda-U.K.)," *Variety*, October 12, 2001.
42 Cieplak, "Nick Hughes," 227.
43 Dauge-Roth, *Writing and Filming the Genocide of the Tutsis in Rwanda*, 189.
44 Baldwin, "Constructing Identity Through Commemoration," 358-359.
45 Baldwin, "Constructing Identity Through Commemoration," 372.
46 Edwards, "*100 Days*," 158.
47 *Report on the Situation of Human Rights in Rwanda*, 7.
48 Marie-Eve Hamel, "Ethnic Belonging of the Children Born out of Rape in Postconflict Bosnia-Herzegovina and Rwanda," *Nation and Nationalism* 22:2 (2016), 298-300.
49 Cieplak, "Nick Hughes," 221.
50 Edwards, "*100 Days*," 156.
51 Cieplak, "Nick Hughes," 225. The priest was Father Athanase Seromba, who killed 2,000 Tutsis at the event. Seromba was sentenced to fifteen years in prison by the ICTR in 2007. George Obulutsa, "Former Priest Gets 15 Years for Rwanda Genocide," Reuters, January 20, 2007, https://www.reuters.com/article/us-rwanda-genocide-idUSWAL35282420061213, accessed March 15, 2023.
52 Cieplak, "Nick Hughes," 224.
53 Cieplak, "The Rwandan Genocide and the Bestiality of Representation in *100 Days* (2001) and *Shooting Dogs* (2005)," 57-59.
54 Dauge-Roth, *Writing and Filming the Genocide of the Tutsis in Rwanda*, 150, and Bromley, "After Such Knowledge," 192. See also Portfleet, "The Films of Eric Kabera," 102-103.
55 For more information about the Aegis Trust, see their homepage: https://www.aegistrust.org/what-we-do/, accessed March 15, 2023.
56 Caplan, "'Never Again'," 20.
57 The eighth emblematic image of "Skeletons and Clothes" is not featured in the film.
58 The third film includes brief stories of people who saved others during the genocide, with an emphasis on the Muslim community in Kigali. It should be noted that many Rwandan Muslims are Hutus who converted to Islam, but this is not mentioned in the film nor in the exhibition.
59 Kavila Matu has primarily worked as an editor, editing films such as *100 Days* and *Keepers of Memory*.
60 James Munyaneza, "Tribute to Massacred Nyange Students," *The New Times*, January 30, 2009.
61 Young, "'We are all Rwandans," 1, 29.
62 Edwards, "*100 Days*," 162-163.
63 Hron, "Interview with Film Producer Eric Kabera," 167-168. On the DVD cover, Eric Kabera is credited as co-director.
64 In December 2019, Domitilla Mukantaganzwa was appointed as the Chairperson of the Rwanda Law Reform Commission (RLRC). James Karuhanga, "Domitilla

Mukantaganzwa Appointed Chairperson of Law Reform Commission," *The New Times*, December 5, 2019.
65 Hron, "Interview with Film Producer Eric Kabera," 170.
66 Erika Dahlmanns, "New Community, Old Tradition: The Intore Warrior as a Symbol of the New Man. Rwanda's Itorero-Policy of Societal Recreation," *Modern Africa: Politics, History and Society* 3:1 (2015), 113-114.
67 Dahlmanns, "New Community, Old Tradition," 143-144.
68 Young, "*We are all Rwandans*," 191.
69 For more information about HROC, see HROC Rwanda, https://healingandrebuildingourcommunities.org/, accessed March 15, 2023.
70 Eric Aoki and Kyle M. Jonas, two American Communications Studies scholars, analyze *Icyizere: Hope* as a document of representational space and collective memory, but they are clearly hesitant as to whether the content of the documentary is true and representative. Eric Aoki and Kyle M. Jonas, "Collective Memory and Sacred Space in Post-genocide Rwanda: Reconciliation and Rehumanization Processes in Mureithi's ICYIZERE," *Journal of International and Intercultural Communication* 9:3 (2016), 240-258.
71 This was a project commissioned by the Goethe-Institut in collaboration with GIZ, Partnership Rhineland-Palatinate, Rwanda, KfW German Development Bank, and Plan International Rwanda. "Three Make it to 'Reconciliation Film' Finals," *The New Times*, March 12, 2014. Jean-Paul Samputu is also one of the featured artists in Kabera's *Intore* (2014).
72 The short film won the Golden Impala Award at the Amakula Film Festival in Uganda in 2010, and the award for Best Short Film at the Silicon Valley African Film Festival in 2010. The feature version won the Nile Grand Prize, Luxor African Film Festival in 2014, and was also nominated in different categories at the Chicago International Film Festival, the Hamburg Film Festival, and the Africa Movie Academy Awards, all in 2013.
73 Kanyekanye, "AFRIKAMERA—Re-Imaging Africa 2013: Imbabazi," Queer View, November 13, 2013, https://www.facebook.com/photo/?fbid=221653694673547&set=a.221225988049651.1073741831.189782614527322, accessed March 15, 2023.
74 Dauge-Roth, *Writing and Filming the Genocide of the Tutsis in Rwanda*, 212.
75 However, in May 2022 Bamporiki fell from grace and was placed under house arrest amid a corruption investigation. Aurore Teta Ufitiwabo, "Bamporiki Placed under House Arrest amid Corruption Investigation," *The New Times*, May 5, 2022.
76 See, for example, Junior Sabena Mutabazi, "Kwibuka21: Why the Youth Must Continue to Remember," *The New Times*, April 2, 2015, and Junior Sabena Mutabazi, "Your Country Needs You to Speak Up Against Genocide Denial," *The New Times*, April 9, 2015.
77 Caroline Losneck, "The Rwandan Candidate: An Interview with Filmmaker Gilbert Ndahayo" (Summer 2010), http://carolinelosneck.blogspot.com/2011/, accessed March 15, 2023.
78 Young, "*We are all Rwandans*," 219.

79 "Rwanda: Beyond the Deadly Pit: Awards," IMDb, https://www.imdb.com/title/tt1679658/awards/?ref_=tt_awd, accessed March 15, 2023.
80 Edwin Musoni, "How Ndahayo Filmed His Way to Hollywood Screens," *The New Times*, November 10, 2013.
81 Karirima Ngarambe Aimable, "African Premiere of Ndahayo's Film THE RWANDAN NIGHT," IGIHE, June 18, 2014, https://en.igihe.com/entertainment/african-premiere-of-ndahayo-s-film-the-rwandan.html, accessed March 15, 2023.
82 "The Rwandan Night Press Kit" (2013), 2, https://ndahayogilbert.files.wordpress.com/2012/03/trn_template_svaff_20131.pdf, accessed March 15, 2023.
83 Prunier, *The Rwanda Crisis*, 62.
84 "The Rwandan Night Press Kit," 2–3.
85 *The Rwandan Night* was supposed to be the first installment in a trilogy on the Rwandan genocide directed by Ndahayo, but the two sequels, "The Rwandan Day" and "The Rwandan Silence," have not seen the light of day, and another film, "The Blood of the Chosen," has been noted as "under production" at IMDb since 2015.
86 Kerner, *Film and the Holocaust*, 5–8.
87 "Daddy Ruhorahoza," CINU México, YouTube, April 17, 2009, https://www.youtube.com/watch?v=2t3mix8zpZA, accessed March 15, 2023.
88 Kristen McCracken, "Awards Announced: 2011 Tribeca Film Festival," Tribeca News, April 28, 2011, https://tribecafilm.com/news/512c0ffd1c7d76d9a9000724-awards-announced-2011-tri, accessed March 15, 2023.
89 Matthias De Groof, "Grey Matter: An Interview with Director Kivu Ruhorahoza," in *The Rwandan Genocide on Film: Critical Essays and Interviews*, Matthew Edwards, ed. (Jefferson, NC: McFarland 2018), 193–194. This view on humanity is a recurrent theme in Ruhorahoza's film production, for example in the non-genocide film *Father's Day* (2022).
90 Noosim Naimasiah, "In Conversation with Kivu Ruhorahoza," Warscapes, June 15, 2015, http://www.warscapes.com/conversations/conversation-kivu-ruhorahoza, accessed March 15, 2023.
91 Zylberman, "From Invisibility to Recognition," 94–95; Mick Broderick, "Not Reconciled: *Grey Matter* (Ruhorahoza 2011) and the Lacunae of Post-genocide Rwandan Cinema," *Critical Arts: South-North Cultural and Media Studies* 31:5 (2017), 78–86.
92 Piotr Cieplak, "History, Trauma and Remembering in Kivu Ruhorahoza's *Grey Matter* (2011)," *Journal of African Cultural Studies* 30:2 (2018), 167, 173.
93 Cieplak, "History, Trauma and Remembering," 174.
94 Naimasiah, "In Conversation with Kivu Ruhorahoza."
95 David DeWitt, "'Grey Matter'—A Rwandan Film," *The New York Times*, January 18, 2012.
96 Howard Feinstein, "Grey Matter," Screen Daily, April 22, 2011, https://www.screendaily.com/grey-matter/5026534.article, accessed March 15, 2023.
97 Anon., "Rwandan Filmmaker Shines at Tribeca Film Festival," *The New Times*,

May 2, 2011; Anon., "Critically Acclaimed 'Grey Matter' Screens in Kacyiru," *The New Times*, September 12, 2012: Quartz, "Rwanda Wins Prestigious Film Prizes in Spain," *The New Times*, October 22, 2012; Collins Mwai, "Movies that Tell the Genocide Story," *The New Times*, April 10, 2014.

98 Anon., "Movie: Grey Matter," *The New Times*, April 10, 2013.
99 Hron, "Interview with Film Producer Eric Kabera," 168–169. See also, Eyder Peralta, "Filmmaker Dreams Of A Romantic Comedy Set In Rwanda," NPR, July 27, 2017, https://www.npr.org/2017/07/27/539825474/filmmaker-dreams-of-a-romantic-comedy-set-in-rwanda, accessed March 15, 2023; Joseph Njata, "Pomp and Joy as Karani Ngufu Premieres in Kigali," *The New Times*, October 21, 2019.
100 Naimasiah, "In Conversation with Kivu Ruhorahoza."
101 Ntayombya, "We Need to Bring our Heroes to Life on Film and Television," *The New Times*, January 31, 2023.
102 Interview with Eric Kabera, conducted in Kigali by the author, April 21, 2015. The title "Inkotanyi" with Eric Kabera as producer has been listed as under production on IMDb since 2017. IMDb, https://www.imdb.com/title/tt4720774/?ref_=nm_knf_t_4, accessed March 15, 2023.
103 Anon., "Kabera on Impact of Movies in Telling the Rwandan Story."

Bibliography

Adhikari, Mohamed, "Hotel Rwanda: Too Much Heroism, Too Little History—or Horror?," in *Black and White in Colour: Africa's History on Screen*, Vivian Bickford-Smith and Richard Mendelsohn, eds. (Athens: Ohio University Press 2006).

Adorno, Theodore W. and Max Horkheimer, *Dialectic of Enlightenment* (Stanford, CA: Stanford University Press 2002).

Aoki, Eric and Kyle M. Jonas, "Collective Memory and Sacred Space in Post-genocide Rwanda: Reconciliation and Rehumanization Processes in Mureithi's ICYIZERE," *Journal of International and Intercultural Communication* 9:3 (2016).

Arendt, Hannah, *Eichmann in Jerusalem: A Report on the Banality of Evil* (London: Penguin Books 1996).

Armstrong II, David A., Christian Davenport, and Allan Stam, "Casualty Estimates in the Rwandan Genocide," *Journal of Genocide Research* 22:1 (2020).

Ashenden, Samantha, James Brown, and Philip Spencer, "Justice Seekers and The Arrows of Truth: An Interview with Antonio Ribeiro," in *The Rwandan Genocide on Film: Critical Essays and Interviews*, Matthew Edwards, ed. (Jefferson, NC: McFarland 2018).

Baldwin, Gretchen, "Constructing Identity Through Commemoration: Kwibuka and the Rise of Survivor Nationalism in Post-conflict Rwanda," *Journal of Modern African Studies* 57:3 (2019).

Barash, Jeffrey Andrew, *Collective Memory and the Historical Past* (Chicago and London: University of Chicago Press 2016).

Barlet, Oliver, *Contemporary African Cinema* (East Lansing: Michigan State University Press 2016).

Barnett, Michael, *Eyewitness to a Genocide: The United Nations and Rwanda* (New York: Cornell University Press 2003).

Berns, Pagnoni, Fernando Gabriel, and Juan Ignacio Juvé, "Let Us Speak of Rwanda (and Argentina and France)," in *The Rwandan Genocide on Film: Critical Essays and Interviews*, Matthew Edwards, ed. (Jefferson, NC: McFarland 2018).

Blockbuster Movies, Julian Stringer, ed. (London and New York: Routledge 2003).

Bolin, Annalisa, "Dignity in Death and Life: Negotiating Agaciro for the Nation in Preservation Practice at Nyamata Genocide Memorial, Rwanda," *Anthropological Quarterly* 92:2 (2019).

Bondebjerg, Ib, *Screening Twentieth Century Europe: Television, History, Memory* (London: Palgrave Macmillan 2020).
Bratu Hansen, Miriam, "*Schindler's List* Is Not Shoah: Second Commandment, Popular Modernism, and Public Memory," in *Spielberg's Holocaust. Critical Perspectives on Schindler's List*, Yosefa Loshitzky, ed. (Bloomington and Indianapolis: Indiana University Press 1997).
Broderick, Mick, "Not Reconciled: *Grey Matter* (Ruhorahoza 2011) and the Lacunae of Post-genocide Rwandan Cinema," *Critical Arts: South-North Cultural and Media Studies* 31:5 (2017).
Bromley, Roger, "After Such Knowledge, What Forgiveness? Cultural Representations of Reconciliation in Rwanda," *French Cultural Studies* 20:2 (2008).
Bruguière, Jean-Louis, *Délivrance de mandats d'arret internationaux*, 97.295.2303/0, Tribunal de Grande Instance de Paris, November 17, 2006.
Bruzzi, Stella, *New Documentary* (London and New York: Routledge 2006).
Bufacchi, Vittorio, "Two Concepts of Violence," *Political Studies Review* 3 (2005).
Bundervoet, Tom, "Livestock, Land and Political Power: The 1993 Killings in Burundi," *Journal of Peace Research* 46:3 (2009).
Cantrell II, Phillip A., "Reconciliation in Post-Genocide Rwanda as Presented in the Film As We Forgive," in *The Rwandan Genocide on Film: Critical Essays and Interviews*, Matthew Edwards, ed. (Jefferson, NC: McFarland 2018).
Cantrell II, Philip A., "'We Were a Chosen People': The East African Revival and Its Return to Post-Genocide Rwanda," *Church History* 83:3 (2014).
Caplan, Pat, "'Never Again': Genocide Memorials in Rwanda," *Anthropology Today* 23:1 (2007).
Chaon, Anne, "Who Failed in Rwanda, Journalists or the Media?," in *The Media and the Rwanda Genocide*, Allan Thompson, ed. (London and Ann Arbor, MI: Pluto Press 2007).
Chaudhuri, Shohini, *Cinema of the Dark Side: Atrocity and the Ethics of Film Spectatorship* (Edinburgh: Edinburgh University Press 2014).
Chopra-Gant, Mike, *Cinema and History: The Telling of Stories* (London and New York: Wallflower Press 2008).
Chrétien, Jean-Pierre, "RTLM Propaganda: The Democratic Alibi," in *The Media and the Rwanda Genocide*, Allan Thompson, ed. (London and Ann Arbor, MI: Pluto Press 2007).
Cieplak, Piotr, "History, Trauma and Remembering in Kivu Ruhorahoza's *Grey Matter* (2011)," *Journal of African Cultural Studies* 30:2 (2018).
Cieplak, Piotr A., "Nick Huges, Director of *100 Days* (2001), Interviewed By," in *Film & Genocide*, Kristi M. Wilson and Tomás F. Crowder-Taraborrelli, eds. (Madison and London: The University of Wisconsin Press 2012).
Cieplak, Piotr A., "The Rwandan Genocide and the Bestiality of Representation in *100 Days* (2001) and *Shooting Dogs* (2005)," *Journal of African Cinemas* 2:1 (2010).
Cohen, Jared A., *One Hundred Days of Silence: America and the Rwanda Genocide* (Lanham, MD and New York: Rowman & Littlefield 2006).

Cohen, Stanley, *States of Denial: Knowing about Atrocities and Suffering* (Cambridge: Polity Press 2007).
Collins, Barrie, *Rwanda 1994: The Myth of the Akazu Genocide Conspiracy and its Consequences* (London and New York: Palgrave Macmillan 2014).
Conrad, Sebastian, *What Is Global History?* (Princeton, NJ: Princeton University Press 2017).
Courtmanche, Gil, *A Sunday at the Pool in Kigali* (Edinburgh: Canongate 2018).
Cruvellier, Thierry and Chari Voss, *Court of Remorse: Inside the International Criminal Tribunal for Rwanda* (Madison: University of Wisconsin Press 2010).
Dahlmanns, Erika, "New Community, Old Tradition: The Intore Warrior as a Symbol of the New Man. Rwanda's Itorero-Policy of Societal Recreation," *Modern Africa: Politics, History and Society* 3:1 (2015).
Dallaire, Roméo (with Brent Beardsley), *Shake Hands with the Devil. The Failure of Humanity in Rwanda* (New York: Carroll & Graf Publishers 2005).
Dauge-Roth, Alexandre, *Writing and Filming the Genocide of the Tutsis in Rwanda: Disremembering and Remembering Traumatic History* (Lanham, MD and Boulder, CO: Lexington Books 2010).
De Groof, Matthias, "Grey Matter: An Interview with Director Kivu Ruhorahoza," in *The Rwandan Genocide on Film: Critical Essays and Interviews*, Matthew Edwards, ed. (Jefferson, NC: McFarland 2018).
de la Guardia, Virginia, *Genocide in Rwanda. The Role of the Media in Confusing Public Opinion and Encouraging the Killings* (Kindle Digital Edition 2012).
Des Forges, Alison, "Call to Genocide: Radio in Rwanda, 1994," in *The Media and the Rwanda Genocide*, Allan Thompson, ed. (London and Ann Arbor, MI: Pluto Press 2007).
Des Forges, Alison, *"Leave None to Tell the Story": Genocide in Rwanda* (New York: Human Rights Watch 1999).
Desser, David, "Race and Culture in the Vietnam War Films," in *Inventing Vietnam: The War in Film and Television*, Michael Anderegg, ed. (Philadelphia, PA: Temple University Press 1991).
Diawara, Mamadou, "Remembering the Past, Reaching for the Future: Aspects of African Historical Memory in an International Context," in *Historical Memory in Africa: Dealing with the Past, Researching for the Future in a Intercultural Context*, Mamadou Diawara, Bernard Lategan, and Jörn Rüsen, eds. (New York and Oxford: Berghahn 2013).
Diawara, Mamadou, Bernard Lategan, and Jörn Rüsen, "Introduction," in *Historical Memory in Africa: Dealing with the Past, Researching for the Future in an Intercultural Context*, Mamadou Diawara, Bernard Lategan, and Jörn Rüsen, eds. (New York and Oxford: Berghahn 2013).
Dooley, Andrea, "Implicated Geographies: Public Memorials and the Topographies of Genocide," *Sightlines* 8 (June 2010).
Doyle, Mark, "Reporting the Genocide," in *The Media and the Rwanda Genocide*, Allan Thompson, ed. (London and Ann Arbor, MI: Pluto Press 2007).

Drumbl, Mark A., *Atrocity, Punishment, and International Law* (Cambridge and New York: Cambridge University Press 2007).

Drumbl, Mark A., "'She Makes Me Ashamed to Be a Woman': The Genocide Conviction of Pauline Nyiramasuhuko, 2011," *Michigan Journal of International Law* 34 (2012).

Edwards, Matthew, "As We Forgive: An Interview with Director Laura Waters Hinson," in *The Rwandan Genocide on Film: Critical Essays and Interviews*, Matthew Edwards, ed. (Jefferson, NC: McFarland 2018).

Edwards, Matthew, "*Munyurangbo*: An Interview with Director Lee Isaac Chung," in *The Rwandan Genocide on Film: Critical Essays and Interviews*, Matthew Edwards, ed. (Jefferson, NC: McFarland 2018).

Edwards, Matthew, "*100 Days*: An Interview with Nick Hughes," in *The Rwandan Genocide on Film: Critical Essays and Interviews*, Matthew Edwards, ed. (Jefferson, NC: McFarland 2018).

Edwards, Matthew, "*Sweet Dreams*: An Interview with Director Lisa Fruchtman," in *The Rwandan Genocide on Film: Critical Essays and Interviews*, Matthew Edwards, ed. (Jefferson, NC: McFarland 2018).

Ezra, Elisabeth and Terry Rowden, "General Introduction," in *Transnational Cinema. The Reader*, Elisabeth Ezra and Terry Rowden, eds. (London and New York: Routledge 2006).

Fair, Jo Ellen and Lisa Parks, "Africa on Camera: Television News Coverage and Aerial Imaging of Rwanda Refugees," *Africa Today* 48:2 (2001).

Faye, Gaël, *Petit pays* (Paris: Le Livre de poche 2017).

Fegley, Randall, *A History of Rwandan Identity and Trauma: The Mythmakers' Victims* (Lanham, MD: Lexington Books 2016).

Ferguson, Tamara J., Daniel Brugman, Jennifer White, and Heidi L. Eyre, "Shame and Guilt as Morally Warranted Experiences," in *The Self-Conscious Emotions. Theory and Research*, Jessica L. Tracy, Richard W. Robins, and June Price Tangney, eds. (New York and London: Guilford Press 2007).

Fisher, Duncan and Jolyon Mitchell, "Portraying Forgiveness through Documentary Film," *Studies in World Christianity* 18:2 (2012).

Giles, Tom, "Media Failure over Rwanda's Genocide," in *The Media and the Rwanda Genocide*, Allan Thompson, ed. (London and Ann Arbor, MI: Pluto Press 2007).

Glassner, Barry, *The Culture of Fear: Why Americans are Afraid of the Wrong Things* (New York: Basic Books 1999).

Glover, Jonathan D., "Genocide, Human Rights, and the Politics of Memorialization: 'Hotel Rwanda' and Africa's World War," *South Atlantic Review* 75:2 (2010).

Goode, Erich and Nachman Ben-Yehudea, *Moral Panics. The Social Construction of Deviance* (Malden, MA and Oxford: Wiley-Blackwell 2009).

Gourevitch, Philip, *We Wish to Inform You That Tomorrow We Will Be Killed with Our Families: Stories from Rwanda* (London: Picador 2000).

Gray, Michael, "Twenty Years On: Finding a Place for the Rwandan Genocide in Education," *Intercultural Education* 25:5 (2014).

Grunfelt, Fred and Anke Huijboom, *The Failure to Prevent Genocide in Rwanda. The Role of Bystanders* (Leiden and Boston: Martinus Nijhoff Publishers 2007).
Gustafsson, Tommy, *Det var en gång: historia för barn i svensk television under det långa 1970-talet* (Malmö: Roos & Tegnér/Universus Academic Press 2014).
Gustafsson, Tommy, "A Fight over Souls: Documentary Films on the Rwandan Genocide with a Christian Theme," *Journal of Religion and Film* 21:2 (2017).
Gustafsson, Tommy, "Filmen som historisk källa. Historiografi, pluralism, representativitet," *Historisk tidskrift* 126:3 (2006).
Gustafsson, Tommy, "*The Last Dog in Rwanda*: Swedish Educational Films and Film Teaching Guides on the History of Genocide," in *Regional Aesthetics: Locating Swedish Media*, Erik Hedling, Olof Hedling, and Mats Jönsson, eds. (Stockholm: National Library of Sweden 2010).
Gustafsson, Tommy, "Swedish Television News Coverage and the Historical Media Memory of the Rwandan Genocide," *Scandia* 76:2 (2010).
Gustafsson, Tommy, "The Visual Re-creation of Black People in a 'White' Country: Oscar Micheaux and Swedish Film Culture in the 1920s," *Cinema Journal* 47:4 (2008), 30–49.
Gustafsson, Tommy and Klara Arnberg, *Moralpanik och lågkultur: genus- och mediehistoriska analyser 1900–2012* (Stockholm: Atlas Akademi 2013).
Guttenplan, D. D., *The Holocaust on Trial: Justice and the David Irving Libel Case* (New York and London: W. W. Norton & Company 2002).
Hadenius, Stig and Lennart Weibull, *Massmedier: En bok om press, radio & TV* (Stockholm: Albert Bonniers förlag 2005).
Hall, Stuart, "When was 'The Postcolonial' Thinking at the Limit," in *The Post-Colonial Question: Common Skies, Divided Horizons*, Iain Chambers and Lidia Curtis, eds. (London and New York: Routledge 1996).
Hamel, Marie-Eve, "Ethnic Belonging of the Children Born out of Rape in Postconflict Bosnia-Herzegovina and Rwanda," *Nation and Nationalism* 22:2 (2016).
Harvey, Daniel C., "The Invisible Genocide: An Analysis of ABC, CBS, and NBC Television News Coverage of the 1994 Genocide in Rwanda" (University of Western Ontario—Electronic Thesis and Dissertation Repository 2012).
Hatzfelt, Jean, *Machete Season: The Killers in Rwanda Speak* (New York: Picador 2005).
Hatzfelt, Jean, *Pappas blod* (Stockholm: Weyler bokförlag 2015).
Hedlund, Anna, *Exile Warriors: Violence and Community Among Hutu Rebels in the Eastern Congo* (Lund: Lund University 2014).
Herman, Edward S. and David Peterson, *Enduring Lies: The Rwandan Genocide in the Propaganda System, 20 Years Later* (The Real New Books 2014).
Higson, Andrew, *English Heritage, English Cinema: Costume Drama Since 1980* (Oxford and New York: Oxford University Press 2003).
Hilsum, Lindsay, "Reporting Rwanda: The Media and the Aid Agencies," in *The Media and the Rwanda Genocide*, Allan Thompson, ed. (London and Ann Arbor, MI: Pluto Press 2007).
Hirsch, Joshua, *AfterImage: Film, Trauma, and the Holocaust* (Philadelphia, PA: Temple University Press 2004).

Holmes, Georgina, *Women and War in Rwanda: Gender, Media and the Representation of Genocide* (London and New York: I. B.Tauris 2014).

Horowitz, Sara, "But Is It Good for the Jews? Spielberg's Schindler and the Aesthetics of Atrocity," in *Spielberg's Holocaust: Critical Perspectives on Schindler's List*, Yosefa Loshitzky, ed. (Bloomington and Indianapolis: Indiana University Press 1997).

Hron, Madelaine, "Genres of 'Yet An Other Genocide': Cinematic Representations of Rwanda," in *Film & Genocide*, Kristi M. Wilson and Tomás F. Crowder-Taraborrelli, eds. (Madison and London: The University of Wisconsin Press 2012).

Hron, Madelaine, "Interview with Film Producer Eric Kabera," in *The Rwandan Genocide on Film: Critical Essays and Interviews*, Matthew Edwards, ed. (Jefferson, NC: McFarland 2018).

Hughes, Nick, "Exhibit 467: The Genocide Through a Lens," in *The Media and the Rwanda Genocide*, Allan Thompson, ed. (London and Ann Arbor, MI: Pluto Press 2007).

Hughey, Matthew, *The White Savior Film: Content, Critics, and Consumption* (Philadelphia, PA: Temple University Press 2014).

Ingelaere, Bert, "Do We Understand Life after Genocide? Center and Periphery in the Construction of Knowledge in Postgenocide Rwanda," *African Studies Review* 53:1 (2010).

Ingelaere, Bert, "The Gacaca Courts in Rwanda," in *Traditional Justice and Reconciliation after Violent Conflict: Learning from African Experiences*, Luc Huyse and Mark Salter, eds. (Stockholm: International IDEA 2008).

Iriye, Akira, *Global and Transnational History: The Past, Present, and Future* (London: Palgrave Pivot 2013).

Jenkins, Keith, "Modernist Disavowals and Postmodern Reminders of the Condition of History Today: On Jean François Lyotard," *Rethinking History* 8:3 (2004).

Jessee, Erin and Sarah E. Watkins, "Good Kings, Bloody Tyrants, and Everything In Between: Representations of the Monarchy in Post-Genocide Rwanda," *History in Africa* 41 (2014).

Jönsson, Mats, *Film och historia: historisk hollywoodfilm 1960–2000* (Lund: KFS 2004).

Kamilindi, Thomas, "Journalism in a Time of Hate Media," in *The Media and the Rwanda Genocide*, Allan Thompson, ed. (London and Ann Arbor, MI: Pluto Press 2007).

Kamukara, Dixon, *Rwanda Conflict: Its Roots and Regional Implications* (Kampala: Fountain Publishers 1997).

Karlsson, Klas-Göran, "The Holocaust as a Problem of Historical Culture," in *Echos of the Holocaust: Historical Cultures in Contemporary Europe*, Klas-Göran Karlsson and Ulf Zander Zander, eds. (Lund: Nordic Academic Press 2003).

Kayihura, Edouard and Kerry Zukas, *Inside Hotel Rwanda: The Surprising True Story . . . And Why It Matters Today* (Dallas, TX: BenBella Books 2014).

Kerner, Aaron, *Film and the Holocaust: New Perspectives on Dramas, Documentaries, and Experimental Films* (New York: Continuum 2011).

Kimani, Mary, "RTLM: The Medium that Became a Tool for Mass Murder," in *The Media and the Rwanda Genocide*, Allan Thompson, ed. (London and Ann Arbor, MI: Pluto Press 2007).

LaMarre, Heather L. and Kristen D. Landreville, "When is Fiction as Good as Fact? Comparing the Influence of Documentary and Historical Reenactment Films on Engagement, Affect, Issue Interest, and Learning," *Mass Communication and Society* 12:4 (2009).

Lev Niv, Kobi, *Life is Beautiful, But not for Jews: Another View of the Film by Benigni* (New York: Scarecrow Press 2003).

Lipstadt, Deborah, *Denying the Holocaust: The Growing Assault on Truth and Memory* (New York: Free Press 1993).

Livingston, Steven, "Limited Vision: How Both the American Media and Government Failed Rwanda," in *The Media and the Rwanda Genocide*, Allan Thompson, ed. (London and Ann Arbor, MI: Pluto Press 2007).

Loshitsky, Yosefa, "Introduction," in *Spielberg's Holocaust. Critical Perspectives on Schindler's List*, Yosefa Loshitzky, ed. (Bloomington and Indianapolis: Indiana University Press 1997).

Ludvigsson, David, *The Historian-Filmmaker's Dilemma. Historical Documentaries in Sweden in the Era of Häger and Villius* (Uppsala: Acta Universitatis Upsaliensis 2003).

Lyons, Terrence, "The Importance of Winning: Victorious Insurgent Groups and Authoritarian Politics," *Comparative Politics* 38:2 (2016).

McCrisken, Trevor and Andrew Pepper, *American History and Contemporary Hollywood Film* (New Brunswick, NJ: Rutgers University Press 2005).

MacGregor, Alexander, "Gladiator," *Filmhäftet* 29:2 (2001).

Magubane, Zine, "Saviors and Survivors: Western Passivity, African Resistance, and the Politics of Genocide in Hotel Rwanda (2004)," in *Through a Lens Darkly: Films of Genocide, Ethnic Cleansing, and Atrocities*, John J. Michalczyk and Raymond G. Helmick, Sr., eds. (New York: Peter Lang 2013).

Mamdani, Mahmood, *When Victims Become Killers. Colonialism, Nativism, and the Genocide in Rwanda* (Princeton, NJ: Princeton University Press 2001).

Marcus, Alan S. and Thomas H. Levine, "Exploring the Past with Feature Film," in *Celluloid Blackboard. Teaching History with Film*, Alan S. Marcus, ed. (Charlotte, NC: Information Age Publishing 2006).

Mboti, Nyasha, "Song and Genocide: Investigating the Function of Yvonne Chaka Chaka's 'Umqombothi' in Hotel Rwanda," *Critical Arts: A South-North Journal of Cultural & Media Studies*, 26:5 (2012).

Melvern, Linda, *Att förråda ett folk. Västmakterna och folkmordet i Rwanda* (Stockholm: Ordfront 2003).

Melvern, Linda, *Conspiracy to Murder: The Rwandan Genocide* (London and New York: Verso 2004).

Melvern, Linda, *Intent to Deceive: Denying the Genocide of the Tutsi* (London and New York: Verso 2020).

Melvern, Linda, "Missing the Story," in *The Media and the Rwanda Genocide*, Allan Thompson, ed. (London and Ann Arbor, MI: Pluto Press 2007).

Metz, Christian, *The Imaginary Signifier: Psychoanalysis and the Cinema* (Bloomington and Indianapolis: Indiana University Press 1986).

Michalczyk, John J., "Village Justice: *In the Tall Grass* (2006)," in *Through a Lens Darkly:*

Films of Genocide, Ethnic Cleansing, and Atrocities, John J. Michalczyk and Raymond G. Helmick, Sr., eds. (New York: Peter Lang 2013).

Mironko, Charles, "The Effect of RTLM's Rhetoric of Ethnic Hatred in Rural Rwanda," in *The Media and the Rwanda Genocide*, Allan Thompson, ed. (London and Ann Arbor, MI: Pluto Press 2007).

Moeller, Susan, *Compassion Fatigue: How the Media Sell Disease, Famine, War, and Death* (New York: Routledge 1999).

Möller, Frank, "Rwanda Revisualized: Genocide, Photography, and the Era of the Witness," *Alternatives* 35:2 (2010).

Mosse, George L., *Fallen Soldiers: Reshaping the Memory of the World Wars* (Oxford and New York: Oxford University Press 1990).

Mukangendo, Marie-Consolee, "Caring for Children Born of Rape in Rwanda," in *Born of War: Protecting Children of Sexual Violence Survivors in Conflict Zones*, R. Charli Carpenter, ed. (Bloomfield, CT: Kumarian Press 2007).

Ndahiro, Alfred and Privat Rutazibwa, *Hotel Rwanda: Or The Tutsi Genocide as Seen by Hollywood* (Paris: L'Harmattan 2008).

Newbury, Catharine, *The Cohesion of Oppression. Clientship and Ethnicity in Rwanda, 1860–1960* (New York: Columbia University Press 1988).

Nichols, Bill, *Introduction to Documentary* (Bloomington and Indianapolis: Indiana University Press 2010).

Nowrojee, Binaifer, "A Lost Opportunity for Justice: Why Did the ICTR Not Prosecute Gender Propaganda?," in *The Media and the Rwanda Genocide*, Allan Thompson, ed. (London and Ann Arbor, MI: Pluto Press 2007).

O'Connell, Richard, "Interview with Greg Barker, Director of *Ghost of Rwanda* (2004)," in *Film & Genocide*, Kristi M. Wilson and Tomás F. Crowder-Taraborrelli, eds. (Madison and London: The University of Wisconsin Press 2012).

Olin-Scheller, Christina, *Såpor istället för Strindberg? Litteraturundervisning i ett nytt medielandskap* (Stockholm: Natur och Kultur 2008).

Paisley, Fiona and Pamela Scully, *Writing Transnational History* (London and New York: Bloomsbury 2019).

Péan, Pierre, *Noires fureurs, blancs menteurs: Rwanda 1990–1994* (Paris: Hachette Pluriel 2014).

Perspectives on European Film and History, Leen Engelen and Roel Vande Winkel, eds. (Gent: Academia Press 2007).

Portfleet, Dianne R., "The Films of Eric Kabera, the Kwetu Film Institute and Hillywood," in *The Rwandan Genocide on Film: Critical Essays and Interviews*, Matthew Edwards, ed. (Jefferson, NC: McFarland 2018).

Prunier, Gérard, *Africa's World War: Congo, the Rwandan Genocide, and the Making of a Continental Catastrophe* (Oxford: and New York: Oxford University Press 2009).

Prunier, Gérard, *The Rwanda Crisis: History of a Genocide* (Kampala: Fountain Publishers Limited 1999).

Ransel, David L., "Reflections on Transnational and World History in the USA and its Applications," *Historisk tidskrift* 127:4 (2007).

Rees, Ellen, "The Nordic 'Quirky' Feel-Good," in *Nordic Genre Film: Small Nation*

Film Cultures in the Global Marketplace, Tommy Gustafsson and Pietari Kääpä, eds. (Edinburgh: Edinburgh University Press 2015).

Rever, Judi, *In Praise of Blood: The Crimes of the Rwandan Patriotic Front* (Toronto: Penguin Random House 2018).

Rittner, Carol, "Rape, Religion, and Genocide: An Unholy Silence," in *Confronting Genocide: Judaism, Christianity, Islam*, Steven Leonard Jacobs, ed. (Plymouth: Lexington Books 2009).

Rittner, Carol, *Rape: Weapon of War and Genocide* (St. Paul, MN: Paragon House 2012).

Rosenstone, Robert A., *History on Film/Film on History* (Harlow: Pearson Education Ltd 2006).

Rousso, Henry, *The Vichy Syndrome: History and Memory in France since 1944* (Cambridge, MA: Harvard University Press 1991).

Rubin, Sara L., "Specificity in Genocide Portrayal on Film: *Sometimes in April* (2005)," in *Through a Lens Darkly: Films of Genocide, Ethnic Cleansing, and Atrocities*, John J. Michalczyk and Raymond G. Helmick, Sr., eds. (New York: Peter Lang 2013).

Rusesabagina, Paul (with Tom Zoellner), *An Ordinary Man: An Autobiography* (London: The Penguin Group 2006).

Rwafa, Urther, "Film Representations of the Rwandan Genocide," *African Identities* 8:4 (2010).

Sakota-Kokot, Tanja, "When the Past Talks to the Present: Fiction Narrative and the 'Other' in Hotel Rwanda," *Critical Arts: A South-North Journal of Cultural & Media Studies* 27:2 (2013).

Sharlach, Lisa, "Rape as Genocide: Bangladesh, the Former Yugoslavia, and Rwanda," *New Political Science* 1:22 (2000).

Shermer, Michael and Alex Grobman, *Denying History: Who Says the Holocaust Never Happened and Why Do They Say It?* (Oakland: University of California Press 2009).

Shohat, Ella and Robert Stam, *Unthinking Eurocentrism: Multiculturalism and the Media* (London and New York: Routledge 2014).

Silencing Cinema: Film Censorship around the World, Daniel Biltereyst and Roel Vande Winkel, eds. (London and New York: Palgrave Macmillan 2013).

Smith, Anthony D., *Nations and Nationalism in a Global Era* (Oxford: Polity Press 1995).

Smith, James and Carol Rittner, "Churches as Memorial Sites, A Photo Essay," in *Genocide in Rwanda: Complicity of the Churches?*, Carol Rittner, ed. (Newark: Aegis 2004).

Sniegon, Tomas, *Den försvunna historien. Förintelsen i tjeckisk och slovakisk historiekultur* (Lund: Lund University 2008).

Spielberg's Holocaust. Critical Perspectives on Schindler's List, Yosefa Loshitzky, ed. (Bloomington and Indianapolis: Indiana University Press 1997).

Stam, Robert and Louise Spence, "Colonialism, Racism, and Representation: An Introduction," in *Film Theory and Criticism*, Leo Braudy and Marshall Cohen, eds. (Oxford and New York: Oxford University Press 2009).

Straus, Scott, "The Limits of a Genocide Lens: Violence against Rwandans in the 1990s," *Journal of Genocide Research* 21:4 (2019).

Taylor, Gabriele, *Pride, Shame, and Guilt. Emotions of Self-Assessment* (Oxford: Clarendon Press 1985).

Temple-Raston, Dina, *Justice on the Grass: Three Rwandan Journalists, Their Trials for War Crimes, and a Nation's Quest for Redemption* (New York and London: Free Press 2005).

The Media and the Rwanda Genocide, Allan Thompson, ed. (London and Ann Arbor, MI: Pluto Press 2007).

The Men Who Killed Me: Rwandan Survivors of Sexual Violence, Anne-Marie De Brouwer and Sandra Ka Hon Chu, eds. (Vancouver: Douglas & McIntyre 2009).

The Persistence of History: Cinema, Television and the Modern Event, Vivian Sobchack, ed. (London and New York: AFI and Routledge 1996).

The Rwandan Genocide on Film: Critical Essays and Interviews, Matthew Edwards, ed. (Jefferson, NC: McFarland 2018).

Toland, Patsy, "Sometimes in April," *Policy & Practice: A Development Education Review* 5 (2007).

Toplin, Robert Brent, *Reel History: In Defense of Hollywood* (Lawrence: University Press of Kansas 2002).

Verwimp, Philip, *A Quantitative Analysis of Genocide in Kibuye Prefecture, Rwanda* (Leuven: Catholic University of Leuven 2001).

Verwimp, Philip, "Testing the Double-Genocide Thesis for Central and Southern Rwanda," *The Journal of Conflict Resolution* 47:4 (2003).

Vianney Higiro, Jean-Marie, "Rwandan Private Print Media on the Eve of the Genocide," in *The Media and the Rwanda Genocide*, Allan Thompson, ed. (London and Ann Arbor, MI: Pluto Press 2007).

Wall, Melissa, "An Analysis of News Magazine Coverage of the Rwanda Crisis in the United States," in *The Media and the Rwanda Genocide*, Allan Thompson, ed. (London and Ann Arbor, MI: Pluto Press 2007).

Wallis, Andrew, *Silent Accomplice: The Untold Story of France's Role in the Rwandan Genocide* (London: I. B. Tauris 2006).

Weeks, Rebecca, *History by HBO: Televising the American Past* (Lexington: The University of Kentucky Press 2022).

White, Hayden, *Metahistory: The Historical Imagination in Nineteenth-Century Europe* (Baltimore, MD and London: The Joshua Hopkins University Press 1975).

Wood, Sophia, "Film and Atrocity: The Holocaust as Spectacle," in *Film & Genocide*, Kristi M. Wilson and Tomás F. Crowder-Taraborrelli, eds. (Madison and London: The University of Wisconsin Press 2012).

Wyatt, Justin, *High Concept: Movies and Marketing in Hollywood* (Austin: University of Texas Press 1994).

Young, Andrew Phillip, *'We are all Rwandans': Imagining the Post-Genocidal Nation Across Media* (Unpublished Dissertation, Los Angeles: University of California 2016).

Zander, Ulf, *Clio på bio: Om amerikansk film, historia och identitet* (Lund: Historiska media 2006).

Zander, Ulf, "Holocaust at the Limits: Historical Culture and the Nazi Genocide in the

Television Era," in *Echoes of the Holocaust. Historical Cultures in Contemporary Europe*, Klas-Göran Karlsson and Ulf Zander, eds. (Lund: Nordic Academic Press 2003).

Zylberman, Lior, "From Invisibility to Recognition: Archive and Cultural Memory of the Rwandan Genocide," in *The Rwandan Genocide on Film: Critical Essays and Interviews*, Matthew Edwards, ed. (Jefferson, NC: McFarland 2018).

Filmography of the Rwandan Genocide

Narrative Films

100 Days (Nick Hughes, UK, Rwanda 2001)
Hotel Rwanda (Terry George, UK, USA, Italy, South Africa, Canada 2004)
Angel of Hate (Michael Marks, USA 2005) short
Shooting Dogs (a.k.a. *Beyond the Gates*, Michael Caton-Jones, UK, Germany 2005)
Sometimes in April (Raoul Peck, France, USA 2005)
A Love Letter to My Country (Thierry Dushimirimana, Rwanda 2006) short
Den sista hunden i Rwanda (*The Last Dog in Rwanda*, Jens Assur, Sweden 2006) short
Un dimanche à Kigali (*A Sunday in Kigali*, Robert Favreau, Canada 2006)
Ibrahim (Manyar I. Parwani, Denmark 2007)
Munyurangabo (Lee Isaac Chung, Rwanda, USA 2007)
Opération Turquoise (Alain Tasma, France 2007)
Shake Hands with the Devil (Roger Spottiswoode, Canada 2007)
Confession (Kivu "Daddy" Ruhorahoza, Rwanda 2008) short
We are all Rwandans (Debs Gardner-Paterson, Rwanda, UK 2008)
Charcoal (Ikara, Yves Gahinde, Tega Mutimura, Rwanda 2009) short
Fora (Ayuub Kasasa Mago, Rwanda 2009) short
Le jour où Dieu est parti en voyage (*The Day God Walked Away*, Philippe Van Leeuw, France, Belgium 2009)
Lignes de front (*Black Out*, Jean-Christophe Klotz, France 2009)
Long Coat (Edouard Bamporiki, Rwanda 2009)
The Pardon (Joël Karekezi, Rwanda 2009) short
Waramutsebo (Kouemo Auguste Bernard, France, Belgium, Cameroon 2009) short
Maibobo (Yves Montand Niyongabo, Rwanda 2010) short
Kinyarwanda (Alrick Brown, USA, France 2011)
Lyzia (Marie-Clementine Dusabejambo, Rwanda 2011) short
Matière Grise (*Grey Matter*, Kivu Ruhorahoza, Rwanda 2011)
Shema (Kayambi Musafari, Rwanda 2011) short
Strength in Fear (Ella Mutuyimana, Rwanda 2012) short
The Pardon (*Imbabazi*, Joël Karekezi, Rwanda 2013)
Crossing Lines (Samuel Ishimwe, Rwanda 2014) short

Hutsi–Akaliza Keza (Philbert Aimé Mbabazi, Rwanda 2014) short
Umurabyo (Charles Gasana, Rwanda 2015)
Mugabo (Amelia Umuhire, Rwanda, Switzerland 2016) short
Imfura (Samuel Ishimwe, Rwanda, Switzerland 2017) short
Ptaki spiewaja w Kigali (*Birds Are Singing in Kigali*, Joanna Kos-Krauze, Krzysztof Krauzse, Poland 2017)
'94 Terror (Richard Mulindwa, Uganda 2018)
Black Earth Rising (Hugo Blick, UK 2018) television series
91 Nights a Left to Tell story (Ricardo Del Río, USA 2019)
Rwanda (Riccardo Salvetti, Italy 2019)
Petit pays (*Small Country: An African Childhood*, Eric Barbier, France, Belgium 2020)
Trees of Peace (Alanna Brown, USA 2021)

Documentary Films

A Culture of Murder (Steve Bradshaw, UK 1994)
Burundi–un suicide africain (Guillaume Tunzini, Jospeh Bitamba, France 1994)
Journey into Darkness (Fergal Keane, UK 1994) television episode
People of the Apocalypse (UK 1994) short television documentary
World of Death (Marc Fiorini, USA 1994)
Blodsarvet (Maria Rinaldo, Peter Rinaldo, Sweden 1995)
Hand of God, Hand of the Devil (Yvan Patry, Sam Grana, Daniéle Lacourse, Canada 1995)
Rwanda, l'histoire qui mène au génocide (*Rwanda: How History Can Lead to Genocide*, Robert Genoud, France 1995)
Rwanda: Maudits soient les yeux fermés (Frédéric Laffont, France 1995)
Rwanda: The Bloody Tricolour (Steve Bradshaw, UK 1995)
Sitting on a Volcano (Daniéle Lacourse, Canada 1995)
The Dead Are Alive: Eyewitness in Rwanda (Anna van der Wee, Belgium 1995) short
UN Blues (Dorothy Byrne, UK 1995)
Une république devenue folle: Rwanda 1894–1994 (*A Republic Gone Mad: Rwanda*, Luc de Heusch, Kathleen de Béthune, Belgium 1995)
Chronicle of a Genocide Foretold (Yvan Patry, Danièle Lacourse, Canada 1996) three-part television series
Facing Up to Genocide: Valentina's Story (Fergal Keane, UK 1997)
Itsembatsemba: Rwanda One Genocide Later (Alexis Cordesse, Eyal Sivan, France 1997) short
Kisangani Diary (Hubert Sauper, France, Austria 1998)
Naze rinjin wo koroshitaka (Kumiko Igarashi, Japan 1998)
Rwanda: Out of the Darkness (Claude Adams, Patricia Chew, USA 1998)
Triumph of Evil (Steve Bradshaw, USA 1998)
Children in War (Alan Raymond, Susan Raymond, USA 2000)
L'Afrique en morceaux: la tragdie des Grands Lacs (Jihan El-Tahri, France 2000)
The Genocide Factor: Genocide: The Horror Continues (Robert J. Emery, USA 2000)
Blodsbarn (Maria Rinaldo, Peter Rinaldo, Sweden 2001)

France in Rwanda: A Guilty Neutrality (Robert Genoud, France 2001)
Rwanda: Hope in Hell (Kate Broome, UK 2001)
Rwanda: In Search of Hope (Peter Raymont, Canada 2001)
The Last Just Man (Steven Silver, Canada 2001)
Der Mörder meiner Mutter–Eugénie will Gerechtigkeit (Martin Buchholz, Germany 2002)
Gacaca: revivre ensamble au Rwanda? (*Gacaca: Living Together Again in Rwanda?*, Anne Aghion, France, USA 2002)
A Good Man in Hell (Jerry Fowler, USA 2003) short
Ramp: Om historia–Rwanda (Sweden 2003) television episode
A Killer's Homecoming (Daniela Volker, UK 2004) television episode
Après–Un voyage dans le Rwanda (Denis Gheerbrant, France 2004)
Au Rwanda on dit . . . La famille qui ne parle pas meurt (*In Rwanda We Say . . . The Family that Does Not Speak Dies*, Anne Aghion, France, USA 2004)
Dokument utifrån: I Guds namn (Maria Rinaldo, Peter Rinaldo, Sweden 2004) television episode
Gardiens de la mémoire (*Keepers of Memory*, Eric Kabera, Rwanda 2004)
Ghosts of Rwanda (Greg Barker, Darren Kemp, USA 2004)
Killers (Fergal Keane, UK 2004)
Rwanda: Do Scars Ever Fade? (Paul Freedman, USA 2004)
Shake Hands with the Devil: The Journey of Roméo Dallaire (Peter Raymont, Canada 2004)
Through My Eyes: A Film About Rwandan Youth (Kavila Matu, Rwanda 2004)
Tuez-les tous! Rwanda: histoire d'un génocide sans importance (*Kill Them All!: Rwanda the Story of an Unimportant Genocide*, Raphaël Glucksmann, David Hazan, Pierre Mezerette, France 2004)
God Sleeps in Rwanda (Kimberlee Acquaro, Stacy Sherman, USA 2005)
Hunting My Husband's Killers (Jay Knox, Ray Tostevin, UK 2005)
Mothers Courage, Thriving Survivors (*Mères Courage*, Leo Kalinda, Canada, Rwanda 2005)
Rwanda, les collines parlent (*Rwanda: The Hills Speak Out*, Bernard Bellefroid, Belgium 2005)
Rwanda: Living Forgiveness (Ralf Springhorn, Switzerland 2005) short
Yesterday in Rwanda (Davina Pardo, USA, Canada, Rwanda 2005) short
60 Minutes: Hiding from Death (USA 2006) television episode
Back Home (J. B. Rutagarama, USA 2006)
Exploring Rwanda and Darfur (USA 2006) television episode
Facing the Past (James Smith, Nicole Volavka, UK 2006) short
In the Tall Grass: Inside Gacaca (John Coll Metcalfe, USA 2006)
Kigali, des images contre un massacre (Jean-Christophe Klotz, France 2006)
Rwanda. A travers nous, l'humanité . . . (*Rwanda: Through Us, Humanity*, Marie-France Collard, Belgium, France 2006)
Screamers (Carla Garapedian, UK 2006)
The Diary of Immaculée (Peter LeDonne, USA 2006)
Massacre at Murambi (Sam Kauffmann, USA 2007) short
On Our Watch (Neil Docherty, USA 2007) television episode
Reconciling Rwanda (Patricia Boiko, USA 2007) short

Rwanda Rising (C. B. Hackworth, USA 2007)
Triage: Dr James Orbinski's Humanitarian Dilemma (Patrick Reed, Canada 2007)
Behind This Convent (Gilbert Ndahayo, Rwanda 2008)
Better In Than Out (Richmond Runanira, Rwanda 2008) short
D'Arusha à Arusha (*From Arusha to Arusha*, Christophe Gargot, France, Canada 2008)
Flores de Ruanda (*Flowers of Rwanda*, David Muñoz, Spain 2008) short
Flower in the Gun Barrel (Gabriel Cowan, USA 2008)
Intended Consequences: Rwandan Children Born of Rape (Jonathan Torgovnik, USA 2008) short
Iseta: Behind the Roadblock (Juan Reina, Kenya, Rwanda 2008)
Gacaca Justice (Bengt Nilsson, Sweden 2009) short
Icyizere: Hope (Patrick Mureithi, USA, 2009)
Los 100 días que no conmovieron al mundo (*The 100 Days That Didn't Shake the World*, Vanessa Ragone, Argentina 2009)
Mon tueur, Mon voisin (*My Neighbor, My Killer*, Anne Aghion, USA, France 2009)
Mothers of War (Maria Rinaldo, Sweden 2009)
Rwanda: Beyond the Deadly Pit (Gilbert Ndahayo, Rwanda, USA 2009)
Rwanda: Hope Rises (Trevor Meier, Canada, Rwanda 2009)
Rwanda, je me souviens (André St-Pierre, Canada 2009)
Les Cahiers de la Mémoire (*The Notebooks of Memory*, Anne Aghion, USA, France 2009)
Umurage (Gorka Gamarra, Jean Marie Mbarushimana, Sonia Rolley, Spain 2009)
Wounded Healers (Mark Stendal, USA 2009)
As We Forgive (Laura Waters Hinson, USA 2010)
Behind of Full of Sorrow (Olivier Uwayezu, Luck Ndunguye, Rwanda 2010) short
Coexist (Adam Mazo, USA 2010) short
Earth Made of Glass (Deborah Scranton, USA 2010)
Eyes on Rwanda (Allison Stubbmann, USA, Rwanda 2010) short
La lista del console (Alessandro Rocca, Italy, Rwanda 2010)
My Globe Is Broken in Ruanda (*My Globe is Broken in Rwanda*, Katharina von Schroeder, Germany, 2010)
One Drop (Chase Layman, Ryan Scott, USA, Rwanda 2010) short
Raindrops Over Rwanda (Charles Annenberg Weingarten, USA 2010) short
Rwanda' Mama (Marilena Delli, Rwanda, Italy 2010) short
Rwanda: Take Two (Pia Sawhney, Netherlands 2010)
Telling Truth in Arusha (Beate Arnestad, Norway 2010)
The Courage of Neighbors: Stories from the Rwandan Genocide (Iara Lee, USA, Rwanda 2010)
The Power of Gacaca (Olivier Uwayezu, Luck Ndunguye, Rwanda 2010) short
You Must Be Something (Linn Groft, USA 2010)
Duhozanye: A Rwandan Village of Widows (Karoline Frogner, Norway 2011)
If Only We Had Listened (Sean Bloomfield, Immaculee Ilibagiza, USA, Belgium, Rwanda 2011)
Poetry of Resilience (Katja Esson, USA, Canada, Japan, Iraq, Poland, Rwanda 2011) short

Sydämeni taakka (*Burden of My Heart*, Yves Niyongabo, Iris Olsson, Finland, Rwanda 2011)
Beyond Right and Wrong: Stories of Justice and Forgiveness (Lekha Singh, Roger Spottiswoode, USA, UK, Rwanda, Palestine, Israel, Ireland 2012) compilation film
Fight Like Soldiers, Die Like Children (Patrick Reed, Canada 2012)
Fractured Lives: The Aftermath of the Rwanda Genocide (Carol Allen Storey, Edmond Terakopian, UK 2012)
Rising from Ashes (T. C. Johnstone, USA, Rwanda, UK, South Africa 2012)
Sweet Dreams (Lisa Fruchtman, Rob Fruchtman, USA 2012)
FC Rwanda (Joris Postema, Netherlands 2013)
Finding Hillywood (Chris Towey, Leah Warshawski, USA 2013)
Goodness in Rwanda (Gord Rand, John Westheuser, Canada 2013)
Rwanda: The Power of Youth and Sport (Mackie Bryson-Bucci, Jules Le Masson Fletcher, Canada, Rwanda 2013) short
Stomp Out Genocide (Eran Amiel, Ab Andani, Pat Fitzgerald, Eden Klogo, Rip Taggart, USA, Zambia, Rwanda, Georgia, Ethiopia 2013) short
The Rwandan Night (Gilbert Ndahayo, Switzerland, USA, Rwanda 2013)
Through the Valley (Kevin McAfee, USA, Rwanda 2013)
7 jours à Kigali (Mehdi Ba, Jeremy Frey, France 2014)
A Place for Everyone (Hans Ulrich Goessl, Angelos Rallis, Austria, Belgium 2014)
A Snake Gives Birth to a Snake (Michael Lessac, South Africa, USA, France, Serbia, Montenegro, Rwanda, Serbia, Ireland, Bosnia and Herzegovina 2014)
Children of the Genocide (Nina Milligan, USA, Rwanda 2014) short
Coexist (Adam Mazo, USA 2014)
Cut the Tall Trees: The Killing Power of Words (Noah Bennett, Max Cho, USA, Rwanda 2014) short
From Trauma to Peace (Jo Danieli, Diana Gross, Robert C. Stone, USA 2014)
God Is Not Working on Sunday, Eh! (Leona Goldstein, Germany, Rwanda 2014)
I Am Kizito (Mike Mapes, USA, Rwanda 2014) short
I Married My Family's Killer (Emily Kassie, Canada, Rwanda 2014) short
Ibyiza Birimbere: The Best Is Still to Come (Soenke C. Weiss, Rwanda 2014)
I'm Not Leaving (Kevin Ekvall, USA, Rwanda 2014) short
Intore (Eric Kabera, Rwanda 2014)
Justice Seekers (Antonio Rui Ribeiro, UK 2014) television episode
Let the Devil Sleep: Rwanda 20 Years After Genocide (Alan Whelan, Eoghan Rice, Elena Hermosa, Ireland 2014)
Life After Death (Joe Callander, USA, Rwanda 2014)
Playing a Part (Lauren Rothman, USA, Rwanda 2014) short
Rwanda, la vie après–Paroles de méres (*Rwanda, Life Goes On*, Benoit Dervaux, André Versaille, Belgium 2014)
Rwanda: The Untold Story (John Conroy, UK 2014) television episode
The Invincible (Yves Montand Niyongabo, Rwanda 2014) short
The Rhythm of Healing (Imani Cook-Gist, USA, Rwanda 2014) short
The Rwandan Genocide: Reunited Through Polaroids (Colin Crowley, Rwanda 2014) short

Tour (Millie Chen, USA, Canada, Rwanda, Poland, Cambodia 2014) short
Umudugudu! Rwanda 20 Ans Après (Giordano Cossu, France, Rwanda 2014) short
Unversöhnt (*Unforgiven*, Lukas Augustin, Germany, Rwanda 2014)
When I Was Young, I Said I Would Be Happy (Paul J. Lynch, USA 2014)
Women Building Peace (Colleen Wagner, Geneviève Appleton, Canada, Uganda, South Africa, Rwanda, Morocco, Georgia, Germany, France 2014)
A Woman's Story (Azra Rashid, Canada 2015)
I Have Seen My Last Born (Samuel Gray Anderson, Lee Isaac Chung, Rwanda, USA 2015)
The Uncondemned (Nick Louvel, Michele Mitchell, USA, Netherlands, Congo, Rwanda 2015)
Mama Rwanda (Laura Waters Hinson, USA 2016) short
Marguerite (Andrei Loshak, Russia 2016) short
Rwanda & Juliet (Ben Proudfoot, USA 2016)
Inkotanyi (Christophe Cotteret, Belgium, France 2017)
Ishimwa: From Bloodshed to Grace (Cynthia Butare, Rwanda 2017) short
The Faces We Lost (Piotr Cieplak, Rwanda, UK 2017)
A Woman's Place (Azra Rashid, Canada 2018)
Arrows of Truth (Antonio Rui Ribeiro, UK 2018)
Circus Rwanda (Michal Varga, Czech Republic, Slovakia 2018)
The 600: The Soldier's Story (Laurent Basset, Richard Hall, USA 2019)
Generation 94 (Gemma Capdevila, Spain 2021) short

Index

'94 Terror (2018), 129, 133–5, 146, 255n, 256n, 283
100 Days (2001), 12, 67, 132, 192, 196–205, 213, 219, 231, 255n, 267n, 282
60 Minutes: Hiding from Death (USA 2006), 284
600: The Soldiers' Story, The (2019), 144, 287
7 jours à Kigali (2014), 138, 286
91 Nights a Left to Tell story (2019), 258n, 283

A Culture of Murder (1994), 70, 283
A Good Man in Hell (2003), 72, 284
A Killer's Homecoming (2004), 284
A Love Letter to my Country (2006), 225–6, 282
A Place for Everyone (2014), 154, 286
A Snake Gives Birth to a Snake (2014), 286
A Woman's Place (2018), 148, 287
A Woman's Story (2015), 148, 287
ABC, 35, 43
Act of Killing, The (2012), 13, 163
Adhikari, Mohamed, 3, 92
Adorno, Theodore, 11–12, 14, 83
Adventist Development and Relief Agency International, 138
Aegis Trust, 207, 267n
Africa United (2010), 205, 211, 231
Aghion, Anne, 68, 153, 158–62

Akayesu, Jean-Paul, 147
Al Jazeera, 143, 173
Alliance des Forces Démocratiques pour la Libération du Congo-Zaïre (AFDL), 168
Alone in Berlin (2016), 82
Alwyn, Richard, 101
Amahano I Bwami (2014), 193, 232
Angel of Hate (2005), 120, 282
Angnestrand, Leif, 41
Après–Un voyage dans le Rwanda (2004), 142, 284
Ararat (2002), 13
Arendt, Hannah, 12
Arrows of Truth (2018), 143, 168, 172–4, 176, 181, 287
As We Forgive (2010), 154, 156–7, 285
Asiimwe, Arthur, 195
Assur, Jens, 124
Atkins, Michael, 81
Au Rwanda on dit... La famille qui ne parle pas meurt (In Rwanda We Say... The Family that Does Not Speak Dies, 2004), 158, 160–1, 284
Avengers: Endgame (2019), 10

Back Home (2006), 153, 284
Bagosora, Théoneste, 87, 105, 169–72
Baldwin, Gretchen, 201, 206, 219
Bamporiki, Edouard, 132, 220–1, 268n
Barash, Jeffrey Andrew, 65–6

Barker, Greg, 10, 111
Barlet, Oliver, 142
BBC, 19, 33, 67, 70, 90, 97-8, 106, 142, 174, 177, 179, 181-3, 247n
Behind of Full of Sorrow (2010), 216, 285
Behind This Convent (2008), 222, 285
Bellefroid, Bernard, 158
Belton, David, 98, 101
Benigni, Roberto, 14
Bernard, Kouemo Auguste, 130
Better In Than Out (2008), 227, 285
Beyond Right and Wrong: Stories of Justice and Forgiveness (2012), 286
Bikindi, Simon, 139
Bitmaba, Joseph, 67
Bizimana, Augustin, 77
Black Earth Rising (2018), 182-7, 233, 283
Black Hawk Down (2001), 18
Blair, Tony, 179
Blick, Hugo, 183-7
Blodsarvet (1995), 78, 148-9, 167, 283
Blodsbarn (2001), 148-52, 283
Blood Diamond (2006), 80
Boardwalk Empire (2010-2014), 7
Bolin, Annalisa, 200
Bouquet, Michel, 223
Boutros, Boutros Ghali, 54, 56
Bradshaw, Steve, 70, 247n
Bratu Hansen, Miriam, 11, 13
Brideshead Revisited (1981), 7
Broderick, Mick, 229
Bromley, Roger, 93, 161-2
Brown, Alanna, 127, 129
Brown, Alrick, 131
Bruguière, Jean-Louis, 176-7
Brummel, Bill, 114
Bufacchi, Vittorio, 92-3
Burundi–un suicide african (1994), 67-8, 283
Bush, George W., 87
Bushnell, Prudence, 105

Callander, Joe, 162-3, 165
Cantrell II, Phillip A., 157

Caplan, Pat, 138, 207
Caton-Jones, Michael, 101
Cayrol, Jean, 223
CBS, 43
Centro de Información Naciones Unidas Mexico, 227
Ceppi, Jean-Philippe, 51
Chaon, Anne, 35
Charcoal (*Ikara*, 2009), 215, 282
Cheadle, Don, 83
Children in War (2000), 283
Children of the Genocide (2014), 156, 286
Chirac, Jacques, 143
Chronicle of a Genocide Foretold (1996), 68, 76, 167, 247n, 283
Chung, Lee Isaac, 130, 220
Cieplak, Piotr A., 12, 98-9, 102, 204, 229-30
Circus Rwanda (2018), 259n, 287
Clinton, Bill, 1, 48, 71, 106, 179, 206, 222
Coel, Michaela, 186
Coexist (2010), 285
Coexist (2014), 157, 286
Cohen, Jared A., 31, 48
Cohen, Stanley, 35-6, 114
Confession (2008), 226-8, 282
Constant, Raphaël, 169, 171-2
Corbin, Jane, 175, 177-8, 180
Costa, Pierantonio, 138
Coulais, Bruno, 106
Courage of Neighbors: Stories from the Rwandan Genocide, The (2010), 156, 285
Courtemanche, Gil, 125
Crossing Lines (2014), 216-17, 282
Curic, Vjeko, 98
Cut the Tall Trees: The Killing Power of Words (2014), 156, 286

Dahlmanns, Erika, 214
Dallaire, Roméo, 24-5, 42, 71-2, 110, 121, 123, 138, 140, 146
Dark Night, The (2008), 10

D'Arusha à Arusha (From Arusha to Arusha, 2008), 168–72, 174, 176, 285
Darwin's Nightmare (2004), 78
Dauge-Roth, Alexandre, 83–4, 89, 93, 95, 98, 102–3, 105, 125–6, 162, 197, 200–1, 219
Davenport, Christian, 168, 177–9, 181, 261n
de Dieu, Jean, 171–2
de la Guardia, Virginia, 31
Dead Are Alive: Eyewitness in Rwanda, The (1995), 68–9, 78, 283
del Ponte, Carla, 178
Democratic Forces for the Liberation of Rwanda (FDLR), 167
Den sista hunden i Rwanda (The Last Dog in Rwanda, 2006), 122, 124, 282
Der Mörder meiner Mutter–Eugénie will Gerechtigkeit (2002), 284
Diary of Immaculée, The (2006), 155, 258n, 284
Die Letzte Chance (The Last Chance, 1945), 11
Dokument utifrån: I Guds namn (2004), 148, 284
Downton Abbey (2010–2015), 7
Doyle, Mark, 57
Duhozanye: A Rwandan Village of Widows (2011), 147, 285
Dusaida, Claude, 41, 245n
Dushimirimana, Thierry, 225–6

E.T.: The Extra-Terrestrial (1982), 1
Earth Made of Glass (2010), 143, 285
Ebert, Roger, 82–3, 130
Eckhard, Fred, 38
Eichmann, Adolf, 12
Elba, Idris, 107
Erin Brockovich (2000), 82
Exodus (1960), 11
Exploring Rwanda and Darfur (2006), 284
Eyes on Rwanda (2010), 154, 285
Ezra, Elizabeth, 17

Faces We Lost, The (2017), 207, 287
Facing the Past (2006), 284
Facing Up to Genocide: Valentina's Story (1997), 70, 283
Farrow, Mia, 154
Faurisson, Robert, 6
Faye, Gaël, 135
FC Rwanda (2013), 286
Fegley, Randall, 77
Feinstein, Howard, 230
Ferguson, Tamara, 91
Fight Like Solders, Die Like Children (2012), 138, 205, 286
Finding Hillywood (2013), 154, 286
Flores de Ruanda (Flowers of Rwanda, 2008), 157, 285
Flower in the Gun Barrel (2008), 156, 285
Fora (2009), 220, 282
Fossey, Dian, 80, 139
Foundas, Scott, 121
Fractured Lives: The Aftermath of the Rwanda Genocide (2012), 168, 172, 174, 286
Fraisse, Robert, 90
France in Rwanda: A Guilty Neutrality (2001), 69, 284
From Trauma to Peace (2014), 153, 286
Front for Democracy in Burundi (FRODEBU), 68
Fruchtman, Lisa, 153

Gacaca Justice (2009), 154, 285
Gacaca: revivre ensamble au Rwanda? (Gacaca: Living Together Again in Rwanda?, 2002), 68, 153, 158–61, 284
Gaddafi, Muammar, 179
Gandhi (1982), 7
Gardiens de la mémoire (Keepers of Memory, 2004), 205–7, 209, 212, 222, 226, 255n, 267n, 284
Gardner-Paterson, Debs, 211
Gargot, Christophe, 169–72
Gauthier, Alain, 143, 173
Gauthier, Dafroza, 143, 173

Generation 94 (2021), 287
Genocide Factor: Genocide: The Horror Continues, The (2000), 69, 283
Genoud, Robert, 69
George, Terry, 3, 81, 86, 89-90, 92, 97
Gérondal Mwiza, Jessica, 185
Gheerbrant, Denis, 142
Ghosts of Rwanda (2004), 11, 32, 67, 80-1, 108-13, 119-20, 137-8, 199, 284
Gladiator (2000), 5
Glover, Jonathan D., 2
God afton, Herr Wallenberg (*Good Evening, Mr. Wallenberg*, 1990), 82
God Is Not Working on Sunday, Eh! (2014), 286
God Sleeps in Rwanda (2005), 147, 284
Goethe Institute, 193, 268n
Goodness in Rwanda (2013), 286
Gorillas in the Mist: The Story of Dian Fossey (1988), 80
Graduation Day (2006), 232, 265n
Griehsel, Marika, 58-9, 246n
Guerra, Andrea, 90

Habyarimana, Juvénal, 23-4, 67, 69, 123, 126, 171, 177, 179, 181, 197, 206
Hall, Stuart, 122
Hamel, Marie-Eve, 202
Hand of God, Hand of the Devil (1995), 76-7, 167, 283
Harding, Tonya, 34
HBO, 81, 97, 104-5
Hey Mr DJ (2007), 232, 265n
Higson, Andrew, 7
History Channel, 81, 113
Holmes, Georgina, 70, 247n
Holocaust (1978), 11, 13, 15, 96
Honorable Woman, The (2014), 183
Horkheimer, Max, 83
Hotel Rwanda (2004), 2-3, 5, 10, 14-15, 18, 32, 67, 80-98, 101-4, 107, 111, 113-15, 119-21, 129, 131, 135, 175, 180, 186, 192, 196-7, 199, 213, 282

Hron, Madelaine, 96
Hughes, Nick, 12, 42, 67, 71, 74, 181, 192, 196-204, 206, 212-13, 231, 247n
Hunting My Husband's Killers (2005), 155, 284
Hurt, John, 98
Hussein, Saddam, 179
Hutsi-Akaliza Keza (2014), 216, 283

I Am Kizito (2014), 156, 286
I Bwiza (*Tenacity*, 2021), 193
I Have Seen My Last Born (2015), 130, 287
I Married My Family's Killer (2014), 286
Ibrahim (2007), 122, 124, 282
Ibuka, 182, 199
Ibyiza Birimbere: The Best Is Still to Come (2014), 286
Icyizere: Hope (2009), 215, 268n, 285
If Only We Had Listened (2011), 155, 258n, 285
Il portiere di note (*The Night Portier*, 1974), 11
I'm Not Leaving (2014), 138, 286
Imfura (2017), 220, 283
In the Tall Grass: Inside Gacaca (2006), 154, 157, 258n, 284
Ingelaere, Bert, 158-60
Inkotanyi (2017), 144, 287
Intended Consequences: Rwandan Children Born of Rape (2008), 148, 285
Interahamwe, 23-4, 26-7, 72, 87, 94, 98-9, 102, 105, 125, 133, 149, 184, 198, 201, 204-6, 211, 217-18, 222
International Alert, 172
International Criminal Tribunal for Rwanda (ICTR), 78, 105, 138-9, 147, 157, 169-72, 178, 181, 184, 267n
International Red Cross (ICRC), 46
Intore (2014), 213-14, 268n, 286
Invincible, The (2014), 216, 224, 286
Irish Centre for Global Education, 103
Irving, David, 6

Iseta: Behind the Roadblock (2008), 209, 211–13, 285
Ishimwa: From Bloodshed to Grace (2017), 220, 287
Ishimwe, Samuel, 216–17, 220
Itsembatsemba: Rwanda One Genocide Later (1997), 283

Jacob the Liar (1999), 14
James, Fraser, 107
Jean, Wyclef, 90
JFJ (2009), 232
JFK (1991), 82, 106
Jin ling shi san chai (*Flowers of War*, 2014), 82
Jost, Jon, 104
Journey into Darkness (1994), 67–8, 70, 142, 283
Judas and the Black Messiah (2021), 233
Jurassic Park (1993), 1
Justice Seekers (2014), 143, 173–4, 181, 286
Juvé, Juan Ignacio, 124, 139

Kabera, Eric, 185, 188, 192–3, 196, 198, 200, 204–14, 222, 225, 231, 234, 265n, 266n, 267n, 270n
Kabuga, Félicien, 195
Kagame, Paul, 57–8, 87, 109, 113, 143–4, 146, 156, 160, 162, 173–81, 195, 227
Kalinda, Léo, 147
Kambanda, Jean, 46
Kanyamugara, Léonard, 161
Karani Ngufu (2019), 231
Karekezi, Joël, 134, 217, 233
Karlsson, Klas-Göran, 85
Kasasa Mago, Ayuub, 211
Kayihura, Edouard, 80, 86–7
Kayisire, Alice, 234
Keane, Fergal, 67, 142
Kerner, Aaron, 9, 13, 96
Kerrigan, Nancy, 34
Kibirige, Shakira, 134

Kigali, des images contre un massacre (2006), 123, 138, 284
Killers (2004), 142, 284
Killing Fields, The (1984), 13
Kinyarwanda (2011), 129–33, 135, 255n, 282
Kisangani Diary (1998), 78, 283
Klotz, Jean-Christophe, 123, 138
Koehler, Robert, 132
Kouchner, Bernard, 51, 246n
Kulamba, Tony, 49
Kwetu Film Institute, 12, 185, 188, 191–2, 205, 214, 231
Kwezi, John, 193

La caduta degli dei (*The Damned*, 1969), 11
La lista del console (2010), 138, 285
La Vita è Bella (*Life is Beautiful*, 1997), 14
Lacour, Anne, 171
Lacourse, Danièle, 76–7
L'Afrique en morceaux: la tragdie des Grands Lacs (2000), 69, 283
LaMarre, Heather L., 111, 113
Landergård, Max, 73
Landreville, Kristen D., 111, 113
Last Just Man, The (2001), 69, 72, 74, 284
Le jour où Dieu est parti en voyage (*The Day God Walked Away*, 2009), 129–31, 133, 135, 255n, 282
Les Cahiers de la Mémoire (*The Notebooks of Memory*, 2009), 158, 161, 285
Let the Devil Sleep: Rwanda 20 Years After Genocide (2014), 156, 286
Life After Death (2014), 162–7, 224, 286
Lignes de front (*Black Out*, 2009), 122–4, 138, 282
Long Coat (2009), 220–1, 224, 277n, 282
Los 100 días que no conmovieron al mundo (*The 100 Days That Didn't Shake the World*, 2009), 138–9, 285
Love 41, 162–4, 259n
Ludvigsson, David, 8–9
Lyzia (2011), 215, 282

Magubane, Zine, 89
Maibobo (2010), 224-5, 282
Malcolm X (1992), 233
Mama Rwanda (2016), 148, 287
Mamdani, Mahmood, 22
Mandela: Long Walk to Freedom (2013), 107
Marchal, Luc, 71, 176
Marguerite (2016), 287
Massacre at Murambi (2007), 141, 284
Matière Grise (*Grey Matter*, 2011), 227-30, 282
Matu, Kavila, 209-10, 267n
Mboti, Nyasha, 2
Médecins Sans Frontières (MSF), 139
Melvern, Linda, 26, 51, 74, 87, 97, 102, 184
Metz, Christian, 7
Michalczyk, John J., 157
Minari (2020), 130
Misago, Wilson, 182
Mitterrand, François, 123, 143
Möller, Frank, 114
Mon tueur, Mon voisin (*My Neighbor, My Killer*, 2009), 158, 255n, 285
Mon, Christopher J., 157
Mothers Courage, Thriving Survivors (2005), 147, 284
Mothers of War (2009), 148-52, 285
Mouvement Révolutionnaire National pour le Développement (MRND), 78, 148, 199
Mu Buzima (2014), 193
Mugabo (2016), 283
Mukangendo, Marie-Consolee, 160
Mukantaganzwa, Domitilla, 212, 267-8n
Mulindwa, Richard, 133-4
Munson, Dave, 162-3, 166
Munson, Suzette, 162-4
Munyurangabo (2007), 129-30, 132-3, 220, 255n, 282
Mureithi, Patrick, 215
Mutuyimana, Ella, 232

My Globe Is Broken in Ruanda (*My Globe is Broken in Rwanda*, 2010), 156, 234, 285

National Commission for the Fight Against Genocide (CNLG), 181, 199, 207
National Liberation Front (FNL), 87
Naze rinjin wo koroshitaka (1998), 78, 283
NBC, 11, 43
Ndadaye, Melchior, 68
Ndahayo, Gilbert, 221-3, 233, 269n
Ndahiro, Alfred, 86-7
Netflix, 105, 120, 127-8, 182-3, 185, 233
Newbury, Catharine, 21-2
Ngendahayo, Jean Marie, 48
Ngeze, François, 68
Ngirumpatse, Mathieu, 78
Nichols, Bill, 108, 150
Nirere, Ruth, 131
Niyomwungere, Constantin, 195
Niyongabo, Yves Montard, 224-5
Ntariyamira, Cyprien, 23
Ntezimana, Laurien, 169, 171
Nuit et brouillard (*Night and Fog*, 1956), 2, 11, 223
Nwankwo, Blessing Chinwendu, 129
Nyamwasa, Kayumba, 176, 179-80, 261n
Nyheterna, 34, 36-41, 43-7, 50-1
Nyungura, Corneille, 213

O'Donovan, Gerard, 181
Odessa File, The (1974), 11
On Our Watch (2007), 138, 284
One Drop (2010), 154, 285
Opération Turquoise (2007), 122-3, 282
Oppenheimer, Joshua, 163
Orbinski, James, 139-41
Organisation of African Unity (OAU), 177
Ostanti etap (*The Last Stage*, 1948), 11

Pacific Rim (2013), 107
Pagnoni Berns, Fernando Gabriel, 123, 139
Pardon, The (2009), 217-19, 282
Pardon, The (*Imbabazi*, 2013), 217-19, 282
Patriot, The (2000), 82
Patry, Yvan, 76-7
PBS, 33, 81, 111, 138
PDR-Ihumure, 87
Pearson, Kier, 81, 86, 89
Peck, Raoul, 103-7
People of the Apocalypse (UK 1994), 197, 247n, 283
Petit pays (*Small Country: An African Childhood*, 2020), 129, 135-6, 231, 283
Pirates of the Caribbean franchise (2003-2017), 10
Playing a Part (2014), 156, 286
Poetry of Resilience (2011), 154, 285
Portfleet, Dianne R., 132
Power of Gacaca, The (2010), 215, 285
Power, Samantha, 111
Prunier, Gérard, 24, 26
Ptaki spiewaja w Kigali (*Birds Are Singing in Kigali*, 2017), 122, 124-6, 129, 283

Radio Télévision Libre des Mille Collines (RTLM), 23, 26, 71, 100, 105, 143, 169
Raindrops Over Rwanda (2010), 285
Ramp: om historia–Rwanda (Sweden 2003), 73, 284
Ransel, David L., 16, 19
Rapport, 34, 36-48, 50-60
Rashid, Azra, 148
Reconciling Rwanda (2007), 156, 284
Reed, Patrick, 140
Reina, Juan, 212
Republican Democratic Movement (MDR), 171
Reyntjens, Filip, 69, 173, 175-6, 178-9, 181

Rhythm of Healing, The (2014), 156, 286
Ribeiro, Antonio Rui, 143, 173-4
Richardson, Jenny, 98
Rinaldo, Maria, 148, 150
Rinaldo, Peter, 148
Rising from Ashes (2012), 153-4, 286
Roman Catholic Church, 22, 27, 69, 98, 142, 150-1, 156, 163, 196-9, 201-2, 222
Rome (2005-2007), 7
Rosenstone, Robert A., 6-8
Rousso, Henry, 167-8, 172-3
Rowden, Terry, 17
Rubin, Sara L., 105
Rudasingwa, Theogene, 41, 49, 176, 179-80, 246n
Ruggiu, Georges 169-72
Ruhorahoza, Kivu, 226-30, 233, 269n
Rüsen, Jörn, 20
Rusesabagina, Paul, 2, 82-3, 86-8, 129, 175, 195, 249n
Rutaganda, Georges, 87, 94
Rutazibwa, Privat, 86
Rwafa, Urther, 103
Rwamfizi, Abraham, 160-1
Rwanda & Juliet (2016), 154, 287
Rwanda (2019), 120-1, 283
Rwanda Cinema Center, 192
Rwanda Development Board (RDB), 193, 232
Rwanda Film Federation, 193
Rwanda Film Institute, 192, 265n
Rwanda' Mama (2010), 285
Rwanda Rising (2007), 154-5, 285
Rwanda Television (RTV), 191, 195, 215, 264n, 265n
Rwanda, je me souviens (2009), 157, 285
Rwanda, la vie après–Paroles de méres (*Rwanda, Life Goes On*, 2014), 148, 286
Rwanda, les collines parlent (*Rwanda: The Hills Speak Out*, 2005), 158, 284
Rwanda, l'histoire qui mène au génocide (*Rwanda: How history can lead to genocide*, 1995), 68-70, 283

Rwanda. A travers nous, l'humanité... (*Rwanda: Through Us, Humanity* (2006), 284
Rwanda: Beyond the Deadly Pit (2009), 222-3, 285
Rwanda: Do Scars Ever Fade? (2004), 67, 80-1, 108-11, 113-14, 137, 156, 253n, 284
Rwanda: Hope in Hell (2001), 284
Rwanda: Hope Rises (2009), 156, 285
Rwanda: In Search of Hope (2001), 284
Rwanda: Living Forgiveness (2005), 113, 155-6, 284
Rwanda: Maudits soient les yeux fermés (1995), 283
Rwanda: Out of the Darkness (1998), 283
Rwanda: Take Two (2010), 154, 285
Rwanda: The Bloody Tricolour (1995), 69-70, 197, 283
Rwanda: The power of Youth and Sport (2013), 286
Rwanda: The Untold Story (2014), 174-82, 286
Rwandan Armed Forces (FAR), 23-4, 45, 56, 123, 176, 211
Rwandan Broadcasting Agency (RBA), 191, 195
Rwandan Genocide: Reunited Through Polaroids, The (2014), 286
Rwandan National AIDS Commission, 193
Rwandan Night, The (2013), 223, 286
Rwandan Patriotic Army (RPA), 77, 178
Rwandan Patriotic Front (RPF), 2-3, 22-4, 26-7, 35, 41, 45, 49, 53, 56-7, 59-61, 68-70, 76-7, 79, 87, 109, 123, 131, 144, 150, 157, 162, 167-8, 170-1, 174-6, 178-80, 184-5, 198-201, 234, 243n, 248n, 260n

Saddleback Leather Company, 162-3
Sakindi, Fidele, 223
Sakota-Kokot, Tanja, 3, 92, 95
Salvetti, Riccardo, 120
Samputu, Jean-Paul, 216
Sandford, Simon, 58-9, 246n
Sauper, Hupert, 78
Saving Private Ryan (1998), 7
Savlov, Marc, 97
Scars of My Day (2006), 222, 232, 265n
Schindler's List (1993), 1-2, 5, 11, 13-14, 18, 82, 88, 92, 138
Scott, A. O., 130
Scranton, Deborah, 143
Screamers (2006), 140, 284
Shake Hands with the Devil (2007), 121, 197, 255n, 282
Shake Hands with the Devil: The Journey of Roméo Dallaire (2004), 18, 67, 80-1, 108-14, 119, 137, 140, 248n, 284
Sheen, Martin, 156
Shelley, Christine, 50, 71, 105, 109
Shema (2011), 220, 282
Shoah (1985), 18
Shooting Dogs (a.k.a. *Beyond the Gates*, 2005), 67, 80-1, 97-104, 107-8, 114, 129, 197, 233-4, 255n, 282
Simbikangwa, Pascal, 143, 173, 181
Simpson, O. J., 31, 66
Sitting on a Volcano (1995), 76-7, 178, 293
Small, Courtney, 166
Sobchak, Vivian, 7
Sometimes in April (2005), 67, 80-1, 97, 103-7, 205, 255n, 282
Spence, Louise, 122
Spielberg, Steven, 1
Spottiswoode, Roger, 121
Stam, Allan C., 168, 177-9, 181
Stam, Robert, 122
Stein, Ruthe, 103
Sterne (*Stars*, 1959), 11
Stomp Out Genocide (2013), 286
Stone, Oliver, 106
Stranger, The (1946), 11
Strength in Fear (2012), 232, 265n, 282
Swedish Film Institute, 193

Swedish Public Television (SVT), 33-4, 41, 50
Swedish SIDA, 172
Sweet Dreams (2012), 153-4, 286
Sydämeni taakka (*Burden of My Heart*, 2011), 157, 286

Tankian, Serj, 141
Tanzini, Guillaume, 67
Télévision Nationale Rwandaise, 191
Telling Truth in Arusha (2010), 285
Thomas, Annie, 57
Thomas, William, 109
Thor: Love and Thunder (2022), 107
Through My Eyes: A Film About Rwandan Youth (2004), 209-11, 213, 224-5, 232, 284
Through the Valley (2013), 155, 285
Tomorrow Never Dies (1997), 121
Toplin, Robert Brent, 7-8, 18, 82, 89-90
Torgovnik, Jonathan, 148
Tour (2014), 141, 287
Train de vie (*Train of Life*, 1999), 14
Tran Ngoc, Laetitia, 185
Trees of Peace (2021), 120, 127-9, 146, 283
Triage: Dr James Orbinski's Humanitarian Dilemma (2007), 139-41, 285
Triumph of Evil, The (1998), 69-73, 81, 111, 113, 247n, 283
Tuez-les tous! Rwanda: histoire d'un génocide sans importance (*Kill Them All!: Rwanda the Story of an Unimportant Genocide*, 2004), 123, 137-8, 284
TV4 (Sweden), 34, 37, 39, 44, 51
Twagirmungo, Faustin, 171

U571 (2000), 18
UK Holocaust Memorial Day Trust, 98
Ulica Graniczna (*Border Street*, 1948), 11
Umudugudu! Rwanda 20 Ans Après (2014), 287
Umuhire, Eliane, 129
Umurabyo (2015), 231-3, 283

Umurage (2009), 285
Umutoma (2012), 193
UN Blues (1995), 69, 197, 283
Un dimanche à Kigali (*A Sunday in Kigali*, 2006), 122, 125-7, 135, 146, 282
Uncondemned, The (2015), 147, 287
Une république devenue folle: Rwanda 1894-1994 (*Rwanda: A Republic Gone Mad*, 1995), 68, 283
UNHCR, 27
Union for National Progress (UPRONA), 68
United Nation's Security Council, 23-4, 48, 54, 58, 61
United Nations (UN), 19-20, 23-5, 38, 47-53, 56-7, 60-1, 71-2, 92, 100, 102, 110, 132, 182, 184, 199
United Nations Assistance Mission for Rwanda (UNAMIR), 23-4, 27, 69, 71-2, 110
United Nations Assistance Mission for Rwanda II (UNAMIR II), 24, 61, 246n
United States Holocaust Memorial Museum, 72
Unversöhnt (*Unforgiven*, 2014), 157, 287
USAID, 172
USC Shoah Foundation Institute for Visual History and Education, 1
Uwilingiyimana, Agathe, 24
Uwizungemariya, Monica, 174

Van Leeuw, Phillippe, 131
Verpoorten, Marijke, 181

Wallenberg: A Hero's Story (1985), 88
Wallis, Andrew, 180
Waramutsebo (2009), 129-30, 135, 282
Waters Hinson, Laura, 154-6
We Are All Rwandans (2008), 209, 211, 282
Weaver, Sigourney, 80
When I Was Young, I Said I Would Be Happy (2014), 157, 287

White, Hayden, 5
Wienberg Roca, Ines, 139
Wiesel, Eli, 11
Wilkens, Carl, 138, 146
Winter, Roger, 35
Wolstencroft, David, 101
Women Building Peace (2014), 287
World of Death (1994), 78, 283
Wounded Healers (2009), 141, 155-6, 285

Year of Living Dangerously, The (1982), 13
Yesterday in Rwanda (2005), 284
You Must Be Something (2010), 157, 285
Young, Andrew Phillip, 211, 222

Zander, Ulf, 8
Zigiranyirazo, Protais, 139
Zukas, Kerry, 80, 86
Zylberman, Lior, 125-6, 133, 136, 139, 229

EU representative:
Easy Access System Europe
Mustamäe tee 50, 10621 Tallinn, Estonia
Gpsr.requests@easproject.com